A HARMONY
of the
GOSPELS

with Explanations and Essays

Using the Text of the
NEW AMERICAN STANDARD BIBLE

ROBERT L. THOMAS, Editor
STANLEY N. GUNDRY, Associate Editor

MOODY PRESS
CHICAGO

Library of Congress Cataloging in Publication Data

Bible. N.T.—Gospels. English. Harmonies. New American
    Standard. 1978.
    A harmony of the Gospels, with explanations and essays.

    Includes bibliographies.
    1. Bible. N.T. Gospels—Criticism, interpretation, etc.—
Addresses, essays, lectures. I. Thomas, Robert L., 1928-
II. Gundry, Stanley N. III. Title.
BS2560.T43   226'.1   78-16048
ISBN 0-8024-3413-4

7 8 9 10 11 12 Printing/EB/Year 87 86 85 84 83

Printed in the United States of America

TABLE OF CONTENTS

INTRODUCTION TO THE HARMONY

The central person of Christianity is Jesus Christ. The bulk of what we know about Jesus Christ is found in the four gospels, Matthew, Mark, Luke, and John. An indispensable step toward a better understanding of these four books is to harmonize the separate accounts so as to assemble as many details as possible into a chronologically meaningful sequence.

This *Harmony of the Gospels* is introduced as a resource to encourage a deeper understanding of Jesus Christ, His life, death, and resurrection. Other harmonies have been produced in the past and are of value. Yet the study of the gospels has been so intensified in recent years that new information about them is becoming available at a very rapid pace. This creates the necessity for a new work incorporating the latest insights.

Another incentive for a new harmony is the recent availability of the *New American Standard Bible*. The editors of this *Harmony*, after investigating other possibilities, felt this translation to be extremely well-suited to be the basic text for a harmony. Belonging to a tradition of English Bible translation dating back to William Tyndale early in the sixteenth century, this work provides a modern English translation of the gospels which is based on a more literal philosophy of translating the Greek text. Appreciation is expressed to the Lockman Foundation of La Habra, California, for permission to use the NASB.

A harmony of the gospels provides an important means for studying the four gospels at one time. Though it could never replace the four gospels studied individually, it is an indispensable tool for gaining a well-rounded overview of Jesus' life in all its facets. The editors have geared this work to provide such an overview for those studying in a college or seminary setting. Yet a serious student of Scripture studying privately and without a familiarity with New Testament Greek will easily be able to follow the discussion. It goes without saying therefore that detailed and technical issues belonging to more advanced levels of scholarship have not been included in the work.

Besides the text of the *Harmony*, a number of other features have been incorporated. An outline of the *Harmony* which follows the probable chronological sequence of Christ's life is found just after this Introduction. The same outline divides the body of the *Harmony*. This enables one to see at a glance when various events occurred in relation to one another. The geographical location or probable location of every happening is given in the body of the *Harmony*. The maps at the close of the volume provide a means for identifying these places in relation to the rest of Palestine. The sources of Old Testament quotations have also been included, as have the notes clarifying the translation of the Reference Edition of the *New American Standard Bible*.

Sections of the *Harmony* that bear a special resemblance to other sections have also been noted in the harmony proper. All section cross-references are listed in the Table of Section Cross-references found toward the rear of the volume. This table also notes the points of similarity between sections. The next table facilitates locating any passage in the *Harmony* by listing the passages according to chapter and verse sequence. Time lines presenting overviews of various segments of Christ's life have been included just after the Tables for Finding Passages in the *Harmony*.

A rather extensive set of explanatory footnotes has been included with the text of the *Harmony*. These notes are designed to amplify the meaning of the text by touching on various problems of chronology, interpretation, harmonization, and history, or by simply commenting on some of the more significant features of the text.

The editors have selected twelve topics for special treatment. These topics, chosen because of their special relevance to a harmony of the gospels, are treated in essays which come just after the *Harmony* proper. When appropriate, a selected reading list appears at the conclusion of each essay. Those interested in researching any of the subjects further will find these lists beneficial.

A prolonged exposure to the person of Jesus Christ such as has been necessary in the preparation of this *Harmony* has served to increase our appreciation for Him more than ever before. This work is presented with the prayer that it will do the same for others when they study it.

ROBERT L. THOMAS
STANLEY N. GUNDRY

AN OUTLINE FOR A HARMONY OF THE GOSPELS

GROWING FAME AND EMPHASIS ON REPENTANCE

FIRST PUBLIC REJECTION BY JEWISH LEADERS

PARABOLIC MYSTERIES ABOUT THE KINGDOM

To the Crowds by the Sea, Secs. 82-87

To the Disciples in the House, Secs. 88-92

CONTINUING OPPOSITION

FINAL GALILEAN CAMPAIGN

Part Seven: The Ministry of Christ Around Galilee

LESSON ON THE BREAD OF LIFE

Part Eight: The Later Judean Ministry of Christ

12

13

EXPLANATION OF GENERAL FORMAT
OF THE NEW AMERICAN STANDARD BIBLE

QUOTATION MARKS are used in the text in accordance with modern English usage.

"THOU", "THEE", AND "THY" are not used in this translation except in the language of prayer when addressing Deity.

PERSONAL PRONOUNS are capitalized when pertaining to Deity.

ITALICS are used in the text to indicate words that are not found in the original Greek but implied by it. Italics are used in the footnotes to signify alternate readings for the text.

SMALL CAPS in the New Testament are used in the text to indicate Old Testament quotations or obvious allusions to Old Testament texts. Variations of Old Testament wording are found in New Testament citations depending on whether the New Testament writer translated from a Hebrew text, used existing Greek or Aramaic translations, or paraphrased the material. It should be noted that modern rules for the indication of direct quotation were not used in biblical times, thus allowing freedom for omissions or insertions without specific indication of these.

ASTERISK—In regard to the use in Greek of the historical present, the translators recognized that in some contexts the present tense seems more unexpected and unjustified to the English reader than a past tense would have been. But Greek authors frequently used the present tense for the sake of heightened vividness, thereby transporting their readers in imagination to the actual scene at the time of occurrence. However, the translators felt that it would be wise to change these historical presents to English past tenses. Therefore verbs marked with an asterisk (*) represent historical presents in the Greek which have been translated with an English past tense in order to conform to modern usage.

ABBREVIATIONS AND SPECIAL MARKINGS:
Lit. = A literal translation
Or = An alternate translation justified by the Greek
[] = Brackets in the text are around words probably not in the original writings
f, ff = following verse or verses
ms., mss. = manuscript, manuscripts
v., vv. = verse, verses
vs. = verses (NASB notes)

EXPLANATION OF THE HARMONY'S FORMAT

1. THE TEXT OF THE GOSPELS The text of one, two, three, or four gospels, depending on how many describe each episode, is found on each page of the *Harmony*. It is arranged in columns with each column containing the text of one gospel. Material in each column is arranged so as to be adjacent to similar material in other columns. The width of the columns varies in accord with how many gospels record the events of each section. The order of the gospels, from left to right, is the same as their order in the modern editions of the New Testament.

2. SECTION NUMBERS The text of the gospels has been divided into sections and arranged in a probable chronological sequence. Each section has been assigned a number which appears in arabic numerals at the top of that section.

3. SECTION TITLES Each section has been assigned a title which appears just after the section number at the head of that section.

4. SECTION CROSS-REFERENCES Just after some section titles are found parenthetical notations begun by the abbreviation "cf." and followed by other section numbers. These are other sections which contain features that are in some way similar to the section where the cross-reference is indicated. A semicolon divides section numbers where the point of cross-referencing is different. The Table of Section Cross-References on pp. 338-341 indicates the point of similarity between the sections.

5. GEOGRAPHICAL NOTATIONS Below most section titles is found a word or phrase set off by dashes. This indicates the place where the events of that section took place. In a few instances the geographical notation is found instead in the section title.

6. SCRIPTURE REFERENCES Just above each column in the *Harmony* are the book name, chapter(s), and verse(s) that tell which biblical passage is found in that column.

7. OLD TESTAMENT QUOTATIONS The sources of Old Testament quotations that are printed in small capital letters in the text of the *Harmony* are shown in brackets immediately after each quotation.

8. TRANSLATION NOTES Superior numbers within the text refer to literal readings, alternate translations, and explanations of the translation which are found at the end of each section. These notes are those found in the Reference Edition of the *New American Standard Bible*.

17

9. EXPLANATORY FOOTNOTES Superior lower case letters within the text or alongside a heading refer to footnotes at the bottoms of the pages where the letters are found. The explanatory footnotes which pertain to the text of the *Harmony* begin with parentheses containing the Scripture reference(s) to which they relate.

A HARMONY OF THE GOSPELS

PART ONE
A PREVIEW OF WHO JESUS IS

Sec. 1 Luke's purpose for writing a gospel

Luke 1:1-4

1 Inasmuch as [a]many have undertaken to compile an account of the things [1]accomplished among us,

2 just as those who from the beginning [2]were eyewitnesses and [3]servants of the [4]word have handed them down to us,

3 it seemed fitting for [b]me as well, having [5]investigated everything carefully from the beginning, to write it out for you in consecutive order, most excellent Theophilus;

4 so that you might know the exact truth about the things you have been [6]taught.

[1]Or, on which there is full conviction. [2]Lit, became. [3]Or, ministers. [4]I.e., gospel. [5]Or, followed. [6]Or, orally instructed in.

Sec. 2 John's prologue: from pre-incarnation to crucifixion

John 1:1-18

1 In the beginning was the Word, and the Word was with God, and the Word was God.

2 [1]He was in the beginning with God.

3 All things [c]came into being [2]by Him, and apart from Him nothing came into being that has come into being.

4 In Him was life, and the life was the light of men.

5 And the light shines in the darkness, and the darkness did not [3]comprehend it.

6 There [4c]came a man, sent from God, whose name was John.

7 [1]He came for a witness, that he might bear witness of the light, that all might believe through him.

8 [5]He was not the light, but came that he might bear witness of the light.

9 There was the true light [6]which, coming into the world, enlightens every man.

10 He was in the world, and the world was made through Him, and the world did not know Him.

11 He came to His [7]own, and those who were His own did not receive Him.

---

[a](Luke 1:1) Recognizing that other second generation Christians had already undertaken a similar task, Luke joined them in producing an account of Christ's life. His reason for doing so was apparently inadequacies in the other efforts, at least insofar as they failed to meet Theophilus' need. If Luke had been aware of the works by Matthew or Mark, it is doubtful that he would have viewed either of them in this light. He would not have looked on either as the work of another non-eyewitness, nor would he have been likely to imply he could improve on them. His sources therefore are best restricted to oral and written tradition which has been long ago replaced by the canonical gospels.

[b](Luke 1:3) Luke, probably the only Gentile writer of Scripture (cf. Col. 4:11, 14), is responsible for two books, Luke and Acts. These are the two longest books in the New Testament. From the standpoint of volume, then, Luke is the most prolific New Testament writer, even though Paul and John each wrote more books.

19

John 1:1-18 (cont'd)

12 But as many as received Him, to them He gave the right to become children of God, *even* to those who believe in His name,

13 who were [8]born not of [9]blood, nor of the will of the flesh, nor of the will of man, but of God.

14 And the Word [c]became flesh, and [10]dwelt among us, and we beheld His glory, glory as of [11]the only begotten from the Father, full of grace and truth.

15 John *bore witness of Him, and cried out, saying, "This was He of whom I said, 'He who comes after me [12]has a higher rank than I, for He existed before me.'"

16 For of His fulness [13]we have all received, and [14]grace upon grace.

17 For the Law was given through Moses; grace and truth [c]were realized through Jesus Christ.

18 No man has seen God at any time; the only begotten [15]God, who is in the bosom of the Father, He has explained *Him.*

[1]Lit., *This one.* [2]Or, *through.* [3]Or, *overpower.* [4]Or, *came into being.* [5]Lit., *That one.* [6]Or, *which enlightens every man coming into the world.* [7]Or, *own things, possessions, domain.* [8]Or, *begotten.* [9]Lit., *bloods.* [10]Or, *tabernacled.* [11]Or, *unique, only one of His kind.* [12]Lit., *is become before me.* [13]Lit., *we all received.* [14]Lit., *grace for grace.* [15]Some later mss. read Son.

Sec. 3   [d]Jesus' legal lineage through Joseph and natural lineage through Mary

Matt. 1:1-17	Luke 3:23b-38
1 The book of the genealogy of Jesus Christ, the son of David, the son of Abraham.	being [11]supposedly *the* son of Joseph, the son of [12]Eli,
2 To Abraham was born Isaac; and to Isaac, Jacob; and to Jacob, [1]Judah and his brothers;	**24** the *son* of Matthat, the *son* of Levi, the *son* of Melchi, the *son* of Jannai, the *son* of Joseph,
3 and to Judah were born Perez and Zerah by Tamar; and to Perez was born Hezron; and to Hezron, [2]Ram;	**25** the *son* of Mattathias, the *son* of Amos, the *son* of Nahum, the *son* of [13]Hesli, the *son* of Naggai,
4 and to Ram was born Amminadab; and to Amminadab, Nahshon; and to Nahshon, Salmon;	**26** the *son* of Maath, the *son* of Mattathias, the *son* of Semein, the *son* of Josech, the *son* of Joda,
5 and to Salmon was born Boaz by Rahab; and to Boaz was born Obed by Ruth; and to Obed, Jesse;	**27** the *son* of Joanan, the *son* of Rhesa, the *son* of Zerubbabel, the *son* of [8]Shealtiel, the *son* of Neri,
6 and to Jesse was born David the king. And to David was born Solomon by her *who had been the wife* of Uriah;	**28** the *son* of Melchi, the *son* of Addi, the *son* of Cosam, the *son* of Elmadam, the *son* of Er,
7 and to Solomon was born Rehoboam; and to Rehoboam, Abijah; and to Abijah, [3]Asa;	**29** the *son* of [14]Joshua, the *son* of Eliezer, the *son* of Jorim, the *son* of Matthat, the *son* of Levi,
8 and to Asa was born Jehoshaphat; and to Jehoshaphat, [4]Joram; and to Joram, Uzziah;	**30** the *son* of Simeon, the *son* of [15]Judah, the *son* of Joseph, the *son* of Jonam, the *son* of Eliakim,
	31 the *son* of Melea, the *son* of Menna, the *son* of Mattatha, the *son* of

[c]John seems to organize his introduction around four significant happenings, each referred to by a use of the Greek verb *egeneto*: the creation (1:3), the coming of the forerunner John (1:6), the incarnation of Christ (1:14), and the crucifixion of Christ (1:17). These four reflect the progress of the gospel as it moves toward its climax in the passion of Christ.

[d]For discussion of the two genealogies see essay 9 at the end of this volume (pp. 313-319).

| Matt. 1:1-17 (cont'd) | Luke 3:23b-38 (cont'd) |

9 and to Uzziah was born [5]Jotham; and to Jotham, Ahaz; and to Ahaz, Hezekiah;

10 and to Hezekiah was born Manasseh; and to Manasseh, [6]Amon; and to Amon, Josiah;

11 and to Josiah were born [7]Jeconiah and his brothers, at the time of the deportation to Babylon.

12 And after the deportation to Babylon, to Jeconiah was born [8]Shealtiel; and to Shealtiel, Zerubbabel;

13 and to Zerubbabel was born [9]Abiud; and to Abiud, Eliakim; and to Eliakim, Azor;

14 and to Azor was born Zadok; and to Zadok, Achim; and to Achim, Eliud;

15 and to Eliud was born Eleazar; and to Eleazar, Matthan; and to Matthan, Jacob;

16 and to Jacob was born Joseph the husband of Mary, by whom was born Jesus, who is called [10]Christ.

17 Therefore all the generations from Abraham to David are fourteen generations; and from David to the deportation to Babylon fourteen generations; and from the deportation to Babylon to *the time of* [10]Christ fourteen generations.

Nathan, the *son* of David,

32 the *son* of Jesse, the *son* of Obed, the *son* of Boaz, the *son* of [16]Salmon, the son of [17]Nahshon,

33 the *son* of Amminadab, the *son* of Admin, the *son* of [18]Ram, the *son* of Hezron, the *son* of Perez, the *son* of Judah,

34 the *son* of Jacob, the *son* of Isaac, the *son* of Abraham, the *son* of Terah, the *son* of Nahor,

35 the *son* of Serug, the *son* of [19]Reu, the *son* of Peleg, the *son* of [20]Heber, the son of Shelah,

36 the *son* of Cainan, the *son* of Arphaxad, the *son* of Shem, the *son* of Noah, the *son* of Lamech,

37 the *son* of Methuselah, the *son* of Enoch, the *son* of Jared, the *son* of Mahalaleel, the *son* of Cainan,

38 the *son* of Enosh, the *son* of Seth, the *son* of Adam, the *son* of God.

---

[1]Gr., *Judas.* Names of Old Testament characters will be given in their Old Testament form. [2]Gr., *Aram.* [3]Gr., *Asaph.* [4]Gr., *Jehoram.* [5]Gr., *Joatham.* [6]Gr., *Amos.* [7]Or, *Jehoiachin.* [8]Gr., *Salathiel.* [9]Gr., *Abihud.* [10]I.e., the Messiah. [11]Lit., *as it was being thought.* [12]Also spelled *Heli.* [13]Also spelled *Esli.* [14]Gr., *Jesus.* [15]Gr., *Judas.* [16]Gr., *Sala.* [17]Gr., *Naasson.* [18]Gr., *Arni.* [19]Gr., *Ragau.* [20]Gr., *Eber.*

PART TWO
THE EARLY YEARS OF JOHN THE BAPTIST

Sec. 4   John's birth foretold to Zacharias (cf. Secs. 5, 11)
– Jerusalem, in the Temple –

Luke 1:5-25

5   [e]In the days of Herod, king of Judea, there [1]was a certain priest named [2]Zacharias, of the division of [3]Abijah; and he had a wife [4]from the daughters of Aaron, and her name was Elizabeth.

6   And they were both righteous in the sight of God, walking blamelessly in all the commandments and requirements of the Lord.

7   And they had no child, because Elizabeth was barren, and they were both advanced in [5]years.

8   Now it came about, while he was performing his priestly service before God in the *appointed* order of his division,

9   according to the custom of the priestly office, he was [f]chosen by lot to enter the temple of the Lord and burn incense.

10   And the whole multitude of the people were in prayer outside at the hour of the incense offering.

11   And an angel of the Lord appeared to him, standing to the right of the altar of incense.

12   And Zacharias was troubled when he saw *him*, and fear [6]gripped him.

13   But the angel said to him, "Do not be afraid, Zacharias, for your petition has been heard, and your wife Elizabeth will bear you a son, and you will [7]give him the name John.

14   "And you will have joy and gladness, and many will rejoice at his birth.

15   "For he will be great in the sight of the Lord, and he will drink no wine or liquor; and he will be filled with the Holy Spirit, [8]while yet in his mother's womb.

16   "And he will turn back many of the sons of Israel to the Lord their God.

17   "And it is he who will go *as a forerunner* before Him in the spirit and power of Elijah, TO TURN THE HEARTS OF THE FATHERS BACK TO THE CHILDREN [Mal. 4:6], and the disobedient to the attitude of the righteous; so as to make ready a people prepared for the Lord."

18   And Zacharias said to the angel, "How shall I know this *for certain*? For I am an old man, and my wife is advanced in [5]years."

19   And the angel answered and said to him, "I am Gabriel, who [9]stands in the presence of God; and I have been sent to speak to you, and to bring you this good news.

---

[e](Luke 1:5) At 1:5 Luke departs from the idiomatic, classical Greek writing style found in Luke 1:1-4. His accounts of the early years of John and Christ (Luke 1:5—2:52) are quite distinctly Hebraistic Greek, probably due to the Aramaic sources on which he depended for that material. Then too, he knew well the Hebraic style from the Septuagint and from his associations with Paul. Good indications exist that much in these first two chapters of the third gospel came from Mary, the mother of Jesus, or some oral and written tradition traceable to her.

[f](Luke 1:9) Because of the large number of priests like Zacharias, he probably was called on to perform this daily service only once in his entire life. This obligation of representing Israel on such a rare occasion doubtless weighed heavily on the shoulders of this righteous man.

Luke 1:5-25 (cont'd)

20 "And behold, you shall be silent and unable to speak until the day when these things take place, because you did not believe my words, which shall be fulfilled in their proper time."

21 And the people were waiting for Zacharias, and were wondering at his delay in the temple.

22 But when he came out, he was unable to speak to them; and they realized that he had seen a vision in the temple; and he kept [10]making signs to them, and remained mute.

23 And it came about, when the days of his priestly service were ended, that he went back home.

24 And after these days Elizabeth his wife became pregnant; and she [11]kept herself in seclusion for five months, saying,

25 "This is the way the Lord has dealt with me in the days when He looked *with favor* upon *me*, to take away my disgrace among men."

---

[1]Lit., *came into being.* [2]I.e., Zechariah. [3]Gr., *Abia.* [4]I.e., of priestly descent. [5]Lit., *days.* [6]Or, *fell upon.* [7]Lit., *call his name.* [8]Lit., *even from.* [9]Lit., *stand beside.* [10]Or, *beckoning to or nodding to.* [11]Lit., *was hidden.*

Sec. 5   Jesus' birth foretold to Mary (cf. Secs. 4, 11)
  – Nazareth –

Luke 1:26-38

26 Now in the sixth month the angel Gabriel was sent from God to a city in Galilee, called Nazareth,

27 to a virgin engaged to a man whose name was Joseph, of the [1]descendants of David; and the virgin's name was Mary.

28 And coming in, he said to her, "Hail, [2]favored one! The Lord [3]*is* with you.[4]"

29 But she was greatly troubled at *this* statement, and kept pondering what kind of salutation this might be.

30 And the angel said to her, "Do not be afraid, Mary; for you have found favor with God.

31 "And behold, you will conceive in your womb, and bear a son, and you shall name Him Jesus.

32 "He will be great, and will be called the Son of the Most High; and the Lord God will give Him the [g]throne of His father David;

33 and He will reign over the house of Jacob forever; and His kingdom will have no end."

34 And Mary said to the angel, "How [5]can this be, since I [6]am a [h]virgin?"

35 And the angel answered and said to her, "The Holy Spirit will come upon you, and the power of the Most High will overshadow you; and for that reason the [7]holy offspring shall be called the Son of God.

36 "And behold, even your relative Elizabeth has also conceived a son in her old age; and [8]she who was called barren is now in her sixth month.

---

[g](Luke 1:32) The language Gabriel uses undoubtedly reflects the strong Old Testament belief in the earthly rule of Israel's Messiah. Just as David, from whom Mary was descended, had a throne located on earth, so will the One whose miraculous birth is promised to Mary. Unlike David's kingdom, however, Jesus' Kingdom will be endless (Luke 1:33).

[h](Luke 1:34) Among New Testament writers, only Luke (in this section) and Matthew (Sec. 11) directly teach the virgin birth of Jesus. Galatians 4:4 probably does not refer to this specific teaching. John 1:13 apparently refers to this belief indirectly by using language related to the virgin birth when describing the new birth of Christians. Since earliest times in the history of the church this doctrine has been an integral part of orthodox Christianity.

Luke 1:26-38 (cont'd)

37 "For [9]nothing will be impossible with God."

38 And [10]Mary said, "Behold, the [11]bondslave of the Lord; be it done to me according to your word." And the angel departed from her.

[1]Lit., *house.*   [2]Or, *O woman richly blessed.*   [3]Or, *be.*   [4]*Later mss. add you are blessed among women.*   [5]Lit., *shall.*   [6]Lit., *know no man.*   [7]Lit., *the holy thing begotten.*   [8]Lit., *this is the sixth month to her who.*   [9]Lit., *not any word.*   [10]Gr., *Mariam; i.e., Miriam;* so throughout Luke.   [11]I.e., female slave.

Sec. 6   Mary's visit to Elizabeth (cf. Secs. 7, 9, 15)
     — Hill country of Judea —

Luke 1:39-45

39 Now [1]at this time Mary arose and went with haste to the hill country, to a city of Judah,

40 and entered the house of Zacharias and greeted Elizabeth.

41 And it came about that when Elizabeth heard Mary's greeting, the baby leaped in her womb; and Elizabeth was filled with the Holy Spirit.

42 And she cried out with a loud voice, and said, "Blessed among women *are* you, and blessed *is* the fruit of your womb!

43 "And [2]how has it *happened* to me, that the mother of my Lord should come to me?

44 "For behold, when the sound of your greeting reached my ears, the baby leaped in my womb for joy.

45 "And blessed *is* she who believed [3]that there would be a fulfillment of what had been spoken to her [4]by the Lord."

[1]Lit., *in these days.*   [2]Lit., *whence this to me.*   [3]Or possibly, *because there will be.*   [4]Lit., *from.*

Sec. 7   Mary's song of joy (cf. Secs. 6, 9, 15)
     — Hill country of Judea —

Luke 1:46-56

46 And Mary said:
     "[1]My soul [1]exalts the Lord,

47 "And my spirit has rejoiced in God my Savior.

48 "For He has had regard for the humble state of His [2]bondslave;
     For behold, from this time on all generations will count me blessed.

49 "For the Mighty One has done great things for me;
     And holy is His name.

50 "AND HIS MERCY IS [3]UPON GENERATION AFTER GENERATION
     TOWARDS THOSE WHO FEAR HIM [Psalm 103:17].

51 "He has done [4]mighty deeds with His arm;
     He has scattered *those who were* proud in the [5]thoughts of their heart.

52 "He has brought down rulers from *their* thrones,
     And has exalted those who were humble.

53 "HE HAS FILLED THE HUNGRY WITH GOOD THINGS [Psalm 107:9];
     And sent away the rich empty-handed.

[1](Luke 1:46) This song has frequently been called "The Magnificat," a title derived from the first word of the Latin translation of it. This "vocal meditation" of Mary recalls the type of literature found in the Old Testament Psalms. Mary describes God's actions with seven past tense (Greek aorist tense) verbs (1:51-54). From the nature of the circumstances, however, it is obvious that these are anticipations of what God was going to do in the future through the child in her womb. Hence, these verbs are probably "prophetic aorists" after the analogy of the Hebrew "prophetic perfect."

Luke 1:46-56 (cont'd)

54 He has given help to Israel His servant,
[6]In remembrance of His mercy,
55 As He spoke to our fathers,
To Abraham and his [7]offspring forever."
56 And Mary stayed with her about three months, and then returned to her home.

[1]Lit., *makes great.* [2]I.e., *female slave.* [3]Lit., *unto generations and generations.* [4]Lit., *might.*
[5]Lit., *thought, attitude.* [6]Lit., *So as to remember.* Lit., *seed.*

Sec. 8 John's birth
— Hill country of Judea —

Luke 1:57-66

57 Now the time [1]had come for Elizabeth to give birth, and she brought forth a son.
58 And her neighbors and her relatives heard that the Lord had [2]displayed His great mercy toward her; and they were rejoicing with her.
59 And it came about that on the eighth day they came to circumcise the child, and they were going to call him Zacharias, [3]after his father.
60 And his mother answered and said, "No indeed; but he shall be called John."
61 And they said to her, "There is no one among your relatives who is called by that name."
62 And they made signs to his father, as to what he wanted him called.
63 And he asked for a tablet, and wrote as follows, "His name is John." And they were all astonished.
64 And at once his mouth was opened and his tongue *loosed,* and he *began* to speak in praise of God.
65 And fear came on all those living around them; and all these matters were being talked about in all the hill country of Judea.
66 And all who heard them kept them in mind, saying, "What then will this child turn out to be?" For the hand of the Lord was certainly with him.

[1]Lit., *was fulfilled.* [2]Lit., *magnified.* [3]Lit., *after the name of.*

Sec. 9 Zacharias' prophetic song (cf. Secs. 6, 7, 15)
— Hill country of Judea —

Luke 1:67-79

67 And his father Zacharias was filled with the Holy Spirit, and prophesied, saying:
68 "[1]Blessed be the Lord God of Israel,
For He has visited us and accomplished redemption for His people,
69 And has raised up a horn of salvation for us
In the house of David His servant—

[1](Luke 1:68) "Benedictus" is the name often applied to this song because this is the first word of the song in Latin. Here is a literary form modeled after the Old Testament prophecies. Like Mary, Zacharias anticipates the redemption and salvation of his nation Israel from the enemy's oppression (1:68, 71). In line with this hope, he alludes to three prominent covenants (agreements or contracts) God made with his people: the Abrahamic (1:72-74; cf. Gen. 15:12-21; 17:7; Psalm 105:8-9), the Davidic (1:69-71; cf. 1 Sam. 2:10; 2 Sam. 7:8-17; Psalm 89), and the New (1:77; cf. Jer. 31:31-34). Of course, Messiah's political deliverance (1:68-74) is inseparable from a moral preparation of His people (1:75-79). Zacharias' son, the forerunner of Messiah, was commissioned to accomplish this latter task (1:76-79).

Luke 1:67-79 (cont'd)

70   As He spoke by the mouth of His holy prophets from of old—
71   ¹Salvation FROM OUR ENEMIES,
     And FROM THE HAND OF ALL WHO HATE US [Psalm 106:10];
72   To show mercy toward our fathers,
     And to remember His holy covenant,
73   The oath which He swore to Abraham our father,
74   To grant us that we, being delivered from the hand of our enemies,
     Might serve Him without fear,
75   In holiness and righteousness before Him all our days.
76   "And you, child, will be called the prophet of the Most High;
     For you will go on BEFORE THE LORD TO PREPARE HIS WAYS [Mal. 3:1];
77   To give to His people the knowledge of salvation
     ²By the forgiveness of their sins,
78   Because of the tender mercy of our God,
     With which the Sunrise from on high shall visit us,
79   To SHINE UPON THOSE WHO SIT IN DARKNESS AND THE SHADOW OF DEATH [Isa.
     9:1-2],
     To guide our feet into the way of peace."

¹Or, *Deliverance.*   ²Or, *Consisting in.*

Sec. 10   John's growth and early life
     – *Judean wilderness* –

Luke 1:80

80   And the child continued to grow, and to become strong in spirit, and he
lived in the deserts until the day of his public appearance to Israel.

PART THREE
THE EARLY YEARS OF JESUS CHRIST

Sec. 11   Circumstances of Jesus' birth explained to Joseph (cf. Secs. 4, 5)
— Nazareth —

Matt. 1:18-25

18 Now the birth of Jesus Christ was as follows. When His mother Mary had been betrothed to Joseph, before they came together she was [k]found to be with child by the Holy Spirit.

19 And Joseph her husband, being a righteous man, and not wanting to disgrace her, desired [1]to put her away secretly.

20 But when he had considered this, behold, an angel of the Lord appeared to him in a dream, saying, "Joseph, son of David, do not be afraid to take Mary as your wife; for that which has been [2]conceived in her is of the Holy Spirit.

21 "And she will bear a Son; and you shall call His name Jesus, for it is He who will save His people from their sins."

22 Now all this [3]took place that what was spoken by the Lord through the prophet might be fulfilled, saying,

23 "BEHOLD, THE VIRGIN SHALL BE WITH CHILD, AND SHALL BEAR A SON, AND THEY SHALL CALL HIS NAME [4]IMMANUEL" [Isa. 7:14], which translated means, "GOD WITH US."

24 And Joseph arose from his sleep, and did as the angel of the Lord commanded him, and took her as his wife,

25 and [5]kept her a virgin until she gave birth to a Son; and he called His name Jesus.

[1]Or, *to divorce her.*   [2]Lit., *begotten.*   [3]Or, *has taken place.*   [4]Or, *Emmanuel.*   [5]Lit., *was not knowing her.*

Sec. 12   Birth of Jesus
— Bethlehem —

Luke 2:1-7

1 Now it came about in those days that a [1]decree went out from Caesar Augustus, that a census be taken of all [1]the inhabited earth.

---

[k](Matt. 1:18) Since Mary probably stayed with Elizabeth until after the birth of John (Luke 1:56), Joseph had not seen her for about four months. By the time of her return her pregnancy was obvious, so that Joseph was forced to do one of two things, either have Mary stoned (Deut. 22:23-27) or divorce her privately. He had already decided on the latter course when the angel came and explained the unique situation. As a righteous man, Joseph had not yet considered what the angel suggested, that is, proceeding with the marriage arrangements. When informed of the nature of the conception, however, he dismissed all thoughts of divorce.

[1](Luke 2:1) Luke, perhaps because of his special attention to Jesus' humanity, is anxious to locate His life in the mainstream of human history. His chronological notations, such as those in 2:1-2, are part of this effort (see essay 11, pp. 324-328 for more discussion of chronology). At one time opponents of biblical infallibility criticized the accuracy of Luke's historical notations in this paragraph, but a careful study of ancient history and archaeological discoveries has overwhelmingly vindicated his reliability. Objections to Luke's accuracy have pertained particularly to the dating of Quirinius' governorship in Syria, but with further research, satisfactory answers to these have surfaced. (For further discussion, see Harold W. Hoehner, *Chronological Aspects of the Life of Christ* [Grand Rapids: Zondervan, 1977], pp. 13-23.)

Luke 2:1-7 (cont'd)

2 [2]This was the first census taken while [3]Quirinius was governor of Syria.

3 And all were proceeding to register for the census, everyone to his own city.

4 And Joseph also went up from Galilee, from the city of Nazareth, to Judea, to the city of David, which is called Bethlehem, because he was of the house and family of David,

5 in order to register, along with Mary, who was engaged to him, and was with child.

6 And it came about that while they were there, the days were completed for her to give birth.

7 And she gave birth to her first-born son; and she wrapped Him in cloths, and laid Him in a [4]manger, because there was no room for them in the inn.

[1]I.e., the Roman empire. [2]Or, *This took place as a first census.* [3]Gr., *Kyrenios.* [4]Or, *feeding trough.*

Sec. 13   Witness of the shepherds
     – Fields near Bethlehem –

Luke 2:8-20

8 And in the same region there were *some* shepherds staying out in the fields, and keeping watch over their flock by night.

9 And an angel of the Lord suddenly stood before them, and the glory of the Lord shone around them; and they were terribly frightened.

10 And the angel said to them, "Do not be afraid; for behold, I bring you good news of a great joy which shall be for all the people;

11 for today in the city of David there has been born for you a Savior, who is [1]Christ the Lord.

12 "And this *will be* a sign for you: you will find a baby wrapped in cloths, and lying in a [2]manger."

13 And suddenly there appeared with the angel a multitude of the heavenly host praising God, and saying,

14 "Glory to God in the highest,
And on earth peace among men [3]with whom He is pleased."

15 And it came about when the angels had gone away from them into heaven, that the shepherds *began* saying to one another, "Let us go straight to Bethlehem then, and see this thing that has happened which the Lord has made known to us."

16 And they came in haste and found their way to Mary and Joseph, and the baby as He lay in the [2]manger.

17 And when they had seen this, they made known the statement which had been told them about this Child.

18 And all who heard it wondered at the things which were told them by the shepherds.

19 But [m]Mary treasured up all these things, pondering them in her heart.

20 And the shepherds went back, glorifying and praising God for all that they had heard and seen, just as had been told them.

[1]I.e., Messiah. [2]Or, *feeding trough.* [3]Lit., *of good pleasure;* or possibly, *of good will.*

[m]Luke 2:19 is one of the strong indications that Mary, the mother of Jesus, was a principal source of Luke's information found in the early chapters of his gospel.

Sec. 14   Circumcision of Jesus
— *Bethlehem* —

Luke 2:21

21   And when eight days were completed [1]before His circumcision, His name was then called Jesus, the name given by the angel before He was conceived in the womb.

[1]Lit., *so as to circumcise Him.*

Sec. 15   Jesus presented in the Temple (cf. Secs. 6, 7, 9)
— *Jerusalem* —

Luke 2:22-38

22   And when the days for their purification according to the law of Moses were completed, they brought Him up to Jerusalem to present Him to the Lord

23   (as it is written in the Law of the Lord, "EVERY first-born MALE THAT OPENS THE WOMB SHALL BE CALLED HOLY TO THE LORD") [Exod. 13:2, 12],

24   and to offer a sacrifice according to what was said in the Law of the Lord, "A PAIR OF TURTLEDOVES, OR TWO YOUNG PIGEONS" [Lev. 5:11; 12:8].

25   And behold, there was a man in Jerusalem whose name was Simeon; and this man was righteous and devout, looking for the consolation of Israel; and the Holy Spirit was upon him.

26   And it had been revealed to him by the Holy Spirit that he would not see death before he had seen the Lord's [1]Christ.

27   And he came in the Spirit into the temple; and when the parents brought in the child Jesus, [2]to carry out for Him the custom of the Law,

28   then he took Him into his arms, and blessed God, and said,

29   "[n]Now Lord, Thou dost let Thy bond-servant depart
        In peace, according to Thy word;

30   For my eyes have seen Thy salvation,

31   Which Thou hast prepared in the presence of all peoples,

32   A LIGHT [3]OF REVELATION TO THE GENTILES [Isa. 42:6; 49:6],
        And the glory of Thy people Israel."

33   And His father and mother were amazed at the things which were being said about Him.

34   And Simeon blessed them, and said to Mary His mother, "Behold, this Child is appointed for the fall and [4]rise of many in Israel, and for a sign to be opposed —

35   and a sword will pierce even your own soul — to the end that thoughts from many hearts may be revealed."

36   And there was a prophetess, [5]Anna the daughter of Phanuel, of the tribe of Asher. She was advanced in [6]years, having lived with a husband seven years after her [7]marriage,

37   and then as a widow to the age of eighty-four. And she never left the temple, serving night and day with fastings and prayers.

38   And at that very [8]moment she came up and *began* giving thanks to God, and continued to speak of Him to all those who were looking for the redemption of Jerusalem.

[1]I.e., Messiah.   [2]Lit., *to do for Him according to.*   [3]Or, *for.*   [4]Or, *resurrection.*   [5]Or, *Hannah.*   [6]Lit., *days.*   [7]Lit., *virginity.*   [8]Lit., *hour.*

[n](Luke 2:29) The song of Simeon, often referred to as the "Nunc Dimittis" (the first two words of the Latin translation), portrays the expectation of Israel's Messianic deliverance by yet another of the godly remnant. For other songs see Sections 7 and 9.

Sec. 16   Return to Nazareth

Luke 2:39

39   And when they had performed everything according to the Law of the Lord, they °returned to Galilee, to their own city of Nazareth.

Sec. 17   Visit of the Magi
– Jerusalem and Bethlehem –

Matt. 2:1-12

1   Now after Jesus was born in Bethlehem of Judea in the days of ᴾHerod the king, behold, ¹magi from the east arrived in Jerusalem, saying,

2   "Where is He who has been born King of the Jews? For we saw His star in the east, and have come to worship Him."

3   And when Herod the king heard it, he was troubled, and all Jerusalem with him.

4   And gathering together all the chief priests and scribes of the people, he *began* to inquire of them where ²the Christ was to be born.

5   And they said to him, "In Bethlehem of Judea, for so it has been written ³by the prophet,

6   'AND YOU, BETHLEHEM, LAND OF JUDAH,
     ARE BY NO MEANS LEAST AMONG THE LEADERS OF JUDAH;
     FOR OUT OF YOU SHALL COME FORTH A RULER,
     WHO WILL SHEPHERD MY PEOPLE ISRAEL'" [Mic. 5:2].

7   Then Herod secretly called the magi, and ascertained from them ⁴the time the star appeared.

8   And he sent them to Bethlehem, and said, "Go and make careful search for the Child; and when you have found *Him*, report to me, that I too may come and worship Him."

9   And having heard the king, they went their way; and lo, the star, which they had seen in the east, went on before them, until it came and stood over where the Child was.

10   And when they saw the star, they rejoiced exceedingly with great joy.

11   And they came into the house and saw the Child with Mary His mother; and they fell down and worshiped Him; and opening their treasures they presented to Him gifts of gold and frankincense and myrrh.

12   And having been warned *by God* in a dream not to return to Herod, they departed for their own country by another way.

¹Pronounced may-ji, a caste of wise men specializing in astrology, medicine and natural science.   ²I.e., the Messiah.   ³Lit., *through.*   ⁴Lit., *the time of the appearing star.*

°(Luke 2:39) Whether this return to Nazareth came before or after the events of Matthew 2:1-18 (Secs. 17-18) is not easily determined. Plummer suggests the family returned immediately to Bethlehem because the parents thought it most appropriate to rear the Son of David in the city of David (Alfred Plummer, *A Critical and Exegetical Commentary on the Gospel According to Luke,* International Critical Commentary on the Holy Scriptures of the Old and New Testaments [N.Y.: Scribners, 1896], pp. 73-74). If this be true, the return of Luke 2:39 came after the visit of the Magi and the flight into Egypt (Matt. 2:1-18). The sequence preferred in this *Harmony,* however, finds them returning to Nazareth from Jerusalem, as the wording of Luke 2:39 implies. Their purpose was to fetch as many of their personal belongings as possible and move their home to Bethlehem, which they did. Matthew 2, then, finds them in their own home (Matt. 2:11) some time after they have been back to Nazareth (Luke 2:39). That they had already transported their household goods to Bethlehem is seen from Joseph's initial plan to return to Bethlehem, not Nazareth, from Egypt (Matt. 2:21-22) (William F. Arndt, *The Gospel According to Luke* [St. Louis: Concordia, 1956], pp. 97-98).

ᴾ(Matt. 2:1) This Herod (Herod the Great) ruled Palestine for the Roman government from 37 B.C. to 4 B.C. He considered himself to be "king of the Jews." The question asked by the Magi aggravated his already insane jealousy to the point of committing another of his characteristic atrocities. The murder of the infants (Matt. 2:16, Sec. 18) was his attempt to rid himself of another rival to the throne. The number slain, however, was not as large as some have supposed. In a village the size of Bethlehem probably not more than twenty babies were involved in this "Massacre of the Innocents," as it has been traditionally called.

Sec. 18 Flight into Egypt
– Bethlehem and Egypt –

Matt. 2:13-18

13 Now when they had departed, behold, an angel of the Lord *appeared to Joseph in a dream, saying, "Arise and take the Child and His mother, and flee to Egypt, and remain there until I tell you; for Herod is going to search for the Child to destroy Him."

14 And he arose and took the Child and His mother by night, and departed for Egypt;

15 and was there until the death of Herod, that what was spoken by the Lord through the prophet might be fulfilled, saying, "OUT OF EGYPT DID I CALL MY SON" [Hos. 11:1].

16 Then when Herod saw that he had been tricked by the magi, he became very enraged, and sent and slew all the male children who were in Bethlehem and in all its environs, from two years old and under, according to the time which he had ascertained from the magi.

17 Then that which was spoken through Jeremiah the prophet was fulfilled, saying,

18 "A VOICE WAS HEARD IN RAMAH,
WEEPING AND GREAT MOURNING,
RACHEL WEEPING FOR HER CHILDREN;
AND SHE REFUSED TO BE COMFORTED,
BECAUSE THEY WERE NO MORE" [Jer. 31:15].

Sec. 19 New home in Nazareth

Matt. 2:19-23

19 But when Herod was dead, behold, an angel of the Lord *appeared in a dream to Joseph in Egypt, saying,

20 "Arise and take the Child and His mother, and go into the land of Israel; for those who sought the Child's life are dead."

21 And he arose and took the Child and His mother, and came into the land of Israel.

22 But when he heard that Archelaus was reigning over Judea in place of his father Herod, he was afraid to go there. And being warned *by God* in a dream, he departed for the regions of Galilee,

23 and came and resided in a city called Nazareth, that what was spoken through the [q]prophets might be fulfilled, "He shall be called a Nazarene."

Sec. 20 Growth and early life of Jesus
– Nazareth –

Luke 2:40

40 And the Child continued to [r]grow and become strong, [1]increasing in wisdom; and the grace of God was upon Him.

[1]Lit., *becoming full of.*

---

[q](Matt. 2:23) No Old Testament prophecy can be singled out as the source of this statement. Probably the reference is to a number of prophecies which together anticipated the low estate and rejection of Messiah (cf. Psalms 22:6-8, 13; 69:8, 20, 21; Isa. 11:1; 49:7; 53:2, 5, 8; Dan. 9:26). Of particular prominence is Isaiah 11:1 where the Hebrew word for "branch" *(neser)* is built around the same consonants as "Nazarene."

[r](Luke 2:40) Luke's attention to Jesus' humanity is perhaps nowhere more clearly seen than in this statement. His was a development along the same line as his cousin John (cf. Luke 1:80, Sec. 10). Yet the two were not exactly the same, because in Jesus for the first time a human being was developing under ideal conditions, unimpeded by hereditary or acquired defects. See also Luke 2:52 (Sec. 22).

Sec. 21   Jesus' first Passover in Jerusalem

Luke 2:41-50

41   And His parents used to go to Jerusalem every year at the Feast of the Passover.

42   And when He became twelve, they went up there according to the custom of the Feast;

43   and as they were returning, after spending the full number of days, the boy Jesus stayed behind in Jerusalem. And His parents were unaware of it,

44   but supposed Him to be in the caravan, and went a day's journey; and they began looking for Him among their relatives and acquaintances.

45   And when they did not find Him, they returned to Jerusalem, looking for Him.

46   And it came about that after three days they found Him in the temple, sitting in the midst of the teachers, both listening to them, and asking them questions.

47   And all who heard Him were amazed at His understanding and His answers.

48   And when they saw Him, they were astonished; and His mother said to Him, "¹Son, why have You treated us this way? Behold, Your father and I ²have been anxiously looking for You."

49   And He said to them, "ˢWhy is it that you were looking for Me? Did you not know that I had to be in My Father's ³house?"

50   And they did not understand the statement which He ⁴had made to them.

¹Lit., *Child*.   ²Lit., *are looking*.   ³Or, *affairs; lit., in the things of My Father*.   ⁴Lit., *had spoken*.

Sec. 22   Jesus' adolescence and early manhood
– Nazareth –

Luke 2:51-52

51   And He went down with them, and came to Nazareth; and He continued in subjection to them; and His mother ¹treasured all *these* ²things in her heart.

52   And Jesus kept ˡincreasing in wisdom and ³stature, and in favor with God and men.

¹Lit., *was treasuring*.   ²Lit., *words*.   ³Or, *age*.

ˢ(Luke 2:49) These are the first recorded words of Jesus. When he referred to God as "My Father," He was probably responding to his mother's words, "Your father and I." His deity as the only begotten Son of God and His virgin birth lay behind His statement (cf. Luke 10:21-22, Sec. 140).

ˡ(Luke 2:52) As Luke 2:40 summarizes Jesus' boyhood until age twelve, Luke 2:52 furnishes a summary of His adolescence and early manhood, that is, the approximately eighteen years until He was about thirty (cf. Luke 3:23, Sec. 27). We have no detailed information about this latter period, beyond the statement of this verse. Some general data about the eighteen years can be assumed, however. Jesus grew up as the oldest of the children in a rather large family (cf. Mark 6:3, Sec. 97). Joseph supported the family through carpentry in which Jesus assisted. Joseph apparently died during the period before Jesus' public appearance and, by implications in the gospels and early church Fathers, we can presume Jesus became the provider for His mother and younger brothers and sisters (Mark 6:3). He therefore seemingly continued to work at carpentry until the beginning of His public ministry. His frequent mention of articles of furniture, houses, plows, yokes, and the like in His teaching reflects an intimate acquaintance with items built by carpenters.

PART FOUR
THE PUBLIC MINISTRY OF JOHN THE BAPTIST

Sec. 23 His ministry launched
– Judean wilderness –

Mark 1:1	Luke 3:1-2
1 The beginning of the gospel of Jesus Christ, [1]the Son of God.	**1** Now in the fifteenth year of the reign of [u]Tiberius Caesar, when Pontius Pilate was governor of Judea, and Herod was tetrarch of Galilee, and his brother Philip was tetrarch of the region of Ituraea and Trachonitis, and Lysanias was tetrarch of Abilene, **2** in the high priesthood of Annas and Caiaphas, the word of God came to John, the son of Zacharias, in the wilderness.

[1]Many mss. do not contain *the Son of God.*

Sec. 24 His person, proclamation, and baptism (cf. Sec. 29)
– Judean wilderness and region around the Jordan River –

Matt. 3:1-6	Mark 1:2-6	Luke 3:3-6
1 Now in those days John the Baptist * [1]came, [2v]preaching in the wilderness of Judea, saying, **2** "Repent, for the kingdom of [3]heaven [4]is at hand." **3** For this is the one referred to [5]by Isaiah the prophet, saying, "THE VOICE OF ONE CRYING IN THE WILDERNESS, MAKE READY THE WAY OF THE LORD,	**2** As it is written in Isaiah the prophet, "BEHOLD, I SEND MY MESSENGER BEFORE YOUR FACE, WHO WILL PREPARE YOUR WAY [Mal. 3:1]; **3** THE VOICE OF ONE CRYING IN THE WILDERNESS. 'MAKE READY THE WAY OF THE LORD, MAKE HIS PATHS STRAIGHT '" [Isa.	**3** And he came into all the district around the Jordan, [v]preaching a baptism of repentance for forgiveness of sins; **4** as it is written in the book of the words of Isaiah the prophet, "THE VOICE Of ONE CRYING IN THE WILDERNESS, 'MAKE READY THE WAY OF THE LORD, MAKE HIS PATHS STRAIGHT.

[u](Luke 3:1) See essay 11, "Chronology of the Life of Christ" (pp. 324-328). In fixing the date of John's ministry, Luke lists five political leaders and two religious leaders. They are, in order, the Roman emperor, rulers of the three divisions of the "kingdom of the Jews," the ruler of the territory just to the north of the Jewish territory, and the father-son combination that presided over worship in Jerusalem for so many years. The Lysanias mentioned comes later than the Lysanias who was king of Abila until 36 B.C. An archaeological discovery at Abila has confirmed that there was a later Lysanias who was tetrarch during the reign of Tiberius (A.D. 14-37).

[v](Matt. 3:1; Luke 3:3) The mission of John was comparable to that of an Oriental courier who preceded his monarch to proclaim the king's coming and the need for citizens to prepare the roads for his arrival. John's preparation, however, was in matters pertaining to moral behavior and outlook. To receive the Kingdom promised them by the Old Testament prophets, Israel's people needed to repent. John's baptism then identified the remnant that had achieved such moral preparation.

Matt. 3:1-6 (cont'd)	Mark 1:2-6 (cont'd)	Luke 3:3-6 (cont'd)
MAKE HIS PATHS STRAIGHT!'" [Isa. 40:3].	40:3].	5 'EVERY RAVINE SHALL BE FILLED UP,
4 Now John himself had [6]a garment of camel's hair, and a leather belt about his waist; and his food was locusts and wild honey.	4 John the Baptist appeared in the wilderness [7]preaching a baptism of repentance for the forgiveness of sins.	AND EVERY MOUNTAIN AND HILL SHALL BE [9]BROUGHT LOW; AND THE CROOKED SHALL BECOME STRAIGHT,
5 Then Jerusalem was going out to him, and all Judea, and all the district around the Jordan;	5 And all the country of Judea was going out to him, and all the people of Jerusalem; and they were being baptized by him in the Jordan River, confessing their sins.	AND THE ROUGH ROADS SMOOTH;
6 and they were being baptized by him in the Jordan River, as they confessed their sins.	6 And John was clothed with camel's hair and wore a leather belt around his waist, and [8]his diet was locusts and wild honey.	6 AND ALL [10]FLESH SHALL SEE THE SALVATION OF GOD'" [Isa. 40:3-5].

[1]Or, arrived. [2]Or, proclaiming as a herald. [3]Lit., the heavens. [4]Lit., has come near. [5]Lit., through. [6]Lit., his garment. [7]Or, proclaiming. [8]Lit., he was eating. [9]Or, leveled. [10]Or, mankind.

Sec. 25 His messages to the Pharisees, Sadducees, multitudes, tax-gatherers, and soldiers
– Judean wilderness and region around the Jordan River –

Matt. 3:7-10	Luke 3:7-14
7 But when he saw many of the Pharisees and Sadducees coming for baptism, he said to them, "You brood of vipers, who warned you to flee from the [w]wrath to come?	7 He therefore began saying to the multitudes who were going out to be baptized by him, "You brood of vipers, who warned you to flee from the [w]wrath to come?
8 "Therefore bring forth fruit in keeping with repentance;	8 "Therefore bring forth fruits in keeping with repentance, and do not begin to say [1]to yourselves, 'We have Abraham for our father,' for I say to you that God is able from these stones to raise up children to Abraham.
9 and do not suppose that you can say to yourselves, 'We have Abraham for our father'; for I say to you, that God is able from these stones to raise up children to Abraham.	
10 "And the axe is already laid at the root of the trees; every tree therefore that does not bear good fruit is cut down and thrown into the fire.	9 "And also the axe is already laid at the root of the trees; every tree therefore that does not bear good fruit is cut down and thrown into the fire."
	10 And the multitudes were questioning him, saying, "Then what shall we do?"

[w](Matt. 3:7; Luke 3:7) The well-known "wrath to come" will immediately precede Christ's second advent. The Old Testament fixes this time at the beginning of "the day of the LORD", and makes it a prelude to Messiah's reign (Isa. 3:16-24; 13:9-11; Jer. 30:7; Ezek. 38-39; Amos 5:18-19; Zeph. 1:14-18; cf. Matt. 24:21; 1 Thess. 1:10; 5:9; Rev. 6:16-17). Messiah's first coming to die for sin was not in John's mind at this moment. His theme for those not yet morally prepared was the threat of coming judgment. Being a member of the covenant nation was not synonymous with enjoying the benefits of the covenants, as so many Jews thought. Personal moral preparation was also necessary.

Luke 3:7-14 (cont'd)

11 And he would answer and say to them, "Let the man who has two tunics share with him who has none; and let him who has food do likewise."

12 And *some* ²tax-gatherers also came to be baptized, and they said to him, "Teacher, what shall we do?"

13 And he said to them, "³Collect no more than what you have been ordered to."

14 And *some* ⁴soldiers were questioning him, saying, "And *what about us,* what shall we do?" And he said to them, "Do not take money from anyone by force, or accuse *anyone* falsely, and be content with your wages."

¹Or, in. ²I.e., Collectors of Roman taxes for profit. ³Or, *Exact.* ⁴I.e., men in active military service.

Sec. 26 His description of the Christ (cf. Sec. 29)
– *Region around Jordan River* –

Matt. 3:11-12	Mark 1:7-8	Luke 3:15-18
11 "As for me, I baptize you ¹with water for repentance, ˣbut He who is coming after me is mightier than I, and I am not fit to remove His sandals; He will baptize you with the Holy Spirit and fire.	**7** And he was ²preaching, and saying, "After me One is coming who is mightier than I, and I am not fit to stoop down and untie the thong of His sandals.	**15** Now while the people were in a state of expectation and all were ³wondering in their hearts about John, as to whether he might be the ⁴Christ,
	8 "I baptized you ¹with water; ˣbut He will baptize you ¹with the Holy Spirit."	**16** John answered and said to them all "As for me, I baptize you ¹with water; ˣbut One is coming who is mightier than I, and I am not fit to untie the thong of His sandals; He will baptize you with the Holy Spirit and fire.
12 "And His winnowing fork is in His hand, and He will thoroughly clear His threshing floor; and He will gather His wheat into the barn, but He will burn up the chaff with unquenchable fire."		**17** "And His winnowing fork is in His hand to thoroughly clear His threshing floor, and to gather the wheat into His barn; but He will burn up the chaff with unquenchable fire."
		18 So with many other exhortations also he preached the gospel to the people.

¹The Gr. here can be translated *in, with* or *by.* ²Or, *proclaiming.* ³Or, *reasoning* or *debating.* ⁴I.e., the Messiah.

ˣ(Matt. 3:11; Mark 1:8; Luke 3:16) In contrasting Christ's baptism with the Holy Spirit and his own baptism with water, John had in mind the promised coming of the Holy Spirit in accord with such prophecies as Joel 2:28-29.

PART FIVE

THE END OF JOHN'S MINISTRY AND THE BEGINNING OF CHRIST'S

– largely in Judea –

Sec. 27 Jesus' baptism by John (cf. Secs. 30; 121)
– ʸBethany beyond Jordan –

Matt. 3:13-17	Mark 1:9-11	Luke 3:21-23a
13 ᶻThen Jesus *arrived from Galilee at the Jordan coming to John, to be baptized by him. **14** But John tried to prevent Him, saying, "I have need to be baptized by You, and do You come to me?" **15** But Jesus answering said to him, "Permit it at this time; for in this way it is fitting for us to fulfill all righteousness." Then he *ᵃpermitted Him.	**9** And it came about in those days that Jesus came from Nazareth in Galilee, and was ᵃbaptized by John in the Jordan.	
16 And after being baptized, Jesus went up immediately from the water; and behold, the heavens were opened, and ¹he saw the Spirit of God descending as a dove, and coming upon Him, **17** and behold, a voice out of the heavens, saying, "This is ²My beloved Son, in whom I am well-pleased."	**10** And immediately coming up out of the water, He saw the heavens ³opening, and the Spirit like a dove descending upon Him; **11** and a voice came out of the heavens: "Thou art My beloved Son, in Thee I am well-pleased."	**21** Now it came about when all the people were ᵃbaptized, that Jesus also was baptized, and while He was praying, heaven was opened, **22** and the Holy Spirit descended upon Him in bodily form like a dove, and a voice came out of heaven, "Thou art My beloved Son, in Thee I am well-pleased." **23** And when He began His ministry, Jesus Himself was about thirty years of age,

¹Or, He. ²Lit., My Son, the Beloved. ³Or, being parted.

ʸ See John 1:28 (Sec. 29).

ᶻ (Matt. 3:13) Jesus' first Passover following His baptism (John 2:13-22, Sec. 34) came in April, of course. Calculating the amount of time occupied by the events between His baptism and Passover leads to the probable conclusion that He was baptized in the summer or spring of the previous year.

ᵃ (Matt. 3:15; Mark 1:9; Luke 3:21) The baptism of Jesus was a very significant event for several reasons:
1. His baptism was different from the baptism of others because He had not sinned and did not need to repent.
2. By it He became publicly identified with the group whom John recognized as morally prepared for the Kingdom.
3. It is recognized by other New Testament sources as the formal beginning of Christ's public ministry (Acts 1:21-22; 10:37-38).

Sec. 28 Jesus' temptation in the wilderness
– *Judean wilderness* –

Matt. 4:1-11	Mark 1:12-13	Luke 4:1-13
1 Then Jesus was led up by the Spirit into the wilderness to be tempted by the devil.	**12** And immediately the Spirit *impelled Him *to go* out into the wilderness.	**1** And Jesus, full of the Holy Spirit, returned from the Jordan and was led about [6]by the Spirit in the wilderness
2 And [b]after He had fasted forty days and forty nights, He [1]then became hungry.	**13** And He was in the wilderness forty days being tempted by Satan; and He was with the wild beasts,	**2** for forty days, being tempted by the devil. And He ate nothing during those days; and when they had ended, He became hungry.
3 And the tempter came and said to Him, "If You are the Son of God, command that these stones become [2]bread."		**3** And the devil said to Him, "If You are the Son of God, tell this stone to become bread."
4 But He answered and said, "It is written, 'MAN SHALL NOT LIVE ON BREAD ALONE, BUT ON EVERY WORD THAT PROCEEDS OUT OF THE MOUTH OF GOD'" [Deut. 8:3].		**4** And Jesus answered him, "It is written, 'MAN SHALL NOT LIVE ON BREAD ALONE'" [Deut. 8:3].
5 Then the devil *took Him into the holy city; and he had Him stand on the pinnacle of the temple,		**5** And he led Him up and showed Him all the kingdoms of [7]the world in a moment of time.
6 and *said to Him, "If You are the Son of God throw Yourself down; for it is written, 'HE WILL GIVE HIS ANGELS CHARGE CONCERNING YOU'; and 'ON their HANDS THEY WILL BEAR YOU UP, LEST YOU STRIKE YOUR FOOT AGAINST A STONE'" [Psalm 91:11-12].		**6** And the devil said to Him, "I will give You all this domain and [8]its glory; for it has been handed over to me, and I give it to whomever I wish.
		7 "Therefore if You [9]worship before me, it shall all be Yours."
7 Jesus said to him, "[3]On the other hand, it is written, 'YOU SHALL NOT [4]PUT THE LORD YOUR GOD TO THE TEST'" [Deut. 6:16].		**8** And Jesus answered and said to him, "It is written, 'YOU SHALL WORSHIP THE LORD YOUR GOD AND SERVE HIM ONLY'" [Deut. 6:13].
		9 And he led Him to Jerusalem and had Him stand on the pinnacle of the temple, and said to Him, "If You are the Son of God, throw Yourself down from here;

[b](Matt. 4:2) The three temptations in the paragraph came at the close of the forty days, when Jesus was most vulnerable. The sequence of temptations in Matthew is preferred over that in Luke (cf. "then," Matt. 3:5). Jesus' victorious encounter with the devil places Him in contrast with Adam (Gen. 3) and the Israelites in the wilderness. He drew each of His responses to the devil from Deuteronomy, which recounts the wilderness experiences. Failure in the wilderness has now become triumph in the wilderness. Now Christians have a basis for confidence in overcoming temptation through Jesus' sympathetic help (Heb. 2:18; 4:14-16).

Matt. 4:1-11 (cont'd)	Mark 1:12-13 (cont'd)	Luke 4:1-13 (cont'd)
8 Again, the devil *took Him to a very high mountain, and *showed Him all the kingdoms of the world, and their glory; **9** and He said to Him, "All these things will I give You, if You fall down and worship me." **10** Then Jesus *said to him, "Begone, Satan! For it is written, 'YOU SHALL WORSHIP THE LORD YOUR GOD, AND ⁵SERVE HIM ONLY'" [Deut. 6:13].		**10** for it is written, 'HE WILL GIVE HIS ANGELS CHARGE CONCERNING YOU TO GUARD YOU,' **11** and, 'ON *their* HANDS THEY WILL BEAR YOU UP, LEST YOU STRIKE YOUR FOOT AGAINST A STONE'" [Psalm 91:11-12]. **12** And Jesus answered and said to him, "It is said, 'YOU SHALL NOT ⁴PUT THE LORD YOUR GOD TO THE TEST'" [Deut. 6:16]. **13** And when the devil had finished every temptation, he departed Him until an opportune time.
11 Then the devil *left Him; and behold, angels came and *began* to minister to Him.	and the angels were ministering to Him.	

¹Lit., *later, afterward.* ²Lit., *loaves.* ³Lit., *Again.* ⁴Or, *tempt . . . God.* ⁵Or, *fulfill religious duty to Him.* ⁶Or, *under the influence of;* lit., *in.* ⁷Lit., *the inhabited earth.* Lit., *their* (referring to the kingdoms). ⁹Or, *bow down.*

Sec. 29   John's self-identification to the priests and Levites (cf. Secs. 24; 26)
— ᶜ*Bethany beyond Jordan* —

John 1:19-28

19 And this is the witness of John, when the Jews sent to him priests and Levites from Jerusalem to ask him, "Who are you?"

20 And he confessed, and did not deny, and he confessed, "I am not ¹the Christ."

21 And they asked him, "What then? Are you Elijah?" And he *said, "ᵈI am not." "Are you the Prophet?" And he answered, "No."

22 They said then to him, "Who are you, so that we may give an answer to those who sent us? What do you say about yourself?"

23 He said, "I am A VOICE OF ONE CRYING IN THE WILDERNESS, 'MAKE STRAIGHT THE WAY OF THE LORD' [Isa. 40:3], as Isaiah the prophet said."

24 Now they had been sent from the Pharisees.

25 And they asked him, and said to him, "Why then are you baptizing, if you are not ¹the Christ, nor Elijah, nor the Prophet?"

ᶜThis Bethany is to be distinguised from the Bethany near Jerusalem (Sec. 142; cf. also Secs. 143-152).

ᵈ(John 1:21) John's relationship to Malachi's prophecy about Elijah (Mal. 4:5-6) is difficult to determine in light of his response to this question. Perhaps the key is found in the condition "if you care to accept it" (Matt. 11:14, Sec. 75). At any rate, John was certainly unaware that he was fulfilling the prophecy, if he was.

John 1:19-28 (cont'd)

26 John answered them saying, "I baptize [2]in water, but among you stands One whom you do not know.

27 "It is He who comes after me, the thong of whose sandal I am not worthy to untie."

28 These things took place in Bethany beyond the Jordan, where John was baptizing.

[1]I.e., the Messiah. [2]The Gr. here can be translated *in, with* or *by*.

Sec. 30   John's identification of Jesus as the Son of God (cf. Sec. 27)
— *Bethany beyond Jordan* —

John 1:29-34

29 The next day he *saw Jesus coming to him, and *said, "[e]Behold, the Lamb of God who takes away the sin of the world!

30 "This is He on behalf of whom I said, 'After me comes a Man who [1]has a higher rank than I, for He existed before me.'

31 "And I did not recognize [2]Him, but in order that He might be manifested to Israel, I came baptizing [3]in water."

32 And John bore witness saying, "I have beheld the Spirit descending as a dove out of heaven, and He remained upon Him.

33 "And I did not recognize [2]Him, but He who sent me to baptize [3]in water said to me, 'He upon whom you see the Spirit descending and remaining upon Him, this is the one who baptizes [3]in the Holy Spirit.'

34 "And I have seen, and have borne witness that this is the Son of God."

[1]Lit., *has become before me*. [2]I.e., as the Messiah. [3]The Gr. here can be translated *in, with* or *by*.

Sec. 31   Jesus' first [f]followers (cf. Secs. 47, 51, 54)
— *Bethany beyond Jordan and Galilee* —

John 1:35-51

35 Again the next day John was standing, [1]with two of his disciples,

36 and he looked upon Jesus as He walked, and *said, "Behold, the Lamb of God!"

37 And the two disciples heard him speak, and they followed Jesus.

38 And Jesus turned, and beheld them following, and *said to them, "What do you seek?" And they said to Him, "Rabbi (which translated means Teacher), where are You staying?"

39 He *said to them, "Come, and you will see." They came therefore and saw where He was staying; and they stayed with Him that day, for it was about [2]the tenth hour.

40 One of the two who heard John speak, and followed Him, was Andrew, Simon Peter's brother.

[e](John 1:29) John was a student of the Old Testament, particularly of Isaiah's prophecy (cf. Sec. 24 with Isa. 40:3-5). It is no surprise, therefore, that he focuses on Messiah's soteriological work ("Behold, the Lamb of God," cf. Isa. 53:6-7) as well as His eschatological ("The kingdom of heaven is at hand," Matt. 3:2, Sec. 24). John did not completely comprehend how the two ministries would combine (Matt. 11:2-3, Sec. 75; cf. 1 Pet. 1:10-11). Even those closest to Christ did not see, until after His resurrection, why He must die.

[f]These followers were won through a variety of means: the first two were won by the testimony of John (v. 36); Simon Peter by the testimony of one of these two, namely, Andrew (vv. 40-42); Philip by the invitation of Jesus (v. 43); and Nathanael by the testimony of Philip (vv. 46-47). Each seems to have acknowledged Jesus' Messiahship (vv. 41, 45, 49) on the basis of John's testimony (vv. 29, 34, 36). Yet they did not become His permanent followers at this point, since at least two of them returned to their occupation as fishermen. See Section 47.

John 1:35-51 (cont'd)

41   He *found first his own brother Simon, and *said to him, "We have found the Messiah" (which translated means ³Christ).

42   He brought him to Jesus. Jesus looked at him, and said, "You are Simon the son of ⁴John; you shall be called Cephas" (which translated means ⁵Peter).

43   The next day He purposed to go forth into Galilee, and He *found Philip. And Jesus *said to him, "Follow Me."

44   Now Philip was from Bethsaida, of the city of Andrew and Peter.

45   Philip *found ᵍNathanael and *said to him, "We have found Him of whom Moses in the Law and *also* the Prophets wrote, Jesus of Nazareth, the son of Joseph."

46   And Nathanael *said to him, "Can any good thing come out of Nazareth?" Philip *said to him, "Come and see."

47   Jesus saw Nathanael coming to Him, and *said of him, "Behold, an Israelite indeed, in whom is no guile!"

48   Nathanael *said to Him, "How do You know me?" Jesus answered and said to him, "Before Philip called you, when you were under the fig tree, I saw you."

49   Nathanael answered Him, "Rabbi, You are the Son of God; You are the King of Israel."

50   Jesus answered and said to him, "Because I said to you that I saw you under the fig tree, do you believe? You shall see greater things than these."

51   And He *said to him, "Truly, truly, I say to you, you shall see the heavens opened, and the angels of God ascending and descending on ʰthe Son of Man."

¹Lit., *and*. ²Perhaps 10 a.m. (Roman time). ³Gr., *Anointed One*. ⁴Gr., *Joannes*. ⁵I.e., Rock or Stone.

Sec. 32   First miracle, water becomes wine
– *Cana of Galilee* –

John 2:1-11

1   And ¹on the third day there was a wedding in Cana of Galilee, and the mother of Jesus was there;

2   and Jesus also was invited, and His disciples, to the wedding.

3   And when the wine gave out, the ʲmother of Jesus *said to Him, "They have no wine."

4   And Jesus *said to her, "Woman, ¹what do I have to do with you? My hour has not yet come."

5   His mother *said to the servants, "Whatever He says to you, do it."

6   Now there were six stone waterpots set there for the Jewish custom of purification, containing ²twenty or thirty gallons each.

ᵍ(John 1:45) If Nathanael became one of the twelve, he should probably be identified with Bartholomew in the lists found in the synoptic gospels and Acts. It cannot be concluded dogmatically, however, that he was one of this select group.

ʰ(John 1:51) "The Son of Man" was a very frequent self-designation adopted by the Lord. Its source was Daniel 7:13-14. The nature of the title both alluded to His Messiahship and veiled it. Listeners probably read into the title as much as they apprehended of Jesus and no more. Its scope of meaning is broad, including overtones of deity, undertones of humanity, and redemption of lost man among other connotations.

ⁱ(John 2:1) "On the third day" marks the conclusion of a week about which we have a rather full account. Beginning with 1:19-28 as the first day, we have then the second day in vv. 29-34, the third in vv. 35-43, the fourth in vv. 43-51, and the seventh in 2:1-11.

ʲ(John 2:3) Jesus' mother showed the same lack of understanding as John the Baptist and Peter did later on (Matt. 11:2-3, Sec. 75; 16:22, Sec. 119). Though they were right as to the fact of His Messiahship, they were wrong as to the time and manner of its glorious manifestation (John 2:4). Jesus did perform a miracle to meet the need, but in a manner that revealed His identity to only a few (John 2:9, 11).

John 2:1-11 (cont'd)

7 Jesus *said to them, "Fill the waterpots with water." And they filled them up to the brim.

8 And He *said to them, "Draw *some* out now, and take it to the ³head-waiter." And they took it to him.

9 And when the headwaiter tasted the water which had become wine, and did not know where it came from (but the servants who had drawn the water knew), the headwaiter *called the bridegroom,

10 and *said to him, "Every man serves the good wine first, and when men ⁴have drunk freely, then that which is poorer; you have kept the good wine until now."

11 This beginning of His ⁵signs Jesus did in Cana of Galilee, and manifested His glory, and His disciples believed in Him.

¹Lit., *what to Me and to you* (a Hebrew idiom). ²Two or three metretai. ³Or, *steward.* ⁴Or, *have become drunk.* ⁵Or, *attesting miracles;* i.e., one which points to the supernatural power of God in redeeming grace.

Sec. 33   Visit at Capernaum with His disciples

John 2:12

12 After this He went down to Capernaum, He and His mother, and His brothers, and His disciples; and there they stayed a few days.

Sec. 34   ᵏFirst cleansing of the Temple at the Passover (cf. Sec. 189)
– Jerusalem –

John 2:13-22

13 And the ¹Passover of the Jews was at hand, and Jesus went up to Jerusalem.

14 And He found in the temple those who were selling oxen and sheep and doves, and the moneychangers seated.

15 And He made a scourge of cords, and drove them all out of the temple, with the sheep and the oxen; and He poured out the coins of the moneychangers, and overturned their tables;

16 and to those who were selling the doves He said, "Take these things away; stop making My Father's house a house of merchandise."

17 His disciples remembered that it was written, "ZEAL FOR THY HOUSE WILL CONSUME ME" [Psalm 69:9].

18 The Jews therefore answered and said to Him, "What sign do You show to us, seeing that You do these things?"

19 Jesus answered and said to them, "Destroy this ¹temple, and in three days I will raise it up."

20 The Jews therefore said, "It took ᵐforty-six years to build this ¹temple, and will You raise it up in three days?"

ᵏThis cleansing of the Temple should be kept distinct from the one at the close of the Lord's ministry (cf. Sec. 189). The differences in wording and setting, along with John's chronological placement of it, verify that the two narratives refer to two different events. Three years between the two is more than ample for the practice of buying and selling to have arisen again on the Temple premises, especially in light of the avaricious tendencies of the Jewish leaders.

¹(John 2:13) This is the first of four Passovers that provide a chronological framework for Jesus' public ministry. See essay 11, "Chronology of the Life of Christ" (pp. 324-328).

ᵐ(John 2:20) Forty-six years is to be reckoned from either the initiation of Herod's rebuilding project in 20/19 B.C., or from completion of the work on the sanctuary (*naos*) proper in 18/17 B.C. See essay 11, "Chronology of the Life of Christ" (pp. 324-328).

John 2:13-22 (cont'd)

21 But He was speaking of the [1]temple of His body.

22 When therefore He was raised from the dead, His disciples remembered that He said this; and they believed the Scripture, and the word which Jesus had spoken.

[1]Or, *sanctuary.*

Sec. 35   An early response to Jesus' miracles
— *Jerusalem* —

John 2:23-25

23 Now when He was in Jerusalem at the Passover, during the feast, many believed in His name, beholding His signs which He was doing.

24 But Jesus, on His part, was not entrusting Himself to them, for He knew all men,

25 and because He did not need anyone to bear witness concerning man for He Himself [n]knew what was in man.

Sec. 36   Nicodemus' interview with Jesus
— *Jerusalem* —

John 3:1-21

1 Now there was a man of the Pharisees, named Nicodemus, a ruler of the Jews;

2 this man came to Him by night, and said to Him, "Rabbi, we know that You have come from God *as* a teacher; for no one can do these [1]signs that You do unless God is with him."

3 Jesus answered and said to him, "Truly, truly, I say to you, unless one is [o]born [2]again, he cannot see the kingdom of God."

4 Nicodemus *said to Him, "How can a man be born when he is old? He cannot enter a second time into his mother's womb and be born, can he?"

5 Jesus answered, "Truly, truly, I say to you, unless one is born of water and the Spirit, he cannot enter into the kingdom of God.

6 "That which is born of the flesh is flesh, and that which is born of the Spirit is spirit.

7 "Do not marvel that I said to you, 'You must be born [2]again.'

8 "The wind blows where it wishes and you hear the sound of it, but do not know where it comes from and where it is going; so is everyone who is born of the Spirit."

9 Nicodemus answered and said to Him, "How can these things be?"

10 Jesus answered and said to him, "Are you the teacher of Israel, and do not understand these things?

11 "Truly, truly, I say to you, we speak that which we know, and bear witness of that which we have seen; and you do not receive our witness.

---

[n](John 2:25) Jesus, being God as well as man, was omniscient. His awareness of human depravity revealed the basically selfish reasons of those attracted to Him at this point. The moral preparation of these prospective subjects was not yet sufficient for their participation in the Kingdom of which He and John the Baptist spoke.

[o](John 3:3) Being "born again" is not specifically mentioned in the Old Testament. The ideas closest to it are those of a new heart and a special activity of the Spirit in conjunction with the inauguration of the New Covenant and Israel's Kingdom (Jer. 31:31-34; Ezek. 36:26-27; Joel 2:28-32).

John 3:1-21 (cont'd)

12 "If I told you earthly things and you do not believe, how shall you believe if I tell you heavenly things?

13 "And no one has ascended into heaven, but He who descended from heaven, even the Son of Man.[3]

14 "And as Moses lifted up the serpent in the wilderness, even so must the Son of Man be lifted up;

15 that whoever [4]believes may in Him have eternal life.

16 "[p]For God so loved the world, that He gave His [5]only begotten Son, that whoever believes in Him should not perish, but have eternal life.

17 "For God did not send the Son into the world to judge the world, but that the world should be saved through Him.

18 "He who believes in Him is not judged; he who does not believe has been judged already, because he has not believed in the name of the [5]only begotten Son of God.

19 "And this is the judgment, that the light is come into the world, and men loved the darkness rather than the light; for their deeds were evil.

20 "For everyone who does evil hates the light, and does not come to the light, lest his deeds should be exposed.

21 "But he who practices the truth comes to the light, that his deeds may be manifested as having been wrought in God."

[1]Or, *attesting miracles.*   [2]Or, *from above.*   [3]Later manuscripts add *who is in heaven.*   [4]Some mss. read *believes in Him may have eternal life.*   [5]Or, *unique, only one of His kind.*

Sec. 37   John superseded by Jesus
— Aenon near Salim —

John 3:22-36

22 [q]After these things Jesus and His disciples came into the land of Judea, and there He was spending time with them and baptizing.

23 And John also was baptizing in Aenon near Salim, because there was [1]much water there; and they were coming and were being baptized.

24 For John had not yet been thrown into prison.

25 There arose therefore a discussion on the part of John's disciples with a Jew about purification.

26 And they came to John and said to him, "Rabbi, He who was with you beyond the Jordan, to whom you have borne witness, behold, He is baptizing, and all are coming to Him."

27 John answered and said, "A man can receive nothing, unless it has been given him from heaven.

28 "You yourselves bear me witness, that I said, 'I am not the [2]Christ,' but, 'I have been sent before Him.'

29 "He who has the bride is the bridegroom; but the friend of the bridegroom, who stands and hears him, rejoices greatly because of the bridegroom's voice. And so this joy of mine has been made full.

30 "He must increase, but I must decrease.

[p](John 3:16) John the apostle is noted for his reflective sections in this gospel, and John 3:16-21 may be one of them. It seems a more natural assumption, however, to view these verses as continuing the Lord's teaching already in progress.

[q](John 3:22) Suggestions that relocate John 3:22-30 after 2:12 or after 3:36 are not well-founded. No convincing reason for doing this has been forthcoming. Besides, John 3:31 does not follow smoothly after 3:21.

John 3:22-36 (cont'd)

31 "[r]He who comes from above is above all, he who is of the earth is from the earth and speaks of the earth. He who comes from heaven is above all.

32 "What He has seen and heard, of that He bears witness; and no man receives His witness.

33 "He who has received His witness has set his seal to this, that God is true.

34 "For He whom God has sent speaks the words of God; [3]for He gives the Spirit without measure.

35 "The Father loves the Son, and has given all things into His hand.

36 "He who believes in the Son has eternal life; but he who does not [4]obey the Son shall not see life, but the wrath of God abides on him."

[1]Lit., many waters.   [2]I.e., Messiah.   [3]Lit., for He does not give the Spirit by measure.   [4]Or, believe.

Sec. 38   Jesus' [s]departure from Judea (cf. Sec. 102)
   — From Judea, through Samaria, to Galilee —

John 4:1-4

1 When therefore the Lord knew that the Pharisees had heard that Jesus was making and baptizing more disciples than John

2 (although Jesus Himself was not baptizing, but His disciples were),

3 He left Judea, and departed again into Galilee.

4 And He had to pass through Samaria.

Luke 3:19-20

19 But when Herod the tetrarch was reproved by him on account of Herodias, his brother's wife, and on account of all the wicked things which Herod had done,

20 he added this also to them all, that he locked John up in prison.

Matt. 4:12	Mark 1:14a	Luke 4:14a
12 Now when He heard that John had been [1]taken into custody, He withdrew into Galilee;	**14** And after John had been [1]taken into custody, Jesus came into Galilee,	**14** And Jesus returned to Galilee in the power of the Spirit;

[1]Lit., delivered up.

Sec. 39   Discussion with a Samaritan woman
   — Sychar in Samaria —

John 4:5-26

5 So He *came to a city of [t]Samaria, called Sychar, near the parcel of ground that Jacob gave to his son Joseph;

---

[r](John 3:31) John 3:31-36 may be a continuation of John the Baptist's speech, the words of Jesus, or reflections of the apostle John. The second possibility is unlikely without relocating some verses. The third possibility is a characteristic of this writer, but comes too much by surprise. The more natural flow is obtained by taking this as a continuation of the Baptist's words.

[s]Jesus had two rather obvious reasons for leaving Judea to go to Galilee at this time: potential opposition from the Pharisees (John 4:1-3) and the imprisonment of John the Baptist (Matt. 4:12; Mark 1:14a; Luke 4:14a). According to Luke, Herod imprisoned John because of being rebuked by John for taking his brother's wife, and also because, according to the secular historian Josephus, Herod feared a revolution led by John.

[t](John 4:5) Among the gospel writers only Luke and John devote special attention to Samaria and Samaritans. Both are especially conscious of how Christ met the needs of non-Jews, since both gospels were composed with readers of Gentile background in view.

John 4:5-26 (cont'd)

6 and Jacob's well was there. Jesus therefore, being wearied from His journey, was sitting thus by the well. It was about [1]the sixth hour.

7 There *came a woman of Samaria to draw water. Jesus *said to her, "Give Me a drink."

8 For His disciples had gone away into the city to buy food.

9 The Samaritan woman therefore *said to Him, "How is it that You, being a Jew, ask me for a drink since I am a Samaritan woman?" (For Jews have no dealings with Samaritans.)

10 Jesus answered and said to her, "If you knew the gift of God, and who it is who says to you, 'Give Me a drink,' you would have asked Him, and He would have given you living water."

11 She *said to Him, "[2]Sir, You have nothing to draw with and the well is deep; where then do You get that living water?

12 "You are not greater than our father Jacob, are You, who gave us the well, and drank of it himself, and his sons, and his cattle?"

13 Jesus answered and said to her, "Everyone who drinks of this water shall thirst again;

14 but whoever drinks of the water that I shall give him shall never thirst; but the water that I shall give him shall become in him a well of water springing up to eternal life."

15 The woman *said to Him, "[2]Sir, give me this water, so I will not be thirsty, nor come all the way here to draw."

16 He *said to her, "Go, call your husband, and come here."

17 The woman answered and said, "I have no husband." Jesus *said to her, "You have well said, 'I have no husband';

18 for you have had five husbands, and the one whom you now have is not your husband; this you have said truly."

19 The woman *said to Him, "[2]Sir, I perceive that You are a prophet.

20 "Our fathers worshiped in this mountain, and you *people* say that in Jerusalem is the place where men ought to worship."

21 Jesus *said to her, "Woman, believe Me, an hour is coming when neither in this mountain, nor in Jerusalem, shall you worship the Father.

22 "You worship that which you do not know; we worship that which we know, for salvation is from the Jews.

23 "But an hour is coming, and now is, when the true worshipers shall worship the Father in spirit and truth; for such people the Father seeks to be His worshipers.

24 "God is [3]spirit, and those who worship Him must worship in spirit and truth."

25 The woman *said to Him, "I know that Messiah is coming (He who is called Christ); when that One comes, He will declare all things to us."

26 Jesus *said to her, "[u]I who speak to you am *He*."

[1]Perhaps 6 p.m. (Roman time).   [2]Or, *Lord.*   [3]Or, *a Spirit.*

[u](John 4:26) This was Jesus' only open declaration of His Messiahship until His trial. See Mark 14:62, Section 229.

Sec. 40   Challenge of a spiritual harvest
    — Sychar in Samaria —

John 4:27-38

27   And at this point His disciples came, and they ᵛmarveled that He had been speaking with a woman; yet no one said, "What do You seek?" or, "Why do You speak with her?"

28   So the woman left her waterpot, and went into the city, and *said to the men,

29   "Come, see a man who told me all the things that I *have* done; this is not ¹the Christ, is it?"

30   They went out of the city, and were coming to Him.

31   In the meanwhile the disciples were requesting Him, saying, "Rabbi, eat."

32   But He said to them, "I have food to eat that you do not know about."

33   The disciples therefore were saying to one another, "No one brought Him *anything* to eat, did he?"

34   Jesus *said to them, "My food is to do the will of Him who sent Me, and to accomplish His work.

35   "Do you not say, 'There are yet four months, and *then* comes the harvest'? Behold, I say to you, lift up your eyes, and look on the fields, that they are white for harvest.

36   "Already he who reaps is receiving wages, and is gathering fruit for life eternal; that he who sows and he who reaps may rejoice together.

37   "For in this *case* the saying is true, 'One sows, and another reaps.'

38   "I sent you to reap that for which you have not labored; others have labored, and you have entered into their labor."

    ¹I.e., the Messiah.

Sec. 41   Evangelization of Sychar

John 4:39-42

39   And from that city many of the Samaritans believed in Him because of the word of the woman who testified. "He told me all the things that I *have* done."

40   So when the Samaritans came to Him, they were asking Him to stay with them; and He stayed there two days.

41   And many more believed because of His word;

42   and they were saying to the woman, "It is no longer because of what you said that we believe, for we have heard for ourselves and know that this One is indeed the ʷSavior of the world."

Sec. 42   Arrival in Galilee (cf. Secs. 43, 45, 97)

John 4:43-45

43   And after the two days He went forth from there into Galilee.

44   For Jesus Himself testified that a prophet has no honor in ˣhis own country.

45   So when He came to Galilee, the Galileans received Him, having seen all the things that He did in Jerusalem at the feast; for they themselves also went to the feast.

    ᵛ(John 4:27) The disciples' surprise arose from Jesus' unconventional conduct. Rabbis would not have carried on a conversation with a woman since they regarded women as inferior in every way. Yet the disciples did not question the action because they had already been with Jesus long enough to know He did not always conform to conventional rabbinic behavior.

    ʷ(John 4:42) Recording the salvation of the Samaritans is John's way of showing his predominantly Gentile readership that salvation in Christ is for all men regardless of race.

    ˣ(John 4:44) "His own country" must be Galilee, not Judea as some have understood. Galilee is the meaning of the expression in the synoptic gospels. A reference to Judea at this point would not fit unless this departure were placed before Jesus' time in Samaria.

PART SIX
THE ʸMINISTRY OF CHRIST IN GALILEE

OPPOSITION AT HOME AND A NEW HEADQUARTERS

Sec. 43   Nature of the ᶻGalilean ministry (cf. Secs. 42, 45, 97)

Matt. 4:17	Mark 1:14b-15	Luke 4:14b-15
17 From that time Jesus began to ¹preach and say, "Repent, for the kingdom of heaven is at hand."	²preaching the gospel of God, **15** and saying, "The ᵃtime is fulfilled, and the kingdom of God is at hand; repent and ³believe in the gospel."	and news about Him spread through all the surrounding district. **15** And He *began* teaching in their synagogues and was praised by all.

¹Or, proclaim.   ²Or, proclaiming.   ³Or, put your trust in.

Sec. 44   Child at Capernaum healed by Jesus while at Cana (cf. Sec. 73)

John 4:46-54

46   He came therefore again to Cana of Galilee where He had made the water wine. And there was a certain royal official, whose son was sick at Capernaum.

47   When he heard that Jesus had come out of Judea into Galilee, he went to Him, and was requesting *Him* to come down and heal his son; for he was at the point of death.

48   Jesus therefore said to him, "ᵇUnless you *people* see ¹signs and wonders, you *simply* will not believe."

49   The royal official *said to Him, "²Sir, come down before my child dies."

50   Jesus *said to him, "Go your way; your son lives." The man believed the word that Jesus spoke to him, and he started off.

ʸFor a discussion of the length of this Galilean ministry, see essay 11, "Chronology of the Life of Christ" (pp. 324-328).

ᶻMatthew, Mark, and Luke devote much space to the period spent in Galilee. Early stages of the period were marked by increasing popularity which reached its peak probably at about the time of the Sermon on the Mount. A rising opposition, beginning with a series of Sabbath controversies with Jewish leaders, is also perceived. This culminated in the first public rejection of Jesus by these leaders. At that point, toward the end of the period, Jesus inaugurated His parabolic teaching ministry so that He might reveal truth to those with receptive hearts while hiding it from the unreceptive.

ᵃ(Mark 1:15) The timing of God's programs in history is a major theme of biblical teaching. The first (Gal. 4:4) and second (Acts 1:7; 3:19-21) comings of Christ are foundational to God's schedule for world history.

ᵇ(John 4:48) Jesus was not rebuking the royal official but lamenting over what was a typical attitude of the Galileans. The official was different in that he believed solely on the basis of Jesus' word (John 4:50).

John 4:46-54 (cont'd)

51 And as he was now going down, *his* slaves met him, saying that his [3]son was living,

52 So he inquired of them the hour when he began to get better. They said therefore to him, "Yesterday at [4]the seventh hour the fever left him."

53 So the father knew that *it was* at that hour in which Jesus said to him, "Your son lives"; and he himself believed, and his whole household.

54 This is again a second [5]sign that Jesus performed, when He had come out of Judea into Galilee.

[1]Or, *attesting miracles.* [2]Or, *Lord.* [3]Or, *boy.* [4]Perhaps 7 p.m. (Roman time). [5]Or, *attesting miracle.*

Sec. 45 Ministry and rejection at Nazareth (cf. Secs. 42, 43, 97)

Luke 4:16-31a

16 And He came to Nazareth, [c]where He had been brought up; and as was His custom, He entered the synagogue on the Sabbath, and stood up to read.

17 And the [1]book of the prophet Isaiah was handed to Him. And He opened the book, and found the place where it was written,

18 "THE SPIRIT OF THE LORD IS UPON ME,
BECAUSE HE ANOINTED ME TO PREACH THE GOSPEL TO THE POOR.
HE HAS SENT ME TO PROCLAIM RELEASE TO THE CAPTIVES,
AND RECOVERY OF SIGHT TO THE BLIND,
TO SET FREE THOSE WHO ARE DOWNTRODDEN,

19 TO PROCLAIM THE FAVORABLE YEAR OF THE LORD" [Isa. 61:1-2].

20 And He closed the [1]book, and gave it back to the attendant, and sat down; and the eyes of all in the synagogue were fixed upon Him.

21 And He began to say to them, "Today this Scripture has been fulfilled in your [2]hearing."

22 And all were [3]speaking well of Him, and wondering at the gracious words which [4]were falling from His lips; and they were saying, "Is this not Joseph's son?"

23 And He said to them, "No doubt you will quote this proverb to Me, 'Physician, heal yourself! Whatever we heard was done at Capernaum, do here in your home town as well.'"

24 And He said, "Truly I say to you, no prophet is welcome in his home town.

25 "But I say to you in truth, there were many widows in Israel in the days of Elijah, when the sky was shut up for three years and six months, when a great famine came over all the land;

26 and yet Elijah was sent to none of them, but only to [5]Zarephath, in the land of Sidon, to a woman who was a widow.

27 "And there were many lepers in Israel in the time of Elisha the prophet; and none of them was cleansed, but only Naaman the Syrian."

28 And all in the synagogue were filled with rage as they heard these things;

29 and they rose up and cast Him out of the city, and led Him to the brow of the hill on which their city had been built, in order to throw Him down the cliff.

30 But passing through their midst, He went His way.

31 And He came down to Capernaum, a city of Galilee.

[1]Or, *scroll.* [2]Lit., *ears.* [3]Or, *testifying.* [4]Lit., *were proceeding out of His mouth.* [5]Gr., *Serepta.*

[c](Luke 4:16) This statement implies that Nazareth had ceased to be Jesus' home already. It had been His boyhood custom to attend the synagogue services in that town. He retained the habit after reaching manhood.

Sec. 46   Move to Capernaum

Matt. 4:13-16

13   and leaving Nazareth, He came and ᵈsettled in Capernaum, which is by the sea, in the region of Zebulun and Naphtali.

14   *This was* to fulfill what was spoken through Isaiah the prophet, saying,

15   "THE LAND OF ZEBULUN AND THE LAND OF NAPHTALI,
¹BY THE WAY OF THE SEA, BEYOND THE JORDAN, GALILEE OF THE ²GENTILES—

16   "THE PEOPLE WHO WERE SITTING IN DARKNESS SAW A GREAT LIGHT,
AND TO THOSE WHO WERE SITTING IN THE LAND AND SHADOW OF DEATH,
UPON THEM A LIGHT DAWNED" [Isa. 9:1-2].

¹Or, *Toward the sea.*   ²Or, *nations.*

DISCIPLES CALLED AND MINISTRY THROUGHOUT GALILEE

Sec. 47   First call of the ᵉfour (cf. Secs. 31, 51, 54)
— By the Sea of Galilee, near Capernaum —

Matt. 4:18-22	Mark 1:16-20
18 And walking by the Sea of Galilee, He saw two brothers, Simon who was called Peter, and Andrew his brother, casting a net into the sea; for they were fishermen.	**16** And as He was going along by the Sea of Galilee, He saw Simon and Andrew, the brother of Simon, casting a net in the sea; for they were fishermen.
19 And He *said to them, "¹Follow Me, and I will make you fishers of men."	**17** And Jesus said to them, "Follow Me, and I will make you become fishers of men."
20 And they immediately left the nets, and followed Him.	**18** And they immediately left the nets and followed Him.
21 And going on from there He saw two other brothers, ²James the *son* of Zebedee, and ³John his brother, in the boat with Zebedee their father, mending their nets; and He called them.	**19** And going on a little farther, He saw ²James the *son* of Zebedee, and John his brother, who were also in the boat mending the nets.
22 And they immediately left the boat and their father, and followed Him.	**20** And immediately He called them; and they left their father Zebedee in the boat with the hired servants, and went away ⁴to follow Him.

¹Lit., *Come here after Me.*   ²Or, *Jacob.*   ³Gr., *Joannes,* Heb., *Johanan.*   ⁴Lit., *after Him.*

ᵈ(Matt. 4:13) Capernaum became Jesus' new home after His unfriendly reception at Nazareth. It had by New Testament times grown into a city, having a tax office (Matt. 9:9, Sec. 54) and a garrison for Roman soldiers (Matt. 8:9, Sec. 73). Jesus had earlier visited Capernaum (John 2:12, Sec. 33). Here a little later He will encounter Peter and Andrew, who had apparently not gone with Him to Nazareth, and James and John, the sons of Zebedee (Matt. 4:18-22; Mark 1:16-20, Sec. 47). He would preach in this city's synagogue which had been built by the good centurion (Luke 7:5, Sec. 73) and of which Jairus was an official (Mark 5:22, Sec. 95). Jesus' famous message on the Bread of Life was delivered here (John 6:59, Sec. 109). It is no wonder that Matthew calls Capernaum Jesus' "own city" (Matt. 9:1, Sec. 53).

ᵉIf, as tradition says, John the son of Zebedee was one of the two unnamed disciples at Bethany (John 1:35, Sec. 31), three of these four fishermen had already followed Jesus for a time without having a specific call. Apparently they responded to His call at this time by temporarily resuming their association with Jesus. Features of Luke 5:1-11 (Sec. 51) are sufficiently distinct from this paragraph to indicate another call later on.

Sec. 48   Teaching in the synagogue of ᶠCapernaum authenticated by healing a demoniac

Mark 1:21-28	Luke 4:31b-37
21 And they *went into Capernaum; and immediately on the Sabbath He entered the synagogue and *began* to teach.	And He was teaching them on the Sabbath;
22 And they were amazed at His teaching; for He was teaching them as *one* having authority, and not as the scribes.	32 and they were amazed at His teaching, for His ²message was with authority.
23 And just then there was in their synagogue a man with an unclean spirit; and he cried out,	33 And there was a man in the synagogue ³possessed by the spirit of an unclean demon, and he cried out with a loud voice,
24 saying, "What do we have to do with You, Jesus ¹of Nazareth? Have You come to destroy us? I know who You are—the Holy One of God!"	34 "⁴Ha! What do we have to do with You, Jesus of ¹Nazareth? Have You come to destroy us? I know who You are — the Holy One of God!"
25 And Jesus rebuked him, saying, "ᵍBe quiet, and come out of him!"	35 And Jesus rebuked him, saying, "ᵍBe quiet and come out of him!" And when the demon had thrown him down in *their* midst, he came out of him without doing him any harm.
26 And throwing him into convulsions, the unclean spirit cried out with a loud voice, and came out of him.	
27 And they were all amazed, so that they debated among themselves, saying, "What is this? A new teaching with authority! He commands even the unclean spirits, and they obey Him."	36 And amazement came upon them all, and they *began* discussing with one another saying, "What is ⁵this message? For with authority and power He commands the unclean spirits, and they come out."
28 And immediately the news about Him went out everywhere into all the surrounding district of Galilee.	37 And the report about Him was getting out into every locality in the surrounding district.

¹Lit., *the Nazarene.* ²Lit., *word.* ³Lit., *having a spirit.* ⁴Or possibly, *Let us alone.* ⁵Or, *this word, that with authority . . . come out?*

Sec. 49   Peter's mother-in-law and others healed
— Capernaum, in Peter's home —

Matt. 8:14-17	Mark 1:29-34	Luke 4:38-41
	29 And immediately ⁴after they had come out of the synagogue, they came into the house of Simon and Andrew, with ⁵James and John.	38 And He arose and *left* the synagogue, and entered Simon's home. Now Simon's mother-in-law was suffering from a high fever; and they made request of Him on her behalf.
14 And when Jesus had come to Peter's ¹home, He saw his mother-in-law	30 Now Simon's mother-in-law was lying sick with a fever; and im-	39 And standing over

ᶠTwo aspects of Jesus' reception at Capernaum stand out. First, the citizens received Him warmly, which was the very opposite of what had happened at Nazareth. Second, Jesus was not criticized for performing a deed like this on the Sabbath as He was so frequently later on (Secs. 57, 60, 61). Apparently Jewish leadership in Jerusalem had not yet become alarmed to the point of sending representatives to Galilee to oppose Him.

ᵍ(Mark 1:25; Luke 4:35) It was altogether inappropriate that Jesus' Messiahship should be proclaimed by representatives of the evil one. Had He allowed this by not silencing the demons, He would have given grounds for a charge brought against Him later by the Pharisees, that of being Satan's ally (Matt. 12:24; Mark 3:22, Sec. 79). Compare also Mark 1:34; Luke 4:41, Sec. 49.

Matt. 8:14-17 (cont'd)	Mark 1:29-34 (cont'd)	Luke 4:38-41 (cont'd)
lying sick in bed with a fever. **15** And He ^htouched her hand, and the fever left her; and she arose, and ²waited on Him. **16** And when evening had come, they brought to Him many who were demon-possessed; and He cast out the spirits with a word, and healed all who were ill **17** in order that what was spoken through Isaiah the prophet might be fulfilled, saying, "HE HIMSELF TOOK OUR INFIRMITIES, AND ³CARRIED AWAY OUR DISEASES" [Isa. 53:4].	mediately they *spoke to Him about her. **31** And ^hHe came to her and raised her up, taking her by the hand, and the fever left her, and she ²waited on them. **32** And when evening had come, after the sun had set, they *began* bringing to Him all who were ill and those who were demon-possessed. **33** And the whole city had gathered at the door. **34** And He healed many who were ill with various diseases, and cast out many demons; and He was not permitting the demons to speak, because they ⁶knew who He was.	her, He ^hrebuked the fever, and it left her; and she immediately arose and ²waited on them. **40** And while the sun was setting, all who had any sick with various diseases brought them to Him; and laying His hands on every one of them, He was healing them. **41** And demons also were coming out of many, crying out and saying, "You are the Son of God!" And rebuking them, He would not allow them to speak, because they knew Him to be ⁷the Christ.

¹Or, *house.*   ²Or, *served.*   ³Or, *removed.*   ⁴Some mss. read *after He had come out, He came.*   ⁵Or, *Jacob.*   ⁶Some mss. read *knew Him to be Christ.*   ⁷I.e., the Messiah.

Sec. 50   Tour of Galilee with Simon and others

Matt. 4:23-24	Mark 1:35-39	Luke 4:42-44
	35 And in the early morning, while it was still dark, He arose and went out and departed to a lonely place, and was praying there. **36** And Simon and his companions hunted for Him; **37** and they found Him, and *said to Him, "Everyone is looking for You." **38** And He *said to them, "Let us go somewhere else to the towns nearby, in order that I may ³preach there also; for that	**42** And when day came, He departed and went to a lonely place; and the multitudes were searching for Him, and came to Him, and tried to keep Him from going away from them. **43** But He said to them, "I must preach the kingdom of God to the other cities also, for I was sent for this purpose."
23 And Jesus was	is what I came out for."	

^h(Matt. 8:15; Mark 1:31; Luke 4:39) The emphases and backgrounds of the synoptic writers differed. Matthew in describing Messiah the King notes that He merely "touched her hand, and the fever left her." Mark describes Messiah the Servant from a slightly different perspective: "He came to her and raised her up, taking her by the hand." Luke the physician, after giving a more professional description of the sickness, pictures Messiah the Man as simply rebuking the fever. Luke alone tells how in the subsequent healings Jesus laid "His hands on every one of them" (4:40), indicating His deep concern for His fellow human beings as individuals.

Matt. 4:23-24 (cont'd)	Mark 1:35-39 (cont'd)	Luke 4:42-44 (cont'd)
going about in all Galilee, [1]teaching in their synagogues, and proclaiming the [1]gospel of the kingdom, and healing every kind of disease and every kind of sickness among the people. **24** And the news about Him went out into all Syria; and they brought to Him all who were ill, taken with various diseases and pains, demoniacs, [2]epileptics, paralytics; and He healed them.	**39** And He went into their synagogues throughout all Galilee, [4]preaching and casting out the demons.	**44** And He kept on preaching in the synagogues of [5]Judea.

[1]Or, *good news.*   [2]Lit., *moon-smitten.*   [3]Or, *proclaim.*   [4]Or, *proclaiming.*   [5]I.e., the country of the Jews (including Galilee); some mss. read *Galilee.*

Sec. 51   [J]Second call of the four (cf. Secs. 31, 47, 54)
– By the Sea of Galilee –

Luke 5:1-11

1 Now it came about that while the multitude were pressing around Him and listening to the word of God, He was standing by the lake of Gennesaret;

2 and He saw two boats lying at the edge of the lake; but the fishermen had gotten out of them, and were washing their nets.

3 And He got into one of the boats, which was Simon's, and asked him to put out a little way from the land. And He sat down and *began* teaching the multitudes from the boat.

4 And when He had finished speaking, He said to Simon, "Put out into the deep water and let down your nets for a catch."

5 And Simon answered and said, "Master, we worked hard all night and caught nothing, but at Your [1]bidding I will let down the nets."

6 And when they had done this, they enclosed a great quantity of fish; and their nets *began* to break;

7 and they signaled to their partners in the other boat, for them to come and help them. And they came, and filled both of the boats, so that they began to sink.

8 But when Simon Peter saw *that,* he fell down at Jesus' [2]feet, saying, "Depart from me, for I am a sinful man, O Lord!"

9 For amazement had seized him and all his companions because of the catch of fish which they had taken;

[1](Matt. 4:23) The threefold thrust of Jesus' ministry is reflected here: He taught in Jewish synagogues, He proclaimed the Kingdom of God, and He healed diseases and sicknesses in certification of the authority of His teaching and preaching.

[J]The sequence of Luke's account, along with several differences in detail from Matthew and Mark, probably indicates this call came later than the one described in Section 47. For example, Simon and Andrew were not fishing from a boat in Matthew and Mark, but they were in Luke. In Matthew and Mark, Jesus did not enter a boat as He did in Luke. Luke records a great catch of fish, but Matthew and Mark say nothing about one. Hence, it appears that the two pairs of brothers went back to their fishing trade after the tour of Section 50. After responding to this second call, they seem to have remained with Jesus permanently. Following His crucifixion they did, however, return to fishing (cf. Sec. 255).

Luke 5:1-11 (cont'd)

10   and so also ³James and John, sons of Zebedee, who were partners with Simon. And Jesus said to Simon, "Do not fear, from now on you will be catching men."

11   And when they had brought their boats to land, they left everything and followed Him.

¹Or, *word.*   ²Lit., *knees.*   ³Or, *Jacob.*

Sec. 52   Cleansing of a leper followed by much publicity
— In one of the cities by the Sea of Galilee —

Matt. 8:2-4	Mark 1:40-45	Luke 5:12-16
2 And behold, a leper came to Him, and ¹bowed down to Him, saying, "Lord, if You are willing, You can make me clean."	**40** And a leper *came to Him, beseeching Him and falling on his knees before Him, and saying to Him, "If You are willing, You can make me clean."	**12** And it came about that while He was in one of the cities, behold, there *was* a man full of leprosy; and when he saw Jesus, he fell on his face and implored Him, saying, "Lord, if You are willing, You can make me clean."
3 And He stretched out His hand and touched him, saying, "I am willing; be cleansed." And immediately his leprosy was cleansed.	**41** And moved with compassion, He stretched out His hand, and touched him, and*said to him, "I am willing; be cleansed."	**13** And He stretched out His hand, and touched him, saying, "I am willing; be cleansed." And immediately the leprosy left him.
	42 And immediately the leprosy left him and he was cleansed.	
	43 And He sternly warned him and immediately sent him away,	
4 And Jesus *said to him, "ᵏSee that you tell no one; but go, show yourself to the priest, and present the ²offering that Moses commanded, for a testimony to them."	**44** and He *said to him, "ᵏSee that you say nothing to anyone; but go, show yourself to the priest and offer for your cleansing what Moses commanded, for a testimony to them."	**14** And He ordered him to ᵏtell no one, "But go and show yourself to the priest, and make an offering for your cleansing, just as Moses commanded, for a testimony to them."
	45 But he went out and began to proclaim it freely and to spread the news about, to such an extent that Jesus could no longer publicly enter a city, but ³stayed out in unpopulated areas; and they were coming to Him from everywhere.	**15** But the news about Him was spreading even farther, and great multitudes were gathering to hear Him and to be healed of their sicknesses.
		16 But He Himself would *often* slip away ⁴to the ⁵wilderness and pray.

¹Or, *worshiped.*   ²Or, *gift.*   ³Lit., *was.*   ⁴Lit., *in.*   ⁵Or, *lonely places.*

ᵏ(Matt. 8:4; Mark 1:44; Luke 5:14) The proper course would have been for the priests to verify the cleansing and announce to the nation the arrival of Messiah. Whether the cleansed leper complied with this instruction is doubtful in light of his disobedience in telling others besides the priests. Even if he had complied, the willingness of the priests to acknowledge Jesus' Messiahship is not established, as reflected in the Sadducees' attitude toward Him later on.

Sec. 53   Forgiving and healing of a paralytic
– Capernaum –

Matt. 9:1-8	Mark 2:1-12	Luke 5:17-26
1 And getting into a boat, He crossed over, and came to His own city.	1 And when He had come back to Capernaum several days afterward, it was heard that He was at home. 2 And many were gathered together, so that there was no longer room, even near the door; and He was speaking the word to them.	17 And it came about [11]one day that He was teaching; and there were some [1]Pharisees and teachers of the law sitting there, who had come from every village of Galilee and Judea and from Jerusalem; and the power of the Lord was present for Him to perform healing.
2 And behold, they were bringing to Him a paralytic, lying on a bed;	3 And they *came, bringing to Him a paralytic, carried by four men. 4 And being unable to [6]get to Him because of the crowd, they removed the roof [7]above Him; and when they had dug an opening, they let down the pallet on which the paralytic was lying.	18 And behold, some men were carrying on a [12]bed a man who was paralyzed; and they were trying to bring him in, and to set him down in front of Him. 19 And not finding any way to bring him in because of the crowd, they went up on the roof and let him down through the tiles with his stretcher, right in the center, in front of Jesus.
and Jesus seeing their faith said to the paralytic, "Take courage, My [1]son, your sins are [2]forgiven."	5 And Jesus seeing their faith *said to the paralytic, "My [8]son, your sins are forgiven."	20 And seeing their faith, He said, "[13]Friend, your sins are forgiven you."
3 And behold, some of the scribes said [3]to themselves, "This *fellow* blasphemes."	6 But there were some of the scribes sitting there and reasoning in their hearts, 7 "Why does this man speak that way? He is blaspheming; who can forgive sins [9]but God alone?"	21 And the scribes and the Pharisees began to reason, saying, "Who is this man who speaks blasphemies? Who can forgive sins, but God alone?"
4 And Jesus knowing their thoughts	8 And immediately Jesus, aware [10]in His spirit that they were reasoning that way within themselves, *said to them,	22 But Jesus, [14]aware of their reasonings, answered and said to them,
said, "Why are you thinking evil in your hearts?	"Why are you reasoning about these things in your hearts?	"Why are you reasoning in your hearts?
5 "For which is easier, to say, 'Your sins [2]are forgiven,' or to say,	9 "Which is easier, to say to the paralytic, 'Your sins are forgiven'; or to say,	23 "Which is easier, to say, 'Your sins have been forgiven you,' or to say,

[1](Luke 5:17) This is the first mention of the Pharisees in Luke's gospel. This is also the first time that opposition to Jesus from religious leaders appeared in Galilee. It began earlier in Jerusalem because of jealousy (John 4:1-4, Sec. 38), and representatives soon came from Judea to continue their campaign against Him. The recent tour of Galilee (Sec. 50) had created wider interest, and therefore the Jewish leaders felt a need to investigate and thwart, if necessary, this new public figure.

Matt. 9:1-8 (cont'd)	Mark 2:1-12 (cont'd)	Luke 5:17-26 (cont'd)
'Rise, and walk'? **6** "But in order that you may know that the Son of Man has authority on earth to forgive sins"— then He *said to the paralytic—"Rise, take up your bed, and go home." **7** And he rose, and [4]went home. **8** But when the multitudes saw this, they were [5]filled with awe, and glorified God, who had given such authority to men.	'Arise, and take up your pallet and walk'? **10** "But in order that you may know that the Son of Man has authority on earth to forgive sins" —He *said to the paralytic— **11** "I say to you, rise, take up your pallet and go home." **12** And he rose and immediately took up the pallet and went out in the sight of all; so that they were all amazed and were glorifying God, saying, "We have never seen anything like this."	'Rise and walk'? **24** "But in order that you may know that the Son of Man has authority on earth to forgive sins,"—He said to the paralytic—"I say to you, rise, and take up your stretcher and go home." **25** And at once he rose up before them, and took up what he had been lying on, and went home, glorifying God. **26** And they were all seized with astonishment and began glorifying God; and they were filled with fear, saying, "We have seen remarkable things today."

[1]Lit., *child.* [2]Lit., *are being forgiven.* [3]Lit., *among.* [4]Or, *departed.* [5]Or, *afraid.* [6]Lit., *bring to.* [7]Lit., *where He was.* [8]Lit., *child.* [9]Lit., *if not one, God.* [10]Lit., *by.* [11]Lit., *on one of the days.* [12]Or, *stretcher.* [13]Lit., *Man.* [14]Or, *perceiving.*

Sec. 54   Call of Matthew (cf. Secs. 31, 47, 51)
— Capernaum —

Matt. 9:9	Mark 2:13-14	Luke 5:27-28
	13 And He went out again by the seashore; and all the multitude were coming to Him, and He was teaching them.	**27** And after that He went out, and noticed a [2]tax-gatherer named Levi,
9 And as Jesus passed on from there, He saw a man, called Matthew, sitting [1]in the [m]tax office; and He *said to him, "Follow Me!" And he rose, and followed Him.	**14** And as He passed by, He saw Levi the son of Alpheus sitting in the [m]tax office, and He *said to him, "Follow Me!" And he rose and followed Him.	sitting in the [m]tax office, and He said to him, "Follow Me." **28** And he left everything behind, and rose and began to follow Him.

[1]Lit., *at the tax booth.* [2]I.e., Collector of Roman taxes for profit.

[m](Matt. 9:9; Mark 2:14; Luke 5:27) Tax-gatherers such as Matthew (also called Levi) estimated the worth of merchants' goods that were in transit and collected taxes on them for the Roman government. Matthew apparently dealt with the shipping trade on the Sea of Galilee (cf. Mark 2:13). Vague tariff rates allowed the tax-gatherer to levy higher fees so as to increase his own profit. Whether or not Matthew was among the dishonest majority of his occupation is not known, but merely belonging to a class that had been excommunicated by fellow Jews was enough to make him despised. His cooperation with the Romans further alienated him from his countrymen. Jesus went against the theocratic notions of the scribes and Pharisees by calling a person with this background. Matthew responded and left his occupation, never to return to it ("everything," Luke 5:28; cf. Luke 5:11, Sec. 51).

Sec. 55   Banquet at Matthew's house
– Capernaum –

Matt. 9:10-13	Mark 2:15-17	Luke 5:29-32
10 And it happened that as He was reclining at the table in the house, behold many tax-gatherers and [2]sinners came and [3]were dining with Jesus and His disciples. 11 And when the Pharisees saw this, they said to His disciples, "Why is your Teacher eating with the tax-gatherers and sinners?" 12 But when He heard this, He said, "It is not those who are healthy who need a physician, but those who are sick. 13 "But go and learn what this means, 'I DESIRE [4]COMPASSION, [5]AND NOT SACRIFICE' [Hos. 6:6], for I did not come to call the righteous, but sinners."	15 And it [6]came about that He was reclining at the table in his house, and many [1]tax-gatherers and sinners [7]were dining with Jesus and His disciples; for there were many of them, and they were following Him. 16 And when the scribes of the Pharisees saw that He was eating with the sinners and tax-gatherers, they began saying to His disciples, "Why is He eating and drinking with tax-gatherers and sinners?" 17 And hearing this, Jesus *said to them, "It is not those who are healthy who need a physician, but those who are sick; I did not come to call the righteous, but sinners."	29 And Levi gave a [n]big [8]reception for Him in his house; and there was a great crowd of tax-gatherers and other people who were reclining at the table with them. 30 And the Pharisees and their scribes began grumbling at His disciples, saying, "Why do you eat and drink with the tax-gatherers and sinners?" 31 And Jesus answered and said to them, "It is not those who are well who need a physician, but those who are sick. 32 "I have not come to call the righteous but sinners to repentance."

[1]I.e., Collectors of Roman taxes for profit. [2]I.e., irreligious Jews. [3]Lit., reclined with. [4]Or, mercy. [5]I.e., more than. [6]Lit., comes. [7]Lit., were reclining with. [8]Or, banquet.

Sec. 56   [o]Changed conditions with the Messiah present explained by three illustrations
– Capernaum –

Matt. 9:14-17	Mark 2:18-22	Luke 5:33-39
14 Then the disciples of John *came to Him, saying, "Why do we and the Pharisees fast, but Your disciples do not fast?"	18 And John's disciples and the Pharisees were fasting; and they *came and *said to Him, "Why do John's disciples and the disciples of the Pharisees fast, but Your disciples do not fast?" 19 And Jesus said to them, "While the bridegroom is with them, the	33 And they said to Him, "The disciples of John often fast and offer prayers; the disciples of the Pharisees also do [5]the same; but Yours eat and drink." 34 And Jesus said to them, "You cannot make the [1]attendants of the bridegroom fast while the

[n](Luke 5:29) Matthew's willingness to use his wealth to evangelize his friends is reflected in the size of the reception he hosted. Jesus' participation with despised tax-gatherers and sinners marked a departure from customary Jewish procedure and demonstrated His concern for those who were spiritually sick and would admit it. For those who felt themselves righteous, but were actually unrighteous, He could do nothing.

[o]Changed conditions arise when Messiah comes. John the Baptist had indicated this (cf. Sec. 37) but had not dealt specifically with the issue of feasting versus fasting.

Matt. 9:14-17 (cont'd)	Mark 2:18-22 (cont'd)	Luke 5:33-39 (cont'd)
15 And Jesus said to them, "The [1]attendants of the bridegroom cannot mourn as long as the bridegroom is with them, can they? But the days will come when the bridegroom is taken away from them, and then they will fast. **16** "But no one puts a [2]patch of unshrunk cloth on an old garment; for the [3]patch pulls away from the garment, and a worse tear results. **17** "Nor do men put new wine into old [4]wineskins; otherwise the wineskins burst, and the wine pours out, and the wineskins are ruined; but they put new wine into fresh wineskins, and both are preserved."	[1]attendants of the bridegroom do not fast, do they? So long as they have the bridegroom with them, they cannot fast. **20** "But the days will come when the bridegroom is taken away from them, and then they will fast in that day. **21** "No one sews a [2]patch of unshrunk cloth on an old garment; otherwise the [3]patch pulls away from it, the new from the old, and a worse tear results. **22** "And no one puts new wine into old [4]wineskins; otherwise the wine will burst the skins, and the wine is lost, and the skins *as well*; but *one puts* new wine into fresh wineskins."	bridegroom is with them, can you? **35** "But *the* days will come; and when the bridegroom is taken away from them, then they will fast in those days." **36** And He was also telling them a [P]parable: "No one tears a piece from a new [6]garment and puts it on an old [6]garment; otherwise he will both tear the new, and the piece from the new will not match the old. **37** "And no one puts new wine into old [4]wineskins; otherwise the new wine will burst the [4]skins, and it will be spilled out, and the [4]skins will be ruined. **38** "But new wine must be put into fresh wineskins. **39** "And no one, after drinking old *wine* wishes for new; for he says, 'The old is good *enough.*'"

[1]Lit., *sons of the bridal-chamber.*   [2]Lit., *that which is put on.*   [3]Lit., *that which fills up.*   [4]I.e., skins used as bottles.   [5]Or, *likewise.*   [6]Or, *cloak.*

SABBATH CONTROVERSIES AND WITHDRAWAL (cf. Secs. 152, 155, 164)

Sec. 57   A lame man healed in Jerusalem on the Sabbath

John 5:1-9

1 After these things there was [1]a [q]feast of the Jews, and Jesus went up to Jerusalem.

[P](Luke 5:36) By "parable" Luke means "illustration." A more technical sense of "parable" later on marks a major change in the Lord's teaching technique (cf. Secs. 82-92). In this latter sense a parable is designed to hide the truth from unbelievers while revealing truth to believers. The former aspect is not in evidence here.

[q](John 5:1) The two most probable identifications of this feast are Passover and Tabernacles. Of the two, the latter seems the better choice for reasons given in essay 11, "Chronology of the Life of Christ" (pp. 324-328).

John 5:1-9 (cont'd)

2 Now there is in Jerusalem by the sheep *gate* a pool, which is called in [2]Hebrew [3]Bethesda, having five porticoes.

3 In these lay a multitude of those who were sick, blind, lame, and withered, [[4]waiting for the moving of the waters;

4 for an angel of the Lord went down at certain seasons into the pool, and stirred up the water; whoever then first, after the stirring up of the water, stepped in was made well from whatever disease with which he was afflicted.]

5 And a certain man was there, who had been thirty-eight years in his sickness.

6 When Jesus saw him lying there, and knew that he had already been a long time in *that condition*, He *said to him, "Do you wish to get well?"

7 The sick man answered Him, "Sir, I have no man to put me into the pool when the water is stirred up, but while I am coming, another steps down before me."

8 Jesus *said to him, "Arise, take up your pallet, and walk."

9 And immediately the man became well, and took up his pallet and *began* to walk.

Now it was the Sabbath on that day.

[1]Many mss. read *the feast;* i.e., the Passover.   [2]I.e., Jewish Aramaic.   [3]Many mss. read *Bethsaida* or *Bethzatha.*   [4]Many mss. do not contain the remainder of v. 3, nor v. 4.

Sec. 58   Effort to kill Jesus for breaking the Sabbath and saying He was equal with God

– Jerusalem –

John 5:10-18

10 Therefore the Jews were saying to him who was cured, "It is the [r]Sabbath, and it is not permissible for you to carry your pallet."

11 But he answered them, "He who made me well was the one who said to me, 'Take up your pallet and walk.'"

12 They asked him, "Who is the man who said to you, 'Take up your pallet, and walk'?"

13 But he who was healed did not know who it was; for Jesus had slipped away while there was a crowd in *that* place.

14 Afterward Jesus *found him in the temple, and said to him, "Behold, you have become well; do not sin anymore, so that nothing worse may befall you."

15 The man went away, and told the Jews that it was Jesus who had made him well.

16 And for this reason the Jews were persecuting Jesus, because He was doing these things on the Sabbath.

17 But He answered them, "My Father is working until now, and I Myself am working."

18 For this cause therefore the Jews were seeking all the more to kill Him, because He not only was breaking the Sabbath, but also was calling God His own Father, making Himself equal with God.

[r](John 5:10) On no other subject did the religious leaders differ with the Lord more frequently than that of the Sabbath. This is the first of three controversies which came in rather rapid succession (cf. Secs. 60, 61). The rabbis had listed thirty-nine principal works that were forbidden on the Sabbath, one group of which included ordinary house chores. Carrying a pallet violated this. A year and a half of ministry still remained (John 5:18), and already the Jerusalem authorities were ready to kill Him. This animosity spread very quickly to Galilee (cf. Mark 3:6, Sec. 61).

Sec. 59 Discourse demonstrating the Son's [s]equality with the Father
    – Jerusalem –

John 5:19-47

19 Jesus therefore answered and was saying to them, "Truly, truly, I say to you, the Son can do nothing of Himself, unless *it is* something He sees the Father doing; for whatever *the Father* does, these things the Son also does in like manner.

20 "For the Father loves the Son, and shows Him all things that He Himself is doing; and greater works than these will He show Him, that you may marvel.

21 "For just as the Father raises the dead and gives them life, even so the Son also gives life to whom He wishes.

22 "For not even the Father judges anyone, but He has given all judgment to the Son,

23 in order that all may honor the Son, even as they honor the Father. He who does not honor the Son does not honor the Father who sent Him.

24 "Truly, truly, I say to you, he who hears My word, and believes Him who sent Me, has eternal life, and does not come into judgment, but has passed out of death into life.

25 "Truly, truly, I say to you, an hour is coming and now is, when the dead shall hear the voice of the Son of God; and those who hear shall live.

26 "For just as the Father has life in Himself, even so He gave to the Son also to have life in Himself;

27 and He gave Him authority to execute judgment, because He is [1]the Son of Man.

28 "Do not marvel at this; for an hour is coming, in which all who are in the tombs shall hear His voice,

29 and shall come forth; those who did the good *deeds* to a resurrection of life, those who committed the evil *deeds* to a resurrection of judgment.

30 "I can do nothing on My own initiative. As I hear, I judge; and My judgment is just, because I do not seek My own will, but the will of Him who sent Me.

31 "If I *alone* bear witness of Myself, My testimony is not [2]true.

32 "There is another who bears witness of Me, and I know that the testimony which He bears of Me is true.

33 "You have sent to John, and he has borne witness to the truth.

34 "But the witness which I receive is not from man, but I say these things that you may be saved.

35 "He was the lamp that was burning and was shining and you were willing to rejoice for a while in his light.

36 "But the witness which I have is greater than *that of* John; for the works which the Father has given Me to accomplish, the very works that I do, bear witness of Me, that the Father has sent Me.

37 "And the Father who sent Me, He has borne witness of Me. You have neither heard His voice at any time, nor seen His form.

38 "And you do not have His word abiding in you, for you do not believe Him whom He sent.

39 "[3]You search the Scriptures, because you think that in them you have eternal life; and it is these that bear witness of Me;

40 and you are unwilling to come to Me, that you may have life.

41 "I do not receive glory from men;

42 but I know you, that you do not have the love of God in yourselves.

---

[s]This discourse takes its cue from and accepts the accuracy of the statement by the Jews in John 5:18: He "was calling God His own Father, making Himself equal with God."

John 5:19-47 (cont'd)

43 "I have come in My Father's name, and you do not receive Me; if another shall come in his own name, you will receive him.

44 "How can you believe, when you receive glory from one another, and you do not seek the [4]glory that is from the *one and* only God?

45 "Do not think that I will accuse you before the Father; the one who accuses you is Moses, in whom you have set your hope.

46 "For if you believed Moses, you would believe Me; for he wrote of Me.

47 "But if you do not believe his writings, how will you believe My words?"

[1]Or, *a son of man.* [2]I.e., admissible as legal evidence. [3]Or, (a command) *Search the Scriptures!* [4]Or, *honor or fame.*

Sec. 60   Controversy over disciples' picking grain on the Sabbath
— Perhaps in Galilee —

Matt. 12:1-8	Mark 2:23-28	Luke 6:1-5
1 At that [1]time Jesus went on the Sabbath through the grainfields, and His disciples became hungry and began to pick the heads *of grain* and eat.	**23** And it came about that He was passing through the grainfields on the Sabbath, and His disciples began to make their way along while picking the heads *of grain.*	**1** Now it came about that on a *certain* [8]Sabbath He was passing through *some* grainfields; and His disciples were [1]picking and eating the heads *of grain,* rubbing them in their hands.
2 But when the Pharisees saw it, they said to Him, "Behold, Your disciples do what is not lawful to do on a Sabbath."	**24** And the Pharisees were saying to Him, "See here, why are they doing what is not lawful on the Sabbath?"	**2** But some of the Pharisees said, "Why do you do what is not lawful on the Sabbath?"
3 But He said to them, "[u]Have you not read what David did, when he became hungry, he and his companions;	**25** And He *said to them, "Have you never read what David did when he was in need and became hungry, he and his companions:	**3** And Jesus answering them said, "Have you not even read what David did when he was hungry, he and those who were with him,
4 how he entered the house of God, and they ate the [2]consecrated bread, which was not lawful for him to eat, nor for those with him, but for the priests alone?	**26** how he entered the house of God in the time of Abiathar *the* high priest, and ate the [2]consecrated bread, which is not lawful for *anyone* to eat except the priests, and he gave *it* also to those who were with him?"	**4** how he entered the house of God, and took and ate the [2]consecrated bread which is not lawful for any to eat except the priests alone, and gave it to his companions?"
5 "Or have you not read in the Law, that on the Sabbath the priests in the temple [3]break the Sabbath, and are innocent?		
6 "But I say to you, that something greater than the temple is here.		

[1](Luke 6:1) "Picking" and "rubbing" were, according to rabbinic tradition, tantamount to reaping, threshing, winnowing, and preparing food. They thus were labeled Sabbath breakers.

[u](Matt. 12:3) Jesus' fivefold rebuttal to the accusation is given in Matthew: (1) the example of David (12:3-4), (2) the teaching of the Law (12:5), (3) the prophetic anticipation of Someone greater than the Temple (12:6), (4) the purpose of the Sabbath for man (12:7; cf. Mark 2:27), and (5) Messiah's lordship over the Sabbath (12:8).

| Matt. 12:1-8 | Mark 2:23-28 | Luke 6:1-5 |
| (cont'd) | (cont'd) | (cont'd) |

7 "But if you had known what this [4]means, 'I DESIRE [5]COMPASSION, AND NOT A SACRIFICE' [Hos. 6:6], you would not have condemned the innocent. **8** "For the Son of Man is Lord of the Sabbath."

27 And He was saying to them, "The Sabbath [6]was made [7]for man, and not man [7]for the Sabbath. **28** "Consequently, the Son of Man is Lord even of the Sabbath."

5 And He was saying to them, "The Son of Man is Lord of the Sabbath."

[1]Or, occasion. [2]Or, showbread; lit., loaves of presentation. [3]Or, profane. [4]Lit., is. [5]Or, mercy. [6]Or, came into being. [7]Lit., for the sake of. [8]Many mss. read the second-first Sabbath; i.e., the second Sabbath after the first.

Sec. 61   Healing of a man's withered hand on the Sabbath
– In a synagogue in Galilee –

| Matt. 12:9-14 | Mark 3:1-6 | Luke 6:6-11 |

9 And departing from there, He went into their synagogue. **10** And behold, there was a man with a withered hand. And they questioned Him, saying, "Is it lawful to heal on the Sabbath?"—in order that they might accuse Him. **11** And He said to them, "What man shall there be [1]among you, who shall have one sheep, and if it falls into a pit on the Sabbath, will he not take hold of it, and lift it out? **12** "Of how much more value then is a man than a sheep! So then, it is lawful to do [2]good on the Sabbath." **13** Then He *said to the man, "Stretch out your hand!" And he stretched it out, and it was restored to [3]normal, like the other. **14** But the Pharisees went out, and counseled together against Him, as to

1 And He entered again into a [v]synagogue; and a man was there with a withered hand. **2** And they were watching Him to see if He would heal him on the Sabbath, in order that they might accuse Him. **3** And He *said to the man with the withered hand, "[4]Rise and come forward!" **4** And He *said to them, "Is it lawful on the Sabbath to do good or to do harm, to save a life or to kill?" But they kept silent. **5** And after looking around at them with anger, grieved at their hardness of heart, He *said to the man, "Stretch out your hand." And he stretched it out, and his hand was restored. **6** And the Pharisees went out and immediately

6 And it came about on another Sabbath, that He entered the synagogue and was teaching; and there was a man there [6]whose right hand was withered. **7** And the scribes and the Pharisees were watching Him closely, to see if He healed on the Sabbath, in order that they might find reason to accuse Him. **8** But He knew [7]what they were thinking, and He said to the man with the withered hand, "[8]Rise and [w]come forward!" And he rose and [9]came forward. **9** And Jesus said to them, "I ask you, is it lawful on the Sabbath to do good, or to do harm, to save a life, or to destroy it?" **10** And after looking around at them all, He said to him, "Stretch out your hand!" And he did so; and

[v](Mark 3:1) That this synagogue was in Galilee is demonstrated by Mark's association of the event with the Sea of Galilee immediately afterward (Mark 3:7, Sec. 62).

[w](Luke 6:8) Jesus' intent to make this an occasion for a theological confrontation is evidenced in His words, "Come forward" (Luke 6:8). This Sabbath healing received maximum publicity.

Matt. 12:9-14 (cont'd)	Mark 3:1-6 (cont'd)	Luke 6:6-11 (cont'd)
how they might destroy Him.	began [5]taking counsel with the Herodians against Him, *as to* how they might destroy Him.	his hand was restored. **11** But they themselves were filled with [10]rage, and discussed together what they might do to Jesus.

[1]Lit., *of.* [2]Lit., *well.* [3]Lit., *health.* [4]Lit., *Arise into the midst.* [5]Lit., *giving.* [6]Lit., *and his.* [7]Lit., *their thoughts.* [8]Lit., *Stand; or, Stood into the midst.* [9]Lit., *stood.* [10]Lit., *folly.*

Sec. 62   Withdrawal to the Sea of Galilee with a great multitude from many places

Matt. 12:15

15 But Jesus, [1]aware of *this*, withdrew from there. And many followed Him, and He healed them all,

Matt. 4:25

25 And [x]great multitudes followed Him from Galilee and Decapolis and Jerusalem and Judea and *from* beyond the Jordan.

Matt. 12:16-21

16 and warned them not to [2]make Him known,

Mark 3:7-12

7 And Jesus withdrew to the sea with His disciples; and a [x]great multitude from Galilee followed; and *also* from Judea,

8 and from Jerusalem, and from Idumea, and beyond the Jordan, and the vicinity of Tyre and Sidon, a great multitude heard of all that He was doing and came to Him.

9 And He told His disciples that a boat should stand ready for Him because of the multitude, in order that they might not crowd Him;

10 for He had healed many, with the result that all those who had afflictions pressed about Him in order to touch Him.

11 And whenever the unclean spirits beheld Him, they would fall down before Him and cry out, saying, "You are the Son of God!"

12 And He earnestly warned them not to [2]make Him known.

17 in order that what was spoken through Isaiah the prophet, might be fulfilled, saying,

18 "BEHOLD, MY [3]SERVANT WHOM I [4]HAVE CHOSEN;
MY BELOVED IN WHOM MY SOUL [5]IS WELL-PLEASED;
I WILL PUT MY SPIRIT UPON HIM,
AND HE SHALL PROCLAIM [6]JUSTICE TO THE [7]GENTILES.
19 "HE WILL NOT QUARREL, NOR CRY OUT;
NOR WILL ANYONE HEAR HIS VOICE IN THE STREETS.
20 "A BATTERED REED HE WILL NOT BREAK OFF,
AND A SMOLDERING WICK HE WILL NOT PUT OUT,
UNTIL HE [8]LEADS [6]JUSTICE TO VICTORY.
21 "AND IN HIS NAME THE [7]GENTILES WILL HOPE" [Isa. 42:1-4].

[1]Lit., *knowing.* [2]Or, *reveal who He was.* [3]Lit., *Child.* [4]Lit., *chose* [5]Or, *took pleasure.* [6]Or, *judgment.* [7]Or, *nations.* [8]Or, *puts forth.*

[x](Matt. 4:25; Mark 3:7) A widespread interest in Jesus had now developed. Distant as well as nearby regions were represented in these large crowds.

APPOINTMENT OF THE TWELVE AND SERMON ON THE MOUNT

Sec. 63   Twelve apostles named (cf. Sec. 99, Acts 1:13)
— A mountain near the Sea of Galilee —

Mark 3:13-19	Luke 6:12-16
13 And He *went up to the mountain and *summoned those whom He Himself wanted, and they came to Him.	**12** And it was [4]at this time that He went off to the mountain to pray, and He spent the whole night in prayer to God.
14 And He appointed twelve[1], that they might be with Him, and that He might send them out to preach,	**13** And when day came, He called His disciples to Him; and chose twelve of them, whom He also named as apostles:
15 and to have authority to cast out the demons.	
16 And He appointed the twelve: [y]Simon (to whom He gave the name Peter),	**14** [y]Simon, whom He also named Peter, and Andrew his brother; and
17 and [2]James, the son of Zebedee, and John the brother of [2]James (to them He gave the name Boanerges, which means, "Sons of Thunder");	[2]James and John; and Philip and Bartholomew;
18 and Andrew, and Philip, and Bartholomew, and Matthew, and Thomas, and [2]James the son of Alphaeus, and Thaddaeus, and Simon the [3]Zealot;	**15** and Matthew and Thomas; [2]James the son of Alphaeus, and Simon who was called the Zealot;
19 and Judas Iscariot, who also betrayed Him.	**16** Judas the son of [2]James, and Judas Iscariot, who became a traitor.

[1]Some early mss. add *whom He named apostles.* [2]Or, *Jacob.* [3]Or, *Cananaean.* [4]Lit., *in these days.*

Sec. 64   Setting of the Sermon
— A level place on the mountain —

Matt. 5:1-2	Luke 6:17-19
	17 And He descended with them, and stood on a [z]level place; and there was
1 And when He saw the multitudes, He went up on the [1z]mountain; and after He sat down, His disciples came to Him.	a great multitude of His disciples, and a great throng of people from all Judea and Jerusalem and the coastal region of Tyre and Sidon,
2 And opening His mouth He began to teach them, saying,	**18** [2]who had come to hear Him, and to be healed of their diseases; and those

[y](Mark 3:16; Luke 6:14) Two other lists of the twelve are given, in Matthew 10:2-4 (Sec. 99) and Acts 1:13. By noting that Thaddaeus is another name for Judas the brother of James, the lists are seen to agree with one another except in sequence. Simon Peter is first in all four lists, however. All were Galileans, except Judas Iscariot who was a Judean.

[z](Matt. 5:1; Luke 6:17) Though some have suggested that the Sermon on the Mount consists of teachings given at different times, evidence is convincing that it was delivered on a single occasion, as Matthew and Luke describe it. That the two gospels contain the same sermon is also well taken. Similarities between the two are too numerous to allow for two different sermons. Jesus delivered this sermon from a level place on the side of a mountain. It was addressed to His disciples (Matt. 5:1-2; Luke 6:20), but the multitude was not excluded from the benefit of His words (Matt. 7:28, Sec. 72; Luke 6:19; 7:1, Sec. 73). The sermon was probably much longer than the combined accounts that are preserved. Since each writer has recorded things that the other does not, and since differing details in some of the sayings indicate that Jesus repeated Himself by varying His wording, there probably was other matter not included in either gospel account.

Luke 6:17-19 (cont'd)

who were troubled with unclean spirits were being cured.
19 And all the multitude were trying to touch Him, for power was coming from Him and healing *them* all.

[1]Or, *hill.* [2]Most English versions begin v. 18 with *and those who.*

Sec. 65 [a]**Blessings of those who inherit the Kingdom and woes to those who do not**

Matt. 5:3-12

3 "Blessed are the poor in spirit, for theirs is the kingdom of heaven.
4 "Blessed are those who mourn, for they shall be comforted.
5 "Blessed are the [1]gentle, for they shall inherit the earth.
6 "Blessed are those who hunger and thirst for righteousness, for they shall be satisfied.
7 "Blessed are the merciful, for they shall receive mercy.
8 "Blessed are the pure in heart, for they shall see God.
9 "Blessed are the peacemakers, for they shall be called sons of God.
10 "Blessed are those who have been persecuted for the sake of righteousness, for theirs is the kingdom of heaven.
11 "Blessed are you when *men* cast insults at you, and persecute you, and say all kinds of evil against you falsely, on account of Me.
12 "Rejoice, and be glad, for your reward in heaven is great, for so they persecuted the prophets who were before you.

Luke 6:20-26

20 And turning His gaze on His disciples, He *began* to say, "Blessed *are* you *who are* poor, for yours is the kingdom of God.
21 "Blessed *are* you who hunger now, for you shall be satisfied. Blessed *are* you who weep now, for you shall laugh.
22 "Blessed are you when men hate you, and ostracize you, and cast insults at you, and spurn your name as evil, for the sake of the Son of Man.
23 "Be glad in that day, and leap *for joy,* for behold, your reward is great in heaven; for in the same way their fathers used to [2]treat the prophets.
24 "But woe to you who are rich, for you are receiving your comfort in full.
25 "Woe to you who are [3]well-fed now, for you shall be hungry. Woe *to you* who laugh now, for you shall mourn and weep.
26 "Woe *to you* when all men speak well of you, for in the same way their fathers used to [2]treat the false prophets.

[1]Or, *humble, meek.* [2]Lit., *do to.* [3]Lit., *having been filled.*

Sec. 66 **Responsibility while awaiting the Kingdom (cf. Secs. 83, 144; 128, 165)**

Matt: 5:13-16

13 "You are the salt of the earth; but if the salt has become tasteless, how will it be made salty *again?* It is good for nothing anymore, except to be thrown out and trampled under foot by men.
14 "You are the light of the world. A city set on a [1]hill cannot be hidden.
15 "Nor do *men* light a lamp, and put it under the peck-measure, but on the lampstand; and it gives light to all who are in the house.
16 "Let your light shine before men in such a way that they may see your good works, and glorify your Father who is in heaven.

[1]Or, *mountain.*

---

[a]Each beatitude is associated with an Old Testament promise to those who will participate in the future Kingdom. By this means Jesus informed His listeners as to what Kingdom He was discussing.

Sec. 67　Law, righteousness, and the Kingdom (cf. Sec. 168)

Matt. 5:17-20

17 "Do not think that I came to [b]abolish the Law or the Prophets; I did not come to abolish, but to fulfill.

18 "For truly I say to you, until heaven and earth pass away, not the [1]smallest letter or stroke shall pass away from the Law, until all is accomplished.

19 "Whoever then annuls one of the least of these commandments, and so teaches [2]others, shall be called least in the kingdom of heaven; but whoever [3]keeps and teaches *them*, he shall be called great in the kingdom of heaven.

20 "For I say to you, that unless your righteousness surpasses *that* of the scribes and Pharisees, you shall not enter the kingdom of heaven.

[1]Lit., *one iota (yodh) or one projection of a letter (serif).*　　[2]Lit., *the men.*　　[3]Lit., *does.*

[c]Sec. 68　Six [d]contrasts in interpreting the Law (cf. Secs. 128; 150; 168, 176; 199)

Matt. 5:21-48

21 "You have heard that the [1]ancients were told, 'YOU SHALL NOT COMMIT MURDER' [Exod. 20:13; Deut. 5:17] and 'Whoever commits murder shall be [2]liable to the court.'

22 "But I say to you that everyone who is angry with his brother [3]shall be [4]guilty before the court; and whoever shall say to his brother '[5]Raca,' shall be guilty before [6]the supreme court; and whoever shall say, 'You fool,' shall be guilty *enough to go* into the [7]fiery hell.

23 "If therefore you are presenting your [8]offering at the altar, and there remember that your brother has something against you,

24 leave your [8]offering there before the altar, and go your way; first be reconciled to your brother, and then come and present your offering.

25 "Make friends quickly with your opponent at law while you are with him on the way, in order that your opponent may not deliver you to the judge, and the judge to the officer, and you be thrown into prison.

26 "Truly I say to you, you shall not come out of there, until you have paid up the last [9]cent.

27 "You have heard that it was said, 'YOU SHALL NOT COMMIT ADULTERY' [Exod. 20:14; Deut. 5:18];

28 but I say to you, that everyone who looks on a woman to lust for her has committed adultery with her already in his heart.

29 "And if your right eye makes you [10]stumble, tear it out, and throw it from you; for it is better for you that one of the parts of your body perish, [11]than for your whole body to be thrown into [12]hell.

30 "And if your right hand makes you [10]stumble, cut it off, and throw it from you; for it is better for you that one of the parts of your body perish, [11]than for your whole body to go into [12]hell.

---

[b](Matt. 5:17) Far from breaking with Old Testament teachings, Jesus came to bring them to fruition by contrasting the true intent of the Law with the common rabbinic interpretations of His day. The key verse of the sermon, therefore, is Matthew 5:20. The righteousness of the scribes and Pharisees was not adequate to gain entrance into the Kingdom because it dealt only with external behavior. Qualifications for entering this promised Kingdom are what Jesus outlines in this discourse (cf. Matt. 7:21, Sec. 71).

[c]Sections 68-70 deal with the inward conditioning God requires, in contrast to the mere outward conformity with which the scribes and Pharisees were content.

[d]The six contrasts are in vv. 21-22, 27-28, 31-32, 33-35, 38-39, and 43-44. In each case the interpretation of the Jewish tradition is given first, then that of Jesus. Tradition concentrated on outward tangible acts, while Jesus showed that the Law was intended to regulate motives as well. In this regard the teachings of the scribes were deficient.

Matt. 5:21-48 (cont'd)

31 "And it was said, 'WHOEVER [13]SENDS HIS WIFE AWAY, LET HIM GIVE HER A CERTIFICATE OF DIVORCE' [Deut. 24:1, 3];

32 but I say to you that everyone who divorces his wife, except for the cause of unchastity, makes her commit adultery; and whoever marries a divorced woman commits adultery.

33 "Again, you have heard that [1]the ancients were told, '[14]YOU SHALL NOT [15]MAKE FALSE VOWS, BUT SHALL FULFILL YOUR [16]VOWS TO THE LORD' [Lev. 19:12; Num. 30:2; Deut. 23:21].

34 "But I say to you, make no oath at all, either by heaven, for it is the throne of God,

35 or by the earth, for it is the footstool of His feet, or [17]by Jerusalem, for it is THE CITY OF THE GREAT KING [Psalm 48:2].

36 "Nor shall you make an oath by your head, for you cannot make one hair white or black.

37 "But let your statement be, 'Yes, yes' or 'No, no'; and anything beyond these is of [18]evil.

38 "You have heard that it was said, 'AN EYE FOR AN EYE, AND A TOOTH FOR A TOOTH' [Exod. 21:24; Lev. 24:20; Deut. 19:21].

39 "But I say to you, do not resist him who is evil; but whoever slaps you on your right cheek, turn to him the other also.

40 "And if anyone wants to sue you, and take your [19]shirt, let him have your [20]coat also.

41 "And whoever shall force you to go one mile, go with him two.

42 "Give to him who asks of you, and do not turn away from him who wants to borrow from you.

43 "You have heard that it was said, 'YOU SHALL LOVE YOUR NEIGHBOR [Lev. 19:18], and hate your enemy.'

Luke 6:27-30, 32-36

44 "But I say to you, love your enemies, and pray for those who persecute you

45 in order that you may [21]be sons of your Father who is in heaven; for He causes His sun to rise on the evil and the good, and sends rain on the righteous and the unrighteous.

27 "But I say to you who hear, love your enemies, do good to those who hate you,

28 bless those who curse you, pray for those who [23]mistreat you.

29 "Whoever hits you on the cheek, offer him the other also; and whoever takes away your [20]coat, do not withhold your [19]shirt from him either.

30 "Give to everyone who asks of you, and whoever takes away what is yours, do not demand it back.

46 "For if you love those who love you, what reward have you? Do not even the [22]taxgatherers do the same?

47 "And if you greet your brothers only, what do you do more than others? Do not even the Gentiles do the same?

48 "Therefore you are to be perfect, as your heavenly Father is perfect.

32 "And if you love those who love you, what credit is that to you? For even sinners love those who love them.

33 "And if you do good to those who do good to you, what credit is that to you? For even sinners do the same.

34 "And if you lend to those from whom you expect to receive, what credit is that to you? Even sinners lend to sinners, in order to receive back the same amount.

35 "But love your enemies, and do good, and lend, [24]expecting nothing in return; and your reward will be great,

Luke 6:27-30, 32-36 (cont'd)
and you will be sons of the Most High; for
He Himself is kind to ungrateful and evil
men.
    36   "[25]Be merciful, just as your Father
is merciful.

[1]Lit., *it was said to the ancients.* [2]Or, *guilty before.* [3]Some mss. insert *without cause.* [4]Or, *liable to.* [5]Aram. for *empty-head* or *good for nothing.* [6]Lit., *the Sanhedrin.* [7]Lit., *Gehenna of fire.* [8]Or, *gift.* [9]Lit., *quadrans* (equaling two lepta or mites); i.e., 1/64 of a denarius. [10]I.e., *cause to sin.* [11]Lit., *not your whole body.* [12]Gr., *Gehenna.* [13]Lit., *puts away.* [14]you and your are singular here. [15]Or, *break your vows.* [16]Lit., *oaths.* [17]Or, *toward.* [18]Or, *from the evil one.* [19]Or, *tunic*; i.e., garment worn next to the body. [20]Or, *cloak*; i.e., outer garment. [21]Or, *show yourselves to be.* [22]I.e., Collectors of Roman taxes for profit. [23]Or, *revile.* [24]Or, *not despairing at all.* [25]Or, *Become.*

Sec. 69   Three hypocritical [e]practices to be avoided (cf. Secs. 143; 175; 192)

Matt. 6:1-18

1   "Beware of practicing your righteousness before men to be noticed by them; otherwise you have no reward with your Father who is in heaven.

2   "When therefore you [1]give alms, do not sound a trumpet before you, as the hypocrites do in the synagogues and in the streets, that they may be honored by men. Truly I say to you, they have their reward in full.

3   "But when you give alms, do not let your left hand know what your right hand is doing

4   that your [2]alms may be in secret; and your Father who sees in secret will repay you.

5   "And when you pray, you are not to be as the hypocrites; for they love to stand and pray in the synagogues and on the street corners, [3]in order to be seen by men. Truly I say to you, they have their reward in full.

6   "But you, when you pray, go into your inner room, and when you have shut your door, pray to your Father who is in secret, and your Father who sees in secret will repay you.

7   "And when you are praying, do not use meaningless repetition, as the Gentiles do, for they suppose that they will be heard for their many words.

8   "Therefore do not be like them; for your Father knows what you need, before you ask Him.

9   "Pray, then, in this way:
     'Our Father who art in [4]heaven,
     Hallowed be Thy name.

10   'Thy kingdom come.
     Thy will be done,
     On earth as it is in heaven.

11   'Give us this day [5]our daily bread.

12   'And forgive us our debts, as we also have forgiven our debtors.

13   'And do not lead us into temptation, but deliver us from [6]evil. [7][For Thine is the kingdom, and the power, and the glory, forever. Amen.]'

14   "For if you forgive men for their transgressions, your heavenly Father will also forgive you.

15   "But if you do not forgive men, then your Father will not forgive your transgressions.

[e]The three "righteous" practices specified are giving alms (6:2-4), prayer (6:5-15), and fasting (6:16-18). The Pharisees did these for the sake of human recognition and for this reason forfeited all prospects of divine reward.

Matt. 6:1-18 (cont'd)

16 "And whenever you fast, do not put on a gloomy face as the hypocrites *do*, for they [8]neglect their appearance in order to be seen fasting by men. Truly I say to you, they have their reward in full.

17 "But you, when you fast, anoint your head, and wash your face

18 so that you may not be seen fasting by men, but by your Father who is in secret; and your Father who sees in secret will repay you.

[1]Or, *do an act of charity.* [2]Or, *deeds of charity.* [3]Lit., *to be apparent to men.* [4]Lit., *the heavens.* [5]Or, *our bread for the coming day* or *our needful bread.* [6]Or, *the evil one.* [7]This clause omitted in the earliest mss. [8]Lit., *render their faces unrecognizable.*

Sec. 70   Three prohibitions against avarice, harsh judgment, and unwise exposure of sacred things (cf. Secs. 83; 83, 147; 99, 213, 220; 144; 146; 147; 167)

Matt. 6:19—7:6

19 "Do not lay up for yourselves treasures upon earth, where moth and rust destroy, and where thieves break in and steal.

20 "But lay up for yourselves treasures in heaven, where neither moth nor rust destroys, and where thieves do not break in or steal;

21 for where your treasure is, there will your heart be also.

22 "The lamp of the body is the eye; if therefore your eye is [1]clear, your whole body will be full of light.

23 "But if your eye is bad, your whole body will be full of darkness. If therefore the light that is in you is darkness, how great is the darkness!

24 "No one can serve two masters; for either he will hate the one and love the other, or he will hold to one and despise the other. You cannot serve God and [2]mammon.

25 "For this reason I say to you, [3]do not be anxious for your life, *as to* what you shall eat, or what you shall drink; nor for your body, *as to* what you shall put on. Is not life more than food, and the body than clothing?

26 "Look at the birds of the [4]air, that they do not sow, neither do they reap, nor gather into barns, and *yet* your heavenly Father feeds them. Are you not worth much more than they?

27 "And which of you by being anxious can add a *single* [5]cubit to his [6]life's span?

28 "And why are you anxious about clothing? Observe how the lilies of the field grow; they do not toil nor do they spin,

29 yet I say to you that even Solomon in all his glory did not clothe himself like one of these.

30 "But if God so arrays the grass of the field, which is *alive* today and tomorrow is thrown into the furnace, *will He* not much more *do so for* you, O men of little faith?

31 "Do not be anxious then, saying, 'What shall we eat?' or 'What shall we drink?' or 'With what shall we clothe ourselves?'

32 "For all these things the Gentiles eagerly seek; for your heavenly Father knows that you need all these things.

33 "But [7]seek first [8]His kingdom and His righteousness; and all these things shall be [9]added to you.

34 "Therefore do not be anxious for tomorrow; for tomorrow will [10]care for itself. *Each* day has enough trouble of its own.

Matt. 6:19—7:6 (cont'd)

1 "Do not judge lest you be judged.

2 "For in the way you judge, you will be judged; and [11]by your standard of measure, it will be measured to you.

3 "And why do you look at the speck that is in your brother's eye, but do not notice the log that is in your own eye?

4 "Or how [12]can you say to your brother, 'Let me take the speck out of your eye,' and behold, the log is in your own eye?

5 "You hypocrite, first take the log out of your own eye, and then you will see clearly to take the speck out of your brother's eye.

6 "Do not give what is holy to dogs, and do not throw your pearls before swine, lest they trample them under their feet, and turn and tear you to pieces.

Luke 6:37-42

37 "And do not judge and you will not be judged; and do not condemn, and you will not be condemned; [13]pardon, and you will be pardoned.

38 "Give, and it will be given to you; good measure, pressed down, shaken together, running over, they will pour into your lap. For [11]by your standard of measure it will be measured to you in return."

39 And He also spoke a parable to them: "A blind man cannot guide a blind man, can he? Will they not both fall into a pit?

40 "[f]A [14]pupil is not above his teacher; but everyone, after he has been fully trained, will [15]be like his teacher.

41 "And why do you look at the speck that is in your brother's eye, but do not notice the log that is in your own eye?

42 "Or how can you say to your brother, 'Brother, let me take out the speck that is in your eye,' when you yourself do not see the log that is in your own eye? You hypocrite, first take the log out of your own eye, and then you will see clearly to take out the speck that is in your brother's eye.

[1]Or, healthy. [2]Or, riches. [3]Or, stop being anxious. [4]Lit., heaven. [5]I.e., One cubit equals approx. 18 in. [6]Or, height. [7]Or, continually seek. [8]Or, the kingdom. [9]Or, provided. [10]Or, will worry about itself. [11]Lit., by what measure you measure. [12]Lit., will. [13]Lit., release. [14]Or, disciple. [15]Or, reach his teacher's level.

Sec. 71 Application and conclusion (cf. Secs. 79; 143; 162)

Matt. 7:7-27

7 "[1]Ask, and it shall be given to you; [2]seek, and you shall find; [3]knock, and it shall be opened to you.

8 "For everyone who asks receives, and he who seeks finds, and to him who knocks it shall be opened.

Luke 6:31, 43-49

[f](Luke 6:40) The first part of Luke 6:40 is one of the frequent sayings of Christ. In the present context it means the pupil or disciple of the Pharisees will be blind like his teachers. In Matthew 10:24 (Sec. 99) it means that Jesus' disciples can expect no better treatment than He received. On another occasion, in John 15:20 (Sec. 220), a slightly different wording conveys a similar meaning. In John 13:16 (Sec. 213) the saying urges the disciples to follow Christ's example of humility. Also the essence of this proverb lies behind Luke 22:27 (Sec. 215).

Matt. 7:7-27 (cont'd)

9 "Or what man is there among you, [4]when his son shall ask him for a loaf, [5]will give him a stone?

10 "Or [6]if he shall ask for a fish, he will not give him a snake, will he?

11 "If you then, being evil, know how to give good gifts to your children, how much more shall your Father who is in heaven give what is good to those who ask Him!

12 "Therefore, however you want people to treat you, so treat them, for this is the Law and the Prophets.

13 "Enter by the narrow gate; for the gate is wide, and the way is broad that leads to [g]destruction, and many are those who enter by it.

14 "For the gate is small, and the way is narrow that leads to [g]life, and few are those who find it.

15 "Beware of the false prophets, who come to you in sheep's clothing, but inwardly are ravenous wolves.

16 "You will [8]know them by their fruits. [9]Grapes are not gathered from thorn *bushes*, nor figs from thistles, are they?

17 "Even so, every good tree bears good fruit; but the bad tree bears bad fruit.

18 "A good tree cannot produce bad fruit, nor can a bad tree produce good fruit.

19 "Every tree that does not bear good fruit is cut down and thrown into the fire.

20 "So then, you will [8]know them by their fruits.

21 "Not everyone who says to Me, 'Lord, Lord,' will enter the [g]kingdom of heaven; but he who does the will of My Father who is in heaven.

22 "Many will say to Me on that day, 'Lord, Lord, did we not prophesy in Your name, and in Your name cast out demons, and in Your name perform many [10]miracles?'

23 "And then I will declare to them, 'I never knew you; [g]DEPART FROM ME, YOU WHO PRACTICE LAWLESSNESS' [Psalm 6:8].

Luke 6:31, 43-49 (cont'd)

31 "And just as you want people to [15]treat you, treat them in the same way.

43 "For there is no good tree which produces bad fruit; nor, [16]on the other hand, a bad tree which produces good fruit.

44 "For each tree is known by its own fruit. For men do not gather figs from thorns, nor do they pick grapes from a briar bush.

45 "The good man out of the good [17]treasure of his heart brings forth what is good; and the evil *man* out of the evil *treasure* brings forth what is evil; for his mouth speaks from [18]that which fills his heart.

46 "And why do you call Me, 'Lord, Lord,' and do not do what I say?

---

[g](Matt. 7:13-14, 21, 23) In Jesus' teachings, to find life was equivalent to entering the Kingdom, and to meet with destruction was equated with exclusion from it. One's relationship to the anticipated Kingdom was thus of crucial importance.

Matt. 7:7-27 (cont'd)	Luke 6:31, 43-49 (cont'd)
24 "Therefore everyone who hears these words of Mine, and [11]acts upon them, [12]may be compared to a wise man, who built his house upon the rock.	**47** "Everyone who comes to Me, and hears My words, and [11]acts upon them, I will show you whom he is like:
25 "And the rain descended, and the [13]floods came, and the winds blew, and burst against that house; and yet it did not fall, for it had been founded upon the rock.	**48** he is like a man building a house, who [19]dug deep and laid a foundation upon the rock; and when a flood rose, the [20]torrent burst against that house and could not shake it, because it had been well built.
26 "And everyone who hears these words of Mine, and does not [14]act upon them, will be like a foolish man, who built his house upon the sand.	**49** "But the one who has heard, and has not acted *accordingly*, is like a man who built a house upon the ground without any foundation; and the [20]torrent burst against it and immediately it collapsed, and the ruin of that house was great."
27 "And the rain descended, and the [13]floods came, and the winds blew, and burst against that house; and it fell, and great was its fall."	

[1]Or, Keep asking. [2]Or, keep seeking. [3]Or, keep knocking. [4]Lit., whom. [5]Lit., he will not give him a stone, will he? [6]Lit., also. [7]Or, you, too, do so for. [8]Or, recognize. [9]Lit., They do not gather. [10]Or, works of power. [11]Lit., does. [12]Lit., will be compared to. [13]Lit., rivers. [14]Lit., do. [15]Lit., do to. [16]Lit., again. [17]Or, treasury, storehouse. [18]Lit., the abundance of. [19]Lit., dug and went deep. [20]Lit., river.

Sec. 72 Reaction of the multitudes

Matt. 7:28-29

28 [1]The result was that when Jesus had finished these words, the multitudes were amazed at His teaching;

29 for He was teaching them as one having authority, and not as their scribes.

[1]Lit., And it came to pass.

GROWING FAME AND EMPHASIS ON REPENTANCE

Sec. 73 A certain centurion's faith and the healing of his servant (cf. Sec. 44)
— Capernaum —

Matt. 8:1, 5-13	Luke 7:1-10
1 And when He had come down from the mountain, great multitudes followed Him.	**1** When He had completed all His discourse in the hearing of the people, He went to Capernaum.
5 And when He had entered Capernaum, a centurion came to Him, entreating Him,	**2** And a certain centurion's slave, [8]who was highly regarded by him, was sick and about to die.
6 and saying, "[1]Lord, my [2]servant is [3]lying paralyzed at home, [4]suffering great pain."	**3** And when he heard about Jesus, he sent some [9]Jewish elders asking Him to come and [10]save the life of his slave.
	4 And when they had come to Jesus, they earnestly entreated Him, saying, "He is worthy for You to grant this to him;

Matt. 8:1, 5-13 (cont'd)	Luke 7:1-10 (cont'd)

Matt. 8:1, 5-13 (cont'd)

7 And He *said to him, "I will come and heal him."

8 But the centurion answered and said, "¹Lord, I am not worthy for You to come under my roof, but ⁵just say the word, and my ²servant will be healed.

9 "For I, too, am a man under authority, with soldiers under me; and I say to this one, 'Go!' and he goes, and to another, 'Come!' and he comes, and to my slave, 'Do this!' and he does it."

10 Now when Jesus heard this, He marveled, and said to those who were following, "Truly I say to you, I have not found such great faith ⁶with anyone in ʰIsrael.

11 "And I say to you, that many shall come from east and west, and ⁷recline at the table with Abraham, and Isaac, and Jacob, in the kingdom of heaven;

12 but the sons of the kingdom shall be cast out into the outer darkness; in that place there shall be weeping and gnashing of teeth."

13 And Jesus said to the centurion, "Go your way; let it be done to you as you have believed." And the ²servant was healed that very hour.

Luke 7:1-10 (cont'd)

5 for he loves our nation, and it was he who built us our synagogue."

6 Now Jesus started on His way with them; and when He was already not far from the house, the centurion sent friends, saying to Him, "¹Lord, do not trouble Yourself further, for I am not worthy for You to come under my roof;

7 for this reason I did not even consider myself worthy to come to You, but ⁵just say the word, and my ¹¹servant will be healed.

8 "For I, too, am a man under authority, with soldiers under me; and I say to this one, 'Go!' and he goes; and to another, 'Come!' and he comes; and to my slave, 'Do this!' and he does it."

9 Now when Jesus heard this, He marveled at him, and turned and said to the multitude that was following Him, "I say to you, not even in ʰIsrael have I found such great faith."

10 And when those who had been sent returned to the house, they found the slave in good health.

¹Or, Sir. ²Lit., boy. ³Lit., throwing. ⁴Lit., fearfully tormented. ⁵Lit., say with a word. ⁶Some manuscripts read not even in Israel. ⁷Or, dine. ⁸Lit., to whom he was honorable. ⁹Lit., elders of the Jews. ¹⁰Lit., bring safely through, rescue. ¹¹Or, boy.

Sec. 74 A widow's son raised at Nain

Luke 7:11-17

11 And it came about ¹soon afterwards, that He went to a city called Nain; and His disciples were going along with Him, ²accompanied by a large multitude.

12 Now as He approached the gate of the city, behold, ³a dead man was being carried out, the ⁴only son of his mother, and she was a widow; and a sizeable crowd from the city was with her.

ʰ (Matt. 8:10; Luke 7:9) Jesus' dealings with a non-Jewish person such as this centurion were striking in view of His avowed purpose of limiting His ministry to the lost sheep of the house of Israel (cf. Matt. 15:24, Sec. 112). The immediate beneficiaries of His ministry, the Jews, would do well to learn from this Gentile.

Luke 7:11-17 (cont'd)

13 And when the Lord saw her, He felt compassion for her, and said to her, "[5]Do not weep."

14 And He came up and touched the coffin; and the bearers came to a halt. And He said, "Young man, I say to you, arise!"

15 And the [6]dead man [i]sat up, and began to speak. And Jesus gave him back to his mother.

16 And fear gripped them all, and they *began* glorifying God, saying, "A great prophet has arisen among us!" and, "God has [7]visited His people!"

17 And this report concerning Him went out all over Judea, and in all the surrounding district.

[1]Some mss. read *on the next day.*   [2]Lit., *and.*   [3]Lit., *one who had died.*   [4]Or, *only begotten.*   [5]Or, *Stop weeping.*   [6]Or, *corpse.*   [7]Or, *cared for.*

Sec. 75   John the Baptist's relationship to the Kingdom
— Galilee —

Matt. 11:2-19	Luke 7:18-35
2 Now when John in prison heard of the works of Christ, he sent *word* by his disciples,	**18** And the disciples of John reported to him about all these things.
3 and said to Him, "[j]Are You the [1k]Expected One, or shall we look for someone else?"	**19** And summoning [16]two of his disciples, John sent them to the Lord, saying, "[j]Are You the [1k]Expected One, or do we look for someone [17]else?"
	20 And when the men had come to Him, they said, "John the Baptist has sent us to You, saying, 'Are You the [1]Expected One, or do we look for someone else?'"
	21 At that [18]very time He cured many *people* of diseases and afflictions and evil spirits; and He granted sight to many *who were* blind.
4 And Jesus answered and said to them, "Go and report to John what you hear and see:	**22** And He answered and said to them, "Go and report to John what you have seen and heard: *the* BLIND RECEIVE
5 *the* BLIND RECEIVE SIGHT and *the* lame walk, *the* lepers are cleansed and *the* deaf hear, and *the* dead are raised up, and *the* POOR HAVE THE [2]GOSPEL PREACHED TO THEM [Isa. 35:5-6; 61:1].	SIGHT, *the* lame walk, *the* lepers are cleansed, and *the* deaf hear, *the* dead are raised up, *the* POOR HAVE THE GOSPEL PREACHED TO THEM [Isa. 35:5-6; 61:1].
6 "And blessed is he [3]who keeps from [4]stumbling over Me."	**23** "And blessed is he [3]who keeps from stumbling over Me."
7 And as these were going *away*, Jesus began to speak to the multitudes about John, "What did you go out into the wilderness to look at? A reed shaken by the wind?	**24** And when the messengers of John had left, He began to speak to the multitudes about John, "What did you go out into the wilderness to look at? A reed shaken by the wind?

[1](Luke 7:15) Jesus is known to have raised dead persons on other occasions (cf. Secs. 95, 171). Luke 7:22 (Sec. 75) implies that He did so at times that are not specifically described.

[j](Matt. 11:3; Luke 7:19) Some have accused John of a faltering faith at this point. This seems unjust. His question was probably prompted rather by impatience with his own personal plight that grew out of an inability to grasp why the death of Christ had to precede His kingly rule. Prior to the crucifixion no one understood this sequence of events.

[k](Matt. 11:3; Luke 7:19) "The Expected One," or more literally "The Coming One," was a well-known designation of Israel's Messiah. The title describes Him in a manner that views His coming as certain.

Matt. 11:2-19 (cont'd)

8 "[5]But what did you go out to see? A man dressed in soft *clothing*? Behold, those who wear soft *clothing* are in kings' [6]palaces.

9 "[5]But why did you go out? To see a prophet? Yes, I say to you, and one who is more than a prophet.

10 "This is the one about whom it [7]is written,

'BEHOLD, I SEND MY MESSENGER BE-
FORE YOUR FACE,
WHO WILL PREPARE YOUR WAY BE-
FORE YOU' [Mal. 3:1].

11 "Truly, I say to you, among those born of women there has not arisen *any-one* [1]greater than John the Baptist; yet he who is [8]least in the kingdom of heaven is greater than he.

12 "And from the days of John the Baptist until now the kingdom of heaven [9]suffers violence, and violent men [10]take it by force.

13 "For all the prophets and the Law prophesied until John.

14 "And if you care to accept *it*, he himself is Elijah, who [11]was to come.

15 "He who has ears to hear, let him hear.

16 "But to what shall I compare this generation? It is like children sitting in the market places, who call out to the other *children*,

17 and say, 'We played the flute for you, and you did not dance; we sang a dirge, and you did not [12]mourn.'

18 "For John came neither eating nor drinking, and they say, 'He has a demon!'

19 "The Son of Man came eating and drinking, and they say, 'Behold, a glut-tonous man and a [13]drunkard, a friend of [14]tax-gatherers and sinners!' [15]Yet wis-

Luke 7:18-35 (cont'd)

25 "[19]But what did you go out to see? A man dressed in soft [20]clothing? Be-hold, those who are splendidly clothed and live in luxury are *found* in royal palaces.

26 "But what did you go out to see? A prophet? Yes, I say to you, and one who is more than a prophet.

27 "This is the one about whom it [7]is written,

'BEHOLD, I SEND MY MESSENGER BE-
FORE YOUR FACE,
WHO WILL PREPARE YOUR WAY BE-
FORE YOU' [Mal. 3:1].

28 "I say to you, among those born of women, there is no one [1]greater than John; yet he who is [8]least in the kingdom of God is greater than he."

29 And when all the people and the [14]tax-gatherers heard *this*, they [21]acknowledged God's justice, having been baptized with the baptism of John.

30 But the Pharisees and the [22]lawyers rejected God's purpose for themselves, not having been baptized by [23]John.

31 "To what then shall I compare the men of this generation, and what are they like?

32 "They are like children who sit in the market place and call to one another; and they say, 'We played the flute for you, and you did not dance; we sang a dirge, and you did not weep.'

33 "For John the Baptist has come eating no bread and drinking no wine; and you say, 'He has a demon!'"

34 "The Son of Man has come eating and drinking; and you say, 'Behold, a gluttonous man, and a [13]drunkard, a friend of [14]tax-gatherers and sinners!'

---

[1](Matt. 11:11; Luke 7:28) John was greater than those of the past because of his proximity to Mes-siah. Yet those in the Kingdom will be greater than John because they will be even closer to Him.

Matt. 11:2-19 (cont'd)	Luke 7:18-35 (cont'd)
dom is vindicated by her deeds."	**35** "[15]Yet wisdom is vindicated by all her children."

[1]Lit., *Coming One.* [2]Or, *good news.* [3]Lit., *whoever.* [4]Or, *taking offense at.* [5]Or, *Well then,* [6]Lit., *houses.* [7]Lit., *has been written.* [8]Lit., *less.* [9]Or, *is forcibly entered.* [10]Or, *seize it for themselves.* [11]Or, *is to come.* [12]Lit., *beat the breast.* [13]Or, *wine-drinker.* [14]I.e., Collectors of Roman taxes for profit. [15]Lit., *And.* [16]Lit., *a certain two.* [17]Some early mss. read *one who is different.* [18]Lit., *hour.* [19]Or, *Well then, what.* [20]Or, *garments.* [21]Or, *justified God.* [22]I.e., experts in the Mosaic Law. [23]Lit., *him.*

Sec. 76   Woes upon Chorazin and Bethsaida for failure to repent (cf. Sec. 139) — Galilee —

Matt. 11:20-30

20 Then He [m]began to reproach the cities in which most of His [1]miracles were done, because they did not repent.

21 "Woe to you, Chorazin! Woe to you, Bethsaida! For if the [1]miracles had occurred in Tyre and Sidon which occurred in you, they would have repented long ago in sackcloth and ashes.

22 "Nevertheless I say to you, it shall be more tolerable for Tyre and Sidon in *the* day of judgment, than for you.

23 "And you, Capernaum, will not be exalted to heaven, will you? You shall [2]descend to Hades; for if the [1]miracles had occurred in Sodom which occurred in you, it would have remained to this day.

24 "Nevertheless I say to you that it shall be more tolerable for the land of Sodom in *the* day of judgment, than for you."

25 At that [3]time Jesus answered and said, "I [4]praise Thee, O Father, Lord of heaven and earth, that Thou didst hide these things from *the* wise and intelligent and didst reveal them to babes.

26 "Yes, Father, for thus it was well-pleasing in Thy sight.

27 "All things [5]have been handed over to Me by My Father; and no one [6]knows the Son, except the Father; nor does anyone [6]know the Father, except the Son, and anyone to whom the Son wills to reveal *Him*.

28 "Come to Me, all who are [7]weary and [n]heavy-laden, and I will give you rest.

29 "Take My yoke upon you, and learn from Me, for I am gentle and humble in heart; and YOU SHALL FIND REST FOR YOUR SOULS [Jer. 6:16].

30 "For My yoke is [8]easy, and My load is light."

[1]Or, *works of power.* [2]Some mss. read *be brought down.* [3]Or, *occasion.* [4]Or, *acknowledge to Thy praise.* [5]Lit., *were given over.* [6]Or, *perfectly know(s).* [7]Or, *who work to exhaustion.* [8]Or, *kindly or pleasant.*

[m](Matt. 11:20) Another beginning in the ministry of Christ is noted here: His announcement of retribution against those who refused to repent in response to both John the Baptist and Himself. The Lord's language became more severe at this point. For other beginnings, see Matthew 4:17, Section 43 and Matthew 16:21, Section 119.

[n](Matt. 11:28) The heavy load was probably that imposed by the scribes and Pharisees in their man-made traditions (Matt. 23:4, Sec. 199).

Sec. 77   Christ's feet anointed by a sinful, but contrite, woman (cf. Sec. 186)
– Galilee –

Luke 7:36-50

36   Now one of the °Pharisees was requesting Him to ¹dine with him. And He entered the Pharisee's house, and reclined at the table.

37   And behold, there was a ᴾwoman in the city who was a ²sinner; and when she learned that He was reclining at the table in the Pharisee's house, she brought an alabaster vial of perfume,

38   and standing behind Him at His feet, weeping, she began to wet His feet with her tears, and kept wiping them with the hair of her head, and kissing His feet, and anointing them with the perfume.

39   Now when the Pharisee who had invited Him saw this, he said ³to himself, "If this man were ⁴a prophet He would know who and what sort of person this woman is who is touching Him, that she is a ²sinner."

40   And Jesus answered and said to him, "Simon, I have something to say to you." And he ⁵replied, "Say it, Teacher."

41   "A certain moneylender had two debtors: one owed five hundred ⁶denarii, and the other fifty.

42   "When they were unable to repay, he graciously forgave them both. Which of them therefore will love him more?"

43   Simon answered and said, "I suppose the one whom he forgave more." And He said to him, "You have judged correctly."

44   And turning toward the woman, He said to Simon, "Do you see this woman? I entered your house; you gave Me no water for My feet, but she has wet My feet with her tears, and wiped them with her hair.

45   "You gave Me no kiss; but she, since the time I came in, ⁷has not ceased to kiss My feet.

46   "You did not anoint My head with oil, but she anointed My feet with perfume.

47   "For this reason I say to you, her sins, which are many, have been forgiven, for she loved much; but he who is forgiven little, loves little."

48   And He said to her, "Your sins have been forgiven."

49   And those who were reclining at the table with Him began to say ⁸to themselves, "Who is this man who even forgives sins?"

50   And He said to the woman, "Your faith has saved you; go in peace."

¹Lit., eat. ²I.e., an immoral woman. ³Lit., to himself, saying. ⁴Some mss. read the prophet. ⁵Lit., says. ⁶The denarius was equivalent to one day's wage. ⁷Lit., was not ceasing. ⁸Or, among.

FIRST PUBLIC REJECTION BY JEWISH LEADERS

Sec. 78   A tour with the twelve and other followers
– Galilee –

Luke 8:1-3

1   And it came about soon afterwards, that He began going about from one city and village to another, proclaiming and preaching the kingdom of God; and the twelve were with Him,

°(Luke 7:36) The rupture between Jesus and the Pharisees was far advanced by now, but was not complete. Simon seemed to be one who had not as yet decided with whom to side. He believed Jesus to be a prophet (7:39), but his love for Him was meager compared to the sinful woman's.

ᴾ(Luke 7:37) This woman should be distinguished from Mary of Bethany who at a later time also anointed the Lord's feet (cf. Secs. 170, 186).

Luke 8:1-3 (cont'd)

2   and *also* some �q women who had been healed of evil spirits and sicknesses: Mary who was called Magdalene, from whom seven demons had gone out,

3   and Joanna the wife of Chuza, Herod's steward, and Susanna, and many others who were contributing to their support out of their private means.

Sec. 79   Blasphemous accusation by the scribes and Pharisees (cf. Secs. 71; 96, 144; 128, 144; 146)
– Galilee –

Matt. 12:22-37 | Mark 3:20-30

20   And He *came ⁸home, and the multitude *gathered again, to such an extent that they could not even eat ⁹a meal.

21   And when His own ¹⁰people heard *of this*, they went out to take custody of Him; for they were saying, "He has lost His senses."

22   Then there was brought to Him a demon-possessed man *who was* blind and dumb, and He healed him, so that the dumb man spoke and saw.

23   And all the multitudes were amazed, and *began* to say, "ʳThis *man* cannot be the Son of David, can he?"

24   But when the Pharisees heard it, they said, "This man casts out demons only by ¹Beelzebul the ruler of the demons."

22   And the scribes who came down from Jerusalem were saying, "He is possessed by ¹Beelzebul," and "He casts out the demons by the ruler of the demons."

23   And He called them to Himself and began speaking to them in parables, "How can Satan cast out Satan?

24   "And if a kingdom is divided against itself, that kingdom cannot stand.

25   And knowing their thoughts He said to them, "²Any kingdom divided against itself is laid waste; and ²any city or house divided against itself shall not stand.

26   "And if Satan casts out Satan, he ²is divided against himself; how then shall his kingdom stand?

27   "And if I by ¹Beelzebul cast out demons, by whom do your sons cast them out? Consequently they shall be your judges.

25   "And if a house is divided against itself, that house will not be able to stand.

26   "And if Satan has risen up against himself and is divided, he cannot stand, but ¹¹he is finished!

---

q(Luke 8:2) It was not unusual for first century Jewish women to contribute large sums of money to support rabbis. The additional incentive for these to give, however, was the spiritual and physical help they had received from Jesus. This tour, which included female followers and the twelve, is mentioned only by Luke, who gives special prominence to women in his gospel.

r(Matt. 12:23) This question forced the first public showdown in the growing rift between Jesus and the Jewish authorities. "Son of David" was a much used title for Messiah. So the antagonistic representatives of Jewish leadership in Jerusalem (Mark 3:22) were forced to speak out strongly against this identification of Jesus. So tense was the confrontation that Jesus' own family wondered about His sanity (Mark 3:21). This encounter was so crucial that it became a major turning point in Jesus' ministry.

Matt. 12:22-37 (cont'd)	Mark 3:20-30 (cont'd)

28 "But if I cast out demons by the Spirit of God, then the [s]kingdom of God has come upon you.

29 "Or how can anyone enter the strong man's house and carry off his property, unless he first binds the strong man? And then he will plunder his house.

30 "He who is not with Me is against Me; and he who does not gather with Me scatters.

31 "Therefore I say to you, any sin and blasphemy shall be forgiven men, but blasphemy against the Spirit shall not be forgiven.

32 "And whoever shall speak a word

27 "But no one can enter the strong man's house and plunder his property unless he first binds the strong man, and then he will plunder his house.

28 "Truly I say to you, all sins shall be forgiven the sons of men, and whatever blasphemies they utter;

29 but whoever blasphemes against the Holy Spirit never has forgiveness, but is guilty of an [t]eternal sin" —

30 because they were saying, "He has an unclean spirit."

against the Son of Man, it shall be forgiven him; but whoever shall speak against the Holy Spirit, it shall [t]not be forgiven him, either in this age, or in the *age* to come.

33 "Either make the tree good, and its fruit good; or make the tree bad, and its fruit bad; for the tree is known by its fruit.

34 "You brood of vipers, how can you, being evil, speak [4]what is good? For the mouth speaks out of that which fills the heart.

35 "The good man out of *his* good treasure brings forth [4]what is good; and the evil man out of *his* evil treasure brings forth [5]what is evil.

36 "And I say to you, that every [6]careless word that men shall speak, they shall render account for it in the day of judgment.

37 "For [7]by your words you shall be justified, and by your words you shall be condemned."

---

[1]Or, *Beezebul*; others read *Beelzebub.* [2]Lit., *Every.* [3]Lit., *was.* [4]Lit., *good things.* [5]Lit., *evil things.* [6]Or, *useless.* [7]Or, *in accordance with.* [8]Lit., *into a house.* [9]Lit., *bread.* [10]Or, *kinsmen.* [11]Lit., *he has an end.*

Sec. 80　Request for a sign refused (cf. Secs. 115, 144)
　　　　　– Galilee –

Matt. 12:38-45

38 Then some of the scribes and Pharisees answered Him, saying, "Teacher, we want to see a [1]sign from You."

39 But He answered and said to them, "An evil and adulterous generation craves for a sign; and *yet* no [1]sign shall be given to it but the sign of Jonah the prophet;

40 for just as JONAH WAS THREE DAYS AND THREE NIGHTS IN THE BELLY OF THE SEA

---

[s](Matt. 12:28) The arrival of the Kingdom of God coincided with the arrival of the King. Yet the unfavorable response of Israel retarded the full realization of all the Old Testament prophecies about it. Without doubt Jesus also spoke of a future Kingdom when all expectations would be brought to fruition (cf. Matt. 25:31, Sec. 208).

[t]The unforgivable (Matt. 12:32) or eternal (Mark 3:29) sin bore a special relationship to the unusual circumstances of that day. The leaders of Israel publicly demonstrated their deliberate and final rejection of the Holy Spirit's clear attestation to the incarnate Messiah. Such definitive circumstances are not found elsewhere.

Matt. 12:38-45 (cont'd)

MONSTER [Jonah 1:17], so shall the Son of Man be three days and three nights in the heart of the earth.

41 "The men of Nineveh shall stand up with this generation at the judgment, and shall condemn it because they repented at the preaching of Jonah; and behold, something greater than Jonah is here.

42 "The Queen of the South shall rise up with this generation at the judgment and shall condemn it, because she came from the ends of the earth to hear the wisdom of Solomon; and behold, something greater than Solomon is here.

43 "Now when the unclean spirit goes out of a man, it passes through waterless places, seeking rest, and does not find it.

44 "Then it says, 'I will return to my house from which I came'; and when it comes, it finds it unoccupied, swept, and put in order.

45 "Then it goes, and takes along with it seven other spirits more wicked than itself, and they go in and live there; and the last state of that man becomes uworse than the first. That is the way it will also be with this evil generation."

¹Or, *attesting miracle.*

Sec. 81   Announcement of new spiritual ties
— Galilee —

Matt. 12:46-50	Mark 3:31-35	Luke 8:19-21
46 While He was still speaking to the multitudes, behold, ᵛHis mother and brothers were standing outside, seeking to speak to Him.	**31** And His ᵛmother and His brothers *arrived, and standing outside they sent word to Him, and called Him.	
		19 And his ᵛmother and brothers came to Him, and they were unable to get to Him because of the crowd.
47 And someone said to Him, "Behold, Your mother and Your brothers are standing outside seeking to speak to You."	**32** And a multitude was sitting around Him, and they *said to Him, "Behold, Your mother and Your brothers ¹are outside looking for You."	**20** And it was reported to Him, "Your mother and Your brothers are standing outside, wishing to see You."
48 But He answered the one who was telling Him and said, "Who is My mother and who are My brothers?"	**33** And answering them, He *said, "Who are My mother and My brothers?"	**21** But He answered and said to them,
49 And stretching out His hand toward His disciples, He said, "Behold, My mother and My brothers!	**34** And looking about on those who were sitting around Him, He *said, "Behold, My mother and My brothers!	
50 "For whoever does the will of My Father who is in heaven, he is My	**35** "For whoever does the will of God, he is My brother and sister and	"My mother and My brothers are these who hear the

u(Matt. 12:45) Because of the rejection (Section 79), this generation of Israelites had become worse than Nineveh, worse than the Queen of Sheba, and even worse than their own former condition. Their leaders' public rejection, in committing the unforgivable sin, dashed any hopes this generation might have had of receiving the Kingdom blessings.

v(Matt. 12:46; Mark 3:31; Luke 8:19) Though quite sincere in trying to help Him, Jesus' family came with a suspicion that He had lost His sanity. Mary had already evidenced her impatience (John 2:4, Sec. 32), and His brothers were critical of Him (John 7:3-5, Sec. 130). They wanted Him to give up this course of opposition to their religious leaders. Knowing His family's motives, Jesus seized the occasion to declare the primacy of spiritual relationships over physical. What a fitting lesson just after His own people had severed themselves from Him by accusing Him of an alliance with Satan.

Matt. 12:46-50 (cont'd)	Mark 3:31-35 (cont'd)	Luke 8:19-21 (cont'd)
brother and sister and mother."	mother."	word of God and do it."

[1]Later mss. add *and Your sisters.*

PARABOLIC MYSTERIES ABOUT THE KINGDOM

– To the crowds by the Sea, Secs. 82-87 –

Sec. 82 The setting of the parables

Matt. 13:1-3a	Mark 4:1-2	Luke 8:4
1 On that ʷday Jesus went out of the house, and was sitting by the sea. 2 And great multitudes gathered to Him, so that He got into a boat and sat down, and the whole multitude was standing on the beach. 3 And He spoke many things to them in parables, saying,	1 And He began to teach again by the sea. And such a very great multitude [1]gathered to Him that He got into a boat in the sea and sat down; and the whole multitude was by the sea on the land. 2 And He was teaching them many things in parables, and was saying to them in His teaching,	4 And when a great multitude were coming together, and those from the various cities were journeying to Him, He spoke by way of a parable:

[1]Lit., *is gathered.*

Sec. 83 The parable of the soils (cf. Secs. 66, 144; 70; 70, 147; 191)

Matt. 13:3b-23	Mark 4:3-25	Luke 8:5-18
"Behold the sower went out to sow; 4 and as he sowed, some *seeds* fell beside the road, and the birds came and ate them up. 5 "And others fell upon the rocky places, where they [1]did not have much soil; and immediately they sprang up, because they had no depth of soil.	3 "Listen *to this!* Behold, the sower went out to sow; 4 and it came about that as he was sowing, some *seed* fell beside the road, and the birds came and ate it up. 5 "And other *seed* fell on the rocky *ground* where it did not have much soil; and immediately it sprang up because it had no depth	5 "The sower went out to sow his seed; and as he sowed, some fell beside the road; and it was trampled under foot, and the birds of the [11]air ate it up. 6 "And other *seed* fell on rocky *soil*, and as soon as it grew up, it withered away, because it had no moisture.

ʷ(Matt. 13:1) These parables were spoken later on the same day as the landmark events of Sections 79-81. They exhibited a new phase of the Lord's teaching. As a teaching tool, parables enabled Him to continue instructing His disciples without giving His enemies unnecessary opportunities to catch Him in His words (Matt. 13:13 and parallels in Sec. 83). They also provided Him a means of revealing Kingdom characteristics not previously described (Matt. 13:11, 17; Mark 4:11; Luke 8:10). These features depicted a new dimension of the Kingdom in light of the confrontation earlier in the day (Sec. 79). The parables do not invalidate earlier teachings about Christ's reign but add to them.

Matt. 13:3b-23 (cont'd)	Mark 4:3-25 (cont'd)	Luke 8:5-18 (cont'd)
6 "But when the sun had risen, they were scorched; and because they had no root, they withered away. **7** "And others fell ²among the thorns, and the thorns came up and choked them out.	of soil. **6** "And after the sun had risen, it was scorched; and because it had no root, it withered away. **7** "And other *seed* fell among the thorns, and the thorns came up and choked it, and it yielded no crop.	**7** "And other *seed* fell among the thorns; and the thorns grew up with it, and choked it out.
8 "And others fell on the good soil, and *yielded a crop, some a hundredfold, some sixty, and some thirty. **9** "He who has ears, let him hear."	**8** "And other *seeds* fell into the good soil and as they grew up and increased, they yielded a crop and produced thirty, sixty, and a hundredfold." **9** And He was saying, "He who has ears to hear, let him hear."	**8** "And other *seed* fell into the good soil, and grew up, and produced a crop a hundred times as great." As He said these things, He would call out, "He who has ears to hear, let him hear."
10 And the disciples came and said to Him, "Why do You speak to them in parables?" **11** And He answered and said to them, "To you it has been granted to know the mysteries of the kingdom of heaven, but to them it has not been granted. **12** "For whoever has, to him shall *more* be given, and he shall have an abundance; but whoever does not have, even what he has shall be taken away from him.	**10** And as soon as He was alone, ⁹His followers, along with the twelve, *began* asking Him *about* the parables. **11** And He was saying to them, "To you has been given the mystery of the kingdom of God; but those who are outside get everything in parables,	**9** And His disciples *began* questioning Him as to what this parable might be. **10** And He said, "To you it has been granted to know the mysteries of the kingdom of God, but to the rest *it is* in parables, in order that SEEING THEY MAY NOT SEE, AND HEARING THEY MAY NOT UNDERSTAND" [Isa. 6:9].
13 "Therefore I speak to them in parables; because while seeing they do not see, and while hearing they do not hear, nor do they understand. **14** "And ³in their case the prophecy of Isaiah is being fulfilled, which says, '⁴YOU WILL KEEP ON HEARING, ⁵BUT WILL NOT UNDERSTAND;	**12** ˣin order that WHILE SEEING, THEY MAY SEE AND NOT PERCEIVE; AND WHILE HEARING, THEY MAY HEAR AND NOT UNDERSTAND LEST THEY RETURN AND BE FORGIVEN" [Isa. 6:9-10].	

ˣ(Mark 4:12) The conclusion that Jesus' desire to hide truth from "outsiders" was prompted by events earlier in the day is very inviting. Whom could He have more in mind than those who, a few hours before, had refused to acknowledge His obvious divine credentials (cf. Sec. 79)?

Matt. 13:3b-23 (cont'd)	Mark 4:3-25 (cont'd)	Luke 8:5-18 (cont'd)
AND ⁶YOU WILL KEEP ON SEEING, BUT WILL NOT PERCEIVE; **15** FOR THE HEART OF THIS PEOPLE HAS BECOME DULL, AND WITH THEIR EARS THEY SCARCELY HEAR, AND THEY HAVE CLOSED THEIR EYES LEST THEY SHOULD SEE WITH THEIR EYES, AND HEAR WITH THEIR EARS, AND UNDERSTAND WITH THEIR HEART AND RETURN, AND I SHOULD HEAL THEM' [Isa. 6:9-10]. **16** "But blessed are your eyes, because they see; and your ears, because they hear. **17** "For truly I say to you, that many prophets and righteous men desired to see what you see, and did not see it; and to hear what you hear, and did not hear it. **18** "Hear then the parable of the sower. **19** "When anyone hears the word of the kingdom, and does not understand it, the evil one comes and snatches away what has been sown in his heart. This is the one on whom seed was sown beside the road. **20** "And the one on whom seed was sown on the rocky places, this is the man who hears the word, and immediately receives it with joy;		
	13 And He *said to them, "Do you not understand this parable? And how will you understand all the parables? **14** "The sower sows the word. **15** "And these are the ones who are beside the road where the word is sown; and when they hear, immediately Satan comes and takes away the word which has been sown in them. **16** "And in a similar way these are the ones on whom seed was sown on the rocky places, who, when they hear the word, immediately receive it with joy;	**11** "Now the parable is this: the seed is the word of God. **12** "And those beside the road are those who have heard; then the devil comes and takes away the word from their heart, so that they may not believe and be saved. **13** "And those on the rocky soil are those who, when they hear, receive the word with joy; and these have no firm root; ¹²they believe for a while, and in time of temptation

Matt. 13:3b-23 (cont'd)	Mark 4:3-25 (cont'd)	Luke 8:5-18 (cont'd)
21 yet he has no *firm* root in himself, but is *only* temporary, and when affliction or persecution arises because of the word, immediately he [7]falls away.	**17** and they have no *firm* root in themselves, but are *only* temporary; then, when affliction or persecution arises because of the word, immediately they [7]fall away.	fall away.
22 "And the one on whom seed was sown among the thorns, this is the man who hears the word, and the worry of the [8]world, and the deceitfulness of riches choke the word, and it becomes unfruitful.	**18** "And others are the ones on whom seed was sown among the thorns; these are the ones who have heard the word,	**14** "And the *seed* which fell among the thorns, these are the ones who have heard, and as they go on their way they are choked with worries and riches and pleasures of *this* life, and bring no fruit to maturity.
23 "And the one on whom seed was sown on the good soil, this is the man who hears the word and understands it; who indeed bears fruit, and brings forth, some a hundredfold, some sixty, and some thirty."	**19** and the worries of the [8]world, and the deceitfulness of riches, and the desires for other things enter in and choke the word, and it becomes unfruitful.	**15** "And the *seed* in the good soil, these are the ones who have heard the word in an honest and good heart, and hold it fast, and bear fruit with [13]perseverance.
	20 "And those are the ones on whom seed was sown on the good soil; and they hear the word and accept it, and bear fruit, thirty, sixty, and a hundredfold."	
	21 And He was saying to them, "A lamp is not brought to be put under a peck-measure, is it, or under a bed? Is it not *brought* to be put on the lampstand?	**16** "Now no one after lighting a lamp covers it over with a container, or puts it under a bed; but he puts it on a lampstand, in order that those who come in may see the light.
	22 "For nothing is hidden, except to be revealed; nor has *anything* been secret, but that it should come to light.	**17** "For nothing is hidden that shall not become evident, nor *anything* secret that shall not be known and come to light.
	23 "If any man has ears to hear, let him hear."	
	24 And He was saying to them, "Take care what you listen to. [10]By your standard of measure it shall be measured to you; and more shall be given you besides.	**18** "Therefore take care how you listen; for whoever has, to him shall *more* be given; and whoever does not have, even what he [14]thinks he has shall be taken away from him."
	25 "For whoever has, to him shall *more* be given; and whoever does not have, even what he has shall be taken away from him."	

¹Lit., *were not having.*   ²Lit., *upon.*   ³Lit., *for them.*   ⁴Lit., *With a hearing you will hear.*   ⁵Lit., *and.*   ⁶Lit., *seeing you will see.*   ⁷Lit., *is (are) caused to stumble.*   ⁸Or, *age.*   ⁹Lit., *those about Him.*   ¹⁰Lit., *By what measure you measure.*   ¹¹Lit., *heaven.*   ¹²Lit., *who believe.*   ¹³Or, *steadfastness.*   ¹⁴ Or, *seems to have.*

Sec. 84   The ʸparable of the seed's spontaneous growth

Mark 4:26-29

26   And He was saying, "The kingdom of God is like a man who casts seed upon the soil;

27   and goes to bed at night and gets up by day, and the seed sprouts up and grows — how, he himself does not know.

28   "The soil produces crops by itself; first the blade, then the head, then the mature grain in the head.

29   "But when the crop permits, he immediately ¹puts in the sickle, because the harvest has come."

¹Lit., *sends forth.*

Sec. 85   The parable of the tares

Matt. 13:24-30

24   He presented another parable to them, saying, "The kingdom of heaven ¹may be compared to a man who sowed good seed in his field.

25   "But while men were sleeping, his enemy came and sowed ²tares also among the wheat, and went away.

26   "But when the ³wheat sprang up and bore grain, then the tares became evident also.

27   "And the slaves of the landowner came and said to him, 'Sir, did you not sow good seed in your field? ⁴How then does it have tares?'

28   "And he said to them, 'An ⁵enemy has done this!' And the slaves *said to him, 'Do you want us, then, to go and gather them up?'

29   "But he *said, 'No; lest while you are gathering up the tares, you may root up the wheat with them.

30   'Allow both to grow together until the harvest; and in the time of the harvest I will say to the reapers, "First gather up the tares and bind them in bundles to burn them up; but gather the wheat into my barn."'"

¹Lit., *was compared to.*   ²Or, *darnel, a weed resembling wheat.*   ³Lit., *grass.*   ⁴Lit., *From where.*   ⁵Lit., *enemy man.*

Sec. 86   The parable of the mustard tree (cf. Sec. 152)

Matt. 13:31-32	Mark 4:30-32
31 He presented another parable to them, saying, "The kingdom of heaven is like a mustard seed, which a man took and sowed in his field;	**30** And He said, "How shall we ²picture the kingdom of God, or by what parable shall we present it?
	31 "*It is* like a mustard seed, which,

ʸThe first four parables (Secs. 83-86) are taken from the agricultural realm. This Marcan parable seems appropriately placed before the parable of the tares (Sec. 85) rather than after it, since it describes the activity of the Word in cases where it falls on "good ground." The tares illustrate the opposite case (cf. Sec. 88).

Matt. 13:31-32 (cont'd)	Mark 4:30-32 (cont'd)
32 and this is ᶻsmaller than all *other* seeds; but when it is full grown, it is larger than the garden plants, and becomes a tree, so that THE BIRDS OF THE ¹AIR come and NEST IN ITS BRANCHES" [Psalm 104:12; Ezek. 17:23; 31:6; Dan. 4:12].	when sown upon the soil, though it is ᶻsmaller than all the seeds that are upon the soil, **32** yet when it is sown, grows up and becomes larger than all the garden plants and forms large branches; so that THE BIRDS OF THE ¹AIR CAN NEST UNDER ITS SHADE" [Psalm 104:12; Ezek. 17:23; 31:6; Dan. 4:12].

¹Or, sky. ²Lit., *compare.*

Sec. 87   The parable of the leavened loaf (cf. Sec. 152)

Matt. 13:33-35	Mark 4:33-34
33 He spoke another parable to them, "The kingdom of heaven is like leaven, which a woman took, and hid in three ¹pecks of meal, until it was all leavened." **34** All these things Jesus spoke to the multitudes in ªparables, and He did not speak to them without a parable, **35** so that what was spoken through the prophet might be fulfilled, saying, "I WILL OPEN MY MOUTH IN PARABLES; I WILL UTTER THINGS HIDDEN SINCE THE FOUNDATION OF THE WORLD" [Psalm 78:2].	**33** And with many such ªparables He was speaking the word to them as they were able to hear it; **34** and He did not speak to them without a parable, but He was explaining everything privately to His own disciples.

¹Gr., *sata.*

To the disciples in the house, Secs. 88-92

Sec. 88   The parable of the tares explained

Matt. 13:36-43

36 Then He left the multitudes, and went into the house. And His disciples came to Him, saying, "ᵇExplain to us the parable of the ¹tares of the field."

37 And He answered and said, "The one who sows the good seed is the Son of Man,

38 and the field is the world; and *as for* the good seed, these are the sons of the kingdom; and the tares are the sons of the evil *one;*

39 and the enemy who sowed them is the devil, and the harvest is the ²end of the age; and the reapers are angels.

ᶻ(Matt. 13:32; Mark 4:31) It is wrong to construe this as a statement of absolute scientific fact and thereby impute error to Jesus and/or the gospel writers. To illustrate another feature of the Kingdom, Jesus was simply resorting to a generally acknowledged characteristic of Palestinian agriculture in that day. That seeds smaller than the mustard seed are known in other times and places is no obstacle to biblical inerrancy. In the circumstances in which it was used, Jesus' statement was completely accurate.

ª(Matt. 13:34; Mark 4:33) Jesus' extensive use of this new pedagogical device suggests that other parables not recorded in this series (Secs. 82-92) were also spoken on this significant day.

ᵇ(Matt. 13:36) A reason for the disciples' asking about this particular parable lay in their inability to reconcile a long delay for gradual ripening of wheat and tares with earlier teachings of John (Matt. 3:2, Sec. 24; Matt. 3:10-12, Secs. 25, 26) and Jesus (Matt. 4:17, Sec. 43) about the impending judgment and Kingdom to follow. Reconciliation of these apparently contradictory teachings probably relates to the new character of Jesus' discussion about the Kingdom that began earlier that day (see note, Sec. 82).

Matt. 13:36-43 (cont'd)

40 "Therefore just as the tares are gathered up and burned with fire, so shall it be at the ²end of the age.

41 "The Son of Man will send forth His angels, and they will gather out of His kingdom all ³stumbling blocks, and those who commit lawlessness,

42 and will cast them into the furnace of fire; in that place there shall be weeping and gnashing of teeth.

43 "Then THE RIGHTEOUS WILL SHINE FORTH AS THE SUN [Dan. 12:3] in the kingdom of their Father. He who has ears, let him hear.

¹Or, *darnel*, a weed resembling wheat.   ²Or, *consummation*.   ³Or, *everything that is offensive*.

Sec. 89   The parable of the hidden treasure

Matt. 13:44

44 "The kingdom of heaven is like a treasure hidden in the field, which a man found and hid; and from joy over it he goes and sells all that he has, and buys that field.

Sec. 90   The parable of the pearl of great price

Matt. 13:45-46

45 "Again, the kingdom of heaven is like a merchant seeking fine pearls,

46 and upon finding one pearl of great value, he went and sold all that he had, and bought it.

Sec. 91   The parable of the ᶜdragnet

Matt. 13:47-50

47 "Again, the kingdom of heaven is like a dragnet cast into the sea, and gathering *fish* of every kind;

48 and when it was filled, they drew it up on the beach; and they sat down, and gathered the good *fish* into containers, but the bad they threw away.

49 "So it will be at the ¹end of the age; the angels shall come forth, and ²take out the wicked from among the righteous,

50 and will cast them into the furnace of fire; there shall be weeping and gnashing of teeth.

¹Or, *consummation*.   ²Or, *separate*.

Sec. 92   The parable of the householder

Matt. 13:51-52

51 "Have you understood all these things?" They *said to Him, "Yes."

52 And He said to them, "Therefore every scribe who has become a disciple of the kingdom of heaven is like a head of a household, who ᵈbrings forth out of his treasure things new and old."

ᶜThough quite similar to the parable of the tares (Sec. 85) and its explanation (Sec. 88), this parable concentrates on the end of the age, while the earlier one gives more details about the period prior to the end.

ᵈ(Matt. 13:52) This parable points up the necessity of understanding these new parabolic teachings properly and, on the basis of such understanding, disseminating them along with previously given teachings about the Kingdom.

CONTINUING OPPOSITION

Sec. 93   Departure across the Sea and calming the storm

Matt. 13:53; 8:18, 23-27	Mark 4:35-41	Luke 8:22-25
53 And it came about that when Jesus had finished these parables, He departed from there.		
18 Now when Jesus saw a crowd around Him, He gave orders to depart to the other side.	**35** And on that day, when evening had come, He *said to them, "Let us go over to the other side."	
23 And when He got into the boat, His disciples followed Him.	**36** And ³leaving the multitude, they *took Him along with them, just as He was, in the boat; and other boats were with Him.	**22** Now it came about on one of those days, that He and His disciples got into a boat, and He said to them, "Let us go over to the other side of the lake." And they launched out.
		23 But as they were sailing along He fell asleep; and a fierce gale of wind descended upon the lake, and they began to be swamped and to be in danger.
24 And behold, there arose ¹a great storm in the sea, so that the boat was covered with the waves; but He Himself was ᵉasleep.	**37** And there *arose a fierce gale of wind, and the waves were breaking over the boat so much that the boat was already filling up.	
25 And they came to Him, and awoke Him, saying, "Save us, Lord; we are perishing!"	**38** And He Himself was in the stern, asleep on the cushion; and they *awoke Him and *said to Him, "Teacher, do You not care that we are perishing?"	
26 And He *said to them, "Why are you timid, you men of little faith?" Then He arose, and rebuked the winds and the sea; and ²it became perfectly ᶠcalm.	**39** And being aroused, He rebuked the wind and said to the sea, "Hush, be still." And the wind died down and ²it became perfectly ᶠcalm.	**24** And they came to Him and woke Him up, saying, "Master, Master, we are perishing!" And being aroused, He rebuked the wind and the surging waves, and they stopped, and ⁴it became ᶠcalm.
	40 And He said to them, "Why are you so timid? How is it that you have no faith?"	**25** And He said to them, "Where is your faith?" And they were fearful and amazed, saying to one another, "ᵍWho then is this, that He commands even the winds and
27 And the men marveled, saying, "ᵍWhat kind of a man is this, that even	**41** And they became very much afraid and said to one another, "ᵍWho	

ᵉ(Matt. 8:24) It is no wonder that Jesus slept so soundly after the taxing day He had been through (Secs. 79-92).

ᶠ(Matt. 8:26; Mark 4:39; Luke 8:24) Here is a double miracle, the cessation of the wind and the immediate calming of the water. Ordinarily the waters would remain rough for a time after the wind stopped, but not this time.

ᵍ(Matt. 8:27; Mark 4:41; Luke 8:25) Though privileged to be insiders in regard to the mysteries of the Kingdom, it is evident that the disciples still needed much strengthening in conviction about the identity of the King. Some of them had begun learning early (Sec. 31), but the process was slow.

Matt. 13:53; 8:18, 23-27 (cont'd)	Mark 4:35-41 (cont'd)	Luke 8:22-25 (cont'd)
the winds and the sea obey Him?"	then is this, that even the wind and the sea obey Him?"	the water, and they obey Him?"

[1]Lit., *a shaking.*   [2]Lit., *a great calm occurred.*   [3]Or, *sending away.*   [4]Lit., *a calm occurred.*

Sec. 94   Healing the Gerasene demoniacs and resultant opposition
   – Gerasa –

Matt. 8:28-34	Mark 5:1-20	Luke 8:26-39
28 And when He had come to the other side into the country of the Gadarenes, [h]two men who were demon-possessed met Him as they were coming out of the tombs; *they were* so exceedingly violent that no one could pass by that road.	**1** And they came to the other side of the sea, into the country of the Gerasenes. **2** And when He had come out of the boat, immediately a [h]man from the tombs with an unclean spirit met Him, **3** and he had his dwelling among the tombs. And no one was able to bind him anymore, even with a chain; **4** because he had often been bound with shackles and chains, and the chains had been torn apart by him, and the shackles broken in pieces, and no one was strong enough to subdue him. **5** And constantly night and day, among the tombs and in the mountains, he was crying out and gashing himself with stones. **6** And seeing Jesus from a distance, he ran up and bowed down before Him;	**26** And they sailed to the country of the [6]Gerasenes, which is opposite Galilee. **27** And when He had come out onto the land, He was met by a certain [h]man from the city who was possessed with demons; and who had not put on any clothing for a long time, and was not living in a house, but in the tombs.
29 And behold, they cried out, saying, "What do we have to do with You, Son of God? Have You come here to torment us before [1]the time?"	**7** and crying out with a loud voice, he *said, "What do I have to do with You, Jesus, Son of the Most High God? I implore You by God, do not torment me!"	**28** And seeing Jesus, he cried out and fell before Him, and said in a loud voice, "What do I have to do with You, Jesus, Son of the Most High God? I beg You, do not torment me." **29** For He [7]had been commanding the unclean spirit to come out of the man. For it had seized him

[h](Matt. 8:28; Mark 5:2; Luke 8:27) Apparently there were two demon-possessed men, but Mark and Luke single out the one who was leader.

Matt. 8:28-34 (cont'd)	Mark 5:1-20 (cont'd)	Luke 8:26-39 (cont'd)
	8 For He had been saying to him, "Come out of the man, you unclean spirit!"	many times; and he was bound with chains and shackles and kept under guard; and yet he would burst his fetters and be driven by the demon into the desert.
	9 And He was asking him, "What is your name?" And he *said to Him, "My name is Legion; for we are many."	**30** And Jesus asked him, "What is your name?" And he said, "Legion"; for many demons had entered him.
	10 And he began to entreat Him earnestly not to send them out of the country.	**31** And they were entreating Him not to command them to depart into the abyss.
30 Now there was at a distance from them a herd of many ¹swine feeding.	**11** Now there was a big herd of ¹swine feeding there on the mountain.	**32** Now there was a herd of many ¹swine feeding there on the mountain; and the demons
31 And the demons began to entreat Him, saying, "If You are going to cast us out, send us into the herd of swine."	**12** And the demons entreated Him, saying, "Send us into the swine so that we may enter them."	entreated Him to permit them to enter ⁸the swine. And He gave them permission.
32 And He said to them, "Begone!" And they came out, and went into the swine, and behold, the whole herd rushed down the steep bank into the sea and perished in the waters.	**13** And He gave them permission. And coming out, the unclean spirits entered the swine; and the herd rushed down the steep bank into the sea, about two thousand of them; and they ³were drowned in the sea.	**33** And the demons came out from the man and entered the swine; and the herd rushed down the steep bank into the lake, and were drowned.
33 And the herdsmen ran away, and went to the city, and reported everything, ²including the incident of the demoniacs.	**14** And their herdsmen ran away and reported it in the city and out in the country. And the people came to see what it was that had happened.	**34** And when the herdsmen saw what had happened, they ran away and reported it in the city and out in the country.
34 And behold, the whole city came out to meet Jesus;	**15** And they *came to Jesus and *observed the man who had been demon-possessed sitting down, clothed and in his right mind, the very man who had had the "legion"; and they became frightened.	**35** And the people went out to see what had happened; and they came to Jesus, and found the man from whom the demons had gone out, sitting down at the feet of Jesus, clothed and in his right mind; and they became frightened.
	16 And those who had seen it described to them how it had happened to	**36** And those who had seen it reported to them how the man who was

---

¹(Matt. 8:30; Mark 5:11; Luke 8:32) The presence of swine in this predominantly Gentile area of Decapolis is not surprising. Swine were unclean animals to the Jews.

Matt. 8:28-34 (cont'd)	Mark 5:1-20 (cont'd)	Luke 8:26-39 (cont'd)
and when they saw Him, they entreated *Him* to depart from their region.	the demon-possessed man, and *all* about the swine. **17** And they began to entreat Him to depart from their region. **18** And as He was getting into the boat, the man who had been demon-possessed was entreating Him that he might [4]accompany Him. **19** And He did not let him, but He *said to him, "Go home to your people and [j]report to them [5]what great things the Lord has done for you, and *how* He had mercy on you." **20** And he went away and began to proclaim in Decapolis [5]what great things Jesus had done for him; and everyone marveled.	demon-possessed had been [9]made well. **37** And all the people of the country of the [6]Gerasenes and the surrounding district asked Him to depart from them; for they were gripped with great fear; and He got into a boat, and returned. **38** But the man from whom the demons had gone out was begging Him that he might [10]accompany Him; but He sent him away, saying, **39** "Return to your house and [j]describe what great things God has done for you." And he went away, proclaiming throughout the whole city what great things Jesus had done for him.

[1]I.e., the appointed time of judgment. [2]Lit., *and.* [3]Lit., *were drowning.* [4]Lit., *be with Him.* [5]Or, *everything that.* [6]Other mss. read *Gergesenes* or *Gadarenes.* [7]Or, *was commanding.* [8]Lit., *them.* [9]Or, *saved.* [10]Lit., *be with.*

Sec. 95 Return to Galilee, healing of woman who touched Christ's garment, and raising of Jairus' daughter

Matt. 9:18-26	Mark 5:21-43	Luke 8:40-56
	21 And when Jesus had crossed over again in the boat to the other side, a great multitude gathered about Him; and He [11]stayed by the seashore. **22** And one of the synagogue [12]officials named Jairus *came up, and upon seeing Him, *fell at His feet,	**40** And as Jesus returned, the multitude welcomed Him, for they had all been waiting for Him.
18 [k]While He was saying these things to them, behold, there came		**41** And behold, there came a man named Jairus, and he was an [2]official of

[j](Mark 5:19; Luke 8:39) Whereas Jesus for various reasons forbade others to speak about their cures, the situation in half-heathen Perea where this miracle was performed was different. Political repercussions from Jewish opponents were nonexistent here. Furthermore, there were no other missionaries to the area.

[k](Matt. 9:18) At times this introductory phrase has been taken to indicate chronological sequence between Matthew 9:14-17 (Sec. 56) and 9:18-26. Even though plausible, this sequence would intolerably disrupt the order of Mark and Luke. Besides, this portion of Matthew's gospel is not chronologically arranged.

Matt. 9:18-26 (cont'd)	Mark 5:21-43 (cont'd)	Luke 8:40-56 (cont'd)
[1]a *synagogue* [2]official, and [3]bowed down before Him, [1]saying, "My daughter has just died; but come and lay Your hand on her, and she will live." **19** And Jesus rose and *began* to follow him, and *so did His disciples.* **20** And behold, a woman who had been suffering from a hemorrhage for twelve years, came up behind Him and touched the fringe of His [4]cloak; **21** for she was saying [5]to herself, "If I only touch His garment, I shall [6]get well."	**23** and *[1]entreated Him earnestly, saying, "My little daughter is at the point of death; *please* come and lay Your hands on her, that she may [6]get well and live." **24** And He went off with him; and a great multitude was following Him and pressing in on Him. **25** And a woman who had had a hemorrhage for twelve years, **26** and had [m]endured much at the hands of many physicians, and had spent all that she had and was not helped at all, but rather had grown worse, **27** after hearing about Jesus, came up in the crowd behind *Him*, and touched His [4]cloak. **28** For she [13]thought, "If I just touch His garments, I shall [6]get well." **29** And immediately the flow of her blood was dried up; and she felt in her body that she was healed of her affliction. **30** And immediately Jesus, perceiving in Himself that the power *proceeding* from Him had gone forth, turned around in the crowd and said, "Who touched My garments?" **31** And His disciples said to Him, "You see the multitude pressing in on You, and You say, 'Who touched Me?'" **32** And He looked around to see the woman who had done this.	the synagogue; and he fell at Jesus' feet, and *began* to [1]entreat Him to come to his house; **42** for he had an [16]only daughter, about twelve years old, and she was dying. But as He went, the multitudes were pressing against Him. **43** And a woman who had a hemorrhage for twelve years, [17]and [m]could not be healed by anyone, **44** came up behind Him, and touched the fringe of His cloak; and immediately her hemorrhage stopped. **45** And Jesus said, "Who is the one who touched Me?" And while they were all denying it, Peter said, [18]"Master, the multitudes are crowding and pressing upon You." **46** But Jesus said,

[1](Matt. 9:18; Mark 5:23; Luke 8:41) Since Jesus had established His headquarters at Capernaum (cf. Sec. 46), it is quite probable that Jairus had previous contact with Him. As a synagogue leader in the city, he probably knew about the healing of the royal official's child (cf. Sec. 44) and of the centurion's servant (cf. Sec. 73). These furnished ample incentive for him to seek Jesus' help.

[m](Mark 5:26; Luke 8:43) Luke the physician is more sympathetic to the efforts of those of his own profession than is Mark.

Matt. 9:18-26 (cont'd)	Mark 5:21-43 (cont'd)	Luke 8:40-56 (cont'd)
	33 But the woman fearing and trembling, aware of what had happened to her, came and fell down before Him, and told Him the whole truth.	"Someone did touch Me, for I was aware that power had gone out of Me."
22 But Jesus turning and seeing her said, "Daughter, take courage; your faith has [7]made you well." And [8]at once the woman was made well.	**34** And He said to her, "Daughter, your faith has [7]made you well; go in peace, and be healed of your affliction."	**47** And when the woman saw that she had not escaped notice, she came trembling and fell down before Him, and declared in the presence of all the people the reason why she had touched Him, and how she had been immediately healed.
	35 While He was still speaking, they *came from the *house of* the synagogue official, saying, "Your daughter has died; why trouble the Teacher anymore?"	**48** And He said to her, "Daughter, your faith has [7]made you well; go in peace."
	36 But Jesus, overhearing what was being spoken, *said to the synagogue official, "Do not be afraid *any longer*, only [14]believe."	
	37 And He allowed no one to follow with Him, except Peter and [15]James and John the brother of James.	**49** While He was still speaking, someone *came from *the house of* the synagogue official, saying, "Your daughter has died; do not trouble the Teacher anymore."
	38 And they *came to the house of the synagogue official; and He *beheld a commotion, and *people loudly weeping and wailing.	**50** But when Jesus heard *this*, He answered him, "Do not be afraid *any longer*; only believe, and she shall [6]be made well."
	39 And entering in, He *said to them,	**51** And when He had come to the house, He did not allow anyone to enter with Him, except Peter and John and James, and the girl's father and mother.
		52 Now they were all weeping and lamenting for her; but He said, "Stop weeping, for she has not died, but is asleep."
23 And when Jesus came into the [9]official's house, and saw the flute-players, and the crowd in noisy disorder,	"Why make a commotion and weep? The child has not died, but is asleep."	**53** And they began laughing at Him, knowing that she had died.
24 He *began* to say, "Depart; for the girl has not died, but is asleep." And they *began* laughing at	**40** And they *began* laughing at Him. But putting them all out, He *took along the child's father and mother and His own companions, and *entered	

Matt. 9:18-26 (cont'd)	Mark 5:21-43 (cont'd)	Luke 8:40-56 (cont'd)
Him. **25** But when the crowd had been put out, He entered and took her by the hand; and the girl [10]arose. **26** And this news went out into all that land.	*the room* where the child was. **41** And taking the child by the hand, He *said to her, "Talitha kum!" (which translated means, "Little girl, I say to you, arise!"). **42** And immediately the girl rose and *began to* walk; for she was twelve years old. And immediately they were completely astounded. **43** And He gave them strict orders that [n]no one should know about this; and He said that *something should be given her to eat.*	**54** He, however, took her by the hand and called, saying, "Child, arise!" **55** And her spirit returned, and she rose immediately; and He gave orders for *something* to be given her to eat. **56** And her parents were amazed; but He instructed them to tell [n]no one what had happened.

[1]Or, one. [2]Lit., ruler. [3]Or, worshiped. [4]Or, outer garment. [5]Lit., in herself. [6]Lit., be saved. [7]Lit., saved you. [8]Lit., from that hour. [9]Lit., ruler's. [10]Or, was raised up. [11]Lit., was. [12]Or, rulers. [13]Lit., was saying. [14]Or, keep on believing. [15]Or, Jacob. [16]Or, only begotten. [17]Some mss. add who had spent all her living upon physicians. [18]Some early mss. add and those with him.

Sec. 96   Three miracles of healing and another blasphemous accusation (cf. Secs. 79, 144; 182)
— Galilee —

Matt. 9:27-34

27 And as Jesus passed on from there, two blind men followed Him, crying out, and saying, "Have mercy on us, Son of David!"

28 And after He had come into the house, the blind men came up to Him, and Jesus *said to them, "Do you believe that I am able to do this?" They *said to Him, "Yes, Lord."

29 Then He touched their eyes, saying, "Be it done to you according to your faith."

30 And their eyes were opened. And Jesus sternly warned them, saying, "See here, [o]let no one know *about this!*"

31 But they went out, and spread the news about Him in all that land.

32 And as they were going out, behold, a dumb man, demon-possessed, [1]was brought to Him.

33 And after the demon was cast out, the dumb man spoke; and the multitudes marveled, saying, "Nothing like this was [2]ever seen in Israel."

[n](Mark 5:43; Luke 8:56) The manner in which the girl was raised from the dead was to be kept from unbelieving and scornful mourners (Mark 5:40; Luke 8:53) and reserved for those who responded to His invitation to believe (Mark 5:36; Luke 8:50). The scene of the incident was Capernaum where earlier (perhaps the same day) His ministry had changed its complexion because of "an eternal sin" (Mark 3:29, Sec. 79). Now He is quite careful as to whom He gives the gospel.

[o](Matt. 9:30) The prohibition intended to silence the healed blind man was prompted by the antagonistic atmosphere that prevailed in Galilee against Jesus. Wrong implications derived from His miraculous deeds furnished an opportunity for further blasphemy against the Holy Spirit (cf. Matt. 9:34; cf. Sec. 79). No further sign was to be given the rejectors (Matt. 12:39, Sec. 80).

Matt. 9:27-34 (cont'd)

34 But the Pharisees were saying, "He casts out the demons by the ruler of the demons."

[1]Lit., *they brought.*   [2]Lit., *ever appeared.*

Sec. 97   Final visit to unbelieving Nazareth (cf. Secs. 42, 43, 45)

Matt. 13:54-58	Mark 6:1-6a
54 And coming to [1]His home town He [2]*began* teaching them in their synagogue, so that they became astonished, and said, "Where *did* this man get this wisdom, and *these* [3]miraculous powers?	**1** And He went out from there, and He *came into [1]His home town; and His disciples *followed Him.
	2 And when the Sabbath had come, He began to teach in the synagogue; and the many listeners were astonished, saying, "Where did this man get these things, and what is *this* wisdom given to Him, and such [6]miracles as these performed by His hands?
55 "Is not this the carpenter's son? Is not His mother called Mary, and His brothers, James and Joseph and Simon and Judas?	**3** "Is not this the carpenter, the son of Mary, and brother of [7]James, and Joses, and Judas, and Simon? Are not His sisters here with us?" And they [4]took offense at Him.
56 "And His sisters, are they not all with us? Where then *did* this man get all these things?"	
57 And they [4]took offense at Him. But Jesus said to them, "A prophet is not without honor except in his [5]home town, and in his *own* household."	**4** And Jesus said to them, "A prophet is not without honor except in his [5]home town and among his *own* relatives and in his *own* household."
58 And He did not do many [6]miracles there because of their [P]unbelief.	**5** And He could do no [6]miracle there except that He laid His hands upon a few sick people and healed them.
	6 And He wondered at their [P]unbelief.

[1]Or, *His own part of the country.*   [2]Or, *was teaching.*   [3]Or, *miracles.*   [4]Lit., *were being made to stumble.*   [5]Or, *his own part of the country.*   [6]Or, *work(s) of power.*   [7]Or, *Jacob.*

FINAL GALILEAN CAMPAIGN

Sec. 98   Shortage of workers (cf. Sec. 99, 139)
     – *Itineration in Galilee* –

Matt. 9:35-38	Mark 6:6b
35 And Jesus was going about all the cities and the villages, teaching in their synagogues, and proclaiming the gospel of the kingdom, and healing every kind of disease and every kind of sickness.	And He was going around the villages teaching.

[P](Matt. 13:58; Mark 6:6a) This visit to Nazareth came about a year after the citizens of the town had attempted to murder Jesus (Luke 4:29, Sec. 45). As their earlier treatment stood in contrast to the belief of the Samaritans (Sec. 41) and the royal official (Sec. 44), so now their unbelief is in marked contrast to the faith of those who benefited from Jesus' ministry in Capernaum (Secs. 95, 96).

Matt. 9:35-38 (cont'd)

36 And seeing the multitudes, He felt compassion for them, because they were [1]distressed and [2]downcast like [q]sheep [3]without a shepherd.

37 Then He *said to His disciples, "The harvest is plentiful, but the workers are few.

38 "Therefore beseech the Lord of the harvest to send out workers into His harvest."

[1]Or, *harassed.*   [2]Lit., *thrown down.*   [3]Lit., *not having.*

Sec. 99   Commissioning of the twelve (cf. Secs. 63, Acts 1:13; 70, 146; 70, 213, 220; 98, 139; 119, 165; 128; 146; 149, 203)
    – Galilee –

Matt. 10:1-42	Mark 6:7-11	Luke 9:1-5
1 And having summoned His twelve disciples, He gave them authority over unclean spirits, to cast them out, and to heal every kind of disease and every kind of sickness.	**7** And He *summoned the twelve and began to send them out in pairs; and He was giving them authority over the unclean spirits;	**1** And He called the twelve together , and gave them power and authority over all the demons, and to heal diseases.
2 Now the names of the twelve apostles are these: The first, Simon, who is called Peter, and Andrew his brother; and [1]James the son of Zebedee, and [2]John his brother;	**8** and He instructed them	**2** And He sent them out to proclaim the kingdom of God, and [29]to perform healing.
3 Philip and [3]Bartholomew; Thomas and Matthew the tax-gatherer; [1]James the son of Alphaeus, and Thaddaeus;		**3** And He said to them,
4 Simon the [4]Zealot, and Judas Iscariot, the one who betrayed Him.		
5 These twelve Jesus sent out after instructing them, saying, "[r]Do not [5]go in the way of the Gentiles,		

[q](Matt. 9:36) The "sheep" are identified more fully in Matt. 10:6 as "the lost sheep of the house of Israel." To evangelize this people more thoroughly was His compassionate objective at this point. Every person had a right to hear the good news about the Kingdom, even though the leadership had already turned its back to the King (cf. Sec. 79).

[r](Matt. 10:5) Jesus at this point continued restricting His outreach—and that of His disciples—to the people to whom the Kingdom had been promised. A broadened responsibility was not outlined until His rejection by this people became more general as reflected in the crucifixion. Then the disciples were told to go to all nations (cf. Sec. 256).

Matt. 10:1-42 (cont'd)	Mark 6:7-11 (cont'd)	Luke 9:1-5 (cont'd)
and do not enter *any* city of the Samaritans; **6** but rather [6]go to the lost sheep of the house of Israel. **7** "And as you [6]go, [7]preach, saying, 'The kingdom of heaven [8]is at hand.' **8** "Heal *the* sick, raise *the* dead, cleanse *the* lepers, cast out demons; freely you received, freely give. **9** "Do not acquire gold, or silver, or copper [9]for your money belts, **10** or a [10]bag for *your* journey, or even two [11]tunics, or sandals, or a staff; for the worker is worthy of his [12]support. **11** "And into whatever city or village you enter, inquire who is worthy in it; and abide there until you go away. **12** "And as you enter the [13]house, give it your greeting. **13** "And if the house is worthy, let your *greeting of* peace come upon it; but if it is not worthy, let your *greeting of* peace return to you. **14** "And whoever does not receive you, nor heed your words, as you go out of that house or that city, shake off the dust of your feet. **15** "Truly I say to you, it will be more tolerable for *the* land of Sodom and Gomorrah in the day of judgment, than for that city.		
	that they should take nothing for *their* journey, except a mere staff; no bread, no [10]bag, no money in their belt; **9** but [26]to wear sandals; and *He added,* "Do not put on two [11]tunics." **10** And He said to them, "Wherever you enter a house, stay there until you [27]leave town.	"Take nothing for your journey, neither a staff, nor a [10]bag, nor bread, nor money; and do not *even* have two [11]tunics apiece. **4** "And whatever house you enter, stay there, and take your leave from there.
	11 "And any place that does not receive you or listen to you, as you go out from there, shake off the dust [28]from the soles of your feet for a testimony against them."	**5** "And as for those who do not receive you, as you go out from that city, shake off the dust from your feet as a testimony against them."

16 "Behold, I send you out as sheep in the midst of wolves; therefore [14]be shrewd as serpents, and innocent as doves.

17 "But beware of men; for they will deliver you up to *the* courts, and scourge you in their synagogues;

18 and you shall even be brought before governors and kings for My sake, as a testimony to them and to the Gentiles.

Matt. 10:1-42 (cont'd)

19 "But when they deliver you up, do not become anxious about how or what you will speak; for it shall be given you in that hour what you are to speak.

20 "For it is not you who speak, but *it is* the Spirit of your Father who speaks in you.

21 "And brother will deliver up brother to death, and a father *his* child; and children will rise up against parents, and [15]cause them to be put to death.

22 "And you will be hated by all on account of My name, but it is the one who has endured to the end who will be saved.

23 "But whenever they persecute you in this city, flee to [16]the next; for truly I say to you, you shall not finish *going through* the cities of Israel, until the Son of Man comes.

24 "A [17]disciple is not above his teacher, nor a slave above his master.

25 "It is enough for the disciple that he become as his teacher, and the slave as his master. [s]If they have called the head of the house [18]Beelzebul, how much more the members of his household!

26 "Therefore do not fear them, for there is nothing covered that will not be revealed, and hidden that will not be known.

27 "What I tell you in the darkness, speak in the light; and what you hear whispered in your ear, proclaim upon the housetops.

28 "And do not fear those who kill the body, but are unable to kill the soul; but rather fear Him who is able to destroy both soul and body in [19]hell.

29 "Are not two sparrows sold for a [20]cent? And yet not one of them will fall to the ground apart from your Father.

30 "But the very hairs of your head are all numbered.

31 "Therefore do not fear; you are of more value than many sparrows.

32 "Everyone therefore who shall confess [21]Me before men, I will also confess [22]him before My Father who is in heaven.

33 "But whoever shall deny Me before men, I will also deny him before My Father who is in heaven.

34 "Do not think that I came to [23]bring peace on the earth; I did not come to bring peace, but a sword.

35 "For I came to SET A MAN AGAINST HIS FATHER, AND A DAUGHTER AGAINST HER MOTHER, AND A DAUGHTER-IN-LAW AGAINST HER MOTHER-IN-LAW;

36 and A MAN'S ENEMIES WILL BE THE MEMBERS OF HIS HOUSEHOLD [Mic. 7:6].

37 "He who loves father or mother more than Me is not worthy of Me; and he who loves son or daughter more than Me is not worthy of Me.

38 "And he who does not take his cross and follow after Me is not worthy of Me.

39 "He who has found his [24]life shall lose it, and he who has lost his [24]life for My sake shall find it.

40 "He who receives you receives Me, and he who receives Me receives Him who sent Me.

41 "He who receives a prophet in the name of a prophet shall receive a prophet's reward; and he who receives a righteous man in the name of a righteous man shall receive a righteous man's reward.

42 "And whoever in the name of a disciple gives to one of these [25]little ones even a cup of cold water to drink, truly I say to you he shall not lose his reward."

[1]Or, *Jacob.* [2]Gr., *Joannes,* Heb., *Johanan.* [3]I.e., son of Talmai (Aram.). [4]Or, *Cananaean.* [5]Or, *go off to.* [6]Or, *proceed.* [7]Or, *proclaim.* [8]Lit., *has come near.* [9]Lit., *into.* [10]Or, *knapsack or beggar's bag.* [11]Or, *inner garments.* [12]Lit., *nourishment.* [13]Or, *household.* [14]Or, *show yourselves to be.* [15]Or, *put them to death.* [16]Lit., *the other.* [17]Or, *pupil.* [18]Or, *Beezebul; others read Beelzebub.* [19]Gr.,

---

[s](Matt. 10:25) Jesus apparently did not expect widespread repentance to result from this mission. In the bulk of the discourse (e.g. Matt. 10:14-39) He anticipated an unfavorable reception of the twelve. This anticipation was based on earlier treatment of Himself (cf. Sec. 79).

Gehenna. [20]Gr., *assarion, the smallest copper coin.* [21]Lit., *in Me.* [22]Lit., *in him.* [23]Lit., *cast.* [24]Or, *soul.* [25]I.e., *humble.* [26]Lit., *being shod with.* [27]Lit., *go out from there.* [28]Lit., *under your feet.* [29]Some mss. read *to heal the sick.*

Sec. 100 Workers sent out
— Itineration in Galilee —

Matt. 11:1	Mark 6:12-13	Luke 9:6
1 And it came about that when Jesus had finished [1]giving instructions to His twelve disciples, He departed from there to teach and [2]preach in their cities.	**12** And they went out and [3]preached that men should repent. **13** And they were casting out many demons and were anointing with oil many sick people and healing them.	**6** And departing, they began going about [4]among the villages, preaching the gospel, and healing everywhere.

[1]Or, *commanding.* [2]Or, *proclaim.* [3]Or, *proclaimed as a herald.* [4]Or, *from village to village.*

Sec. 101 Antipas' mistaken identification of Jesus

Matt. 14:1-2	Mark 6:14-16	Luke 9:7-9
1 At that [1]time Herod the tetrarch [t]heard the news about Jesus, **2** and said to his servants, "This is John the Baptist; [2]he has risen from the dead; and that is why miraculous powers are at work in him."	**14** And King Herod [t]heard *of it,* for His name had become well known; and *people* were saying, "John the Baptist has risen from the dead, and that is why these miraculous powers are at work in Him." **15** But others were saying, *"He is* Elijah." And others were saying, *"He is* a prophet, like one of the prophets *of old."* **16** But when Herod heard *of it,* he kept saying, "John, whom I beheaded, has risen!"	**7** Now Herod the tetrarch [t]heard of all that was happening; and he was greatly perplexed, because it was said by some that John had risen from the dead, **8** and by some that Elijah had appeared, and by others, that one of the prophets of old had risen again. **9** And Herod said, "I myself had John beheaded; but who is this man about whom I hear such things?" And he kept trying to see Him.

[1]Or, *occasion.* [2]Or, *he, himself.*

---

[t](Matt. 14:1; Mark 6:14; Luke 9:7) The multiplied outreach of Jesus' ministry through the twelve (Secs. 99-100) was what brought Him increased fame. Herod Antipas, whose domain included Galilee and Perea, was now forced to give Him attention.

Sec. 102   ᵁEarlier imprisonment and beheading of John the Baptist (cf. Sec. 38)
— Probably Tiberias —

Matt. 14:3-12	Mark 6:17-29
3 For when Herod had John arrested, he bound him, and put him in prison on account of Herodias, the wife of his brother Philip.	**17** For Herod himself had sent and had John arrested and bound in prison on account of Herodias, the wife of his brother Philip, because he had married her.
4 For John had been saying to him, "It is not lawful for you to have her."	**18** For John had been saying to Herod, "It is not lawful for you to have your brother's wife."
5 And although he wanted to put him to death, he feared the multitude, because ¹they regarded him as a prophet.	**19** And Herodias had a grudge against him and wanted to put him to death and could not *do so;*
	20 for Herod was afraid of John, knowing that he was a righteous and holy man, and kept him safe. And when he heard him, he was very perplexed; ⁶but he ⁷used to enjoy listening to him.
	21 And a strategic day came when Herod on his birthday gave a banquet for his lords and military ⁸commanders and the leading men of Galilee;
6 But when Herod's birthday ²came, the daughter of Herodias danced ³before *them* and pleased Herod.	**22** and when the daughter of Herodias herself came in and danced, she pleased Herod and his ⁹dinner guests; and the king said to the girl, "Ask me for whatever you want and I will give it to you."
7 Thereupon he promised with an oath to give her whatever she asked.	**23** And he swore to her, "Whatever you ask of me, I will give it to you; up to half of my kingdom."
	24 And she went out and said to her mother, "What shall I ask for?" And she said, "The head of John the Baptist."
	25 And immediately she came in haste before the king and asked, saying, "I want you to give me right away the head of John the Baptist on a platter."
8 And having been prompted by her mother, she *said, "Give me here on a platter the head of John the Baptist."	**26** And although the king was very sorry, *yet* because of his oaths and because of ⁴his dinner guests, he was unwilling to refuse her.
9 And although he was grieved, the king commanded *it* to be given because of his oaths, and because of ⁴his dinner guests.	**27** And immediately the king sent an executioner and commanded *him* to bring *back* his head. And he went and had him beheaded in the prison.
10 And he sent and had John beheaded in the prison.	
11 And his head was brought on a platter and given to the girl; and she brought *it* to her mother.	**28** and brought his head on a platter, and gave it to the girl; and the girl gave it to her mother.

ᵁThis section is an historical flashback given as background to the execution of John which occurred at this point in the chronology. John's imprisonment began about a year and a half earlier, at the time Jesus began His Galilean ministry (cf. Sec. 38).

Matt. 14:3-12 (cont'd)	Mark 6:17-29 (cont'd)
12 And his disciples came and took away the body and buried ⁵it; and they went and reported to Jesus.	**29** And when his disciples heard *about this,* they came and took away his body and laid it in a tomb.

¹Lit., *they were holding.* ²Lit., *occurred.* ³Lit., *in the midst.* ⁴Lit., *those who reclined at the table with him.* ⁵Lit., *him.* ⁶Lit., *and.* ⁷Lit., *was hearing him gladly.* ⁸I.e., chiliarchs, in command of a thousand troops. ⁹Lit., *those reclining at the table.*

Sec. 103 Return of the workers
– Galilee –

Mark 6:30	Luke 9:10a
30 And the apostles *gathered together with Jesus; and they reported to Him all that they had done and taught.	**10** And when the apostles returned, they gave an account to Him of all that they had done.

PART SEVEN

THE MINISTRY OF CHRIST AROUND GALILEE

LESSON ON THE BREAD OF LIFE

Sec. 104 Withdrawal from Galilee
– From Galilee to ᵛBethsaida, near Julias –

Matt. 14:13-14	Mark 6:31-34	Luke 9:10b-11	John 6:1-3
	31 A n d H e *said to them, "ˣCome away by yourselves to a lonely place and rest a while." (For there were many *people* coming and going, and they did not even have time to eat.)		
13 Now when Jesus heard *it*, He ʷwithdrew from there in a boat, to a lonely place by	32 A n d t h e y went away in the boat to a lonely place by them- selves.	And taking them with Him, He ʷwithdrew by Himself to a city called Bethsaida.	1 After these things Jesus went away to the other side of the Sea of

---

ᵛApparently two communities were named Bethsaida. That of Luke 9:10 should be identified with Bethsaida near Julias on the northeast side of the Sea of Galilee. In Mark 6:45 (Sec. 106) the name designates a village on the western shore, near Capernaum.

ʷ(Matt. 14:13; Luke 9:10) At this point in His ministry, Jesus' relationship with the multitudes changed. Prior to this He made it a point for the most part to go to them, though there were exceptions (e.g. Sec. 93). The following months were especially characterized by His withdrawal from them. In addition to this section, see Sections 106, 112, 113, and 116. Five factors have merit in accounting for these withdrawals:

1. The jealousy of Herod Antipas (cf. Matt. 14:13 with Mark 6:30, Sec. 103). Apparently the arrival of John's disciples with the news of his burial coincided with the return of the twelve from their preaching tour of Galilee, which was part of Herod's domain. Jesus left the area to avoid any further retaliatory steps by Herod because of the widespread publicity resulting from the tour of the twelve.
2. The misguided zeal of followers who sought to force Jesus to accept the throne of Israel prematurely (cf. John 6:15, Sec. 106). Jesus avoided such a confrontation and its probable unfortunate aftereffects.
3. The hostility of Jewish leaders (cf. Mark 7:1-23, Sec. 111). Opposition from those in high places had surfaced as the Galilean ministry progressed, but now it had developed to the point that further ministry in Galilee had to be curtailed radically.
4. The disciples' need for rest after their grueling tours (cf. Mark 6:31). Departure from the hot shores of the Sea of Galilee to the cooler mountain areas afforded an opportunity for this.
5. The opportunity for more personalized instruction of the disciples (cf. Secs. 104-132 where the disciples were either in the role of recipients of instruction or were profiting in a special way from Jesus' dealing with others). Their ministries throughout Galilee had probably created many questions. The Lord thus gave them a different kind of opportunity to learn about and from Him.

ˣ(Mark 6:31) This point marks a shift from a predominantly public ministry to a predominantly private one. Other transitions may be observed in progress at this point: an emphasis on the King replaced an emphasis on the Kingdom; instruction was preparatory for a period of His absence in lieu of His presence; and with the exception of intermittent visits to Galilee, He limited His ministry to outside that area from this point on.

Matt. 14:13-14 (cont'd)	Mark 6:31-34 (cont'd)	Luke 9:10b-11 (cont'd)	John 6:1-3 (cont'd)
Himself; and when the multitudes heard *of this,* they followed Him on foot from the cities.	**33** And *the people* saw them going, and many recognized *them,* and they ran there together on foot from all the cities, and got there ahead of them.		Galilee (or Tiberias). **2** And a great multitude was following Him, because they were seeing the [2]signs which He was performing on those who were sick.
14 And when He went [1]ashore, He saw a great multitude, and felt compassion for them, and healed their sick.	**34** And when He went [1]ashore, He saw a great multitude, and He felt compassion for them because they were like sheep without a shepherd; and He began to teach them many things.	**11** But the multitudes were aware of this and followed Him; and welcoming them, He *began* speaking to them about the kingdom of God and curing those who had need of healing.	**3** And Jesus went up on the mountain, and there He sat with His disciples.

[1]Lit., *out.*   [2]Or, *attesting miracles.*

Sec. 105   Feeding the five thousand (cf. Secs. 114, 116)
— *Bethsaida* —

Matt. 14:15-21	Mark 6:35-44	Luke 9:12-17	John 6:4-13
15 And when it was evening, the [y]disciples came to Him, saying, "The place is desolate, and the time is already past; so send the multitudes away, that they may go into the villages and buy food for themselves."	**35** And when it was already quite late, His [y]disciples came up to Him and *began* saying, "The place is desolate and it is already quite late; **36** send them away so that they may go into the surrounding countryside and villages and buy themselves [1]something to eat."	**12** And the day began to decline, and the [y]twelve came and said to Him, "Send the multitude away, that they may go into the surrounding villages and countryside and find lodging and get [3]something to eat; for here we are in a desolate place."	**4** Now the Passover, the feast of the Jews, was at hand. **5** Jesus therefore lifting up His eyes, and seeing that a great multitude was coming to Him, *said to [y]Philip, "Where are we to buy bread, that these may eat?"
16 But Jesus said to them, "They do not need to go away; you give	**37** But He answered and said to them, "You give them *something* to	**13** But He said to them, "You give them *something* to eat!"	**6** And this He was saying to test him; for He Himself knew what He was

[y](Matt. 14:15; Mark 6:35; Luke 9:12; John 6:5) The prominence of the disciples throughout this episode underscores the importance of the learning experience for them. They learned something about their teacher's power they had not realized before (cf. John 6:12-13). Their doubt (Mark 6:37; John 6:7-8) needed to be replaced by confidence in Him.

Matt. 14:15-21 (cont'd)	Mark 6:35-44 (cont'd)	Luke 9:12-17 (cont'd)	John 6:4-13 (cont'd)
them *something* to eat!"	eat!'' And they *said to Him, "Shall we go and spend ᶻtwo hundred ²denarii on bread and give them *something* to eat?"		intending to do. 7 Philip answered Him, "ᶻTwo hundred ²denarii worth of bread is not sufficient for them, for everyone to receive a little."
1⁷ And they *said to Him, "We have here only five loaves and two fish." 18 And He said, "Bring them here to Me." 19 And ordering the multitudes to recline on the grass,	38 And He *said to them, "How many loaves do you have? Go look!" And when they found out, they *said, "Five and two fish." 39 And He commanded them all to recline by groups on the green grass. 40 And they reclined in companies of hundreds and of fifties.	And they said, "We have no more than five loaves and two fish, unless perhaps we go and buy food for all these people." 14 (For there were about ᵃfive thousand men.) And He said to His disciples, "Have them recline to eat in groups of about fifty each." 15 And they did so, and had them all recline.	8 One of His disciples, Andrew, Simon Peter's brother, *said to Him, 9 "There is a lad here who has five barley loaves and two fish, but what are these for so many people?" 10 Jesus said, "Have the people ⁵sit down." Now there was much grass in the place. So the men sat down, in number about ᵃfive thousand.
He took the five loaves and the two fish, and looking up toward heaven, He blessed *the food, and* breaking the loaves He gave them to the disciples, and the disciples *gave* to the multitudes, 20 and they all ate, and were satisfied. And they picked up what was left over of the broken pieces, twelve full baskets. 21 And there were about ᵃfive thousand men who ate, aside from	41 And He took the five loaves and the two fish, and looking up toward heaven, He blessed *the food* and broke the loaves and He kept giving *them* to the disciples to set before them; and He divided up the two fish among them all. 42 And they all ate and were satisfied. 43 And they picked up twelve full baskets of the broken pieces, and also of the fish. 44 And there were ᵃfive	16 And He took the five loaves and the two fish, and looking up to heaven, He blessed *them,* and broke *them,* and kept giving *them* to the disciples to set before the multitude. 17 And they all ate and were satisfied; and ⁴the broken pieces which they had left over were picked up, twelve baskets *full.*	11 Jesus therefore took the loaves; and having given thanks, He distributed to those who were seated; likewise also of the fish as much as they wanted. 12 And when they were filled, He *said to His disciples, "Gather up the leftover fragments that nothing may be lost." 13 And so they gathered them up, and filled twelve baskets with frag-

ᶻ(Mark 6:37; John 6:7) Two hundred denarii, though not a large amount of money, was probably more than the disciples had in their treasury. Even if they had possessed this much, it would not have been enough.

ᵃ(Matt. 14:21; Mark 6:44; Luke 9:14; John 6:10) The presence of five thousand men strongly implies an equal number of women and at least an equal number of children. The hungry crowd that was fed probably totaled in excess of fifteen thousand.

Matt. 14:15-21 (cont'd)	Mark 6:35-44 (cont'd)		John 6:4-13 (cont'd)
women and children.	thousand men who ate the loaves.		ments from the five barley loaves, which were left over by those who had eaten.

[1]Lit., *what they may eat.* [2]The denarius was equivalent to one day's wage. [3]Lit., *provisions.* [4]Lit., *that which was left over to them of the broken pieces was.* [5]Lit., *recline(d).*

Sec. 106   A premature attempt to make Jesus king blocked
– Alone on the mountain –

Matt. 14:22-23	Mark 6:45-46	John 6:14-15
22 And immediately He [1]made the disciples get into the boat, and go ahead of Him to the other side, while He sent the multitudes away. 23 And after He had sent the multitudes away, He went up to the mountain by Himself to pray; and when it was evening, He was there alone.	45 And immediately He made His disciples get into the boat and go ahead of Him to the other side to Bethsaida, while He Himself was sending the multitude away. 46 And after bidding them farewell, He departed to the mountain to pray.	14 When therefore the people saw the [2]sign which He had performed, they said, "This is of a truth the Prophet who is to come into the world." 15 Jesus therefore perceiving that they were [3]intending to come and take Him by force, to make Him king, [b]withdrew again to the mountain by Himself alone.

[1]Lit., *compelled.* [2]Or, *attesting miracle.* [3]Or, *about.*

Sec. 107   Walking on the water during a storm at sea
– On the Sea of Galilee –

Matt. 14:24-33	Mark 6:47-52	John 6:16-21
24 But the boat was already many [1]stadia away from the land, [2]battered by the waves; for the wind was contrary. 25 And in the [3][c]fourth watch of the night He came to them, walking on the sea.	47 And when it was evening, the boat was in the midst of the sea, and He *was* alone on the land. 48 And seeing them [5]straining at the oars, for the wind was against them, at about the [3][c]fourth watch of the night, He *came to them, walking on the sea; and He intended to pass by them.	16 Now when evening came, His disciples went down to the sea, 17 and after getting into a boat, they *started to* cross the sea to Capernaum. And it had already become dark, and Jesus had not yet come to them. 18 And the sea *began* to be stirred up because a strong wind was blowing.

[b](John 6:15) Once again Jesus refused to accede to popular demand (cf. John 2:23, Sec. 35). He did not deny that He would eventually be King over earthly subjects but was unwilling to assume an active rule until His subjects met the moral prerequisites for entering the kind of Kingdom that He came to institute (cf. Sermon on the Mount, Secs. 64-72). Their recent rejection of Him in Galilee, as well as their selfish motives on the present occasion, were ample proof that they were not ready for His Kingdom.

[c](Matt. 14:25; Mark 6:48) Between nine and twelve hours must have elapsed since Jesus left the disciples. He had left them at about 6:00 P.M. ("evening," Mark 6:47) and rejoined them between 3:00 A.M. the next morning ("the fourth watch"). All this time they were fighting the storm, and He was praying.

Matt. 14:24-33 (cont'd)	Mark 6:47-52 (cont'd)	John 6:16-21 (cont'd)
26 And when the disciples saw Him walking on the sea, they were [4]frightened, saying, "It is a ghost!" And they cried out for fear. **27** But immediately Jesus spoke to them, saying, "Take courage, it is I; do not be afraid." **28** And Peter answered Him and said, "Lord, if it is You, command me to come to You on the water." **29** And He said, "Come!" And Peter got out of the boat, and walked on the water and came toward Jesus. **30** But seeing the wind, he became afraid, and beginning to sink, he cried out, saying, "Lord, save me!" **31** And immediately Jesus stretched out His hand and took hold of him, and *said to him, "O you of little faith, why did you doubt?" **32** And when they got into the boat, the wind stopped. **33** And those who were in the boat worshiped Him, saying, "You are certainly [e]God's Son!"	**49** But when they saw Him walking on the sea, they supposed that it was a ghost, and cried out; **50** for they all saw Him and were [4]frightened. But immediately He spoke with them and *said to them, "Take courage; it is I, do not be afraid." **51** And He got into the boat with them, and [d]the wind stopped; and they were greatly astonished, **52** for they [6]had not gained any insight from the *incident* of the loaves, but [7]their heart was hardened.	**19** When therefore they had rowed about [8]three or four miles, they *beheld Jesus walking on the sea and drawing near to the boat; and they were frightened. **20** But He *said to them, "It is I; [9]do not be afraid." **21** They were willing therefore to receive Him into the boat; and [d]immediately the boat was at the land to which they were going.

[1]A stadion was about 600 feet.   [2]Lit., tormented.   [3]I.e., 3-6 a.m.   [4]Or, troubled.   [5]Lit., harassed in rowing.   [6]Lit., had not understood on the basis of.   [7]Or, their mind was closed, made dull, or insensible.   [8]I.e., 25 or 30 stadia.   [9]Or, stop fearing.

---

[d](Mark 6:51; John 6:21) A twofold miracle occurred: the immediate cessation of the wind and the immediate arrival of the boat at its destination.

[e](Matt. 14:33) Through this experience the disciples advanced one more step in their appreciation of Jesus' person. The double miracle brought them to acknowledge Jesus to be "such a person as the Son of God" (the Greek text has no definite article). It was to be a while yet before they would confess Him to be the "the Son of the living God," however (cf. Matt. 16:16, Sec. 118).

Sec. 108   Healings at ᶠGennesaret

<table>
<tr><td align="center">Matt. 14:34-36</td><td align="center">Mark 6:53-56</td></tr>
<tr>
<td>

34   And when they had crossed over, they came to ¹land at ᵍGennesaret.

35   And when the men of that place ²recognized Him, they sent into all that surrounding district and brought to Him all who were sick;

36   and they *began* to entreat Him that they might just touch the fringe of His cloak; and as many as touched *it* were cured.

</td>
<td>

53   And when they had crossed over they came to land at Gennesaret, and moored to the shore.
54   And when they had come out of the boat, immediately *the people* recognized Him,
55   and ran about that whole country and began to carry about on their pallets those who were sick, to ³the place they heard He was.
56   And wherever He entered villages, or cities, or countryside, they were laying the sick in the market places, and entreating Him that they might just touch the fringe of His cloak; and as many as touched it were being cured.

</td>
</tr>
</table>

¹Lit., *the land.*   ²Or, *knew.*   ³Or, *where they were hearing that He was.*

Sec. 109   Discourse on the true bread of life
– *Capernaum* –

John 6:22-59

22   The next day the multitude that stood on the other side of the sea saw that there was no other small boat there, except one, and that Jesus had not entered with His disciples into the boat, but *that* His disciples had gone away alone.

23   There came other small boats from Tiberias near to the place where they ate the bread after the Lord had given thanks.

24   When the multitude therefore saw that Jesus was not there, nor His disciples, they themselves got into the small boats, and came to Capernaum, seeking Jesus.

25   And when they found Him on the other side of the sea, they said to Him, "Rabbi, when did You get here?"

26   Jesus answered them and said, "Truly, truly, I say to you, you seek Me, not because you saw signs, but because ʰyou ate of the loaves, and were filled.

27   "Do not work for the food which perishes, but for the food which endures to eternal life, which the Son of Man shall give to you, for on Him the Father, *even* God, has set His seal."

28   They said therefore to Him, "What shall we do, that we may work the works of God?"

29   Jesus answered and said to them, "This is the work of God, ⁱthat you believe in Him whom He has sent."

ᶠGennesaret was near Capernaum and Bethsaida. Compare Mark 6:53 with John 6:17 and Mark 6:45.

ᵍLocated on the west coast of the Sea of Galilee, Gennesaret was a fertile plain just south of Capernaum. During this brief visit to Galilee, those who had so recently been party to rejecting Him as Messiah (Secs. 79, 96) were still willing to accept benefit from the miracles that proved His Messiahship.

ʰ(John 6:26) The same selfish motive (cf. Sec. 108) was evident in those who had eaten the loaves and fish on the other side of the sea. They were quite ready for the benefits associated with the Kingdom, but not so ready to comply with its moral responsibilities.

ⁱ(John 6:29) "The food which perishes" (John 6:27) represents the externalities which Israelites of the day thought all important. Jesus constantly sought to correct their misguided efforts. Inward conditioning including faith in Him, not outward conformity, was the crying need of the hour.

John 6:22-59 (cont'd)

30 They said therefore to Him, "What then do You do for a sign, that we may see, and believe You? What work do You perform?

31 "Our fathers ate the manna in the wilderness; as it is written, 'HE GAVE THEM BREAD OUT OF HEAVEN TO EAT'" [Exod. 16:4, 15; Neh. 9:15; Psalm 78:24; 105:40].

32 Jesus therefore said to them, "Truly, truly, I say to you, it is not Moses who has given you the bread out of heaven, but it is My Father who gives you the true bread out of heaven.

33 "For the bread of God is ¹that which comes down out of heaven, and gives life to the world."

34 They said therefore to Him, "Lord, evermore give us this bread."

35 Jesus said to them, "¹I am the bread of life; he who comes to Me shall not hunger, and he who believes in Me shall never thirst.

36 "But I said to you, that you have seen Me, and yet do not believe.

37 "All that the Father gives Me shall come to Me, and the one who comes to Me I will certainly not cast out.

38 "For I have come down from heaven, not to do My own will, but the will of Him who sent Me.

39 "And this is the will of Him who sent Me, that of all that He has given Me I lose nothing, but raise it up on the last day.

40 "For this is the will of My Father, that everyone who beholds the Son and believes in Him, may have eternal life; and I Myself will raise him up on the last day."

41 The Jews therefore were grumbling about Him, because He said, "I am the bread that came down out of heaven."

42 And they were saying, "Is not this Jesus, the son of Joseph, whose father and mother we know? How does He now say, 'I have come down out of heaven'?"

43 Jesus answered and said to them, "Do not grumble among yourselves.

44 "No one can come to Me, unless the Father who sent Me draws him; and I will raise him up on the last day.

45 "It is written in the prophets, 'AND THEY SHALL ALL BE TAUGHT OF GOD' [Isa. 54:13]. Every one who has heard and learned from the Father, comes to Me.

46 "Not that any man has seen the Father, except the One who is from God; He has seen the Father.

47 "Truly, truly, I say to you, he who believes has eternal life.

48 "I am the bread of life.

49 "Your fathers ate the manna in the wilderness, and they died.

50 "This is the bread which comes down out of heaven, so that one may eat of it and not die.

51 "I am the living bread that came down out of heaven; if anyone eats of this bread, he shall live forever; and the bread also which I shall give for the life of the world is My flesh."

52 The Jews therefore began to argue with one another, saying, "How can this man give us His flesh to eat?"

53 Jesus therefore said to them, "Truly, truly, I say to you, unless you eat the flesh of the Son of Man and drink His blood, you have no life in yourselves.

54 "He who eats My flesh and drinks My blood has eternal life, and I will raise him up on the last day.

55 "For My flesh is true food, and My blood is true drink.

56 "He who eats My flesh and drinks My blood abides in Me, and I in him.

---

¹(John 6:35) The "I am" of John's has far-reaching significance. Here as elsewhere it is probably traceable back to Exodus 3:14 and the name of God heard by Moses from the burning bush. This is the first of seven such sayings in Johns's gospel (cf. 8:12; 10:7, 9; 10:11, 14; 11:25; 14:6; 15:1, 5).

John 6:22-59 (cont'd)

57 "As the living Father sent Me, and I live because of the Father, so he who eats Me, he also shall live because of Me.

58 "This is the bread which came down out of heaven; not as the fathers ate, and died, he who eats this bread shall live forever."

59 These things He said in the synagogue, as He taught in Capernaum.

[1]Or, He who comes.

Sec. 110 Defection among the disciples (cf. Sec. 118)
— Capernaum —

John 6:60-71

60 Many therefore of His disciples, when they heard this said, "This is a difficult statement; who can listen to it?"

61 But Jesus, conscious that His disciples grumbled at this, said to them, "Does this cause you to stumble?

62 "What then if you should behold the Son of Man ascending where He was before?

63 "It is the Spirit who gives life; the flesh profits nothing; the words that I have spoken to you are spirit and are life.

64 "But there are some of you who do not believe." For Jesus knew from the beginning who they were who did not believe, and who it was that would [1]betray Him.

65 And He was saying, "For this reason I have said to you, that no one can come to Me, unless it has been granted him from the Father."

66 As a result of this many of His [k]disciples withdrew, and were not walking with Him anymore.

67 Jesus said therefore to the twelve, "You do not want to go away also, do you?"

68 Simon Peter answered Him, "Lord, to whom shall we go? You have words of eternal life.

69 "And we have believed and have come to know that You are [l]the Holy One of God."

70 Jesus answered them, "Did I Myself not choose you, the twelve, and yet one of you is a devil?"

71 Now He meant Judas the son of Simon Iscariot, for he, one of the twelve, [2]was going to betray Him.

[1]Or, deliver Him up.   [2]Or, was intending to.

LESSON ON THE LEAVEN OF THE PHARISEES, SADDUCEES, AND HERODIANS

Sec. 111 Conflict over the tradition of ceremonial defilement
— Galilee, perhaps Capernaum —

---

[k](John 6:66) The strong emphasis on inner response as the only proper basis for external behavior was more than most listeners could bear (John 6:60). As a result, many would-be disciples no longer followed Him. John 6:66 marks a turning point in the use of "disciple" in John's gospel. From this point on, it is found in the more restricted sense of "genuine disciple."

[l](John 6:69) Peter and his fellow disciples at this point reached the threshold of what Jesus was teaching them during this period. Their confession was stronger than the previous one (Matt. 14:33, Sec. 107) but not yet as specific as it would be (Matt. 16:16, Sec. 118). "The Holy One of God" was none other than the One whom God anointed to be King (Psalm 16:10; 71:22; 78:41; 89:18; Isa. 1:4). In spite of public rejection of Him, the disciples were growing into a full appreciation of His person.

Matt. 15:1-20	Mark 7:1-23	John 7:1
1 Then some [m]Pharisees and scribes *came to Jesus from Jerusalem, saying,	**1** And the [m]Pharisees and some of the scribes gathered together around Him when they had come from Jerusalem,	**1** And after these things Jesus was walking in Galilee; for He was unwilling to walk in Judea, because the Jews were seeking to kill Him.
	2 and had seen that some of His disciples were eating their bread with impure hands, that is, unwashed.	
	3 (For the Pharisees and all the Jews do not eat unless they [12][n]carefully wash their hands, thus observing the traditions of the elders;	
	4 and when they come from the market place, they do not eat unless they [13]cleanse themselves; and there are many other things which they have received in order to observe, such as the [14]washing of cups and pitchers and copper pots.)	
	5 And the Pharisees and the scribes *asked Him, "Why do Your disciples not walk according to the tradition of the elders, but eat their bread with impure hands?"	
2 "Why do Your disciples transgress the tradition of the elders? For they do not wash their hands when they eat bread."		
3 And He answered and said to them,	**6** And He said to them, "Rightly did Isaiah prophesy of you hypocrites, as it is written,	
7 "You hypocrites, rightly did Isaiah prophesy of you, saying,		
8 'THIS PEOPLE HONORS ME WITH THEIR LIPS, BUT THEIR HEART IS FAR AWAY FROM ME.	'THIS PEOPLE HONORS ME WITH THEIR LIPS, BUT THEIR HEART IS FAR AWAY FROM ME.	
9 'BUT IN VAIN DO THEY WORSHIP ME,	**7** 'BUT IN VAIN DO THEY WORSHIP ME, TEACHING AS DOCTRINES THE PRE-	

---

[m](Matt. 15:1; Mark 7:1) These represented the official leadership in Jerusalem. Unable to trap Jesus on the issue of Sabbath observance earlier (cf. Secs. 57, 60, 61), they now have come to Galilee to raise another issue, the tradition of the elders about hand washing before eating.

[n](Mark 7:3) The exact requirement of the tradition is not completely clear. The Greek expression is literally "with the fist." Suggestions of the specific meaning have included washing carefully (or diligently), washing by turning a clenched fist around in the hollow of the other hand, washing up to the elbow (or wrist), washing with a handful of water, and washing by rubbing the hand dry with the fist. From evidence available, the most probable solution is washing with a handful of water.

Matt. 15:1-20
(cont'd)

TEACHING AS DOCTRINES THE
PRECEPTS OF MEN'" [Isa. 29:13].

3 "And why do ¹you yourselves transgress the commandment of God for the sake of your tradition?

4 "For God said, 'HONOR YOUR FATHER AND MOTHER,' and, 'HE WHO SPEAKS EVIL OF FATHER OR MOTHER, LET HIM ²BE PUT TO DEATH' [Exod. 20:12; Deut. 5:16].

5 "But you say, '⁰Whoever shall say to *his* father or mother, "Anything of mine you might have been helped by has been ³given *to* God,"

6 he is not to honor his father ⁴or his mother⁵.' And *thus* you invalidated the ⁶word of God for the sake of your tradition.

10 And after He called the multitude to Him, He said to them, "Hear, and understand.

11 "Not what enters into the mouth defiles the man, but what proceeds out of the mouth, this defiles the man."

12 Then the disciples *came and *said to Him, "Do You know that the Pharisees were ⁷offended when they heard this statement?"

13 But He answered and said, "Every plant which My heavenly Father did not plant shall be rooted up.

14 "Let them alone; they are blind guides ⁸of the blind. And if a blind man guides a blind man, both will fall into a pit."

15 And Peter answered and said to Him, "Explain the parable to us."

16 And He said, "Are you still lacking in understanding also?

17 "Do you not understand that everything that goes into the mouth passes into the ⁹stomach, and is ¹⁰eliminated?

Mark 7:1-23
(cont'd)

CEPTS OF MEN' [Isa. 29:13].

8 "Neglecting the commandment of God, you hold to the tradition of men."

9 He was also saying to them, "You nicely set aside the commandment of God in order to keep your tradition.

10 "For Moses said, 'HONOR YOUR FATHER AND YOUR MOTHER'; and, 'HE WHO SPEAKS EVIL OF FATHER OR MOTHER, LET HIM ²BE PUT TO DEATH' [Exod. 20:12; Deut. 5:16];

11 but you say, '⁰If a man says to *his* father or *his* mother, anything of mine you might have been helped by is Corban (that is to say, ³given *to* God),'

12 you no longer permit him to do anything for *his* father or *his* mother;

13 *thus* invalidating the word of God by your tradition which you have handed down; and you do many things such as that."

14 And after He called the multitude to Him again, He *began* saying to them, "Listen to Me, all of you, and understand:

15 there is nothing outside the man which going into him can defile him; but the things which proceed out of the man are what defile the man.

16 ¹⁵["If any man has ears to hear, let him hear."]

17 And when leaving the multitude, He had entered the house, His disciples questioned Him about the parable.

18 And He *said to them, "Are you so lacking in understanding also? Do you not understand that whatever goes into the man from outside cannot defile him;

19 because it does not go into his heart, but into his stomach, and is

---

⁰(Matt. 15:5; Mark 7:11) Here is a specific tradition favored by the scribes and Pharisees. By following this custom they in effect nullified God's commandment about honoring their parents. Their tradition with its emphasis on externalities was diametrically opposed to Jesus' emphasis on the inner man (Matt. 15:11; Mark 7:15). He labored to make this point clear, especially to His disciples (Matt. 15:12-20; Mark 7:17-23).

Matt. 15:1-20 (cont'd)	Mark 7:1-23 (cont'd)
18 "But the things that proceed out of the mouth come from the heart, and those defile the man.	[16]eliminated?" *(Thus He declared all foods clean.)* **20** And He was saying, "That which proceeds out of the man, that is what defiles the man.
19 "For out of the heart come evil thoughts, murders, adulteries, [11]fornications, thefts, false witness, slanders.	**21** "For from within, out of the heart of men, proceed the evil thoughts, [11]fornications, thefts, murders, adulteries, **22** deeds of coveting *and* wickedness, *as well as* deceit, sensuality, [17]envy, slander, [18]pride *and* foolishness.
20 "These are the things which defile the man; but to eat with unwashed hands does not defile the man."	**23** "All these evil things proceed from within and defile the man."

[1]Or, *you also.*   [2]Lit., *die the death.*   [3]Or, *a gift, an offering.*   [4]Many mss. do not contain *or his mother.*   [5]I.e., by supporting them with it.   [6]Some mss. read *law.*   [7]Lit., *caused to stumble.*   [8]Some mss. do not contain *of the blind.*   [9]Lit., *belly.*   [10]Lit., *cast out into the latrine.*   [11]I.e., (acts of) sexual immorality.   [12]Lit., *with the fist.*   [13]Or, *sprinkle.*   [14]Lit., *baptizing.*   [15]Many mss. do not contain this verse.   [16]Lit., *goes out into the latrine.*   [17]Lit., *an evil eye.*   [18]Or, *arrogance.*

Sec. 112   Ministry to a believing Gentile woman in Tyre and Sidon

Matt. 15:21-28	Mark 7:24-30
21 And Jesus went away from there, and withdrew into the district of Tyre and Sidon.	**24** And from there He arose and went away to the region of Tyre[5]. And when He had entered a house, He wanted no one to know *of it;* [6]yet He could not escape notice.
22 And behold, a Canaanite woman came out from that region, and *began to* cry out, saying, "Have mercy on me, O Lord, Son of David; my daughter is cruelly demon-possessed."	**25** But after hearing of Him, a woman whose little daughter had an unclean spirit, immediately came and fell at His feet.
23 But He did not answer her a word. And His disciples came to *Him* and kept asking Him, saying, "Send her away, for she is shouting out after us."	**26** Now the woman was a [7]Gentile, of the Syrophoenician race. And she kept asking Him to cast the demon out of her daughter.
24 But He answered and said, "I was sent [P]only to the lost sheep of the house of Israel."	
25 But she came and *began* [1]to bow down before Him, saying, "Lord, help me!"	
26 And He answered and said, "It is not [2]good to take the children's bread and throw it to the dogs."	**27** And He was saying to her, "Let the children be satisfied first, for it is not [2]good to take the children's bread and throw it to the dogs."
27 But she said, "Yes, Lord; [3]but even	

[P](Matt. 15:24) The continuing exclusive character of Jesus' mission (cf. Matt. 10:5-6, Sec. 99) is nowhere more clearly seen than here. Retreating from His Pharisaic enemies into Gentile territory (Matt. 15:21; Mark 7:24), He at first ignored this woman's request completely (Matt. 15:23). Since she was not of Israel, she had no basis for asking a favor. After she acknowledged that Gentiles receive blessing only indirectly when God blesses Israel, however, Jesus commended her perception and faith and granted her request (Matt. 15:27-28; Mark 7:29-30).

Matt. 15:21-28 (cont'd)

the dogs feed on the crumbs which fall from their masters' table."

28 Then Jesus answered and said to her, "O woman, your faith is great; be it done for you as you wish." And her daughter was healed [4]at once.

Mark 7:24-30 (cont'd)

28 But she answered and *said to Him, "Yes, Lord, but even the dogs under the table feed on the children's crumbs."

29 And He said to her, "Because of this [8]answer go your way; the demon has gone out of your daughter."

30 And going back to her home, she found the child [9]lying on the bed, the demon having departed.

[1]Or, to worship. [2]Or, proper. [3]Lit., for. [4]Lit., from that hour. [5]Some early mss. add and Sidon. [6]Lit., and. [7]Lit., Greek. [8]Lit., word. [9]Lit., thrown.

Sec. 113 Healings in Decapolis
– In Decapolis near the Sea of Galilee –

Matt. 15:29-31

29 And departing from there, Jesus went along by the Sea of Galilee, and having gone up to the mountain, He was sitting there.

30 And great multitudes came to Him, bringing with them those who were lame, crippled, blind, dumb, and many others, and they laid them down at His feet; and He healed them,

31 so that the multitude marveled as they saw the dumb speaking, the crippled [1]restored, and the lame walking, and the blind seeing; and they glorified the God of Israel.

[1]Or, healthy. [2]Or, bond. [3]Lit., was loosed.

Mark 7:31-37

31 And again He went out from the region of Tyre, and [q]came through Sidon to the Sea of Galilee, within the region of Decapolis.

32 And they *brought to Him one who was deaf and spoke with difficulty, and they *entreated Him to lay His hand upon him.

33 And He took him aside from the multitude by himself, and put His fingers into his ears, and after spitting, He touched his tongue with the saliva;

34 and looking up to heaven with a deep sigh, He *said to him, "Ephphatha!" that is, "Be opened!"

35 And his ears were opened, and the [2]impediment of his tongue [3]was removed, and he began speaking plainly.

36 And He [r]gave them orders not to tell anyone; but the more He ordered them, the more widely they continued to proclaim it.

37 And they were utterly astonished, saying, "He has done all things well; He makes even the deaf to hear, and the dumb to speak."

---

[q](Mark 7:31) The long, circuitous route followed by Jesus as He traveled from the Mediterranean coast to the eastern shore of the Sea of Galilee was probably designed to guard His privacy with the disciples. This took Him back to the area where He had healed two Gerasene demoniacs (Sec. 94).

[r](Mark 7:36) The difference between this instruction to keep silent and the earlier one to spread the news widely (Mark 5:19, Sec. 94) is great. Earlier, Jesus was still reaching out to the multitudes, but now more publicity would have impeded His special training of the twelve. When performing the healing, He even made special effort to avoid the multitude's attention (Mark 7:33).

Sec. 114   Feeding the four thousand in Decapolis (cf. Secs. 105, 116)

Matt. 15:32-38	Mark 8:1-9
	1 In those days again, when there was a great multitude and they had nothing to eat, He called His disciples and *said to them,
32 And Jesus called His disciples to Him and said, "I feel compassion for the multitude because they [1]have remained with Me now three days and have nothing to eat; and I do not wish to send them away hungry, lest they faint on the way."	**2** "I feel compassion for the multitude because they have remained with me now three days, and have nothing to eat;
33 And the disciples *said to Him, "[s]Where would we get so many loaves in a desolate place to satisfy such a great multitude?"	**3** and if I send them away hungry to their home, they will faint on the way; and some of them have come from a distance."
34 And Jesus *said to them, "How many loaves do you have?" And they said, "Seven, and a few small fish."	**4** And His disciples answered Him, "[s]Where will anyone be able to find enough to satisfy these men with [3]bread here in a desolate place?"
35 And He directed the multitude to [2]sit down on the ground;	**5** And He was asking them, "How many loaves do you have?" And they said, "Seven."
36 and He took the seven loaves and the fish; and giving thanks, He broke them and started giving them to the disciples, and the disciples in turn, to the multitudes.	**6** And He *directed the multitude to [2]sit down on the ground; and taking the seven loaves, He gave thanks and broke them, and started giving them to His disciples to [4]serve to them, and they served them to the multitude.
	7 They also had a few small fish; and after He had blessed them, He ordered these to be [5]served as well.
37 And they all ate, and were satisfied, and they picked up what was left over of the broken pieces, seven large baskets full.	**8** And they ate and were satisfied; and they picked up seven large baskets full of what was left over of the broken pieces.
38 And those who ate were four thousand men, besides women and children.	**9** And about four thousand were there; and He sent them away.

[1]Lit., *are remaining.*   [2]Lit., *recline.*   [3]Lit., *loaves.*   [4]Lit., *set before.*   [5]Lit., *set before them.*

Sec. 115   Return to Galilee and encounter with the Pharisees and Sadducees (cf. Secs. 80, 144)
– Magadan –

Matt. 15:39—16:4	Mark 8:10-12
39 And sending away the multitudes, He got into the boat, and came to the region of Magadan.	**10** And immediately He entered the boat with His disciples, and came to the district of Dalmanutha.

[s](Matt. 15:33; Mark 8:4) That the disciples would forget the feeding of the five thousand just a short time before (Sec. 105) appears inexplicable. Perhaps they misinterpreted Jesus' strong rebuke of the previous crowds' selfishness (John 6:26-27, Sec. 109) and thought He would not perform such a miracle again. To correct the misimpression, Jesus again miraculously fed a multitude. Patiently He dealt with the twelve to prove His identity to them and to show that nothing was inherently wrong with such a miracle.

Matt. 15:39—16:4 (cont'd)	Mark 8:10-12 (cont'd)
1 And the Pharisees and Sadducees came up, and testing Him asked Him to show them a [1]tsign from heaven.	**11** And the Pharisees came out and began to argue with Him, seeking from Him a [1]sign from heaven, [4]to test Him.
2 [2]But He answered and said to them, "When it is evening, you say, '*It will be* fair weather, for the sky is red.'	
3 "And in the morning, '*There will be* a storm today, for the sky is red and threatening.' Do you know how to discern the [3]appearance of the sky, but cannot *discern* the signs of the times?	
4 "An evil and adulterous generation seeks after a [1]sign; and a [1]sign will not be given it, except the [1]sign of Jonah." And He left them, and went away.	**12** And sighing deeply [5]in His spirit, He *said, "Why does this generation seek for a [1]sign? Truly I say to you, [6]no [1]sign shall be given to this generation."

[1]Or, *attesting miracle.* [2]The earliest mss. do not contain vv. 2, 3. [3]Lit., *face.* [4]Lit., *testing Him.* [5]Or, *to Himself.* [6]Lit., *if a sign shall be given.*

Sec. 116   Warning about the error of the Pharisees, Sadducees, and Herodians (cf. Secs. 105, 114; 146)
– *Crossing to east side of the Sea of Galilee* –

Matt. 16:5-12	Mark 8:13-21
	13 And leaving them, He again embarked and went away to the other side.
5 And the disciples came to the other side and had forgotten to take bread.	**14** And they had forgotten to take bread; and [2]did not have more than one loaf in the boat with them.
6 And Jesus said to them, "Watch out and beware of the [1u]leaven of the Pharisees and Sadducees."	**15** And He was giving orders to them, saying, "Watch out! Beware of the [u]leaven of the Pharisees and the leaven of Herod."
7 And they began to discuss among themselves, saying, "*It is* because we took no bread."	**16** And they *began* to discuss with one another the *fact* that they had no bread.
8 But Jesus, aware of this, said, "You men of little faith, why do you discuss among youselves that you have no bread?	**17** And Jesus, aware of this, *said to them, "Why do you discuss *the fact* that you have no bread? Do you not yet see or understand? Do you have a [3]hardened heart?
9 "Do you not yet understand or remember the five loaves of the five	

[1](Matt. 16:1) No sooner had Jesus set foot in Galilee again than His enemies were upon Him. They asked for a sign, perhaps along the line of what God had done for Moses (Exod. 16:15), Joshua (Josh. 10:13), Samuel (1 Sam. 12:18), Elijah (1 Kings 18:38), and Isaiah (2 Kings 20:11; Isa. 38:8). Jesus stood firm on His previous response, however (Matt. 16:4; Mark 8:12; cf. Matt. 12:39, Sec. 80). For the first time the Sadducees joined the Pharisees in attacking Him. Both parties were willing to forget their differences because of their common animosity toward Him.

[u](Matt. 16:6; Mark 8:15) In the Law, leaven was regarded as symbolic of impurity (Exod. 34:25; Lev. 2:11). Jesus expected His disciples to understand this connotation (Matt. 16:11; Mark 8:17, 21). His recent miracles with the five thousand and the four thousand showed He need not be concerned over a lack of bread (cf. Secs. 105, 114). His recent explanation about the true source of defilement should have been fresh in the disciples' minds (cf. Sec. 111). Just a moment of reflection would have shown them that he was talking about spiritual defilement. The Pharisees, the Sadducees, and the Herodians all had distorted ideas about the Kingdom. The Pharisees would have molded it to conform to the tradition of the elders. By rationalizations the Sadducees explained away Old Testament predictions about it. The Herodians saw some member of Herod's family as the promised king. By ridding themselves of false concepts, the twelve were readied for the true picture of Messiah which was about to surface (cf. Sec. 118).

Matt. 16:5-12 (cont'd)	Mark 8:13-21 (cont'd)
thousand, and how many baskets you took up?	**18** "HAVING EYES, DO YOU NOT SEE? AND HAVING EARS, DO YOU NOT HEAR?
10 "Or the seven loaves of the four thousand, and how many large baskets you took up?	[Ezek. 12:2]. And do you not remember,
11 "How is it that you do not understand that I did not speak to you concerning bread? But beware of the ¹leaven of the Pharisees and Sadducees."	**19** when I broke the five loaves for the five thousand, how many baskets full of broken pieces you picked up?" They *said to Him, "Twelve."
12 Then they understood that He did not say to beware of the leaven of bread, but of the teaching of the Pharisees and Sadducees.	**20** "And when I broke the seven for the four thousand, how many large baskets full of broken pieces did you pick up?" And they *said to Him, "Seven."
	21 And He was saying to them, "Do you not yet understand?"

¹Or, yeast.   ²Lit., were not having.   ³Or, dull, insensible.

Sec. 117   Healing a blind man at Bethsaida
— Bethsaida, near Julias —

Mark 8:22-26

22   And they *came to Bethsaida. And they *brought a blind man to Him, and *entreated Him to touch him.

23   And taking the blind man by the hand, He brought him out of the village; and after spitting on his eyes, and laying His hands upon him, He asked him, "Do you see anything?"

24   And he ¹looked up and said, "I see men, for ²I am seeing them like trees, walking about."

25   Then again He laid His hands upon his eyes; and he looked intently and ᵛwas restored, and began to see everything clearly.

26   And He sent him to his home, saying, "Do not even enter the village."

¹Or, gained sight.   ²Or, they look to me.

LESSON OF MESSIAHSHIP LEARNED AND CONFIRMED

Sec. 118   Peter's identification of Jesus as the Christ, and first prophecy of the church (cf. Sec. 110)
— District of Caesarea Philippi —

Matt. 16:13-20	Mark 8:27-30	Luke 9:18-21
13 Now when Jesus came into the district of ᵂCaesarea Philippi, He began asking His disci-	**27** And Jesus went out, along with His disciples, to the villages of ᵂCaesarea Philippi; and on the way	**18** And it came about that while He was praying alone, the disciples were with Him, and He ques-

ᵛ(Mark 8:25) This is one of two miracles that are recorded by Mark alone (cf. Sec. 113). From each, one might infer that Christ had difficulty in effecting the cure. In each case Jesus made a point of performing the deed privately (Mark 8:23) and avoiding publicity after the healing (Mark 8:26). This case in Bethsaida, occurring as it did in two stages, is the only instance of a gradual cure by Jesus (Mark 8:24-25). Perhaps the twelve needed to learn that every miracle would not be instantaneous. In some cases the victory of divine power over sin and sickness would be gradual.

ᵂ(Matt. 16:13; Mark 8:27) Herod Philip was tetrarch in this territory. Compared to his half brothers Archelaus and Antipas, Philip was a just ruler. He had no reason to be suspicious of Jesus as Antipas was (cf. Sec. 104, note w). Jesus probably remained with His disciples in this region where the inhabitants were predominantly Gentile and where little occasion would arise for Jewish opposition or large crowds.

Matt. 16:13-20 (cont'd)	Mark 8:27-30 (cont'd)	Luke 9:18-21 (cont'd)
ples, saying, "Who do people say that the Son of Man is?"	He questioned His disciples, saying to them, "Who do people say that I am?"	tioned them, saying, "Who do the multitudes say that I am?"
14 And they said, "Some *say* John the Baptist; and others, [1]Elijah; but still others, [2]Jeremiah, or one of the prophets."	**28** And they told Him, saying, "John the Baptist; and others *say* Elijah; but others, one of the prophets."	**19** And they answered and said, "John the Baptist, and others *say* Elijah; but others, that one of the prophets of old has risen again."
15 He *said to them, "But [x]who do you say that I am?"	**29** And He *continued* by questioning them, "But [x]who do you say that I am?" Peter *answered and *said to Him, "Thou art [3]the Christ."	**20** And He said to them, "But [x]who do you say that I am?" And Peter answered and said, "[3]The Christ of God."
16 And Simon Peter answered and said, "[y]Thou art the [3]Christ, the Son of the living God."		
17 And Jesus answered and said to him, "Blessed are you, Simon [4]Barjona, because flesh and blood did not reveal *this* to you, but My Father who is in heaven.		
18 "And I also say to you that you are [5]Peter, and upon this [6]rock I will build My [z]church; and the gates of Hades shall not overpower it.		
19 "I will give you the keys of the kingdom of heaven; and whatever you shall bind on earth shall be bound in heaven, and whatever you shall loose on earth shall be loosed in heaven."		
20 Then He [7]warned the disciples that they	**30** And He [7]warned them to tell [a]no one about	**21** But He [7]warned them, and instructed *them*

[x](Matt. 16:15; Mark 8:29; Luke 9:20) Jesus saw the time was right to solicit a specific identification of Himself. This is the objective toward which He had been moving since leaving Galilee several months earlier (Sec. 104). Practically every activity was designed to lead His disciples to a conviction about His person. It now remained for them to disclose their conclusion in answer to His question.

[y](Matt. 16:16) Matthew retains the fullest record of Peter's reply. The Messiahship and deity of Jesus were not completely new concepts to the twelve (Matt. 14:33, Sec. 107; John 1:41, 49, Sec. 31), but now Peter and the rest, on the basis of what they had seen and heard, could with strong conviction verify His identity as such. The truth thus elicited from Peter was foundational to the further instruction Jesus was to give His immediate followers.

[z](Matt. 16:18) This was the first disclosure of a new work that Jesus was to undertake. It was made to a group that would constitute the nucleus of that body which He called the "church." This inner circle of disciples at this point began to hear of a subject which they were slow to understand, but which was eventually to become the dominant interest of their lives.

[a](Matt. 16:20; Mark 8:30; Luke 9:21) Jesus' Messiahship and deity, though foundational for the church, were not to be broadcast widely. Israel's leadership had by now forfeited its opportunity for a positive response by refusal to acknowledge His credentials (cf. Sec. 79). The populace had exhibited a similar unwillingness to submit to moral requirements in connection with an earthly reign of Messiah (cf. Sec. 106). It was inappropriate to approach them further on these issues until the time for an open declaration of His identity before the Jewish authorities in Jerusalem (cf. Matt. 26:63-64, Sec. 229).

Matt. 16:13-20	Mark 8:27-30	Luke 9:18-21
(cont'd)	(cont'd)	(cont'd)
should tell [a]no one that He was [3]the Christ.	Him.	[a]not to tell this to anyone,

[1]Gr., *Elias.* [2]Gr., *Jeremias.* [3]I.e., the Messiah. [4]I.e., son of Jonah. [5]Gr., *Petros,* a stone. [6]Gr., *petra,* large rock, bed-rock. [7]Or, *strictly admonished.*

Sec. 119　First direct prediction of the rejection, crucifixion, and resurrection (cf. Secs. 99, 165; 121, 122, 125, 180; 190)
– Near Caesarea Philippi –

Matt. 16:21-26	Mark 8:31-37	Luke 9:22-25
21 From that time Jesus Christ [b]began to show His disciples that He must go to Jerusalem, and suffer many things from the elders and chief priests and scribes, and be killed, and be raised up on the third day. **22** And Peter took Him aside and began to rebuke Him, saying, "[1]God forbid it, Lord! This shall never [2]happen to You." **23** But He turned and said to Peter, "Get behind Me, Satan! You are a stumbling block to Me; for you are not setting your mind on [3]God's interests, but man's." **24** Then Jesus said to His disciples, "[c]If anyone wishes to come after Me, let him deny himself, and take up his cross, and follow Me. **25** "For whoever wishes to save his [4]life shall lose it; but whoever loses his [4]life for My sake shall find it.	**31** And He [b]began to teach them that the Son of Man must suffer many things and be rejected by the elders and the chief priests and the scribes, and be killed, and after three days rise again. **32** And He was stating the matter plainly. And Peter took Him aside and began to rebuke Him. **33** But turning around and seeing His disciples, He rebuked Peter, and *said, "Get behind Me, Satan; for you are not setting your mind on [3]God's interests, but man's." **34** And He summoned the multitude with His disciples, and said to them, "[c]If anyone wishes to come after Me, let him deny himself, and take up his cross, and follow Me. **35** "For whoever wishes to save his [4]life shall lose it; but whoever loses his [4]life for My sake and the gospel's shall save it.	**22** saying, "[b]The Son of Man must suffer many things, and be rejected by the elders and chief priests and scribes, and be killed, and be raised up on the third day." **23** And He was saying to them all, "[c]If anyone wishes to come after Me, let him deny himself, and take up his cross daily, and follow Me. **24** "For whoever wishes to save his [4]life shall lose it, but whoever loses his [4]life for My sake, he is the one who will save

[b](Matt. 16:21; Mark 8:31; Luke 9:22) Coming immediately after Peter's confession, this prophecy was apparently triggered by the confession. If it had come any earlier, the twelve would have been unable to receive it without being shaken in their conviction about Him. This is Jesus' first open prediction of the events which were now about one year away, though earlier He had referred to them in veiled terminology (cf. John 2:19, Sec. 34). Peter was unwilling to accept such a revelation because he was now so certain about Jesus' Messiahship (Matt. 16:22; Mark 8:32). His misguided zeal drew the same rebuke the Lord used with Satan after the temptation (Matt. 4:10, Sec. 28).

[c](Matt. 16:24; Mark 8:34; Luke 9:23) After the multitude joined the disciples, Jesus extended the scope of the predicted suffering to anyone who desired to be His follower. The necessity of this was axiomatic in the teachings of Jesus (cf. Matt. 16:25; Mark 8:35; Luke 9:24 with Matt. 10:39, Sec. 99; Luke 17:33, Sec. 174; John 12:25, Sec. 190), and formed a basis for Peter's first epistle many years later (1 Pet. 2:20-21).

Matt. 16:21-26 (cont'd)	Mark 8:31-37 (cont'd)	Luke 9:22-25 (cont'd)
26 "For what will a man be profited, if he gains the whole world, and forfeits his [4]soul? Or what will a man give in exchange for his [4]soul?	**36** "For what does it profit a man to gain the whole world, and forfeit his [4]soul? **37** "For what shall a man give in exchange for his [4]soul?	it. **25** "For what is a man profited if he gains the whole world, and loses or forfeits himself?

[1]Lit., (God be) merciful to You.　　[2]Lit., be.　　[3]Lit., the things of God.　　[4]Or, soul.

Sec. 120　Coming of the Son of Man and judgment
– Near Caesarea Philippi –

Matt. 16:27-28	Mark 8:38—9:1	Luke 9:26-27
27 "For the Son of Man is going to come in the glory of His Father with His angels; and WILL THEN RECOMPENSE EVERY MAN ACCORDING TO HIS [1]DEEDS [Psalm 62:12; Prov. 24:12]. **28** "Truly I say to you, there are some of those who are standing here who shall not taste death until they see the Son of Man coming in His [d]kingdom."	**38** "For whoever is ashamed of Me and My words in this adulterous and sinful generation, the Son of Man will also be ashamed of him when He comes in the glory of His Father with the holy angels." **1** And He was saying to them, "Truly I say to you, there are some of those who are standing here who shall not taste death until they see the [d]kingdom of God after it has come with power."	**26** "For whoever is ashamed of Me and My words, of him will the Son of Man be ashamed when He comes in His glory, and *the glory of the Father and* of the holy angels. **27** "But I say to you truthfully, there are some of those standing here who shall not taste death until they see the [d]kingdom of God."

[1]Lit., doing.

Sec. 121　Transfiguration of Jesus (cf. Secs. 27; 119, 122, 125, 180)
– [e]A high mountain, perhaps Mount Hermon –

[d](Matt. 16:28; Mark 9:1; Luke 9:27) Reference to the judgment of faithfulness at the time of the Son of Man's coming occasioned mention of the Kingdom. This coming of the Son and His Kingdom has been variously identified with Christ's resurrection and ascension, the day of Pentecost, the spread of Christianity, Christ's second advent, or the destruction of Jerusalem in A.D. 70; yet the only interpretation that satisfies the facts of history and the conditions of the context is to understand a reference to the transfiguration scene which immediately followed (Sec. 121). Here a foretaste of the Son's coming with His Kingdom was granted to three of the listeners during their normal lifetime.

[e]The exact location of the mount of transfiguration is unknown. Traditionally it has been identified with Mount Tabor, which rises from the Plain of Esdraelon. But that is too far removed from Caesarea Philippi and Capernaum to be a likely site. Furthermore, it is unlikely that Jesus and His disciples would have gone up a mountain where heathen worship had been carried on. Others have suggested one of several hills near Capernaum. But none of these seems to be high enough to qualify as the "high mountain" spoken of by Matthew and Mark. Mount Hermon does answer to this description and has the advantage of being near Caesarea Philippi, where Jesus had recently been.

Matt. 17:1-8	Mark 9:2-8	Luke 9:28-36a
1 And [f]six days later Jesus *took with Him Peter and [1]James and John his brother, and *brought them up to a high mountain by themselves.	**2** And [f]six days later, Jesus *took with Him Peter and [1]James and John, and *brought them up to a high mountain by themselves. And He was transfigured before them;	**28** And [f]some eight days after these sayings, it came about that He took along Peter and John and James, and went up to the mountain to pray.
2 And He was transfigured before them; and His face shone like the sun, and His garments became as white as light.	**3** and His garments became radiant and exceedingly white, as no launderer on earth can whiten them.	**29** And while He was praying, the appearance of His face became different, and His clothing *became* white *and* [5]gleaming.
3 And behold, Moses and Elijah appeared to them, talking with Him.	**4** And Elijah appeared to them along with Moses; and they were talking with Jesus.	**30** And behold, two men were talking with Him; and they were Moses and Elijah,
		31 who, appearing in [6]glory, were speaking of His [g]departure which He was about to accomplish at Jerusalem.
		32 Now Peter and his companions had been overcome with sleep; but when they were fully awake, they saw His glory and the two men standing with Him.
4 And Peter answered and said to Jesus, "Lord, it is good for us to be here; if You wish, I will make three [2]tabernacles here, one for You, and one for Moses, and one for Elijah."	**5** And Peter answered and *said to Jesus, "Rabbi, it is good for us to be here; and let us make three [2]tabernacles, one for You, and one for Moses, and one for Elijah."	**33** And it came about, as [7]these were parting from Him, Peter said to Jesus, "Master, it is good for us to be here; and let us make three [2]tabernacles: one for You, and one for Moses, and one for Elijah" — not realizing what he was saying.
5 While he was still speaking, behold, a bright cloud overshadowed them; and behold, a voice out of the cloud, saying, "This is My beloved Son, with whom I am well-pleased; listen to Him!"	**6** For he did not know what to answer; for they became terrified.	**34** And while he was saying this, a cloud [3]formed and *began to* overshadow them; and they were afraid as they entered the cloud.
6 And when the disciples heard this, they fell on their faces and were much afraid.	**7** Then a cloud [3]formed, overshadowing them, and a voice came out of the cloud, "This is My beloved Son, [4]listen to Him!"	**35** And a voice came out of the cloud, saying, "This is My Son, *My* Chosen One; listen to Him!"

[f](Matt. 17:1; Mark 9:2; Luke 9:28) Luke's "some eight days" is an approximate figure for the six days of Matthew and Mark. Within a one-week period came Peter's confession, the first prophecy of the church, the first prophecy of crucifixion and resurrection, and now this confirmatory revelation of the King and His Kingdom. The disciples probably wondered how the church and Messiah's predicted incarceration and death would affect the unfulfilled prophecies of His coming Kingdom. The transfiguration reassured them that these prophecies would still receive a literal fulfillment. For at least Peter this was true (2 Pet. 1:16-19).

[g](Luke 9:31) Only Luke discloses the subject of conversation among Moses and Elijah and Jesus. "Departure" probably refers to His death. In this detail, Luke's interest in Jesus' humanity surfaces once again.

Matt. 17:1-8 (cont'd)	Mark 9:2-8 (cont'd)	Luke 9:28-36a (cont'd)
7 And Jesus came to them and touched them and said, "Arise, and do not be afraid." **8** And lifting up their eyes, they saw no one, except Jesus Himself alone.	**8** And all at once they looked around and saw no one with them anymore, except Jesus alone.	**36** And when the voice [8]had spoken, Jesus was found alone.

[1]Or, *Jacob.* [2]Or, *sacred tents.* [3]Or, *occurred.* [4]Or, *give constant heed.* [5]Lit., *flashing like lightning.* [6]Or, *splendor.* [7]Lit., *they.* [8]Lit., *occurred.*

Sec. 122 Command to keep the transfiguration secret (cf. Secs. 119, 121, 125, 180)
– Coming down the mountain –

Matt. 17:9	Mark 9:9-10	Luke 9:36b
9 And as they were coming down from the mountain, Jesus commanded them, saying, "Tell the vision to no one [h]until the Son of Man has risen from the dead."	**9** And as they were coming down from the mountain, He gave them orders not to relate to anyone what they had seen, [1][h]until the Son of Man should rise from the dead. **10** And they [2]seized upon [3]that statement, discussing with one another [4]what rising from the dead might mean.	And they kept silent, and reported to no one in those days any of the things which they had seen.

[1]Lit., *except when.* [2]Or, *kept to themselves.* [3]Lit., *the statement.* [4]Lit., *what was the rising from the dead.*

Sec. 123 Elijah, John the Baptist, and the Son of Man's coming
– Coming down the mountain –

Matt. 17:10-13	Mark 9:11-13
10 And His disciples asked Him, saying, "Why then do the scribes say that Elijah must come first?" **11** And He answered and said, "Elijah is coming and will restore all things; **12** but I say to you, that Elijah already came, and they did not recognize him,	**11** And they asked Him, saying, "Why is it that the scribes say that Elijah must come first?" **12** And He said to them, "Elijah does first come and restore all things. And yet how is it written of the Son of Man that He should suffer many things and be treated with contempt?

[h](Matt. 17:9; Mark 9:9) The time limit placed on the silence is probably a key to seeing why the silence was enjoined. As Mark 9:10 shows, the disciples did not yet understand what it meant for the Son of Man to rise from the dead and would not until they witnessed it. Only after the Son's resurrection could they adequately comprehend the real significance of the transfiguration experience (cf. 2 Pet. 1:16-19).

Matt. 17:10-13
(cont'd)

but did ¹to him whatever they wished. So also the Son of Man is going to suffer ²at their hands."

13 Then the disciples understood that He had spoken to them about ¹John the Baptist.

Mark 9:11-13
(cont'd)

13 "But I say to you, that Elijah has ³indeed come, and they did to him whatever they wished, just as it is written of him."

¹Lit., *in him*; or, *in his case.*   ²Lit., *by them.*   ³Lit., *also.*

LESSONS ON RESPONSIBILITY TO OTHERS

Sec. 124 Healing of demoniac boy, and faithlessness rebuked
– *Near the mount of transfiguration* –

Matt. 17:14-20, [21]	Mark 9:14-29	Luke 9:37-43a
	14 And when they came *back* to the disciples, they saw a large crowd around them, and *some* scribes arguing with them.	
	15 And immediately, when the entire crowd saw Him, they were amazed, and *began* running up to greet Him.	**37** And it came about on the next day, that when they had come down from the mountain, a great multitude met Him.
14 And when they came to the multitude, a man came up to Him, falling on his knees before Him, and saying,	**16** And He asked them, "What are you discussing with them?"	
15 "¹Lord, have mercy on my son, for he is a lunatic, and is very ill; for he often falls into the fire, and often into the water.	**17** And one of the crowd answered Him, "Teacher, I brought You my son, possessed with a spirit which makes him mute;	**38** And behold, a man from the multitude shouted out, saying, "Teacher, I beg You to look at my son, for he is my ¹²only *boy*,
16 "And I brought him to Your disciples, and they could not cure him."	**18** and ⁴whenever it seizes him, it ⁵dashes him *to the ground* and he foams *at the mouth*, and grinds his teeth, and ⁶stiffens out. And I told Your disciples to cast it out, and they could not *do it.*"	**39** and behold, a spirit seizes him, and he suddenly screams, and it throws him into a convulsion with foaming *at the mouth*, and as it mauls him, it scarcely leaves him.
17 And Jesus answered and said, "¹O un-	**19** And He *answered them and *said, "¹O unbe-	**40** "And I begged Your disciples to cast it out, and they could not."

¹(Matt. 17:13) John the Baptist is here identified with Elijah, but earlier John denied such an identification (John 1:21, see note d, Sec. 29). In what sense he fulfilled the prophecy about Elijah (Mal. 4:5-6) is hard to discern. The fulfillment seemed to be contingent on Israel's reception of him and Messiah (Matt. 11:14-15, Sec. 75). Their rejection of the Baptist and Messiah (Matt. 17:12; Mark 9:13) apparently nullified the potential fulfillment.

¹(Matt. 17:17; Mark 9:19; Luke 9:41) This is the only known occasion when Jesus' sensitivity showed itself in the form of momentary impatience with His environment. Coming as a response to the father, the expression probably indicates a connection between the man and the scribes (Mark 9:14). These may have used the man and his son to gather evidence against the nine disciples and, therefore, also against Jesus. The antagonism of the Lord's enemies surfaced once again and was met with this sharp rebuke. Such strong language could hardly be a reprimand of the nine for their inability to perform the miracle, because they did have faith, though it was quite small (cf. Matt. 17:20).

Matt. 17:14-20, [21] (cont'd)	Mark 9:14-29 (cont'd)	Luke 9:37-43a (cont'd)
believing and perverted generation, how long shall I be with you? How long shall I put up with you? Bring him here to Me."	lieving generation, how long shall I be with you? How long shall I put up with you? Bring him to Me!" **20** And they brought [7]the boy to Him. And when he saw Him, immediately the spirit threw him into a convulsion, and falling to the ground, he *began* rolling about and foaming *at the mouth.* **21** And He asked his father, "How long has this been happening to him?" And he said, "From childhood. **22** "And it has often thrown him both into the fire and into the water to destroy him. But if You can do anything, take pity on us and help us!" **23** And Jesus said to him, "'If You can!' All things are possible to him who believes." **24** Immediately the boy's father cried out and *began* saying, "I do believe; help my unbelief." **25** And when Jesus saw that a crowd was [8]rapidly gathering, He rebuked the unclean spirit, saying to it, "You deaf and dumb spirit, [9]I command you, come out of him and do not enter him [10]again." **26** And after crying out and throwing him into terrible convulsions, it came out; and *the boy* became so much like a corpse that most *of them* said, "He is dead!" **27** But Jesus took him by the hand and raised him; and he got up. **28** And when He had come into *the* house, His disciples *began* question-	**41** And Jesus answered and said, "[j]O unbelieving and perverted generation, how long shall I be with you, and put up with you? Bring your son here." **42** And while he was still approaching, the demon [13]dashed him *to the* ground, and threw him into a convulsion.
18 And Jesus rebuked him, and the demon came out of him, and the boy was cured [2]at once.		But Jesus rebuked the unclean spirit, and healed the boy, and gave him back to his father. **43** And they were all amazed at the [14]greatness of God.
19 Then the disciples came to Jesus privately and said, "Why could we		

Matt. 17:14-20, [21] (cont'd)	Mark 9:14-29 (cont'd)
not cast it out?" **20** And He *said to them, "Because of the littleness of your faith; for truly I say to you, if you have faith as a mustard seed, you shall say to this mountain, 'Move from here to there,' and it shall move; and nothing shall be impossible to you. **21** 3["But this kind does not go out except by prayer and fasting."]	ing Him privately, "Why could we not cast it out?" **29** And He said to them, "This kind cannot come out by anything but prayer11."

1Or, Sir. 2Lit., *from that hour.* 3Many mss. do not contain this v. 4Or, *wherever.* 5Or, *tears him.* 6Or, *withers away.* 7Lit., *him.* 8Or, *running together.* 9Or, *I Myself command.* 10Or, *from now on.* 11Many mss. add *and fasting.* 12Or, *only begotten.* 13Or, *tore him.* 14Or, *majesty.*

Sec. 125   Second prediction of the resurrection (cf. Secs. 119, 121, 122, 180)
          – Itineration in Galilee –

Matt. 17:22-23	Mark 9:30-32	Luke 9:43b-45
	30 And from there they went out and *began to go* kthrough Galilee, and He was unwilling for anyone to know *about it.*	But while everyone was marveling at all that He was doing, He said to His disciples,
22 And while they were gathering together in Galilee, Jesus said to them, "The Son of Man is going to be 1delivered into the hands of men;	**31** For He was teaching His disciples and telling them, "The Son of Man is to be 1delivered into the hands of men, and they will kill Him; and when He has been killed, He will rise three days later."	**44** "Let these words sink into your ears; for the Son of Man is going to be 1delivered into the hands of men."
23 and they will kill Him, and He will be raised on the third day." And they were deeply grieved.	**32** But they 2did not understand this statement, and they were afraid to ask Him.	**45** But they 2did not understand this statement, and it was concealed from them so that they might not perceive it; and they were afraid to ask Him about this statement.

1Or, *betrayed.* 2Lit., *were not knowing.*

---

k(Mark 9:30) From the area of Caesarea Philippi and northeast Palestine, Jesus at this point began the journey that would take Him through Galilee and Perea to Judea and Jerusalem where His crucifixion and resurrection would take place about six months later.

Sec. 126　Payment of the Temple tax
– Capernaum –

Matt. 17:24-27

24　And when they had come to Capernaum, those who collected the [1]two-drachma *tax* came to Peter, and said, "Does your teacher not pay the [1]two-drachma *tax?"*

25　He *said, "Yes." And when he came into the house, Jesus [2]spoke to him first, saying, "What do you think, Simon? From whom do the kings of the earth collect [1]customs or poll-tax, from their sons or from strangers?"

26　And upon his saying, "From strangers," Jesus said to him, "Consequently the sons are [3]exempt.

27　"But, lest we [4]give them offense, go to the sea, and throw in a hook, and take the first fish that comes up; and when you open its mouth, you will find a [5]stater. Take that and give it to them for you and Me."

[1]Equivalent to two denarii or two days' wages paid as a temple tax.　[2]Or, *anticipated what he was going to say,*　[3]Or, *free.*　[4]Lit., *cause them to stumble.*　[5]Or, *shekel,* worth four drachmas.

Sec. 127　Rivalry over greatness dispelled (cf. Secs. 177; 213)
– Capernaum –

Matt. 18:1-5	Mark 9:33-37	Luke 9:46-48
1　At that [1]time the disciples came to Jesus, saying, "[m]Who then is [2]greatest in the kingdom of heaven?"	**33**　And they came to Capernaum; and when He [4]was in the house, He *began* to question them, "What were you discussing on the way?"　**34**　But they kept silent, for on the way they had discussed with one another [m]which *of them was* the greatest.	**46**　And an argument [8]arose among them as to [m]which of them might be the greatest.
2　And He called a child to Himself and set him [6]before them,　**3**　and said, "Truly I say to you, unless you [3]are converted and become like children, you shall not enter the kingdom of heaven.　**4**　"Whoever then	**35**　And sitting down, He called the twelve and *said to them, "If anyone wants to be first, [5]he shall be last of all, and servant of all."　**36**　And taking a child, He set him [6]before them, and taking him in His arms, He said to them.	**47**　But Jesus, knowing [9]what they were thinking in their heart, took a child and stood him by His side,

[1](Matt. 17:25) Matthew, himself a former tax collector, demonstrates special interest in this episode, though his former occupation involved collecting taxes for the Roman government, not for the Temple. The tax here sought was to provide sacrificial victims for Temple worship. The regular time for paying this tax was the spring, but it was now early autumn. The Lord and His disciples had been out of the area at the normal time, so the collectors made a special point of approaching them, either to make up the deficit in their quota or to seek yet another avenue for building a case against Jesus.

[m](Matt. 18:1; Mark 9:34; Luke 9:46) In a culture where precedence and rank were the norm, the disciples quite naturally fell into the same mold. The recent choice of those to be with Jesus on the mount of transfiguration (Sec. 121) and the prominence of Peter among them (Secs. 118, 126) gave special occasion for such a discussion at this time. Greatness "in the kingdom of heaven" probably came up also because, with Jerusalem as their destination, a "kingdom fever" had begun to develop (cf. Luke 19:11, Sec. 184). In response, Jesus indicated that humility was not only the condition of greatness (Matt. 18:4), but also a condition for even entering the kingdom (Matt. 18:3).

Matt. 18:1-5 (cont'd)	Mark 9:33-37 (cont'd)	Luke 9:46-48 (cont'd)
humbles himself as this child, he is the greatest in the kingdom of heaven.		
5 "And whoever receives one such child in My name receives Me;	37 "Whoever receives [7]one child like this in My name receives Me; and whoever receives Me does not receive Me, but Him who sent Me."	48 and said to them, "Whoever receives this child in My name receives Me; and whoever receives Me receives Him who sent Me; for he who is [10]least among you, this is the one who is great."

[1]Lit., *hour.* [2]Lit., *greater.* [3]Lit., *are turned.* [4]Lit., *had come.* [5]Or, *let him be.* [6]Lit., *in their midst.* [7]Lit., *one of such children.* [8]Lit., *entered in.* [9]Lit., *the reasoning; or, argument.* [10]Or, *lowliest.*

Sec. 128   Warning against causing believers to stumble (cf. Secs. 66, 165; 68; 79, 144; 99; 166; 169)

– Capernaum –

Matt. 18:6-14	Mark 9:38-50	Luke 9:49-50
	38 John said to Him, "Teacher, we saw someone casting out demons in Your name, and [n]we tried to hinder him because he was not following us."	49 And John answered and said, "Master, we saw someone casting out demons in Your name; and [n]we tried to hinder him because he does not follow along with us."
	39 But Jesus said, "Do not hinder him, for there is no one who shall perform a miracle in My name, and be able soon afterward to speak evil of Me.	50 But Jesus said to him, "Do not hinder *him;* for he who is not against you is [14]for you."
	40 " [o]For he who is not against us is [6]for us.	
	41 "For whoever gives you a cup of water to drink [7]because of your name as *followers* of Christ, truly I say to you, he shall not lose his reward.	
6 but whoever causes one of these little ones who believe in Me to stumble, it is better for him that a [1]heavy millstone be hung around his neck, and that he be drowned in the depth of the sea.	42 "And whoever causes one of these [8]little ones who believe to stumble, it [9]would be better for him if, with a heavy millstone hung around his neck, he [10]had been cast into the sea.	

[n](Mark 9:38; Luke 9:49) Just as Peter had misunderstood God's program earlier (Sec. 119), so John did on this occasion. Later the third honored disciple, James, would do the same (Sec. 181). Each misunderstanding followed shortly after a prediction of Jesus' passion and resurrection.

[o](Mark 9:40) This statement appears to contradict Matthew 12:30 (Sec. 79), but actually it complements it. Matthew 12:30 speaks of the relation of a man's inner life to Christ, while Mark 9:40 refers to his outward conduct. One who is not a declared enemy may be regarded as a friend, especially in this case where he invokes the name of Christ.

Matt. 18:6-14 (cont'd)	Mark 9:38-50 (cont'd)

7 "Woe to the world because of its stumbling blocks! For it is inevitable that stumbling blocks come; but woe to that man through whom the stumbling block comes!

8 "And if your hand or your Pfoot causes you to stumble, cut it off and throw it from you; it is better for you to enter life crippled or lame, than having two hands or two feet, to be cast into the eternal fire.

43 "And if your Phand causes you to stumble, cut it off; it is better for you to enter life crippled, than having your two hands, to go into 11hell, into the unquenchable fire,

44 [12where THEIR WORM DOES NOT DIE, AND THE FIRE IS NOT QUENCHED.]

45 "And if your Pfoot causes you to stumble, cut it off; it is better for you to enter life lame, than having your two feet, to be cast into 11hell,

46 [12where THEIR WORM DOES NOT DIE, AND THE FIRE IS NOT QUENCHED.]

9 "And if your Peye causes you to stumble, pluck it out, and throw it from you. It is better for you to enter life with one eye, than having two eyes, to be cast into the 2fiery hell.

47 "And if your Peye causes you to stumble, cast it out; it is better for you to enter the kingdom of God with one eye, than having two eyes, to be cast into 11hell,

10 "See that you do not despise one of these little ones, for I say to you, that their angels in heaven continually behold the face of My Father who is in heaven.

48 where THEIR WORM DOES NOT DIE, AND THE FIRE IS NOT QUENCHED [Isa. 66:24].

11 3["For the Son of Man has come to save that which was lost.]

49 "For everyone will be salted with fire.

12 "What do you think? If any man 4has a hundred sheep, and one of them has gone astray, does he not leave the ninety-nine on the mountains and go and search for the one that is straying?

50 "qSalt is good; but if the salt becomes unsalty, with what will you 13make it salty *again*? Have salt in yourselves, and be at peace with one another."

13 "And if it turns out that he finds it, truly I say to you, he rejoices over it more than over the ninety-nine which have not gone astray.

14 "Thus it is not *the* will 5of your Father who is in heaven that one of these little ones perish.

1Lit., *millstone turned by a donkey.*   2Lit., *Gehenna of fire.*   3Most ancient mss. do not contain this v.   4Or, *comes to have.*   5Lit., *before.*   6Or, *on our side.*   7Lit., *in a name that you are Christ's.*   8I.e., humble.   9Lit., *is better for him if a millstone turned by a donkey is hung.*   10Lit., *has been cast.*   11Gr., *Gehenna.*   12Vv. 44 and 46, which are indentical with v. 48, are not found in the best ancient mss.   13Lit., *season it.*   14Or, *on your side.*

P(Matt. 18:8-9; Mark 9:43, 45, 47) According to Palestinian custom, Jews did not refer to the abstract sinful act but to the concrete member of the body by which it was liable to be committed. This was thus not a call to self-mutilation but to a refusal to place the body at the disposal of selfish pleasures (cf. Rom. 12:1).

q(Mark 9:50) "The salt of the covenant" (Lev. 2:13) provided for purification and preservation of the sacrifice. As long as the disciples remained pure by not wrangling among themselves over greatness (Sec. 127), they could preserve the world from judgment. The salt of the illustration was salt from the Dead Sea which, unlike modern salt, contained impurities which made it lose its saltiness (cf. Matt. 5:13, Sec. 66).

Sec. 129   Treatment and forgiveness of a sinning brother
   – Capernaum –

Matt. 18:15-35

15 "And if your brother sins[1], go and reprove him [2]in private; if he listens to you, you have won your brother.

16 "But if he does not listen *to you*, take one or two more with you, so that BY THE MOUTH OF TWO OR THREE WITNESSES EVERY [3]FACT MAY BE CONFIRMED [Deut. 19:15].

17 "And if he refuses to listen to them, tell it to the church; and if he refuses to listen even to the church, let him be to you as [4]a Gentile and a [5]tax-gatherer.

18 "Truly I say to you, whatever you shall [6]bind on earth shall be bound in heaven; and whatever you [7]loose on earth shall be loosed in heaven.

19 "Again I say to you, that if two of you agree on earth about anything that they may ask, it shall be done for them [8]by My Father who is in heaven.

20 "For where two or three have gathered together in My name, there I am in their midst."

21 Then Peter came and said to Him, "Lord, how often shall my brother sin against me and I forgive him? Up to [r]seven times?"

22 Jesus *said to him, "I do not say to you, up to seven times, but up to seventy times seven.

23 "For this reason the kingdom of heaven may be compared to a certain king who wished to settle accounts with his slaves.

24 "And when he had begun to settle *them*, there was brought to him one who owed him [9]ten thousand talents.

25 "But since he [10]did not have *the means* to repay, his lord commanded him to be sold, along with his wife and children and all that he had, and repayment to be made.

26 "The slave therefore falling down, prostrated himself before him, saying, 'Have patience with me, and I will repay you everything.'

27 "And the lord of that slave felt compassion and released him and forgave him the [11]debt.

28 "But that slave went out and found one of his fellow slaves who owed him a hundred [12]denarii; and he seized him and *began* to choke *him*, saying, '[s]Pay back what you owe.'

29 "So his fellow slave fell down and *began* to entreat him, saying, 'Have patience with me and I will repay you.'

30 "He was unwilling however, but went and threw him in prison until he should pay back what was owed.

31 "So when his fellow slaves saw what had happened, they were deeply grieved and came and reported to their lord all that had happened.

32 "Then summoning him, his lord *said to him, 'You wicked slave, I forgave you all that debt because you entreated me.

33 'Should you not also have had mercy on your fellow slave, even as I had mercy on you?'

34 "And his lord, moved with anger, handed him over to the torturers until he should repay all that was owed him.

35 "So shall My heavenly Father also do to you, if each of you does not forgive his brother from [13]your heart."

[1]Many mss. add *against you.* [2]Lit., *between you and him alone.* [3]Lit., *word.* [4]Lit., *the.* [5]I.e.,

[r](Matt. 18:21) By suggesting seven acts of forgiveness Peter thought he was being quite generous, because the rabbis required only three. Jesus' response was to require unlimited forgiveness. The Greek expression in verse 22 can be either seventy times seven or seventy-seven, but the effect of either is the same: a number so large as to be, for all practical purposes, limitless.

[s](Matt. 18:28) For a disciple to refuse unlimited forgiveness is like this slave's refusal to forgive a debt of $18 (the amount here) after he himself had been forgiven one of over $10 million (v. 24).

Collector of Roman taxes for profit. ⁶Or, *forbid.* ⁷Or, *permit.* ⁸Lit., *from.* ⁹About $10,000,000 in silver content but worth much more in buying power. ¹⁰Or, *was unable to.* ¹¹Or, *loan.* ¹²The denarius was equivalent to one day's wage. ¹³Lit., *your hearts.*

JOURNEY TO JERUSALEM FOR THE FEAST OF TABERNACLES (Booths)

Sec. 130   Ridicule by the Lord's half-brothers
— *Galilee* —

John 7:2-9

2 Now the feast of the Jews, the Feast of Booths, was at hand.

3 His brothers therefore said to Him, "Depart from here, and go into Judea, that Your disciples also may behold Your works which You are doing.

4 "For no one does anything in secret, ¹when he himself seeks to be known publicly. If You do these things, 'show Yourself to the world."

5 For not even His brothers were believing in Him.

6 Jesus therefore *said to them, "My time is not yet at hand; but your time is always opportune.

7 "The world cannot hate you; but it hates Me because I testify of it, that its deeds are evil.

8 "Go up to the feast yourselves; I do not go up ²to this feast because My time has not yet fully come."

9 And having said these things to them, He stayed in Galilee.

¹Lit., *and.*   ²Some authorities add *yet.*

Sec. 131   Journey through Samaria
— *Start of journey to* ᵘ*Jerusalem* —

Luke 9:51-56	John 7:10
51 And it came about, when the days were approaching for His ¹ascension, that He resolutely set His face to go to Jerusalem;	**10** But when His brothers had gone up to the feast, then He Himself also went up, not publicly, but as it were, in secret.
52 and He sent messengers on ahead of Him. And they went, and entered a village of the Samaritans, to ²make arrangements for Him.	
53 And they did not receive Him, because ³He was journeying with His face toward ᵛJerusalem.	
54 And when His disciples James	

ᵗ(John 7:4) After the last six months of relative obscurity, the Lord's brothers prodded Him to make a dramatic appearance at the impending Feast of Tabernacles in Jerusalem. In their unbelieving state they mockingly asked for a kind of Messianic manifestation that would have been quite untimely in the outworking of God's purpose (v. 8).

ᵘAlthough he was later to return briefly to Galilee (Secs. 173-174), Jesus at this point left Galilee as the sphere of his activity.

ᵛ(Luke 9:53) To go to Jerusalem to worship was a repudiation of the Samaritan temple on Mount Gerizim. In return for animosity, James and John wanted to perform a miracle like Elijah whom they had recently seen (Sec. 121) and destroy the unreceptive (Luke 9:54; cf. 2 Kings 1:10, 12). The two "sons of thunder" probably identified this refusal by the Samaritans with the opposition Jesus had predicted for this Jerusalem visit.

Luke 9:51-56 (cont'd)

and John saw *this*, they said, "Lord, do You want us to command fire to come down from heaven and consume them⁴?"

55 But He turned and rebuked them, [⁵and said, "You do not know what kind of spirit you are of;

56 for the Son of Man did not come to destroy men's lives, but to save them."] And they went on to another village.

¹Lit., *taking up*.   ²Or, *prepare*.   ³Lit., *His face was proceeding toward*.   ⁴Some mss. add, *as Elijah did*.   ⁵Many mss. do not contain bracketed portion.

Sec. 132   Complete commitment required of followers
     – On the road –

Matt. 8:19-22

19 And a certain scribe came and said to Him, "Teacher, I will follow You wherever You go."

20 And Jesus *said to him, "The foxes have holes, and the birds of the ¹air *have* ²nests; but the Son of Man has nowhere to lay His head."

21 And another of the disciples said to Him, "Lord, permit me first to go and bury my father."

22 But Jesus *said to him, "Follow Me; and ʷallow the dead to bury their own dead."

Luke 9:57-62

57 And as they were going along the road, someone said to Him, "I will follow You wherever You go."

58 And Jesus said to him, "The foxes have holes, and the birds of the ¹air *have* ²nests, but the Son of Man has nowhere to lay His head."

59 And He said to another, "Follow Me." But he said, "³Permit me first to go and bury my father."

60 But He said to him, "ʷAllow the dead to bury their own dead; but as for you, go and proclaim everywhere the kingdom of God."

61 And another also said, "I will follow You, Lord; but first permit me to say good-bye to those at home."

62 But Jesus said to him, "No one, after putting his hand to the plow and looking back, is fit for the kingdom of God."

¹Or, *sky*.   ²Or, *roosting-places*.   ³Some mss. add *Lord*.

ʷ (Matt. 8:22; Luke 9:60) The son wished to complete the burial rites for his father who had just died or else to observe the customary thirty-day mourning period. But the call to discipleship had to be accepted when issued, or it would be lost. As for his dead father, there were enough who were still spiritually dead to handle the burial.

PART EIGHT
THE LATER JUDEAN MINISTRY OF CHRIST

TEACHINGS AT THE FEAST OF TABERNACLES (BOOTHS)

Sec. 133 Mixed reaction to Jesus' teaching and miracles
— Jerusalem, in the Temple —

John 7:11-31

11 The Jews therefore were seeking Him at the ˣfeast, and were saying, "Where is He?"

12 And there was much grumbling among the multitudes concerning Him; some were saying, "He is a good man"; others were saying, "No, on the contrary, He leads the multitude astray."

13 Yet no one was speaking openly of Him for fear of the ʸJews.

14 But when it was now the midst of the feast Jesus went up into the temple, and *began to* teach.

15 The Jews therefore were marveling, saying, "ᶻHow has this man become learned, having never been educated?"

16 Jesus therefore answered them, and said, "My teaching is not Mine, but His who sent Me.

17 "If any man is willing to do His will, he shall know of the teaching, whether it is of God, or *whether* I speak from Myself.

18 "He who speaks from himself seeks his own glory; but He who is seeking the glory of the one who sent Him, He is true, and there is no unrighteousness in Him.

19 "Did not Moses give you the law, and *yet* none of you carries out the law? Why do you seek to kill Me?"

20 The multitude answered, "You ¹have a demon! Who seeks to kill You?"

21 Jesus answered and said to them, "I did one ²deed, and you all marvel.

22 "On this account Moses has given you circumcision (not because it is from Moses, but from the fathers), and on *the* Sabbath you circumcise a man.

23 "If a man receives circumcision on *the* Sabbath that the Law of Moses may not be broken, are you angry with Me because I made an entire man well on *the* Sabbath?

24 "Do not judge according to appearance, but ³judge with righteous judgment."

ˣ(John 7:11) This is the Feast of Tabernacles. At this point Jesus returned to Jerusalem, the home ground of His strongest enemies. The inevitable result was strong controversy which dominated the period from beginning to end. The Feast of Dedication marked the conclusion of this period of three months (John 10:22, Sec. 160). By then decisions had been reached regarding the controversial issues, and there remained only the carrying out of the decision to separate Messiah from His people.

ʸ(John 7:13) In John 7-8 (Secs. 133-138), designations of Jesus' enemies include "the Jews" (7:11, 13, 15, 35; 8:22, 48, 52, 57), "the Pharisees" (7:32, 47; 8:13), and "the chief priests and the Pharisees" (7:32, 45). Those who are friendly or mildly friendly to Him are called "the multitude" (7:12, 20, 31-32, 40-41, 43, 49), "Nicodemus" (7:50), and "many who came to believe in Him" (8:30). Those who are as yet undecided are "the multitudes" (7:12-13), "the people of Jerusalem" (7:25), "officers" (7:32, 45), and "those Jews who had believed Him" (8:31). In the rapid movement of the narrative the following mixed reactions are recorded: vague inquiries (7:11), debates (7:12, 40-43), fear (7:13, 30, 44), wonder (7:15, 46), perplexity (7:25-27), sincere belief (7:31; 8:30), open hostility (7:32), unfriendly criticism (7:23-27; 8:48-53), and selfish belief (8:3-44).

ᶻ(John 7:15) Two specific issues dominated the discussion: the source of Jesus' authority (7:15-24) and possible identification of Him as the Messiah (7:25-31).

John 7:11-31 (cont'd)

25   Therefore some of the people of Jerusalem were saying, "Is this not the man whom they are seeking to kill?

26   "And look, He is speaking publicly, and they are saying nothing to Him. The rulers do not really know that this is [4]the Christ, do they?

27   "However we know where this man is from; but whenever the Christ may come, no one knows where He is from."

28   Jesus therefore cried out in the temple, teaching and saying, "You both know Me, and know where I am from; and I have not come of Myself, but He who sent Me is true, whom you do not know.

29   "I know Him; because I am from Him, and He sent Me."

30   They were seeking therefore to seize Him; and no man laid his hand on Him, because His hour had not yet come.

31   But many of the multitude believed in Him; and they were saying, "When [4]the Christ shall come, He will not perform more [5]signs than those which this man has, will He?"

[1]Or, *are demented.*   [2]Or, *work.*   [3]Lit., *judge the righteous judgment.*   [4]I.e., the Messiah.   [5]Or, *attesting miracles.*

Sec. 134   Frustrated attempt to arrest Jesus
— Jerusalem —

John 7:32-52

32   The Pharisees heard the multitude muttering these things about Him; and the chief priests and the Pharisees sent officers to seize Him.

33   Jesus therefore said, "For a little while longer I am with you, then I go to Him who sent Me.

34   "You shall seek Me, and shall not find Me; and where I am, you cannot come."

35   The Jews therefore said to one another, "Where does this man intend to go that we shall not find Him? He is not intending to go to the Dispersion among the Greeks, and teach the Greeks, is He?

36   "What is this statement that He said, 'You will seek Me, and will not find Me; and where I am, you cannot come'?"

37   Now on the last day, the great *day* of the feast, Jesus stood and cried out, saying, "If any man is thirsty, let him [1]come to Me and [a]drink.

38   "He who believes in Me, as the Scripture said, '[2]From his innermost being shall flow rivers of living water.'"

39   But this He spoke of the Spirit, whom those who believed in Him were to receive; [3]for the Spirit was not yet *given*, because Jesus was not yet glorified.

40   *Some* of the multitude therefore, when they heard these words, were saying, "This certainly is the Prophet."

41   Others were saying, "This is the Christ." Still others were saying, "Surely [4]the Christ is not going to come from Galilee, is He?

42   "Has not the Scripture said that the Christ comes from the offspring of David, and from Bethlehem, the village where David was?"

43   So there arose a division in the multitude because of Him.

44   And some of them wanted to seize Him, but no one laid hands on Him.

45   The officers therefore came to the chief priests and Pharisees, and they said to them, "Why did you not bring Him?"

46   The officers answered, "Never did a man speak the way this man speaks."

[a](John 7:37) The Feast of Tabernacles included a daily libation of water to commemorate the miraculous supply of water in the wilderness after Israel departed from Egypt. At the same time, it pointed forward to what the prophets saw as the future blessing of the nation (Ezek. 47:1, 12; Joel 3:18). Jesus claimed ability to fulfill this promise, and the parenthetical interpretation of John 7:39 identifies the fulfillment with the provision of the Holy Spirit following Jesus' glorification.

John 7:32-52 (cont'd)

47 The Pharisees therefore answered them, "You have not also been led astray, have you?

48 "No one of the rulers or Pharisees has believed in Him, has he?

49 "But this multitude which does not know the Law is accursed."

50 Nicodemus *said to them (he who came to Him before, being one of them),

51 "Our Law does not judge a man, unless it first hears from him and knows what he is doing, does it?"

52 They answered and said to him, "You are not also from Galilee, are you? Search, and see that no prophet arises out of Galilee."

¹I.e., let him keep coming to Me and let him keep drinking. ²Lit., *out of his belly.* ³Other mss. read *for the Holy Spirit was not yet given.* ⁴I.e., the Messiah.

Sec. 135 Jesus' forgiveness of an adulteress
— Jerusalem, in the Temple —

[John 7:53—8:11]ᵇ

53 [¹And everyone went to his home.

1 But Jesus went to the Mount of Olives.

2 And early in the morning He came again into the temple, and all the people were coming to Him; and He sat down and *began* to teach them.

3 And the scribes and the Pharisees *brought a woman caught in adultery, and having set her in the midst,

4 they *said to Him, "Teacher, this woman has been caught in adultery, in the very act.

5 "Now in the Law Moses commanded us to stone such women; what then do You say?"

6 And they were saying this, testing Him, in order that they might have grounds for accusing Him. But Jesus stooped down, and with His finger wrote on the ground.

7 But when they persisted in asking Him, He straightened up, and said to them, "He who is without sin among you, let him *be the* first to throw a stone at her."

8 And again He stooped down, and wrote on the ground.

9 And when they heard it, they *began* to go out one by one, beginning with the older ones, and He was left alone, and the woman, *where she had been,* in the midst.

10 And straightening up, Jesus said to her, "Woman, where are they? Did no one condemn you?"

11 And she said, "No one, ²Lord." And Jesus said, "Neither do I condemn you; go your way. From now on sin no more."]

¹John 7:53—8:11 is not found in most of the old mss. ²Or, *Sir.*

Sec. 136 Conflict over Jesus' claim to be the light of the world
— Jerusalem, in the Temple —

John 8:12-20

12 Again therefore Jesus spoke to them, saying, "I am the ᶜlight of the world;

ᵇThis section probably records a historic incident in the life of Christ, but one preserved by Christian tradition and not by the writer of this gospel. Evidence from more reliable textual sources denies this incident a place in John's gospel. Therefore, it is impossible to discover the correct chronological placement of this encounter.

ᶜ(John 8:12) Some have suggested that "light" drew attention to the pillar of fire in the wilderness

John 8:12-20 (cont'd)

he who follows Me shall not walk in the darkness, but shall have the light of life."

13 The Pharisees therefore said to Him, "You are bearing witness of Yourself; Your witness is not [1]true."

14 Jesus answered and said to them, "Even if I bear witness of Myself, My witness is true; for I know where I come from, and where I am going; but you do not know where I come from, or where I am going.

15 "You people judge [2]according to the flesh; I am not judging anyone.

16 "But even if I do judge, My judgment is true; for I am not alone in it, but I and [3]He who sent Me.

17 "Even in your law it has been written, that the testimony of two men is [4]true.

18 "I am He who bears witness of Myself, and the Father who sent Me bears witness of Me."

19 And so they were saying to Him, "Where is Your Father?" Jesus answered, "You know neither Me, nor My Father; if you knew Me, you would know My Father also."

20 These words He spoke in the [d]treasury, as He taught in the temple; and no one seized Him, because His hour had not yet come.

[1]Or, *valid*.　[2]I.e., a carnal standard.　[3]Many ancient mss. read *the Father who sent Me*.　[4]I.e., valid or admissible.

Sec. 137　Invitation to believe in Jesus
　– Jerusalem, in the Temple –

John 8:21-30

21 He said therefore again to them, "I go away, and you shall seek Me, and shall die in your sin; where I am going, you cannot come."

22 Therefore the Jews were saying, "Surely He will not kill Himself, will He, since He says, 'Where I am going, you cannot come'?"

23 And He was saying to them, "You are from below, I am from above; you are of this world, I am not of this world.

24 "I said therefore to you, that you shall die in your sins; [e]for unless you believe that [1]I am He, you shall die in your sins."

25 And so they were saying to Him, "Who are You?" Jesus said to them, "[2]What have I been saying to you *from* the beginning?

26 "I have many things to speak and to judge concerning you, but He who sent Me is true; and the things which I heard from Him, these I speak to the world."

27 They did not realize that He had been speaking to them about the Father.

28 Jesus therefore said, "When you lift up the Son of Man, then you will know that [3]I am He, and I do nothing on My own initiative, but I speak these things as the Father taught Me.

(see note a, Sec. 134). Though an indirect reference to this is probable, the preferable understanding is an allusion to the golden candelabrum which was lit on the first night of the Feast of Tabernacles. This light source in turn was commemorative of the Shekinah which guided the Israelites through the wilderness.

[d](John 8:20) "Treasury" must be a reference to that part of the court of the women in which thirteen trumpet-shaped collection boxes were located (cf. Mark 12:41, 43 and Luke 21:1, Sec. 201). This court was a gathering place for both sexes, and teaching was permitted there. Interestingly, it was quite near the meeting hall of the Sanhedrin, the official council of Judaism that was determined to dispose of Jesus.

[e](John 8:24) Jesus' challenge to believe in Himself as Messiah is met with a positive response by "many" (John 8:30). Whether these were opponents, neutral bystanders, or both is not disclosed.

John 8:21-30 (cont'd)

29   "And He who sent Me is with Me; He [4]has not left Me alone, for I always do the things that are pleasing to Him."

30   As He spoke these things, [e]many came to believe in Him.

[1]Most authorities connect this with Ex. 3:14, *I AM WHO I AM.*   [2]Or, *That which I have been saying to you from the beginning.*   [3]Lit., *I AM* (v. 24 note).   [4]Or, *did not leave.*

Sec. 138   Relationship to Abraham, and attempted stoning
— Jerusalem, in the Temple —

John 8:31-59

31   Jesus therefore was saying to those Jews who had [f]believed Him, "If you abide in My word, then you are truly disciples of Mine;

32   and you shall know the truth, and the truth shall make you free."

33   They answered Him, "[g]We are Abraham's offspring, and have never yet been enslaved to anyone; how is it that You say, 'You shall become free'?"

34   Jesus answered them, "Truly, truly, I say to you, everyone who commits sin is the slave of sin.

35   "And the slave does not remain in the house forever; the son does remain forever.

36   "If therefore the Son shall make you free, you shall be free indeed.

37   "I know that you are Abraham's offspring; yet you seek to kill Me, because My word [1]has no place in you.

38   "I speak the things which I have seen [2]with My Father; therefore you also do the things which you heard from your father."

39   They answered and said to Him, "Abraham is our father." Jesus [*]said to them, "If you are Abraham's children, do the deeds of Abraham.

40   "But as it is, you are seeking to kill Me, a man who has told you the truth, which I heard from God; this Abraham did not do.

41   "You are doing the deeds of your father." They said to Him, "We were not born of fornication; we have one Father, *even* God."

42   Jesus said to them, "If God were your Father, you would love Me; for I proceeded forth and have come from God, for I have not even come on My own initiative, but [3]He sent Me.

43   "Why do you not understand [4]what I am saying? *It is* because you cannot hear My word.

44   "You are of *your* father the devil, and you want to do the desires of your father. He was a murderer from the beginning, and does not stand in the truth, because there is no truth in him. Whenever he speaks [5]a lie, he speaks from his own *nature;* for he is a liar, and the father of [6]lies.

45   "But because I speak the truth, you do not believe Me.

46   "Which one of you convicts Me of sin? If I speak truth, why do you not believe Me?

47   "He who is of God hears the words of God; for this reason you do not hear *them,* because you are not of God."

48   The Jews answered and said to Him, "Do we not say rightly that You are a Samaritan and have a demon?"

[f](John 8:31) The Greek construction is such as to distinguish this group from the sincere believers of John 8:30. "Believe Him" does not carry the same connotation of commitment as "believed in Him." The words of this section are therefore addressed to those who see the plausibility of His Messianic claims but are unwilling to comply with the ethical demands accompanying them.

[g](John 8:33) This is the first of several declarations in the section that portray the animosity of Judaism toward Jesus and His teachings. Here the Jews claimed inheritance of freedom through Abraham so as to contradict Jesus' promise of freedom only if they abide in His word. Their other claims and accusations are found in verses 39, 41, 48, 53, 57.

John 8:31-59 (cont'd)

49 Jesus answered, "I do not have a demon; but I honor My Father, and you dishonor Me.

50 "But I do not seek My glory; there is One who seeks and judges.

51 "Truly, truly, I say to you, if anyone keeps My word he shall never see death."

52 The Jews said to Him, "Now we know that You have a demon. Abraham died, and the prophets *also;* and You say, 'If anyone keeps My word, he shall never taste of death.'

53 "Surely You are not greater than our father Abraham, who died? The prophets died too; whom do You make Yourself out *to be?*"

54 Jesus answered, "If I glorify Myself, My glory is nothing; it is My Father who glorifies Me, of whom you say, 'He is our God';

55 and you have not come to know Him, but I know Him; and if I say that I do not know Him, I shall be a liar like you, but I do know Him, and keep His word.

56 "Your father Abraham rejoiced [7]to see My day; and he saw *it,* and was glad."

57 The Jews therefore said to Him, "You are not yet fifty years old, and have You seen Abraham?"

58 Jesus said to them, "Truly, truly, I say to you, before Abraham [8]was born, I am."

59 Therefore they picked up stones to throw at Him; but Jesus [9]hid Himself, and went out of the temple[10].

[1]Or, *makes no progress.* [2]Or, *in the presence of.* [3]Lit., *that One.* [4]Or, *My mode of speaking.* [5]Lit., *the lie.* [6]Lit., *it.* [7]Lit., *in order that he might see.* [8]Lit., *came into being.* [9]Lit., *was hidden.* [10]Some mss. add *and going through the midst of them went His way and so passed by.*

PRIVATE LESSONS ON LOVING SERVICE AND PRAYER

Sec. 139   Commissioning of the seventy (cf. Secs. 76; 98, 99)
— *Probably in Judea* —

Luke 10:1-16

1 Now after this the Lord appointed [1h]seventy others, and sent them two and two ahead of Him to every city and place where He Himself was going to come.

2 And He was saying to them, "The harvest is plentiful, but the laborers are few; therefore beseech the Lord of the harvest to send out laborers into His harvest.

3 "Go your ways; behold, I send you out as lambs in the midst of wolves.

4 "Carry no purse, no [2]bag, no shoes; and greet no one on the way.

5 "And whatever house you enter, first say, 'Peace *be* to this house.'

6 "And if a [3]man of peace is there, your peace will rest upon him; but if not, it will return to you.

7 "And stay in [4]that house, eating and drinking [5]what they give you; for the laborer is worthy of his wages. Do not keep moving from house to house.

8 "And whatever city you enter, and they receive you, eat what is set before you;

[h](Luke 10:1) Just as Moses appointed seventy elders to help him, Jesus appointed a like number to expedite His mission in the brief time remaining before His arrest and crucifixion. Unlike the twelve, whose ministry had been to Galilee, the seventy were to reach either Perea (Transjordan) or Judea. The twelve had a more independent and permanent impact, but the seventy were commissioned to prepare the towns and villages for a coming visit by Christ.

Luke 10:1-16 (cont'd)

9 and heal those in it who are sick, and say to them, "The kingdom of God has come near to you.'

10 "But whatever city you enter and they do not receive you, go out into its streets and say,

11 'Even the dust of your city which clings to our feet, we wipe off in protest against you; yet [6]be sure of this, that the kingdom of God has come near.'

12 "I say to you, it will be more tolerable in that day for Sodom, than for that city.

13 "Woe to you, Chorazin! Woe to you, Bethsaida! For if the [7]miracles had been performed in Tyre and Sidon which occurred in you, they would have repented long ago, sitting in sackcloth and ashes.

14 "But it will be more tolerable for Tyre and Sidon in the judgment, than for you.

15 "And you, Capernaum, will not be exalted to heaven, will you? You will be brought down to Hades!

16 "The one who listens to you listens to Me, and the one who rejects you rejects Me; and he who rejects Me rejects the One who sent Me."

[1]Some mss. read *seventy-two.*   [2]Or, *knapsack or beggar's bag.*   [3]Lit., *son*   [4]Or, *the house itself.*   [5]Lit., *the things from them.*   [6]Lit., *know.*   [7]Or, *works of power.*

Sec. 140   Return of the seventy
– Probably in Judea –

Luke 10:17-24

17 And the [1]seventy [j]returned with joy, saying, "Lord, even the demons are subject to us in Your name."

18 And He said to them, "I was watching Satan fall from heaven like lightning.

19 "Behold, I have given you authority to tread upon serpents and scorpions, and over all the power of the enemy, and nothing shall injure you.

20 "Nevertheless do not rejoice in this, that the spirits are subject to you, but rejoice that your names are recorded in heaven."

21 At that very [2]time He rejoiced greatly in the Holy Spirit, and said, "I [3]praise Thee, O Father, Lord of heaven and earth, that Thou didst hide these things from the wise and intelligent and didst reveal them to babes. Yes, Father, for thus it was well-pleasing in Thy sight.

22 "All things have been handed over to Me by My Father, and no one knows who the Son is except the Father, and who the Father is except the Son, and anyone to whom the Son wills to reveal Him."

23 And turning to the disciples, He said privately, "Blessed are the eyes which see the things you see,

24 for I say to you, that many prophets and kings wished to see the things which you see, and did not see them, and to hear the things which you hear, and did not hear them."

[1]Some mss. read *seventy-two.*   [2]Lit., *hour.*   [3]Or, *acknowledge to Thy praise.*

---

[1](Luke 10:9) The message is still about the nearness of the Kingdom (cf. Matt. 10:7, Sec. 99). The inhabitants of other areas had a right to this proclamation just as did those in Galilee. This widespread ministry, particularly in Judea, served to prepare Israel for the official offer of her King in the triumphal entry which was less than six months away (cf. Sec. 187).

[j](Luke 10:17) The seventy did not return all at once and probably did not return to the same place. They in all likelihood met Him as He followed them into the places they had entered as His forerunners. After they were all back together, this dialogue took place.

Sec. 141   Story of the good Samaritan (cf. Sec. 197)

– Probably in Judea –

Luke 10:25-37

25 And behold, a certain [1]lawyer stood up and put Him to the test, saying, "Teacher, what shall I do to inherit eternal life?"

26 And He said to him, "What is written in the Law? How [2]does it read to you?"

27 And he answered and said, "YOU SHALL LOVE THE LORD YOUR GOD WITH ALL YOUR HEART, AND WITH ALL YOUR SOUL, AND WITH ALL YOUR STRENGTH, AND WITH ALL YOUR MIND; AND YOUR NEIGHBOR AS YOURSELF" [Lev. 19:18; Deut. 6:5].

28 And He said to him, "You have answered correctly; DO THIS, AND YOU WILL LIVE" [Lev. 18:5].

29 But wishing to justify himself, he said to Jesus, "And who is my neighbor?"

30 Jesus replied and said, "[k]A certain man was going down from Jerusalem to Jericho; and he fell among robbers, and they stripped him and [3]beat him, and went off leaving him half dead.

31 "And by chance a certain priest was going down on that road, and when he saw him, he passed by on the other side.

32 "And likewise a Levite also, when he came to the place and saw him, passed by on the other side.

33 "But a certain Samaritan, who was on a journey, came upon him; and when he saw him, he felt compassion,

34 and came to him, and bandaged up his wounds, pouring oil and wine on *them;* and he put him on his own beast, and brought him to an inn, and took care of him.

35 "And on the next day he took out two [4]denarii and gave them to the innkeeper and said, 'Take care of him; and whatever more you spend, when I return, I will repay you.'

36 "[l]Which of these three do you think proved to be a neighbor to the man who fell into the robbers' *hands?"*

37 And he said, "The one who showed mercy toward him." And Jesus said to him, "Go and do [5]the same."

[1]I.e., an expert in the Mosaic Law. [2]Lit., *do you read?* [3]Lit., *laid blows upon.* [4]The denarius was equivalent to one day's wage. [5]Or, *likewise.*

Sec. 142   Jesus' visit with Mary and Martha

– Bethany near Jerusalem –

Luke 10:38-42

38 Now as they were traveling along, He entered a certain village; and a [1]woman named [m]Martha welcomed Him into her home.

39 And she had a sister called [m]Mary, who moreover was listening to the Lord's word, seated at His feet.

[k](Luke 10:30) Though often referred to as a parable, the possibility of this being an actual occurrence is good. Jesus would hardly have attributed such unbecoming behavior to His enemies (i.e., a priest and a Levite) unless such a thing had actually happened. This is especially true since the lawyer who asked was one of the scribes who was putting Jesus to the test (v. 25).

[l](Luke 10:36) Jesus rephrased and corrected the lawyer's question from "Who is my neighbor?" (v. 29) to "To whom am I neighbor?" What the man should have asked himself was, "To whom do I prove myself to be a neighbor?" Jesus' answer in the story of the good Samaritan is, "Anyone in need, even if he is my avowed enemy." Love, not place, produces neighborhood.

[m](Luke 10:38-39) The pictures of Mary and Martha in this episode agree perfectly with those in John 11:17-44 (Sec. 171) when their brother Lazarus was raised. The former was characterized especially by a life of worship and meditation, while the latter was given more to a life of activity and service. Both are legitimate. The error arose when Martha allowed anxiety to intervene and spoil what otherwise was a necessary service.

Luke 10:38-42 (cont'd)

40 But Martha was distracted with [2]all her preparations; and she came up to Him, and said, "Lord, do You not care that my sister has left me to do all the serving alone? Then tell her to help me."

41 But the Lord answered and said to her, "Martha, Martha, you are worried and bothered about so many things;

42 [3]but *only* a few things are necessary, [4]really *only* one, for Mary has chosen the good part, which shall not be taken away from her."

[1]Lit., *certain woman.*   [2]Lit., *much service.*   [3]Some mss. read *but one thing is necessary.*   [4]Lit., *or.*

Sec. 143   Lesson on how to pray and parable of the importunate friend (cf. Secs. 69; 71; 175)
– *Probably in Judea* –

Luke 11:1-13

1 And it came about that while He was praying in a certain place, after He had finished, one of His disciples said to Him, "Lord, teach us to pray just as John also taught his disciples."

2 And He said to them, "When you pray, say:
'[1]Father, hallowed be Thy name.
Thy kingdom come.

3 'Give us each day our [2]daily bread.

4 'And forgive us our sins,
For we ourselves also forgive everyone who is indebted to us.
And lead us not into temptation.'"

5 And He said to them, "[3]Suppose one of you shall have a friend, and shall go to him at midnight, and say to him, 'Friend, lend me three loaves;

6 for a friend of mine has come to me from a journey, and I have nothing to set before him';

7 and from inside he shall answer and say, 'Do not bother me; the door has already been shut and my children [4]and I are in bed; I cannot get up and give you *anything.*'

8 "I tell you, even though he will not get up and give him *anything* because he is his friend, yet because of his [5][n]persistence he will get up and give him as much as he needs.

9 "And I say to you, [6]ask, and it shall be given to you; [7]seek, and you shall find; [8]knock, and it shall be opened to you.

10 "For everyone who asks, receives; and he who seeks, finds; and to him who knocks, it shall be opened.

11 "Now [9]suppose one of you fathers is asked by his son for a [10]fish; he will not give him a snake instead of a fish, will he?

12 "Or if he is asked for an egg, he will not give him a scorpion, will he?

13 "If you then, being evil, know how to give good gifts to your children, how much more shall your [11]heavenly Father give the Holy Spirit to those who ask Him?"

[1]Some mss. insert phrases from Matt. 6:9-13 to make the two passages closely similar.   [2]Or, *bread for the coming day* or *needful bread.*   [3]Lit., *Which one of you.*   [4]Lit., *with me.*   [5]Or, *shamelessness.*   [6]Or, *keep asking.*   [7]Or, *keep seeking.*   [8]Or, *keep knocking.*   [9]Lit., *which of you, a son, shall ask the father.*   [10]Some early mss. insert *loaf, he will not give him a stone, will he,* or for a.   [11]Lit., *Father from heaven.*

---

[n](Luke 11:8) The ideas of earnestness and urgency are found in the word. In the case of God, as in the case of the inconvenienced friend, the shamelessness of the asker who is thus motivated is what tips the balance in favor of granting the request.

SECOND DEBATE WITH THE SCRIBES AND PHARISEES

Sec. 144　A third blasphemous accusation and a second debate (cf. Secs. 66, 83; 70; 79, 128; 79, 96, 128; 80, 115; 146)
– *Probably in Judea* –

Luke 11:14-36

14　And He was casting out a demon, *and it was* dumb; and it came about that when the demon had gone out, the dumb man spoke; and the multitudes marveled.

15　But some of them said, "°He casts out demons by [1]Beelzebul, the ruler of the demons."

16　And others, [2]to test *Him*, were demanding of Him a [3]sign from heaven.

17　But He knew their thoughts, and said to them, "[4]Any kingdom divided against itself is laid waste; and a house *divided* against [5]itself falls.

18　"And if Satan also is divided against himself, how shall his kingdom stand? For you say that I cast out demons by Beelzebul.

19　"And if I by Beelzebul cast out demons, by whom do your sons cast them out? Consequently they shall be your judges.

20　"But if I cast out demons by the finger of God, then the kingdom of God has come upon you.

21　"When [6]a strong *man*, fully armed, guards his own homestead, his possessions are [7]undisturbed;

22　but when someone stronger than he attacks him and overpowers him, he takes away from him all his armor on which he had relied, and distributes his plunder.

23　"He who is not with Me is against Me; and he who does not gather with Me, scatters.

24　"When the unclean spirit goes out of [6]a man, it passes through waterless places seeking rest, and not finding any, it says, 'I will return to my house from which I came.'

25　"And when it comes, it finds it swept and put in order.

26　"Then it goes and takes *along* seven other spirits more evil than itself, and they go in and live there; and the last state of that man becomes worse than the first."

27　And it came about while He said these things, one of the women in the crowd raised her voice, and said to Him, "Blessed is the womb that bore You, and the breasts at which You nursed."

28　But He said, "On the contrary, blessed are those who hear the word of God, and observe it."

29　And as the crowds were increasing, He began to say, "This generation is a wicked generation; it seeks for a [3]sign, and yet no sign shall be given to it but the [3]sign of Jonah.

30　"For just as Jonah became a [3]sign to the Ninevites, so shall the Son of Man be to this generation.

31　"The Queen of the South shall rise up with the men of this generation at the judgment and condemn them, because she came from the ends of the earth to hear the wisdom of Solomon; and behold, something greater than Solomon is here.

°(Luke 11:15) The same accusation was made about a year before when a similar debate ensued. Jesus used the same three arguments He had used on the earlier occasion. That the two encounters were distinct from each other is seen by three factors:

1. Luke appears to place this debate in Judea while the earlier one was in Galilee.
2. In Luke's account the man healed is dumb, but in Matthew's he is dumb and blind. Luke, in line with his medical orientation, would hardly have failed to mention the blindness if this were the man's condition.
3. Events that follow the two episodes are quite different, namely, the initiation of parabolic teaching in the earlier case and breakfast with a Pharisee in the later.

Luke 11:14-36 (cont'd)

32 "The men of Nineveh shall stand up with this generation at the judgment and condemn it, because they repented at the preaching of Jonah; and behold, something greater than Jonah is here.

33 "No one, after lighting a lamp, puts it away in a cellar, nor under a peck-measure, but on the lampstand, in order that those who enter may see the light.

34 'The lamp of your body is your eye; when your eye is [8]clear, your whole body also is full of light; but when it is bad, your body also is full of darkness.

35 "Then watch out that the light in you may not be darkness.

36 "If therefore your whole body is full of light, with no dark part in it, it shall be wholly illumined, as when the lamp illumines you with its rays."

[1]Here and in vv. 18 and 19 some mss. read *Beezebul.*   [2]Lit., *were testing.*   [3]Or, *attesting miracle.*   [4]Lit., *every.*   [5]Lit., *a house.*   [6]Lit., *the.*   [7]Lit., *in peace.*   [8]Or, *healthy.*

Sec. 145   Woes against the scribes and Pharisees while eating with a Pharisee (cf. Sec. 199)
– *Probably in Judea* –

Luke 11:37-54

37 Now when He had spoken, a Pharisee *asked Him to have lunch with him; and He went in, and reclined *at the table.*

38 And when the [P]Pharisee saw it, he was surprised that He had not first [1]ceremonially washed before the [2]meal.

39 But the Lord said to him, "Now you Pharisees clean the outside of the cup and of the platter; but [3]inside of you, you are full of robbery and wickedness.

40 "You foolish ones, did not He who made the outside make the inside also?

41 "But give that which is within as charity, and [4]then all things are clean for you.

42 "But woe to you Pharisees! For you pay tithe of mint and rue and every *kind of* garden herb, and *yet* disregard justice and the love of God; but these are the things you should have done without neglecting the others.

43 "Woe to you Pharisees! For you love the front seats in the synagogues, and the respectful greetings in the market places.

44 "Woe to you! For you are like [5]concealed tombs, and the people who walk over *them* are unaware *of it.*"

45 And one of the [6]lawyers *said to Him in reply, "Teacher, when You say this, You insult us too."

46 But He said, "Woe to you lawyers as well! For you weigh men down with burdens hard to bear, [7]while you yourselves will not even touch the burdens with one of your fingers.

47 "Woe to you! For you build the [8]tombs of the prophets, and *it was* your fathers *who* killed them.

48 "Consequently, you are witnesses and approve the deeds of your fathers; because it was they who killed them, and you build *their tombs.*

49 "For this reason also the wisdom of God said, 'I will send to them prophets and apostles, and *some* of them they will kill and *some* they will [9]persecute,

[P](Luke 11:38) The contrary inner disposition of Jesus' host is clear. Though the formal decision to destroy Jesus had not yet been reached (John 11:53, Sec. 172), the intentions of the Sanhedrin were obvious to its members (Secs. 134, 138). Thus the scribes and Pharisees had one of their number invite Him to a meal so they could watch Him more closely to find basis for a formal complaint. As a result of this encounter their hostility was intensified even more (vv. 53-54). At an earlier meal with a Pharisee in Galilee the host had not been so antagonistic (Sec. 77).

Luke 11:37-54 (cont'd)

50 in order that the blood of all the prophets, shed since the foundation of the world, may be [10]charged against this generation,

51 from the blood of Abel to the blood of Zechariah, who perished between the altar and the house *of God*; yes, I tell you, it shall be [10]charged against this generation.'

52 "Woe to you [6]lawyers! For you have [q]taken away the key of knowledge; you did not enter in yourselves, and those who were entering in you hindered."

53 And when He left there, the scribes and the Pharisees began to be very hostile and to question Him closely on many subjects,

54 plotting against Him, to catch *Him* in [11]something He might say.

[1]Lit., *baptized.* [2]Or, *lunch.* [3]Lit., *your inside is full.* [4]Lit., *behold.* [5]Or, *indistinct, unseen.* [6]I.e., *experts in the Mosaic Law.* [7]Lit., *and.* [8]Or, *monuments to.* [9]Or, *drive out.* [10]Or, *required of.* [11]Lit., *something out of His mouth.*

Sec. 146 **Warning the disciples about hypocrisy (cf. Secs. 70, 99; 70, 79, 144; 99; 116; 203)**

– *Probably in Judea* –

Luke 12:1-12

1 Under these circumstances, after [1]so many thousands of the multitude had gathered together that they were stepping on one another, He began saying to His [r]disciples first *of all,* "Beware of the leaven of the Pharisees, which is [s]hypocrisy.

2 "But there is nothing covered up that will not be revealed, and hidden that will not be known.

3 "Accordingly, whatever you have said in the dark shall be heard in the light, and what you have [2]whispered in the inner rooms shall be proclaimed upon the housetops.

4 "And I say to you, My friends, do not be afraid of those who kill the body, and after that have no more that they can do.

5 "But I will [3]warn you whom to fear: fear the One who after He has killed has authority to cast into [4]hell; yes, I tell you, fear Him!

6 "Are not five sparrows sold for two [5]cents? And yet not one of them is forgotten before God.

7 "Indeed the very hairs of your head are all numbered. Do not fear; you are of more value than many sparrows.

8 "And I say to you, everyone who confesses Me before men, the Son of Man shall confess him also before the angels of God;

9 but he who denies Me before men shall be denied before the angels of God.

10 "And everyone who will speak a word against the Son of Man, it shall be forgiven him; but he who blasphemes against the Holy Spirit, it shall not be forgiven him.

---

[q](Luke 11:52) Jesus' denunciation of the Pharisees (vv. 39-44) and the lawyers (or scribes, vv. 45-51) was brought to a climax when He charged the lawyers with taking away the key of knowledge. The key to a knowledge of God was the Old Testament, the true meaning of which they had hidden by their erroneous interpretations and man-made traditions. These experts in the Law refused to enter into an accurate appreciation of God, and in addition kept those whom they taught from doing so by imposing their own ideas on the Scriptures.

[r](Luke 12:1) Luke 12:1-59 (Secs. 146-150) is a continuous oration against the backdrop of strong opposition. A very large crowd, most of which was probably hostile, was present. What Jesus said, however, was largely addressed to His disciples (vv. 1-12, 22-53), though in the hearing of the crowd.

[s](Luke 12:1) Pharisaic pretense in general prompted by the fear of man (vv. 1-7) and pretense in particular in denying Jesus in word or work (vv. 8-12) are the two parts to this warning.

Luke 12:1-12 (cont'd)

11 "And when they bring you before the synagogues and the rulers and the authorities, do not become anxious about how or what you should speak in your defense, or what you should say;

12 for the Holy Spirit will teach you in that very hour what you ought to say."

[1]Lit., *myriads.* [2]Lit., *spoken in the ear.* [3]Or, *show.* [4]Gr., *Gehenna.* [5]Gr., *assaria,* the smallest of copper coins.

Sec. 147   Warning about greed and trust in wealth (cf. Sec. 70)
– Probably in Judea –

Luke 12:13-34

13 And someone [1]in the crowd said to Him, "'Teacher, tell my brother to divide the *family* inheritance with me."

14 But He said to him, "Man, who appointed Me a judge or arbiter over you?"

15 And He said to them, "Beware, and be on your guard against every form of greed; for not *even* when one has an abundance does his life consist of his possessions."

16 And He told them a parable, saying, "The land of a certain rich man was very productive.

17 "And he began reasoning to himself, saying, 'What shall I do, since I have no place to store my crops?'

18 "And he said, 'This is what I will do: I will tear down my barns and build larger ones, and there I will store all my grain and my goods.

19 'And I will say to my soul, "Soul, you have many goods laid up for many years *to come;* take your ease, eat, drink *and* be merry."'

20 "But God said to him, 'You fool! This *very* night [2]your soul is required of you; and *now* who will own what you have prepared?'

21 "So is the man who lays up treasure for himself, and is not rich toward God."

22 And He said to His disciples, "For this reason I say to you, do not be anxious for *your* [3]life, *as to* what you shall eat; nor for your body, *as to* what you shall put on.

23 "For life is more than food, and the body than clothing.

24 "Consider the ravens, for they neither sow nor reap; and they have no storeroom nor barn; and *yet* God feeds them; how much more valuable you are than the birds!

25 "And which of you by being anxious can add a *single* [4]cubit to his [5]life's span?

26 "If then you cannot do even a very little thing, why are you anxious about other matters?

27 "Consider the lilies, how [6]they grow; they neither toil nor spin; but I tell you, even Solomon in all his glory did not clothe himself like one of these.

28 "But if God so arrays the grass in the field, which is *alive* today and tomorrow is thrown into the furnace, how much more *will He clothe* you, O men of little faith!

29 "And do not seek what you shall eat, and what you shall drink, and do not keep worrying.

30 "For [7]all these things the nations of the world eagerly seek; but your Father knows that you need these things.

[1](Luke 12:13) This request reflected the pronounced tendency of the Pharisees toward avarice (Luke 16:14, Sec. 168) with which Jesus had already dealt (Matt. 6:19-24, Sec. 70).

Luke 12:13-34 (cont'd)

31 "But seek for His kingdom, and these things shall be added to you.

32 "Do not be afraid, little flock, for your Father has chosen gladly to give you the kingdom.

33 "Sell your possessions and give to charity; make yourselves purses which do not wear out, an unfailing treasure in heaven, where no thief comes near, nor moth destroys.

34 "For where your treasure is, there will your heart be also.

¹Lit., *out of.* ²Lit., *they are demanding your soul from you.* ³Or, *soul.* ⁴I.e., One cubit equals approx. 18 in. ⁵Or, *height.* ⁶Some mss. omit *they grow.* ⁷Or, *these things all the nations of the world.*

Sec. 148   Warning against being unprepared for the Son of Man's coming (cf. Sec. 207)

– Probably in Judea –

Luke 12:35-48

35 "¹Be dressed in ᵘreadiness, and *keep* your lamps alight.

36 "And be like men who are waiting for their master when he returns from the wedding feast, so that they may immediately open *the door* to him when he comes and knocks.

37 "Blessed are those slaves whom the master shall find on the alert when he comes; truly I say to you, that he will gird himself *to serve,* and have them recline *at the table,* and will come up and wait on them.

38 "Whether he comes in the ²second watch, or even in the ³third, and finds *them* so, blessed are those *slaves.*

39 "And ⁴be sure of this, that if the head of the house had known at what hour the thief was coming. he would not have allowed his house to be ⁵broken into.

40 "You too, be ready; for the Son of Man is coming at an hour that you do not ⁶expect."

41 And Peter said, "Lord, are You addressing this parable to us, or to everyone *else* as well?"

42 And the Lord said, "Who then is the faithful and sensible steward, whom his master will put in charge of his ⁷servants, to give them their rations at the proper time?

43 "Blessed is that slave whom his ⁸master finds so doing when he comes.

44 "Truly I say to you, that he will put him in charge of all his possessions.

45 "But if that slave says in his heart, 'My master ⁹will be a long time in coming,' and begins to beat the slaves, *both* men and women, and to eat and drink and get drunk;

46 the master of that slave will come on a day when he does not expect *him,* and at an hour he does not know, and will cut him in pieces, and assign him a place with the unbelievers.

47 "And that slave who knew his master's will and did not get ready or act in accord with his will, shall receive many lashes.

48 but the one who did not know *it,* and committed deeds worthy of ¹⁰a flogging, will receive but few. And from everyone who has been given much shall much be required; and to whom they entrusted much, of him they will ask all the more.

¹Lit., *Let your loins be girded.* ²I.e., 9 p.m. to midnight. ³I.e., midnight to 3 a.m. ⁴Lit., *know.* ⁵Lit., *dug through.* ⁶Lit., *think, suppose.* ⁷Lit., *service.* ⁸Or, *lord.* ⁹Lit., *is delaying to come.* ¹⁰Lit., *blows.*

ᵘ(Luke 12:35) A state of constant readiness for the Kingdom that is promised the "little flock" (Luke 12:31-32, Sec. 147), and that will be ushered in by the coming of the Son of Man (Luke 12:40), is the only way to avoid future punishment (Luke 12:47-48).

Sec. 149   Warning about the coming division (cf. Sec. 99)
    – *Probably in Judea* –

Luke 12:49-53

49   "I [1]have come to cast fire upon the earth; and [2]how I wish it were already kindled!

50   "But I have a baptism to [3]undergo, and how distressed I am until it is accomplished!

51   "Do you suppose that I came to grant peace on earth? I tell you, no, but rather [v]division;

52   for from now on five *members* in one household will be divided, three against two, and two against three.

53   "They will be divided, father against son, and son against father; mother against daughter, and daughter against mother; mother-in-law against daughter-in-law, and daughter-in-law against mother-in-law."

[1]Or, *came.*   [2]Lit., *what do I wish if. . . ?*   [3]Lit., *be baptized with.*

Sec. 150   Warning against failing to discern the present time (cf. Sec. 68)
    – *Probably in Judea* –

Luke 12:54-59

54   And He was also saying to the multitudes, "When you see a cloud rising in the west, immediately you say, 'A shower is coming,' and so it turns out.

55   "And when you see a south wind blowing, you say, 'It will be a hot day,' and it turns out *that way.*

56   "You hypocrites! You know how to analyze the appearance of the earth and the sky, but [1]why do you not analyze this [w]present time?

57   "And why do you not even on your own initiative judge what is right?

58   "For while you are going with your opponent to appear before the magistrate, on your way *there* make an effort to [2]settle with him, in order that he may not drag you before the judge, and the judge turn you over to the constable, and the constable throw you into prison.

59   "I say to you, you shall not get out of there until you have paid the very last [3]cent."

[1]Lit., *how.*   [2]Lit., *be released from him.*   [3]Gr., *lepton;* i.e., 1/128 of a denarius.

Sec. 151   Two alternatives: repent or perish
    – *Probably in Judea* –

Luke 13:1-9

1   Now on the same occasion there were some present who reported to Him about the Galileans, whose blood Pilate had [1]mingled with their sacrifices.

2   And He answered and said to them, "Do you suppose that these Galileans were *greater* sinners than all *other* Galileans, because they suffered this *fate?*

3   "I tell you, [x]no, but, unless you [2]repent, you will all likewise perish.

[v](Luke 12:51) The division of which Jesus spoke was none other than the one represented in the crowd before Him. Where there was adamant refusal to meet His terms of inner purity (refusal pictured by the self-indulgence of the wicked slave of the foregoing illustration [Luke 12:45, Sec. 148]), nothing but division could result.

[w](Luke 12:56) "This present time" was a period characterized mainly by the nearness of the Kingdom (cf. Sec. 148). To the unfriendly members of the crowd, the signs of the times should have been just as obvious as the weather signs. Yet they pretended not to notice them, just as they purposely ignored the unambiguous evidence that Jesus was the Messiah.

[x](Luke 13:3, 5) The false notion, prevailing from the time of Job, that a person's extreme sinfulness was always to blame for great calamity was flatly rejected by Jesus. Yet it was true that the suffering of a whole nation might be produced by that nation's sin. Christ foresaw the approaching judgment of Israel and therefore warned of the consequences of failure to repent.

Luke 13:1-9 (cont'd)

4 "Or do you suppose that those eighteen on whom the tower in Siloam fell and killed them, were worse [3]culprits than all the men who live in Jerusalem?

5 "I tell you, [x]no, but, unless you repent, you will all likewise perish."

6 And He *began* telling this parable: "A certain man had a [y]fig tree which had been planted in his vineyard; and he came looking for fruit on it, and did not find any.

7 "And he said to the vineyard-keeper, 'Behold, for three years I have come looking for fruit on this fig tree [4]without finding any. Cut it down! Why does it even use up the ground?'

8 "And he answered and said to him, 'Let it alone, sir, for this year too, until I dig around it and put in fertilizer;

9 and if it bears fruit next year, *fine*; but if not, cut it down.'"

[1]Or, *shed along with.*   [2]Or, *are repentant.*   [3]Lit., *debtors.*   [4]Lit., *and I do not find.*

Sec. 152   Opposition from a synagogue official for healing a woman on the Sabbath (cf. Secs. 57-61, 155, 164; 86; 87)
       – *Probably in Judea* –

Luke 13:10-21

10 And He was teaching in one of the synagogues on the Sabbath.

11 And behold, there was a woman who for eighteen years had had a sickness caused by a spirit; and she was bent double, and could not straighten up at all.

12 And when Jesus saw her, He called her over and said to her, "Woman, you are freed from your sickness."

13 And He laid His hands upon her; and immediately she was made erect again, and *began* glorifying God.

14 And the synagogue official, indignant because Jesus had healed on the Sabbath, *began* saying to the multitude in response, "There are six days in which work should be done; therefore come during them and get healed, and not on the Sabbath day."

15 But the Lord answered him and said, "You hypocrites, does not each of you on the Sabbath untie his ox or his donkey from the stall, and lead him away to water *him?*

16 "And this woman, a daughter of Abraham as she is, whom Satan has bound for eighteen long years, should she not have been released from this bond on the Sabbath day?"

17 And as He said this, all His opponents were being humiliated; and the entire multitude was rejoicing over all the glorious things being done by Him.

18 [z]Therefore He was saying, "What is the kingdom of God like, and to what shall I compare it?

---

[y](Luke 13:6) In conjuction with the narrative of 13:1-5, the fig tree must symbolize this generation of Jewish people (cf. Hos. 9:10; Joel 1:7; Matt. 21:19 and Mark 11:13, Sec. 187). Just as a fig tree has three years to reach maturity, so Israel had been exposed to three years of Christ's ministry. The additional year covered the remainder of Christ's ministry, His postresurrection ministry, and some of the post-Pentecostal ministry of the early church. If the symbolism is carried further, the owner of the vineyard is the Father, the vineyard-keeper is Christ, and the "using up" of the ground (v. 7) depicts Israel's standing in the way of God's mericiful purpose to others (cf. Rom. 9:19).

[z](Luke 13:18) "Therefore" connects the two following parables with verses 11-17. With what it connects in those verses is not so easy to decide. Yet this determines the meaning of the parables. The two principal possibilities are the enthusiasm of the multitude for His miracles and the presence of opposition within the Kingdom at this early stage.

Luke 13:10-21 (cont'd)

19 "It is like a mustard seed, which a man took and threw into his own garden; and it grew and became a tree; AND THE BIRDS OF THE ¹AIR NESTED IN ITS BRANCHES" [Psalm 104:12; Ezek. 17:23; 31:6; Dan. 4:12].

20 And again He said, "To what shall I compare the kingdom of God?

21 "It is like leaven, which a woman took and hid in three ²pecks of meal, until it was all leavened."

¹Or, *sky.*   ²Gr., *sata.*

TEACHING AT THE FEAST OF DEDICATION

Sec. 153   Healing of a man born blind
     – *Jerusalem* –

John 9:1-7

1 And ᵃas He passed by, He saw a man blind from birth.

2 And His disciples asked Him, saying, "Rabbi, who sinned, this man or his parents, that he should be born blind?"

3 Jesus answered, "It was neither *that* this man sinned, nor his parents; but *it was* in order that the works of God might be displayed in him.

4 "We must work the works of Him who sent Me, as long as it is day; night is coming, when no man can work.

5 "While I am in the world, I am the light of the world."

6 When He had said this, He spat on the ground, and made clay of the spittle, and applied the clay to his eyes,

7 and said to him, "Go, wash in the pool of Siloam" (which is translated, Sent). And so he went away and washed, and came *back* seeing.

Sec. 154   Reaction of the blind man's neighbors
     – *Jerusalem* –

John 9:8-12

8 The neighbors therefore, and those who previously saw him as a beggar, were saying, "Is not this the one who used to sit and beg?"

9 Others were saying, "This is he," *still* others were saying, "No, but he is like him." He kept saying, "I am the one."

10 Therefore they were saying to him, "How then were your eyes opened?"

11 He answered, "The ᵇman who is called Jesus made clay, and anointed my eyes, and said to me, 'Go to Siloam, and wash'; so I went away and washed, and I received sight."

ᵃ(John 9:1) Though some place the events of John 9:1—10:21 (Secs. 153-159) on the same day as the events of John 8:31-59 (Sec. 138) at the Feast of Tabernacles, it is better to see them as happening at the Feast of Dedication (John 10:22, Sec. 160) for the following reasons:
1. The Jews would hardly have sought to stone Jesus (John 8:59) on the Sabbath (John 9:14, Sec. 155).
2. Elapsed time is required after the attempted stoning (John 8:59) to allow antagonism to die down before another public encounter like that in John 9:1—10:21.
3. "At that time" in John 10:22 (Sec. 160) shows the events prior to 10:22 to be part of Jesus' attendance at the Feast of Dedication.
4. The subject of discussion in 9:1—10:21 (sheep) has most affinity with 10:22-29.
5. The tone of 9:1—10:21 is markedly different from the turmoil and debate that dominated the Feast of Tabernacles. In the later section the Jewish listeners had become confirmed in their rejection, and Jesus turned His attention to those outside Israel.

ᵇ(John 9:11) At this point the healed blind man has little apprehension of who Jesus is. As events unfold, however, his appreciation of Him grows rapidly. In verse 17 (Sec. 155) he calls Him a prophet. In verses 27-28 (Sec. 155) he has become His disciple. In verse 31 he describes Him as God-fearing. In verse 33 he acknowledges Him to be from God. In verses 35 and 38 (Sec. 156) he accepts Him as the Son of Man.

John 9:8-12 (cont'd)

12 And they said to him, "Where is He?" He *said, "I do not know."

Sec. 155 Examination and excommunication of the blind man by the Pharisees (cf. Secs. 57-61, 152, 164)

— Jerusalem —

John 9:13-34

13 They *brought to the Pharisees him who was formerly blind.

14 Now it was a Sabbath on the day when Jesus made the clay, and opened his eyes.

15 Again, therefore, the Pharisees also were asking him how he received his sight. And he said to them, "He applied clay to my eyes, and I washed, and I see."

16 Therefore some of the Pharisees were saying, "ᶜThis man is not from God, because He does not keep the Sabbath." But others were saying, "How can a man who is a sinner perform such ¹signs?" And there was a division among them.

17 They *said therefore to the blind man again, "What do you say about Him, since He opened your eyes?" And he said, "He is a prophet."

18 The Jews therefore did not believe *it* of him, that he had been blind, and had received sight, until they called the parents of the very one who had received his sight,

19 and questioned them, saying, "Is this your son, who you say was born blind? Then how does he now see?"

20 His parents answered them and said, "We know that this is our son, and that he was born blind;

21 but how he now sees, we do not know; or who opened his eyes, we do not know. Ask him; he is of age, he shall speak for himself."

22 His parents said this because they were afraid of the Jews; for the Jews had already agreed, that if anyone should confess Him to be ²Christ, he should be ᵈput out of the synagogue.

23 For this reason his parents said, "He is of age; ask him."

24 So a second time they called the man who had been blind, and said to him, "Give glory to God; we know that this man is a sinner."

25 He therefore answered, "Whether He is a sinner, I do not know; one thing I do know, that, whereas I was blind, now I see."

26 They said therefore to him, "What did He do to you? How did He open your eyes?"

27 He answered them, "I told you already, and you did not listen; why do you want to hear *it* again? You do not want to become His disciples too, do you?"

28 And they reviled him, and said, "You are His disciple; but we are disciples of Moses.

29 "We know that God has spoken to Moses; but as for this man, we do not know where He is from."

ᶜ(John 9:16) The regress of the Pharisees during this encounter is pronounced. In verse 16 the dominant group says Jesus is not from God. In verse 18 they question His miracle. In verse 24 they call Him a sinner. In verse 29 they acknowledge their ignorance about Him. In verse 41 (Sec. 157) they are pronounced to be blind sinners.

ᵈ(John 9:22) A form of excommunication as a penalty for those who confessed Jesus to be the Messiah had by now been adopted by some Jewish leaders and perhaps by the Sanhedrin. Severe and final, the punishment resulted in severance from the religious and social life of Israel. This punishment was apparently not implemented with consistency; Christians in Acts moved in synagogue circles with a good bit of freedom.

John 9:13-34 (cont'd)

30   The man answered and said to them, "Well, here is an amazing thing, that you do not know where He is from, and yet He opened my eyes.

31   "We know that God does not hear sinners; but if anyone is God-fearing, and does His will, he hears him.

32   "³Since the beginning of time it has never been heard that anyone opened the eyes of a person born blind.

33   "If this man were not from God, He could do nothing."

34   They answered and said to him, "You were born entirely in sins, and are you teaching us?" And they ᵉput him out.

¹Or, *attesting miracles.*   ²I.e., the Messiah.   ³Lit., *From antiquity it was not heard.*

Sec. 156   Jesus' identification of Himself to the blind man
– Jerusalem –

John 9:35-38

35   Jesus heard that they had put him out; and finding him, He said, "Do you believe in the Son of Man?"

36   He answered and said, "And who is He, ¹Lord, that I may believe in Him?"

37   Jesus said to him, "You have both seen Him, and He is the one who is talking with you."

38   And he said, "Lord, I believe." And he ᶠworshiped Him.

¹Or, *Sir.*

Sec. 157   Spiritual blindness of the Pharisees
– Jerusalem –

John 9:39-41

39   And Jesus said, "For judgment I came into this world, that those who do not see may see; and that those who see may become blind."

40   Those of the Pharisees who were with Him heard these things, and said to Him, "We are not blind too, are we?"

41   Jesus said to them, "ᵍIf you were blind, you would have no sin; but since you say, 'We see,' your sin remains.

Sec. 158   Allegory of the Good Shepherd and the thief
– Jerusalem –

John 10:1-18

1   "Truly, truly, I say to you, ʰhe who does not enter by the door into the fold of the sheep, but climbs up some other way, he is a thief and a robber.

ᵉ(John 9:34) The excommunication so greatly feared by the parents (vv. 22-23) was here carried out against the son because of his tenacious defense of Jesus.

ᶠ(John 9:38) The man's devotion to Jesus here reaches its climax. In John's gospel the word for "worship" describes a reverence that is due God alone.

ᵍ(John 9:41) If the Pharisees had been willing to admit their spiritual blindness, they would have yearned for spiritual light and could have found forgiveness. Since they professed to see and consequently refused to acknowledge Jesus to be the Messiah, their case was hopeless. They were fully persuaded they were right and refused to learn the truth about Him. Any prospect of being freed from sin was thereby removed (cf. Matt. 9:13; Mark 2:17; Luke 5:32, Sec. 55).

ʰ(John 10:1) The occasion for this allegory was furnished by the excommunication of the blind man whom Jesus healed (John 9:34, Sec. 155). The healed man was one of the sheep who are the godly

John 10:1-18 (cont'd)

2 "But he who enters by the door is a shepherd of the sheep.

3 "To him the doorkeeper opens, and the sheep hear his voice, and he calls his own sheep by name, and leads them out.

4 "When he puts forth all his own, he goes before them, and the sheep follow him because they know his voice.

5 "And a stranger they simply will not follow, but will flee from him, because they do not know the voice of strangers."

6 This figure of speech Jesus spoke to them, but they did not understand what those things were which He had been saying to them.

7 Jesus therefore said to them again, "Truly, truly, I say to you, I am the door of the sheep.

8 "All who came before Me are thieves and robbers, but the sheep did not hear them.

9 "I am the door; if anyone enters through Me, he shall be saved, and shall go in and out, and find pasture.

10 "The thief comes only to steal, and kill, and destroy; I came that they might have life, and might [1]have *it* abundantly.

11 "I am the good shepherd; the good shepherd lays down His life for the sheep.

12 "He who is a hireling, and not a shepherd, who is not the owner of the sheep, beholds the wolf coming, and leaves the sheep, and flees, and the wolf snatches them, and scatters *them*.

13 *"He flees* because he is a hireling, and is not concerned about the sheep.

14 "I am the good shepherd; and I know My own, and My own know Me,

15 even as the Father knows Me and I know the Father; and I lay down My life for the sheep.

16 "And I have other sheep, which are not of this fold; I must bring them also, and they shall hear My voice; and they shall become one flock *with* one shepherd.

17 "For this reason the Father loves Me, because I lay down My life that I may take it again.

18 "No one [2]has taken it away from Me, but I lay it down on My own initiative. I have authority to lay it down, and I have [1]authority to take it up again. This commandment I received from My Father."

[1]Or, *have abundance.* [2]Many Greek mss. read *takes.*

Sec. 159　Further division among the Jews
　　　— Jerusalem —

John 10:19-21

19 There arose a [j]division again among the Jews because of these words.

20 And many of them were saying, "He has a demon and is insane. Why do you listen to Him?"

21 Others were saying, "These are not the sayings of one demon-possessed. A demon cannot open the eyes of the blind, can he?"

remnant of Israel, and the Pharisees were identified with the thieves (10:1, 8), the stranger (10:5), and the hireling (10:12-13). The "fold" of which He spoke (10:1, 16) represented Judaism of Christ's day from which He led the remnant (10:3). The "other sheep" (10:16) were those of the Gentile world who were to believe in Christ. "One flock" (10:16) anticipated formation of the body of Christ composed of the godly remnant of Israel and Gentile believers. Jesus is both the door of access into the flock (10:7, 9) and the Good Shepherd who cares for the flock (10:11, 14).

[1](John 10:18) Only here and in John 2:19 (Sec. 34) does Jesus claim to raise Himself or have authority to do so. Elsewhere the agent in raising the Son is always the Father.

[j](John 10:19) In John, earlier instances of such division include 6:52 (Sec. 109), 7:43 (Sec. 134), and 9:16 (Sec. 155). Jesus' function as divider of men had already become quite evident (Matt. 10:34-36, Sec. 99; Luke 12:51-53, Sec. 149).

Sec. 160   Another attempt to stone or arrest Jesus for blasphemy
– Jerusalem –

John 10:22-39

22   At that time the Feast of the Dedication took place at Jerusalem;

23   it was winter, and Jesus was walking in the temple in the portico of Solomon.

24   The Jews therefore gathered around Him, and were saying to Him, "How long will You keep us in suspense? If You are [1]the [k]Christ, tell us plainly."

25   Jesus answered them, "I told you, and you do not believe; the works that I do in My Father's name, these bear witness of Me.

26   "But you do not believe, because you are not of My sheep.

27   "My sheep hear My voice, and I know them, and they follow Me;

28   and I give eternal life to them, and they shall never perish; and no one shall snatch them out of My hand.

29   "[2]My Father, who has given *them* to Me, is greater than all; and no one is able to snatch *them* out of the Father's hand.

30   "I and the Father are [3]one."

31   The Jews took up stones again to stone Him.

32   Jesus answered them, "I showed you many good works from the Father; for which of them are you stoning Me?"

33   The Jews answered Him, "For a good work we do not stone You, but for blasphemy; and because You, being a man, make Yourself out *to be* God."

34   Jesus answered them, "Has it not been written in your Law, 'I SAID, YOU ARE GODS'? [Psalm 82:6].

35   "If he called them gods, to whom the word of God came (and the Scripture cannot be broken),

36   do you say of Him, whom the Father sanctified and sent into the world, 'You are blaspheming,' because I said, '[l]I am the Son of God'?

37   "If I do not do the works of My Father, do not believe Me;

38   but if I do them, though you do not believe Me, believe the works, that you may [4]know and understand that the Father is in Me, and I in the Father."

39   Therefore they were seeking again to seize Him, and He eluded their grasp.

[1]I.e., the Messiah.   [2]Some early mss. read *What My Father has given Me is greater than all.*   [3]Lit., (neuter) *a unity;* or, *one essence.*   [4]Lit., *know and continue knowing.*

---

[k](John 10:24) The heart of the whole dispute was whether or not Jesus was Israel's promised Messiah. As proofs that He was, Jesus offered His works (v. 25), His impartation of eternal life to His sheep (v. 28) and, as a climax, His unity with the Father (v. 30). This claim was more than His enemies could bear so they sought both to stone Him again (v. 31) and to arrest Him (v. 39).

[l](John 10:36) It is wrong to conclude that Jesus was claiming to be no more than a man among men. His words mean that if the Psalm quoted in 10:35 applies the term "gods" to men it may with even greater propriety be applied to Him who is one in essence with the Father (cf. 10:30).

PART NINE
THE MINISTRY OF CHRIST IN AND AROUND PEREA
PRINCIPLES OF DISCIPLESHIP

Sec. 161   From Jerusalem to Perea

John 10:40-42

40   And He ^mwent away again beyond the Jordan to the place where John was
first baptizing, and He was staying there.
41   And many came to Him, and were saying, "While John performed no sign,
yet everything John said about this man was true."
42   And many believed in Him there.

Sec. 162   Question about salvation and entering the Kingdom (cf. Secs. 71; 178, 179)
– Itineration toward Jerusalem while in Perea –

Luke 13:22-30

22   And He was passing through from one city and village to another, teaching, and proceeding on His way to Jerusalem.
23   And someone said to Him, "ⁿLord, are there *just* a few who are being
saved?" And He said to them,
24   "Strive to enter by the narrow door; for many, I tell you, will seek to enter
and will not be ¹able.
25   "Once the head of the house gets up and shuts the door, and you begin to
stand outside and knock on the door, saying, 'Lord, open up to us!' ²then He will
answer and say to you, 'I do not know where you are from.'
26   "Then you will begin to say, 'We ate and drank in Your presence, and You
taught in our streets';
27   and He will say, 'I tell you, I do not know where you are from; DEPART
FROM ME, ALL YOU EVILDOERS' [Psalm 6:8].
28   "There will be weeping and gnashing of teeth there when you see Abraham and Isaac and Jacob and all the prophets in the kingdom of God, but yourselves being cast out.
29   "And they will come from east and west, and from north and south, and
will recline *at the table* in the kingdom of God.
30   "And behold, *some* are last who will be first and *some* are first who will
be last."

¹Or, *able, once.*   ²Lit., *and.*

---

^m(John 10:40) The period begun by this departure lasted about three and one-half months, from the
Feast of Dedication until the week before Passover. Response to Jesus' ministry in Perea (v. 42) was in
sharp contrast to the recent response in Jerusalem (John 10:37-39, Sec. 160).

ⁿ(Luke 13:23) The question, provoked by the surprisingly small number who were following Mes-
siah faithfully, related to being saved so as to enter Messiah's Kingdom. While Jesus only implied a
positive answer here, He earlier explicitly stated, "Few are those who find it" (Matt. 7:14, Sec. 71).
Those who thought they could claim admission solely through their relation to Abraham will be excluded (Luke 13:28-29).

Sec. 163 Anticipation of His coming death and lament over Jerusalem (cf. Sec. 200)
– Itineration toward Jerusalem while in Perea –

Luke 13:31-35

31 Just at that time some Pharisees came up, saying to Him, "Go away and depart from here, for °Herod wants to kill You."

32 And He said to them, "Go and tell that fox, 'Behold, I cast out demons and perform cures today and tomorrow, and the third *day* I ¹reach My goal.'

33 "Nevertheless I ᴾmust journey on today and tomorrow and the next *day;* for it cannot be that a prophet should perish outside of Jerusalem.

34 "O Jerusalem, Jerusalem, *the city* that kills the prophets and stones those sent to her! How often I wanted to gather your children together, just as a hen *gathers* her brood under her wings, and you would not *have it!*

35 "Behold, your house is left to you ²desolate; and I say to you, you shall not see Me until *the time* comes when you say, 'BLESSED IS HE WHO COMES IN THE NAME OF THE LORD!'" [Psalm 118:26].

¹Or possibly, *am perfected.*   ²Later mss. add *desolate.*

Sec. 164 Healing of a man with dropsy while eating with a Pharisaic leader on the Sabbath (cf. Secs. 57-61, 152, 155)
– Probably in Perea –

Luke 14:1-24

1 And it came about when He went into the house of one of the ¹ᵈleaders of the Pharisees on *the* Sabbath to eat bread, that they were watching Him closely.

2 And ²there, in front of Him was a certain man suffering from dropsy.

3 And Jesus answered and spoke to the ³lawyers and Pharisees, saying, "Is it lawful to heal on the Sabbath, or not?"

4 But they kept silent. And He took hold of him, and healed him, and sent him away.

5 And He said to them, "Which one of you shall have a ⁴son or an ox fall into a well, and will not immediately pull him out on a Sabbath day?"

6 And they could make no reply to this.

7 And He *began* speaking a parable to the invited guests when He noticed ʳhow they had been picking out the places of honor *at the table;* saying to them,

8 "When you are invited by someone to a wedding feast, do not ⁵take the

°(Luke 13:31) Perea belonged to Herod Antipas' jurisdiction as did Galilee. These Pharisees sought to capitalize on Jesus' past encounters with Antipas (Sec. 104, note w) so as to force Him back into Judea where the Sanhedrin had more direct control. On the other hand, their story about Herod was not fabricated, because the Lord in His reply (vv. 32-35) refrained from denouncing them for deceit in the matter.

ᴾ(Luke 13:33) Divine decree determined that Messiah's mission would not be cut short by Herod and that His death take place in Jerusalem, not Perea. In the process of carrying out this mission, therefore, He would not flee immediately because of Herod's animosity but would remain a few days longer in Perea before resuming that journey that would eventually carry Him to His crucifixion in Jerusalem.

ᵈ(Luke 14:1) It is surprising to find Jesus eating at the home of a Pharisaic leader, in view of His recent denunciation of them (Luke 11:37-54, Sec. 145). Clearly the occasion was staged to furnish them an opportunity to watch Him (v. 1) and thereby gain evidence against Him. They wanted to catch Him in the act of breaking the Sabbath when He healed the sick man.

ʳ(Luke 14:7) Jesus used the occasion of this meal to teach three important lessons needed by those present:
1. the importance of humility instead of maneuvering to secure the places of honor (vv. 7-11);
2. the importance of impartiality in choosing whom to invite to such an occasion, (vv. 12-14; and,
3. the importance of making the Kingdom of God, viewed here as a "big dinner," one's highest priority and not forfeiting the right to enter the same (vv. 15-24).
Jesus' host and fellow guests were in need of all three lessons.

Luke 14:1-24 (cont'd)

place of honor, lest someone more distinguished than you may have been invited by him,

9   and he who invited you both shall come and say to you, 'Give place to this man,' and then in disgrace you [6]proceed to occupy the last place.

10   "But when you are invited, go and recline at the last place, so that when the one who has invited you comes, he may say to you, 'Friend, move up higher'; then you will have honor in the sight of all who [7]are at the table with you.

11   "For everyone who exalts himself shall be humbled, and he who humbles himself shall be exalted."

12   And He also went on to say to the one who had invited Him, "When you give a luncheon or a dinner, do not invite your friends or your brothers or your relatives or rich neighbors, lest they also invite you in return, and repayment come to you.

13   "But when you give a [8]reception, invite *the* poor, *the* crippled, *the* lame, *the* blind,

14   and you will be [9]blessed, since they [10]do not have *the means* to repay you; for you will be repaid at the resurrection of the righteous."

15   And when one of those who were reclining *at the table* with Him heard this, he said to Him, "Blessed is everyone who shall eat bread in the kingdom of God!"

16   But He said to him, "A certain man was giving a big dinner, and he invited many;

17   and at the dinner hour he sent his slave to say to those who had been invited, 'Come; for everything is ready now.'

18   "But they all alike began to make excuses. The first one said to him, 'I have bought a [11]piece of land and I need to go out and look at it; [12]please consider me excused.'

19   "And another one said, I have bought five yoke of oxen, and I am going to try them out; please consider me excused.'

20   "And another one said, 'I have married a wife, and for that reason I cannot come.'

21   "And the slave came *back* and reported this to his master. Then the head of the household became angry and said to his slave, 'Go out at once into the streets and lanes of the city and bring in here the poor and crippled and blind and lame.'

22   "And the slave said, 'Master, what you commanded has been done, and still there is room.'

23   "And the master said to the slave, 'Go out into the highways and along the hedges, and compel *them* to come in, that my house may be filled.

24   'For I tell you, none of those men who were invited shall taste of my dinner.'"

[1]I.e., members of the Sanhedrin.   [2]Lit., *behold.*   [3]I.e., experts in Mosaic Law.   [4]Some ancient mss. read *donkey.*   [5]Lit., *recline at.*   [6]Lit., *begin.*   [7]Lit., *recline at the table.*   [8]Or, *banquet.*   [9]Or, *happy.*   [10]Or, *are unable to.*   [11]Or, *field.*   [12]Lit., *I request you.*

Sec. 165   Cost of discipleship (cf. Secs. 66, 128; 99, 119)
    – *Probably in Perea* –

Luke 14:25-35

25   Now [s]great multitudes were going along with Him; and He turned and said to them,

[s](Luke 14:25) Jesus' ministry in Perea had attracted very wide attention. The people's persuasion that Jesus was Messiah dictated that they remain near Him, especially in light of the nearing national crisis in relation to the Kingdom of God. As He approached Jerusalem, they did not want to miss any blessings of the occasion. Jesus took this opportunity to discourage any who may have joined the throng for superficial reasons. His disciples had to be prepared to face adversity of the severest sort.

Luke 14:25-35 (cont'd)

26 "If anyone comes to Me, and does not [1]hate his own father and mother and wife and children and brothers and sisters, yes, and even his own life, he cannot be My disciple.

27 "Whoever does not carry his own cross and come after Me cannot be My disciple.

28 "For which one of you, when he wants to build a tower, does not first sit down and calculate the cost, to see if he has enough to complete it?

29 "Otherwise, when he has laid a foundation, and is not able to finish, all who observe it begin to ridicule him,

30 saying, 'This man began to build and was not able to finish.'

31 "Or what king, when he sets out to meet another king in battle, will not first sit down and take counsel whether he is strong enough with ten thousand men to encounter the one coming against him with twenty thousand?

32 "Or else, while the other is still far away, he sends [2]a delegation and asks terms of peace.

33 "So therefore, no one of you can be My disciple who does not give up all his own possessions.

34 "Therefore, salt is good; but if even salt has become tasteless, with what will it be seasoned?

35 "It is useless either for the soil or for the manure pile; [3]it is thrown out. He who has ears to hear, let him hear."

[1]I.e., by comparison of his love for Me.   [2]Or, *an embassy.*   [3]Lit., *they throw it out.*

Sec. 166   Parables in defense of associations with sinners (cf. Sec. 128)
– *Probably in Perea* –

Luke 15:1-32

1 Now all the [1]tax-gatherers and the [2]sinners were coming near Him to listen to Him.

2 And both the Pharisees and the scribes *began* to [3]grumble, saying, "'This man receives sinners and eats with them."

3 And He told them this parable, saying,

4 "What man among you, if he has a hundred sheep and has lost one of them, does not leave the ninety-nine in the [4]open pasture, and go after the one which is lost, until he finds it?

5 "And when he has found it, he lays it on his shoulders, rejoicing.

6 "And when he comes home, he calls together his friends and his neighbors, saying to them, 'Rejoice with me, for I have found my sheep which was lost!'

7 "I tell you that in the same way, there will be *more* joy in heaven over one sinner who repents, than over ninety-nine righteous persons who need no repentance.

8 "Or what woman, if she has ten [5]silver coins and loses one coin, does not light a lamp and sweep the house and search carefully until she finds it?

9 "And when she has found it, she calls together her [6]friends and neighbors, saying, 'Rejoice with me, for I have found the coin which I had lost!'

10 "In the same way, I tell you, there is joy in the presence of the angels of God over one sinner who repents."

11 And He said, "A certain man had two sons;

---

[1](Luke 15:2) At least two significant features prompted the giving of three parables:
1. The enemies of Jesus were still scrutinizing His every move with evil intent.
2. They totally lacked the loving concern of Jesus which the tax-gatherers and sinners found so appealing. They lacked the loving heart of the Father and a readiness to receive one who repents (vv. 7, 10, 20-25).

Luke 15:1-32 (cont'd)

12 and the younger of them said to his father, 'Father, give me the share of the estate that falls to me.' And he divided his [7]wealth between them.

13 "And not many days later, the younger son gathered everything together and went on a journey into a distant country, and there he squandered his estate with loose living.

14 "Now when he had spent everything, a severe famine occurred in that country, and he began to be in need.

15 "And he went and [8]attached himself to one of the citizens of that country, and he sent him into his fields to feed swine.

16 "And he was longing [9]to fill his [10]stomach with the [11]pods that the swine were eating, and no one was giving *anything* to him.

17 "But when he came to [12]his senses, he said, 'How many of my father's hired men have more than enough bread, but I am dying here with hunger!

18 'I will get up and go to my father, and will say to him, "Father, I have sinned against heaven, and [13]in your sight;

19 "I am no longer worthy to be called your son; make me as one of your hired men."'

20 "And he got up and came to [14]his father. But while he was still a long way off, his father saw him, and felt compassion *for him*, and ran and [15]embraced him, and [16]kissed him.

21 "And the son said to him, 'Father, I have sinned against heaven and in your sight; I am no longer worthy to be called your son.[17]'

22 "But the father said to his slaves, 'Quickly bring out the best robe and put it on him, and put a ring on his hand and sandals on his feet;

23 and bring the fattened calf, kill it, and let us eat and be merry;

24 for this son of mine was dead, and has come to life again; he was lost, and has been found.' And they began to be merry.

25 "Now his older son was in the field, and when he came and approached the house, he heard music and dancing.

26 "And he summoned one of the servants and *began* inquiring what these things might be.

27 "And he said to him, 'Your brother has come, and your father has killed the fattened calf, because he has received him back safe and sound.'

28 "But he became angry, and was not willing to go in; and his father came out and *began* entreating him.

29 "But he answered and said to his father, 'Look! For so many years I have been serving you, and I have never [18]neglected a command of yours; and *yet* you have never given me a [19]kid, that I might be merry with my friends;

30 but when this son of yours came, who has devoured your [7]wealth with harlots, you killed the fattened calf for him.'

31 "And he said to him, 'My child, you [20]have always been with me, and all that is mine is yours.

32 'But [21]we had to be merry and rejoice, for this brother of yours was dead and *has* begun to live, and *was* lost and has been found.'"

[1]I.e., Collectors of Roman taxes for profit. [2]I.e., irreligious or non-practicing Jews. [3]Lit., *grumble among themselves*. [4]Lit., *wilderness*. [5]Gr., *drachmas*, one drachma was equivalent to a day's wages. [6]Lit., *women friends and neighbors*. [7]Lit., *living*. [8]Lit., *was joined to*. [9]Some mss. read *to be satisfied with*. [10]Lit., *belly*. [11]I.e., of the carob tree. [12]Lit., *himself*. [13]Lit., *before you*. [14]Lit., *his own*. [15]Lit., *fell on his neck*. [16]Lit., *kissed him again and again*. [17]Some ancient mss. add *make me as one of your hired men*. [18]Or, *disobeyed*. [19]Or, *young goat*. [20]Lit., *are always with me*. [21]Lit., *it was necessary*.

Sec. 167 Parable to teach the proper use of money (cf. Sec. 70)
  – *Probably in Perea* –

Luke 16:1-13

1 Now He was also saying to the disciples, "There was a certain rich man who had a steward, and this *steward* was [1]reported to him as squandering his possessions.

2 "And he called him and said to him, 'What is this I hear about you? Give an account of your stewardship, for you can no longer be steward.'

3 "And the steward said to himself, 'What shall I do, since my [2]master is taking the stewardship away from me? I am not strong enough to dig; I am ashamed to beg.

4 'I [3]know what I shall do, so that when I am removed from the stewardship, they will receive me into their homes.'

5 "And he summoned each one of his [4]master's debtors, and he *began* saying to the first, 'How much do you owe my master?'

6 "And he said, 'A hundred [5]measures of oil.' And he said to him, 'Take your bill, and sit down quickly and write fifty.'

7 "Then he said to another, 'And how much do you owe?' And he said, 'A hundred [6]measures of wheat.' He *said to him, 'Take your bill, and write eighty.'

8 "And his [2]master praised the unrighteous steward because he had acted shrewdly; for the sons of this age are more shrewd in relation to their own [7]kind than the sons of light.

9 "And I say to you, [u]make friends for yourselves by means of the [8]mammon of unrighteousness; that when it fails, they may receive you into the eternal dwellings.

10 "He who is faithful in a very little thing is faithful also in much; and he who is unrighteous in a very little thing is unrighteous also in much.

11 "If therefore you have not been faithful in the use *of* unrighteous [8]mammon, who will entrust the true *riches* to you?

12 "And if you have not been faithful in *the use of* that which is another's, who will give you that which is [9]your own?

13 "No [10]servant can serve two masters; for either he will hate the one, and love the other, or else he will hold to one, and despise the other. You cannot serve God and [8]mammon."

[1]Or, *accused.* [2]Or, *lord.* [3]Lit., *have come to the knowledge of.* [4]Or, *lord's.* [5]Gr., *baths,* one bath equals between 8 and 9 gal. [6]Gr., *kors,* one kor equals between 10 and 12 bu. [7]Lit., *generation.* [8]Or, *riches.* [9]Some mss. read *our own.* [10]Or, *house-servant.*

Sec. 168   Story to teach the danger of wealth (cf. Secs. 67; 68, 176)
– Probably in Perea –

Luke 16:14-31

14 [v]Now the Pharisees, who were lovers of money, were listening to all these things, and they were scoffing at Him.

15 And He said to them, "You are those who justify yourselves [1]in the sight of men, but God knows your hearts; for that which is [2]highly esteemed among men is detestable [3]in the sight of God.

[u](Luke 16:9) The wisdom of using material possessions to provide for the future is commended but not the dishonesty by which the steward procured the possessions. Money in itself is not sinful. Money can be used to bring blessing to others and thereby make provision for a warm welcome by others in an eternal home. Thereby perishable riches can be transformed into imperishable heavenly treasures.

[v](Luke 16:14) This highly condensed paragraph (vv. 14-18) introduces the story of the rich man and Lazarus. The avaricious Pharisees were addressed because of their reaction to His words to the disciples about mammon (Luke 16:13, Sec. 167). He therefore spoke to the Pharisees in light of their persuasion that God had given them their wealth because they carefully kept the Law. Their system of external observances did not satisfy God (v. 15) but amounted to an attempt to force their way into the Kindgom of God (v. 16). By breaking the Law through such traditions as those which permitted divorce, they endeavored to change statutes which cannot be changed (vv. 17-18). Riches therefore were not a sign of God's favor as the following story goes on to show (vv. 19-31).

Luke 16:14-31 (cont'd)

16 "The Law and the Prophets *were* proclaimed until John; since then the gospel of the kingdom of God is preached, and everyone is forcing his way into it.

17 "But it is easier for heaven and earth to pass away than for one [4]stroke of a letter of the Law to fail.

18 "Everyone who divorces his wife and marries another commits adultery; and he who marries one who is divorced from a husband commits adultery.

19 "Now there was a certain rich man, and he habitually dressed in purple and fine linen, gaily living in splendor every day.

20 "And a certain poor man named [w]Lazarus was laid at his gate, covered with sores,

21 and longing to be fed with the *crumbs* which were falling from the rich man's table; besides, even the dogs were coming and licking his sores.

22 "Now it came about that the poor man died and he was carried away by the angels to Abraham's bosom; and the rich man also died and was buried.

23 "And in [x]Hades [5]he lifted up his eyes, being in torment, and *saw Abraham far away, and Lazarus in his bosom.

24 "And he cried out and said, 'Father Abraham, have mercy on me, and send Lazarus, that he may dip the tip of his finger in water and cool off my tongue; for I am in agony in this flame.'

25 "But Abraham said, 'Child, remember that during your life you received your good things, and likewise Lazarus bad things; but now he is being comforted here, and you are in agony.

26 'And [6]besides all this, between us and you there is a great chasm fixed, in order that those who wish to come over from here to you may not be able, and *that* none may cross over from there to us.'

27 "And he said, 'Then I beg you, Father, that you send him to my father's house —

28 for I have five brothers—that he may warn them, lest they also come to this place of torment.'

29 "But Abraham *said, 'They have Moses and the Prophets; let them hear them.'

30 "But he said, 'No, Father Abraham, but if someone goes to them from the dead, they will repent!'

31 "But he said to him, 'If they do not listen to Moses and the Prophets, neither will they be persuaded if someone rises from the dead.'"

[1]Lit., *before men.* [2]Lit., *high.* [3]Lit., *before God.* [4]I.e., projection of a letter (serif). [5]Lit., *having lifted up.* [6]Lit., *in all these things.*

Sec. 169   Four lessons on discipleship (cf. Sec. 128)
  – Probably in Perea –

Luke 17:1-10

1 And He said to His disciples, "It is inevitable that [1]stumbling blocks should come, but [y]woe to him through whom they come!

[w](Luke 16:20) Nowhere else does Jesus use a person's name in a parable. This story is often referred to as a parable, but is nowhere in the biblical text called one. It is therefore impossible to be sure that it was a parable and not a real happening.

[x](Luke 16:23) Hades in the New Testament is the abode of souls loosed from their bodies at death. For the ungodly it is a place of temporary retribution until their bodies are raised for judgment at the great white throne (Rev. 20:11-15). In this incident representing conditions before the resurrection of Christ, the godly are not specifically connected with Hades, but they are pictured in a state of rest in the underworld where Hades is located (Luke 16:26). Jesus was in Hades between His death and resurrection (Acts 2:27, 31). Since His resurrection, the godly are always found in His immediate presence (Phil. 1:23).

[y](Luke 17:1) The first of the four lessons is a warning against causing others to sin (vv. 1-2). The

Luke 17:1-10 (cont'd)

2 "It would be better for him if a millstone were hung around his neck and he were thrown into the sea, than that he should cause one of these [2]little ones to stumble.

3 "[3]Be on your guard! If your brother sins, rebuke him; and if he repents, forgive him.

4 "And if he sins against you seven times a day, and returns to you seven times, saying, 'I repent,' [4]forgive him."

5 And the apostles said to the Lord, "Increase our faith!"

6 And the Lord said, "If you had faith like a mustard seed, you would say to this mulberry tree, 'Be uprooted and be planted in the sea'; and it would [5]obey you.

7 "But which of you, having a slave plowing or tending sheep, will say to him when he has come in from the field, 'Come immediately and [6]sit down to eat'?

8 "But will he not say to him, 'Prepare something for me to eat, and properly [7]clothe yourself and serve me until I have eaten and drunk; and [8]afterward you will eat and drink'?

9 "He does not thank the slave because he did the things which were commanded, does he?

10 "So you too, when you do all the things which are commanded you, say, 'We are unworthy slaves; we have done *only* that which we ought to have done.'"

[1]Or, *temptations to sin.* [2]I.e., humble. [3]Lit., *Take heed to yourselves.* [4]Lit., *you shall forgive.* [5]Or, *have obeyed.* [6]Lit., *recline.* [7]Lit., *gird.* [8]Lit., *after these things.*

RAISING OF LAZARUS AND A BRIEF TOUR THROUGH SAMARIA AND GALILEE

Sec. 170   Sickness and death of Lazarus
– From Perea to Bethany near Jerusalem –

John 11:1-16

1 Now a certain man was sick, Lazarus of Bethany, of the village of Mary and her sister Martha.

2 And it was the Mary who anointed the Lord with ointment, and wiped His feet with her hair, whose brother Lazarus was sick.

3 The sisters therefore sent to Him, saying, "Lord, behold, he whom You love is sick."

4 But when Jesus heard it, He said, "This sickness is not unto death, but for the glory of God, that the Son of God may be glorified by it."

5 Now Jesus loved Martha, and her sister, and Lazarus.

6 When [2]therefore He heard that he was sick, He stayed then two days *longer* in the place where He was.

7 Then after this He *said to the disciples, "Let us go to Judea again."

---

other three deal with the duty of forgiving a repentant brother (vv. 3-4), the power of faith (vv. 5-6), and the insufficiency of works to gain special honor (vv. 7-10).

[2](John 11:6) Four unusual uses of the Greek particle *oun* mark the incident involving Lazarus. They apparently indicate four steps by which Jesus followed a sequence predetermined by the Father in carrying out this miracle:
1. "Therefore" in verse 6 shows how He purposely delayed going to the scene.
2. "So" in verse 17 (Sec. 171) indicates the plan was for Him to arrive four days after the death.
3. "Therefore" in verse 33 (Sec. 171) points out His appointed response to the bereaved.
4. "Therefore" in verse 38 (Sec. 171) shows the final step of going to the tomb to accomplish the miracle.
This procedure was clearly designed to bring glory to God and His Son (v. 4).

John 11:1-16 (cont'd)

8   The disciples *said to Him, "Rabbi, [a]the Jews were just now seeking to stone You, and are You going there again?"

9   Jesus answered, "Are there not twelve hours in the day? If anyone walks in the day, he does not stumble, because he sees the light of this world.

10   "But if anyone walks in the night, he stumbles, because the light is not in him."

11   This He said, and after that He *said to them, "Our friend Lazarus has fallen asleep; but I go, that I may awaken him out of sleep."

12   The disciples therefore said to Him, "Lord, if he has fallen asleep, he will [1]recover."

13   Now Jesus had spoken of his death, but they thought that He was speaking of [2]literal sleep.

14   Then Jesus therefore said to them plainly, "Lazarus is dead,

15   and I am glad for your sakes that I was not there, so that you may believe; but let us go to him."

16   Thomas therefore, who is called [3]Didymus, said to his fellow disciples, "Let us also go, that we may die with Him."

[1]Lit., *be saved.*   [2]Lit., *the slumber of sleep.*   [3]I.e., the Twin.

Sec. 171   Lazarus raised from the dead
– Bethany near Jerusalem –

John 11:17-44

17   So when Jesus came, He found that he had already been in the tomb four days.

18   Now Bethany was near Jerusalem, about [1]two miles off;

19   and many of the Jews had come to Martha and Mary, to console them concerning their brother.

20   Martha therefore, when she heard that Jesus was coming, went to meet Him; but Mary still sat in the house.

21   Martha therefore said to Jesus, "Lord, if You had been here, my brother would not have died.

22   "Even now I know that whatever You ask of God, God will give You."

23   Jesus *said to her, "Your brother shall rise again."

24   Martha *said to Him, "I know that he will rise again in the resurrection on the last day."

25   Jesus said to her, "I am the resurrection and the life; he who believes in Me shall live even if he dies,

26   and everyone who lives and believes in Me shall never die. Do you believe this?"

27   She *said to Him, "Yes, Lord; [b]I have believed that You are [2]the Christ, the Son of God, even [3]He who comes into the world."

28   And when she had said this, she went away, and called Mary her sister, saying secretly, "The Teacher is here, and is calling for you."

29   And when she heard it, she *arose quickly, and was coming to Him.

30   Now Jesus had not yet come into the village, but was still in the place where Martha met Him.

[a](John 11:8) Bethany was only about two miles from Jerusalem, and the disciples remembered the recent attempted stoning in Jerusalem (John 10:31, Sec. 160). Jesus' response was that He, like everyone else, had to use His opportunities while present or else lose them. Danger could not be a deterrent.

[b](John 11:27) Whatever fault she may have had (cf. Luke 10:41, Sec. 142), Martha was a woman of faith in and conviction about the person of Christ. Her threefold confession here represents the highest view of Him one can hold.

John 11:17-44 (cont'd)

31   The Jews then who were with her in the house, and consoling her, when they saw that Mary rose up quickly and went out, followed her, supposing that she was going to the tomb to [4]weep there.

32   Therefore, when Mary came where Jesus was, she saw Him, and fell at His feet, saying to Him, "Lord, if You had been here, my brother would not have died."

33   When Jesus therefore saw her weeping, and the Jews who came with her, *also* [5]weeping, He was deeply moved in spirit, and [6]was troubled,

34   and said, "Where have you laid him?" They *said to Him, "Lord, come and see."

35   [c]Jesus wept.

36   And so the Jews were saying, "Behold how He [7]loved him!"

37   But some of them said, "Could not this man, who opened the eyes of him who was blind, [8]have kept this man also from dying?"

38   Jesus therefore again being deeply moved within, *came to the tomb. Now it was a cave, and a stone was lying against it.

39   Jesus *said, "Remove the stone." Martha, the sister of the deceased, *said to Him, "Lord, by this time [9]there will be a stench; for he has been *dead* four days."

40   Jesus *said to her, "Did I not say to you, if you believe, you will see the glory of God?"

41   And so they removed the stone. And Jesus raised His eyes, and said, "Father, I thank Thee that Thou heardest Me.

42   "And I knew that Thou hearest Me always; but because of the people standing around I said it, that they may believe that Thou didst send Me."

43   And when He had said these things, He cried out with a loud voice, "Lazarus, come forth."

44   [d]He who had died came forth, bound hand and foot with wrappings; and his face was wrapped around with a cloth. Jesus *said to them, "Unbind him, and let him go."

[1]I.e., 15 stadia (9,090 ft.).   [2]I.e., the Messiah.   [3]The Coming One was the Messianic title.   [4]Lit., *wail.*   [5]Lit., *wailing.*   [6]Lit., *troubled Himself.*   [7]Lit., *was loving.*   [8]Lit., *have caused that this man also not die.*   [9]Lit., *he stinks.*

Sec. 172   Decision of the Sanhedrin to put Jesus to death
— Jerusalem and [e]Ephraim near the wilderness —

John 11:45-54

45   Many therefore of the Jews, who had come to Mary and beheld what He had done, believed in Him.

---

[c](John 11:35) This verse has been subjected to a wide variety of interpretations. Certainly He did not weep because of the loss of Lazarus whom He was about to raise. His intense emotion (cf. v. 33) probably related somehow to the dominance of sin in these surroundings. Through sin death had gained its power. Through it the mourners were misguided in their concept of death. Because of it He was about to call Lazarus from a far better existence back to mortality. Because of it Jesus Himself became a criminal in the eyes of the authorities (Sec. 172). It is no wonder that John used a word usually reserved for anger when describing His response to the situation ("was deeply moved," v. 33).

[d](John 11:44) It has been of great concern to many that the synoptic gospels say nothing of this highly significant miracle. For some reason the synoptic writers pass over other significant Jerusalem miracles (Secs. 57, 153) too. They are likewise noticeably silent about other happenings that came one to two months before Passion Week. Apparently they felt that the two resurrections already recorded (Secs. 74, 95) were sufficient to show Jesus' power over death.

[e]Ephraim was probably in northern Judea and near the rough terrain (wilderness) that leads down to the Jordan Valley.

John 11:45-54 (cont'd)

46 But some of them went away to the Pharisees, and told them the things which Jesus had done.

47 Therefore the ʳchief priests and the Pharisees convened a council, and were saying, "What are we doing? For this man is performing many ¹signs.

48 "If we let Him go on like this, all men will believe in Him, and the Romans will come and take away both our place and our nation."

49 But a certain one of them, Caiaphas, who was high priest that year, said to them, "You know nothing at all,

50 nor do you take into account that ᵍit is expedient for you that one man should die for the people, and that the whole nation should not perish."

51 Now this he did not say ²on his own initiative; but being high priest that year, he prophesied that Jesus was going to die for the nation,

52 and not for the nation only, but that He might also gather together into one the children of God who are scattered abroad.

53 So from that day on ʰthey planned together to kill Him.

54 Jesus therefore no longer continued to walk publicly among the Jews, but went away from there to the country near the wilderness, into a city called Ephraim; and there He stayed with the disciples.

¹Or, *attesting miracles.* ²Lit., *from himself.*

Sec. 173   Healing of ten lepers while passing through Samaria and Galilee

Luke 17:11-21

11 And it came about while He was on the way to Jerusalem, that He was passing ¹ⁱbetween Samaria and Galilee.

12 And as He entered a certain village, ten leprous men who stood at a distance met Him;

13 and they raised their voices, saying, "Jesus, Master, have mercy on us!"

14 And when He saw them, He said to them, "Go and show yourselves to the priests." And it came about that as they were going, they were cleansed.

15 Now one of them, when he saw that he had been healed, turned back, glorifying God with a loud voice,

16 and he fell on his face at His feet, giving thanks to Him. And he was a Samaritan.

17 And Jesus answered and said, "Were there not ten cleansed? But the nine—where are they?

ʳ(John 11:47) The chief priests belonged to the Sadducean hierarchy which took the lead in opposing Jesus from this point until the end. (The Pharisees had now become secondary opponents.) Now that the resurrection of a dead person had become the center of attention in Jerusalem, the Sadducees could do no other because of their teaching which denied resurrection.

ᵍ(John 11:50) As Caiaphas intended them, these words meant that Jesus must be put to death for his privileged class of Jews to maintain its authority under Roman occupation. But John observes that God, because of Caiaphas' high priestly office, was using his cynicism to voice something altogether different. Unwittingly the high priest predicted the substitutionary death of Christ for Israel and for all Gentiles who were destined to believe in Him (vv. 51-52; cf. John 10:16, Sec. 158).

ʰ(John 11:53) This occasion marked the official agreement of the Sanhedrin (cf. v. 47) to have Jesus executed, even though this may well have not been a formal meeting of the council. On the basis of Caiaphas' advice, these leaders came to a settled decision as to what must be done to rid themselves of this rival authority figure.

ⁱ(Luke 17:11) This verse may be translated so as to indicate either that Jesus passed between Samaria and Galilee, or that He passed through Samaria and Galilee. It is difficult to know what the former might mean, except perhaps that it might describe a journey through a stretch of disputed territory between Samaria and Galilee. The editors prefer the translation "through." It fits best the probable sequence, so far as it can be reconstructed. Jesus had gone to Ephraim, a city in a remote northern district of Judea and near Samaria (Sec. 172). From there He went through Samaria and Galilee, probably to join the pilgrims traveling from Galilee, through Perea, to Jerusalem for the Passover. This explains why He would go north (through Samaria and Galilee) to go south (to Jerusalem).

Luke 17:11-21 (cont'd)

18 "[2]Was no one found who turned back to give glory to God, except this foreigner?"

19 And He said to him, "Rise, and go your way; your faith [3]has made you well."

20 Now having been questioned by the Pharisees as to when the kingdom of God was coming, He answered them and said, "The kingdom of God is not coming with [4]signs to be observed;

21 nor will they say, 'Look, here it is!' or, 'There it is!' For behold, the kingdom of God is [5]jin your midst."

[1]Lit., through the midst of; or, along the borders of.   [2]Lit., Were there not found those who.   [3]Or, has saved you.   [4]Lit., observation.   [5]Or, within you.

Sec. 174 Instructions regarding the Son of Man's coming (cf. Secs. 204-206)
– Samaria or Galilee –

Luke 17:22-37

22 And He said to the disciples, "The days shall come when you will long to see one of the days of the Son of Man, and you will not see it.

23 "And they will say to you, 'Look there! Look here!' Do not go away, and do not run after them.

24 "For just as the lightning, when it flashes out of one part of the sky, shines to the other part [1]of the sky, so will the Son of Man be in His day.

25 "But first He must suffer many things and be rejected by this generation.

26 "And just as it happened in the days of Noah, so it shall be also in the days of the Son of Man:

27 they were eating, they were drinking, they were marrying, they were being given in marriage, until the day that Noah entered the ark, and the flood came and destroyed them all.

28 "[2]It was the same as happened in the days of Lot: they were eating, they were drinking, they were buying, they were selling, they were planting, they were building;

29 but on the day that Lot went out from Sodom it rained fire and [3]brimstone from heaven and destroyed them all.

30 "It will be [4]just the same on the day that the Son of Man is revealed.

31 "On that day, let not the one who is on the housetop and whose goods are in the house go down to take them away; and likewise let not the one who is in the field turn back.

32 "Remember Lot's wife.

33 "Whoever seeks to keep his [5]life shall lose it, and whoever loses his life shall preserve it.

34 "I tell you, on that night there will be two men in one bed; [k]one will be taken, and the other will be left.

35 "There will be two women grinding at the same place; [k]one will be taken, and the other will be left.

---

[j](Luke 17:21) The Kingdom of God was certainly not "within" the Pharisees who were the ones addressed, though usage of the expression permits this meaning. The historical situation requires a reference to the Kingdom as present "among" the Pharisees. This is the Kingdom whose arrival Jesus had already announced (Matt. 12:28, Sec. 79; Luke 11:20, Sec. 144), but that for the present was found in a form not predicted in the Old Testament (Matt. 13:1-52, Secs. 82-92) because of His rejection by Israel. In subsequent verses Jesus proceeds to speak of the coming of the Kingdom as the disciples knew it from the Old Testament (Sec. 174). This would come only after the Son of Man's rejection by that generation, however (Luke 17:24-25, Sec. 174).

[k](Luke 17:34-35) A final separation will come when the Son of Man is revealed. The unprepared, who are dominated by worldly pursuits, will be overtaken by judgment as in the illustrations above (vv. 26-29, 32), but the faithful will enter the joys of the Kingdom.

Luke 17:22-37 (cont'd)

36 6["Two men will be in the field; one will be taken and the other will be left."]

37 And answering they *said to Him, "Where, Lord?" And He said to them, "Where the body *is*, there also will the 7vultures be gathered."

¹Lit., *under heaven.* ²Lit., *In the same way as.* ³Or, *sulphur.* ⁴Lit., *according to the same things.* ⁵Or, *soul.* ⁶Many mss. do not contain this v. ⁷Or, *eagles.*

TEACHING WHILE ON FINAL JOURNEY TO JERUSALEM

Sec. 175 Two parables on prayer: the importunate widow and the Pharisee and the publican (cf. Secs. 69; 143)
   – Itineration toward Jerusalem –

Luke 18:1-14

1 Now He was telling them a parable to show that at all times they ought to pray and not to lose heart,

2 saying, "There was in a certain city a judge who did not fear God, and did not respect man.

3 "And there was a widow in that city, and she kept coming to him, saying, '¹Give me legal protection from my opponent.'

4 "And for a while he was unwilling; but afterward he said to himself, 'Even though I do not fear God nor respect man,

5 yet because this widow bothers me, I will ²give her legal protection, lest by continually coming she ³wear me out.'"

6 And the Lord said, "Hear what the unrighteous judge *said;

7 now shall not God bring about justice for His elect, who cry to Him day and night, ⁴and will He delay long over them?

8 "I tell you that ¹He will bring about justice for them speedily. However, when the Son of Man comes, will He find ⁵faith on the earth?"

9 And He also told this parable to ᵐcertain ones who trusted in themselves that they were righteous, and viewed others with contempt:

10 "Two men went up into the temple to pray, one a Pharisee, and the other a ⁶tax-gatherer.

11 "The Pharisee stood and was praying thus to himself, 'God, I thank Thee that I am not like other people: swindlers, unjust, adulterers, or even like this ⁶tax-gatherer.

12 'I fast twice a week; I pay tithes of all that I get.'

13 "But the ⁶tax-gatherer, standing some distance away, was even unwilling to lift up his eyes to heaven, but was beating his breast, saying, 'God, be ⁷merciful to me, the sinner!'

14 "I tell you, this man went down to his house justified rather than the other; for everyone who exalts himself shall be humbled, but he who humbles himself shall be exalted."

¹Lit., *Do me justice.* ²Lit., *do her justice.* ³Lit., *hit me under the eye.* ⁴Or, *and yet He is longsuffering over them.* ⁵Lit., *the faith.* ⁶I.e., *Collector of Roman taxes for profit.* ⁷Or, *propitious.*

---

¹(Luke 18:8) Continuing the theme of the previous section (Sec. 174), the Lord went on to prepare His disciples for a delay in His return. The parable taught them not to be discouraged by the delay but to persist in faith and prayer, knowing that He will certainly return to institute justice speedily.

ᵐ(Luke 18:9) The parable was probably addressed to Pharisees, perhaps the ones who had asked a little while earlier when the Kingdom of God was coming (Luke 17:20, Sec. 173). Their proud attitude completely hindered their prayers being heard. Such as the publican, on the other hand, were heard because of their humility.

Sec. 176   Conflict with the Pharisaic teaching on divorce (cf. Secs. 68, 168)
  – Perea –

Matt. 19:1-12

1 And it came about that when Jesus had finished these words, He departed from Galilee, and came into the region of Judea beyond the Jordan;

2 and great multitudes followed Him, and He healed them there.

3 And *some* Pharisees came to Him, testing Him, and saying, "Is it lawful *for a man* to divorce his wife for any cause at all?"

4 And He answered and said,

"Have you not read, that He who created *them* from the beginning MADE THEM MALE AND FEMALE" [Gen. 1:27; 5:2],

5 and said, 'FOR THIS CAUSE A MAN SHALL LEAVE HIS FATHER AND MOTHER, AND SHALL CLEAVE TO HIS WIFE; AND THE TWO SHALL BECOME ONE FLESH'? [Gen. 2:24].

6 "Consequently they are no longer two, but one flesh. What therefore God has joined together, let no man separate."

7 They *said to Him, "[n]Why then did Moses command to GIVE HER A CERTIFICATE OF DIVORCE AND SEND her AWAY?" [Deut. 24:1-4].

8 He *said to them, "[1]Because of your hardness of heart, Moses permitted you to divorce your wives; but from the beginning it has not been this way.

9 "And I say to you, whoever divorces his wife, except for [2]immorality, and marries another woman [3]commits adultery[4]."

10 The disciples *said to Him, "If the relationship of the man with his wife is like this, it is better not to marry."

11 But He said to them, "Not all men *can* accept this statement, but *only* those to whom it has been given.

12 "For there are eunuchs who were born that way from their mother's womb;

Mark 10:1-12

1 And rising up, He *went from there to the region of Judea, and beyond the Jordan; and crowds *gathered around Him again, and, according to His custom, He once more *began* to teach them.

2 And *some* Pharisees came up to Him, testing Him, and *began* to question Him whether it was lawful for a man to divorce a wife.

3 And He answered and said to them, "What did Moses command you?"

4 And they said, "Moses permitted *a man* TO WRITE A CERTIFICATE OF DIVORCE AND [5]SEND her AWAY" [Deut. 24:1-4].

5 But Jesus said to them, "[1]Because of your hardness of heart he wrote you this commandment.

6 "But from the beginning of creation, *God* MADE THEM MALE AND FEMALE [Gen. 1:27; 5:2].

7 "FOR THIS CAUSE A MAN SHALL LEAVE HIS FATHER AND MOTHER[6],

8 AND THE TWO SHALL BECOME ONE FLESH [Gen. 2:24]; consequently they are no longer two, but one flesh.

9 "What therefore God has joined together, let no man separate."

10 And in the house the disciples *began* questioning Him about this again.

11 And He *said to them, "Whoever divorces his wife and marries another woman commits adultery against her;

12 and if she herself divorces her husband and marries another man, she is committing adultery."

---

[n](Matt. 19:7) In light of Jesus' view of the indissolubility of the marriage union, His enemies thought they had finally caught Him teaching contrary to Moses. Jesus easily relieved the contradiction, however, by showing that Moses only permitted divorce because of the moral insensitivity that prevailed following the slavery in Egypt. The Pharisees gave more attention to the *concession* of Deuteronomy 24:1-4 than they did to the *institution* of marriage of Genesis 2:24. Moses commanded the latter (Mark 10:3), but he only permitted the former (Matt. 19:8).

Matt. 19:1-12 (cont'd)

and there are eunuchs who were made eunuchs by men; and there are *also* eunuchs who made themselves eunuchs for the sake of the kingdom of heaven. He who is able to accept *this*, let him accept *it*."

¹Or, *With reference to.* ²I.e., sexual immorality. ³Some early mss. read *makes her commit adultery.* ⁴Some early mss. add *and he who marries a divorced woman commits adultery.* ⁵Or, *divorce her.* ⁶Some mss. add *and shall cleave to his wife.*

Sec. 177 Example of little children in relation to the Kingdom (cf. Sec. 127)
— *Perea* —

Matt. 19:13-15	Mark 10:13-16	Luke 18:15-17
13 Then *some* children were brought to Him so that He might lay His hands on them and pray; and the disciples rebuked them. **14** But Jesus said, "'Let the children alone, and do not hinder them from coming to Me; for the kingdom of heaven belongs to such as these." **15** And after laying His hands on them, He departed from there.	**13** And they were bringing children to Him so that He might touch them; and the disciples rebuked them. **14** But when Jesus saw this, He was indignant and said to them, "Permit the children to come to Me; do not hinder them; for the kingdom of God belongs to such as these. **15** "Truly I say to you, whoever does not receive the kingdom of God like a child shall not enter it *at all.*" **16** And He took them in His arms and *began* blessing them, laying His hands upon them.	**15** And they were bringing even their babies to Him so that He might touch them, but when the disciples saw it, they *began* rebuking them. **16** But Jesus called for them, saying, "Permit the children to come to Me, and do not hinder them, for the kingdom of God belongs to such as these. **17** "Truly I say to you, whoever does not receive the kingdom of God like a child shall not enter it *at all.*"

¹Or, *Permit the children.*

Sec. 178 Riches and the Kingdom (cf. Secs. 162, 179)
— *Perea* —

Matt. 19:16-30	Mark 10:17-31	Luke 18:18-30
16 And behold, one came to Him and said, "Teacher, what good thing shall I do that I may obtain eternal life?" **17** And He said to him, "Why are you asking Me about what is good? There is *only* One who is good;	**17** And as He was setting out on a journey, a man ran up to Him and knelt before Him, and *began* asking Him, "Good Teacher, what shall I do to inherit eternal life?" **18** And Jesus said to him, "Why do you call Me	**18** And a certain ruler questioned Him, saying, "Good Teacher, what shall I do to inherit eternal life?" **19** And Jesus said to him, "Why do you call Me good? No one is good except God alone.

Matt. 19:16-30
(cont'd)

but if you wish to enter into life, keep the commandments."

18 He *said to Him, "Which ones?" And Jesus said, "YOU SHALL NOT COMMIT MURDER; YOU SHALL NOT COMMIT ADULTERY; YOU SHALL NOT STEAL; YOU SHALL NOT BEAR FALSE WITNESS;

19 HONOR YOUR FATHER AND MOTHER [Exod. 20:12-16; Deut. 5:16-20]; and YOU SHALL LOVE YOUR NEIGHBOR AS YOURSELF" [Lev. 19:18].

20 The young man *said to Him, "All these things I have kept; what am I still lacking?"

21 Jesus said to him, "If you wish to be [1]complete, go and sell your possessions and give to the poor, and you shall have treasure in heaven; and come, follow Me."

22 But when the young man heard this statement, he went away grieved; for he was one who owned much property.

23 And Jesus said to His disciples, "Truly I say to you, it is hard for a rich man to enter the kingdom of heaven.

24 "And again I say to you, it is easier for a camel to go through the eye of a needle, than for a rich man to enter the kingdom of God."

25 And when the disciples heard this, they

Mark 10:17-31
(cont'd)

good? No one is good except God alone.

19 "You know the commandments, 'DO NOT MURDER, DO NOT COMMIT ADULTERY, DO NOT STEAL, DO NOT BEAR FALSE WITNESS, Do not defraud, HONOR YOUR FATHER AND MOTHER'" [Exod. 20:12-16; Deut. 5:16-20].

20 And he said to Him, "Teacher, I have kept all these things from my youth up."

21 And looking at him, Jesus felt a love for him, and said to him, "One thing you lack: go and sell all you possess, and give to the poor, and you shall have treasure in heaven; and come, follow Me."

22 But at these words [5]his face fell, and he went away grieved, for he was one who owned much property.

23 And Jesus, looking around, *said to His disciples, "How hard it will be for those who are wealthy to enter the kingdom of God!"

24 And the disciples were amazed at His words. But Jesus *answered again and *said to them, "Children, how hard it is [6]to enter the kingdom of God!

25 "It is easier for a camel to go through the eye of [7]a needle than for a rich man to enter the kingdom of God."

26 And they were [0]even more astonished and said [8]to Him, "[9]Then

---

Luke 18:18-30
(cont'd)

20 "You know the commandments,

'DO NOT COMMIT ADULTERY, DO NOT MURDER, DO NOT STEAL, DO NOT BEAR FALSE WITNESS, HONOR YOUR FATHER AND MOTHER'" [Exod. 20:12-16; Deut. 5:16-20].

21 And he said, "All these things I have kept from my youth."

22 And when Jesus heard this, He said to him, "One thing you still lack; sell all that you possess, and distribute it to the poor, and you shall have treasure in heaven; and come, follow Me."

23 But when he had heard these things, he became very sad; for he was extremely rich.

24 And Jesus looked at him and said, "How hard it is for those who are wealthy to enter the kingdom of God!

25 "For it is easier for a camel to [11]go through the

Matt. 19:16-30 (cont'd)	Mark 10:17-31 (cont'd)	Luke 18:18-30 (cont'd)
were °very astonished and said, "Then who can be saved?"	who can be saved?"	eye of a needle, than for a rich man to enter the kingdom of God."
26 And looking upon *them* Jesus said to them, "With men this is impossible, but with God all things are possible."	**27** Looking upon them, Jesus *said, "With men it is impossible, but not with God; for all things are possible with God."	**26** And they who heard it said, "⁹Then who can be saved?"
27 Then Peter answered and said to Him, "Behold, we have left everything and followed You; what then will there be for us?"	**28** Peter began to say to Him, "Behold, we have left everything and followed You."	**27** But He said, "The things impossible with men are possible with God."
28 And Jesus said to them, "Truly I say to you, that you who have followed Me, in the ᵖregeneration when the Son of Man will sit on ²His glorious throne, you also shall sit upon twelve thrones, judging the twelve tribes of Israel.	**29** Jesus said, "Truly I say to you,	**28** And Peter said, "Behold, we have left ¹²our own *homes*, and followed You."
29 "And everyone who has left houses or brothers or sisters or father or mother³ or children or farms for My name's sake, shall receive ⁴many times as much,	there is no one who has left house or brothers or sisters or mother or father or children or farms, for My sake and for the gospel's sake,	**29** And He said to them, "Truly I say to you, there is no one who has left house or wife or brothers or parents or children, for the sake of the kingdom of God,
	30 but that he shall receive a hundred times as much now in the ¹⁰present age, houses and brothers and sisters and mothers and children and farms, along with persecutions;	**30** who shall not receive many times as much at this time and in the age to come, eternal life."
and shall inherit eternal life.	and in the age to come, eternal life.	
30 "But many *who are* first will be last; and *the* last, first.	**31** "But many *who are* first, will be last; and the last, first."	

¹Or, *perfect.* ²Lit., *the throne of His glory.* ³Many mss. add *or wife.* ⁴Many mss. read *a hundredfold.* ⁵Or, *he became gloomy.* ⁶Later mss. insert *for those who trust in wealth.* ⁷Lit., *the.* ⁸Later mss. read *to one another.* ⁹Lit., *And.* ¹⁰Lit., *this time.* ¹¹Lit., *enter.* ¹²Lit., *our own things.*

°(Matt. 19:25; Mark 10:26) It was inconceivable in contemporary Judaism that wealth should be a hindrance to entering the Kingdom of God since this was considered to be a sign of God's favor. When properly used to help the needy (Deut. 15:7-8, 11), wealth did give opportunity for demonstrating personal piety and could be construed as a work of God's blessing (Job 1:10; 42:10), but too many of Jesus' day, including this ruler, had succumbed to the temptation to place a higher premium on material things than on God.

ᵖ(Matt. 19:28) "Regeneration" describes the world's restored condition when Messiah returns to fulfil the long-anticipated Old Testament promises of the Kingdom. The people of Israel will once again be central objects in God's dealings with the world, and these twelve (excluding Judas, of course) will occupy places of authority over them. This teaching, following Jesus' shocking statement about how hard it is to enter the Kingdom of God (Mark 10:24), must have been quite a relief to them.

Sec. 179 Parable of the landowner's sovereignty (cf. Secs. 162, 178)
– *Perea* –

Matt. 20:1-16

1 "For the kingdom of heaven is like [1]a landowner who went out early in the morning to hire laborers [2]for his vineyard.

2 "And when he had agreed with the laborers for a [3]denarius for the day, he sent them into his vineyard.

3 "And he went out about the [4]third hour and saw others standing idle in the market place;

4 and to those he said, 'You too go into the vineyard, and whatever is right I will give you.' And so they went.

5 "Again he went out about the [5]sixth and the ninth hour, and did [6]the same thing.

6 "And about the [7]eleventh *hour* he went out, and found others standing; and he said to them, 'Why have you been standing here idle all day long?'

7 "They *said to him, 'Because no one hired us.' He *said to them, 'You too go into the vineyard.'

8 "And when evening had come, the [8]owner of the vineyard *said to his foreman, 'Call the laborers and pay them their wages, beginning with the last *group* to the first.'

9 "And when those *hired* about the eleventh hour came, each one received a [3]denarius.

10 "And when those *hired* first came, they thought that they would receive more; and they also received each one a [3]denarius.

11 "And when they received it, they grumbled at the landowner,

12 saying, 'These last men have worked *only* one hour, and you have made them equal to us who have borne the burden and the scorching heat of the day.'

13 "But he answered and said to one of them, 'Friend, I am doing you no wrong; did you not agree with me for a [3]denarius?

14 'Take what is yours and go your way, but I wish to give to this last man the same as to you.

15 '[q]Is it not lawful for me to do what I wish with what is my own? Or is your eye [9]envious because I am [10]generous?'

16 "Thus the last shall be first, and the first last."

[1]Lit., *a man, a landowner*. [2]Lit., *into*. [3]The denarius was equivalent to one day's wage. [4]I.e., 9 a.m. [5]I.e., Noon and 3 p.m. [6]Lit., *similarly*. [7]I.e., 5 p.m. [8]Or, *lord*. [9]Lit., *evil*. [10]Lit., *good*.

Sec. 180 Third prediction of the resurrection (cf. Secs. 119, 121, 122, 125)
– *On the road up to Jerusalem* –

Matt. 20:17-19	Mark 10:32-34	Luke 18:31-34
17 And as Jesus was about to go up to Jerusalem,	**32** And they were on the road, going up to Jerusalem, and Jesus was walking on ahead of them; and they were amazed, and those who followed	

[q](Matt. 20:15) In further response to Peter's question of Matt. 19:27 (Sec. 178), Jesus warned against the twelve's assuming that their favored position in the Kingdom would be the result of longer service or more work performed. Ultimately all rewards will issue from the sovereign grace of God who may, on the basis of His judgment of men's motives, grant richer rewards to those who have labored less.

Matt. 20:17-19 (cont'd)	Mark 10:32-34 (cont'd)	Luke 18:31-34 (cont'd)
He took the twelve disciples aside by themselves, and on the way He said to them, **18** "Behold, we are going up to Jerusalem; and the Son of Man will be [1]delivered to the chief priests and scribes, and they will condemn Him to death, **19** and will deliver Him to the Gentiles to mock and scourge and crucify *Him*, and on the third day He will be raised up."	were [r]fearful. And again He took the twelve aside and began to tell them what was going to happen to Him, **33** saying, "Behold, we are going up to Jerusalem, and the Son of Man will be [1]delivered to the chief priests and the scribes; and they will condemn Him to death, and will [2]deliver Him to the Gentiles. **34** "And they will mock Him and spit upon Him, and scourge Him, and kill *Him*, and three days later He will rise again."	**31** And He took the twelve aside and said to them, "Behold, we are going up to Jerusalem, and all things which are written through the prophets about the Son of Man will be accomplished. **32** "For He will be [1]delivered to the Gentiles, and will be mocked and mistreated and spit upon, **33** and after they have scourged Him, they will kill Him; and the third day He will rise again." **34** And they understood none of these things, and this saying was hidden from them, and they did not comprehend the things that were said.

[1]Or, *betrayed.*   [2]Or, *betray.*

Sec. 181   Warning against ambitious pride (cf. Sec. 215)
– On the road up to Jerusalem –

Matt. 20:20-28	Mark 10:35-45
20 Then the mother of the sons of Zebedee came to Him with her sons, bowing down, and making a [s]request of Him. **21** And He said to her, "What do you wish?" She *said to Him, "Command that in Your kingdom these two sons of mine may sit, one on Your right and one on Your left."	**35** And [2]James and John, the two sons of Zebedee, *came up to Him, [s]saying to Him, "Teacher, we want You to do for us whatever we ask of You." **36** And He said to them, "What do you want Me to do for you?" **37** And they said to Him, "[3]Grant that we may sit in Your glory, one on Your right, and one on Your left."

[r](Mark 10:32) This was probably a fear of what Jesus' enemies would do to Him once He arrived in Jerusalem (cf. John 11:8, Sec. 170). In spite of His reiterated prophecy of suffering and resurrection, the twelve did not comprehend yet (Luke 18:34) because they still anticipated a mighty Messianic conqueror who would establish His Kingdom on earth. In three years of instruction Jesus had not denied them this hope, but taught them that this hope must wait a little longer before realization (cf. Sec. 184).

[s](Matt. 20:20; Mark 10:37) This request for places of honor showed a continuing feeling among the disciples that Jesus was going to Jerusalem to restore the glory of the fallen throne and Kingdom of David. This was a normal, though selfish, reaction to Jesus' recent words about the twelve's occupancy of twelve thrones in that Kingdom (Matt. 19:28, Sec. 178). Not only had James and John missed the point in regard to humility, they had also failed to grasp the necessity of delay because of Messiah's coming passion.

Matt. 20:20-28 (cont'd)

22 But Jesus answered and said, "You do not know what you are asking for. Are you able to drink the cup that I am about to drink?" They *said to Him, "We are able."

23 He *said to them, "My cup you shall drink;

but to sit on My right and on My left, this is not Mine to give, but it is for those for whom it has been prepared by My Father."

24 And hearing *this*, the ten became indignant with the two brothers.

25 But Jesus called them to Himself, and said, "You know that the rulers of the Gentiles lord it over them, and *their* great men exercise authority over them.

26 "It is not so among you, but whoever wishes to become great among you shall be your servant,

27 and whoever wishes to be first among you shall be your slave;

28 just as the Son of Man did not come to be served, but to serve, and to give His ¹life a ransom for many."

Mark 10:35-45 (cont'd)

38 But Jesus said to them, "You do not know what you are asking for. Are you able to drink the cup that I drink, or to be baptized with the baptism with which I am baptized?"

39 And they said to Him, "We are able." And Jesus said to them, "The cup that I drink you shall drink; and you shall be baptized with the baptism with which I am baptized.

40 "But to sit on My right or on *My* left, this is not Mine to give; but it is for those for whom it has been prepared."

41 And hearing this, the ten began to feel indignant with ²James and John.

42 And calling them to Himself, Jesus *said to them, "You know that those who are recognized as rulers of the Gentiles lord it over them; and their great men exercise authority over them.

43 "But it is not so among you, but whoever wishes to become great among you shall be your servant;

44 and whoever wishes to be first among you shall be slave of all.

45 "For even the Son of Man did not come to be served, but to serve, and to give His ¹life a ransom for many."

¹Or, *soul*.   ²Or, *Jacob*.   ³Lit., *Give to us*.

Sec. 182   Healing blind Bartimaeus and his companion (cf. Sec. 96)
— Jericho —

Matt. 20:29-34	Mark 10:46-52	Luke 18:35-43
29 And as they were going out from Jericho, a great multitude followed Him.	**46** And they *came to Jericho. And as He was going out from Jericho with His disciples and a great multitude, ᵗa blind beggar *named* Bartimaeus, the son of Timaeus, was sitting by the road.	**35** And it came about that as He was approaching Jericho, ᵗa certain blind man was sitting by the road, begging.
		36 Now hearing a multitude going by, he *began* to inquire what this might be.
30 And behold, ᵗtwo blind men sitting by the	**47** And when he heard that it was Jesus the	**37** And they told him that Jesus of Nazareth was

ᵗ(Matt. 20:30; Mark 10:46; Luke 18:35) As in an earlier case, Matthew describes two victims while Mark and Luke write about only one (Sec. 94). The second and third gospels single out the more vocal of the pair. The miracle was apparently performed as Jesus left the city (Matt. 20:29; Mark 10:46) though He first encountered the men when He approached the city (Luke 18:35).

Matt. 20:29-34 (cont'd)	Mark 10:46-52 (cont'd)	Luke 18:35-43 (cont'd)
road, hearing that Jesus was passing by, cried out, saying, "Lord, have mercy on us, Son of David!" **31** And the multitude sternly told them to be quiet; but they cried out all the more, saying, "Lord, have mercy on us, ᵘSon of David!" **32** And Jesus stopped and called them,	Nazarene, he began to cry out and say, "Jesus, Son of David, have mercy on me!" **48** And many were sternly telling him to be quiet, but he kept crying out all the more, "ᵘSon of David, have mercy on me!" **49** And Jesus stopped and said, "Call him here. And they *called the blind man, saying to him, "Take courage, arise! He is calling for you." **50** And casting aside his cloak, he jumped up, and came to Jesus. **51** And answering him, Jesus said, "What do you want Me to do for You?" And the blind man said to Him, "¹Rabboni, I want to regain my sight!" **52** And Jesus said to him, "Go your way; your faith has ²made you well." And immediately he regained his sight and began following Him on the road.	passing by. **38** And he called out, saying, "Jesus, Son of David, have mercy on me!" **39** And those who led the way were sternly telling him to be quiet; but he kept crying out all the more, "ᵘSon of David, have mercy on me!" **40** And Jesus ³stopped and commanded that he be brought to Him; and when he had come near, He questioned him, **41** "What do you want Me to do for you?" And he said, "Lord, I want to regain my sight!" **42** And Jesus said to him, "⁴Receive your sight; your faith has ²made you well." **43** And immediately he regained his sight, and began following Him, glorifying God; and when all the people saw it, they gave praise to God.
and said, "What do you want Me to do for you?" **33** They *said to Him, "Lord, we want our eyes to be opened." **34** And moved with compassion, Jesus touched their eyes; and immediately they regained their sight and followed Him.		

¹I.e., *My Master.*   ²Lit., *saved you.*   ³Lit., *stood.*   ⁴Or, *Regain.*

Sec. 183   Salvation of Zaccheus
— Jericho —

Luke 19:1-10

1   And He entered and was passing through Jericho.

2   And behold, there was a man called by the name of Zaccheus; and he was a chief ¹tax-gatherer, and he was rich.

3   And he was trying to see who Jesus was, and he was unable because of the crowd, for he was small in stature.

4   And he ran on ahead and climbed up into a ²sycamore tree in order to see Him, for He was about to pass through that way.

ᵘ(Matt. 20:31; Mark 10:48; Luke 18:38) The title "Son of David" is a Messianic title. Like the twelve, these blind men looked upon Jesus not only as one who could restore their sight (Isa. 35:5) but also as one who would fulfil the promises made to David (2 Sam. 7:12-16; Psalm 89; Isa. 11:1-9; Jer. 23:5-6; Ezek. 34:23-24).

Luke 19:1-10 (cont'd)

5 And when Jesus came to the place, He looked up and said to him, "Zaccheus, hurry and come down, for today I must stay at your house."

6 And he hurried and came down, and received Him ³gladly.

7 And when they saw it, they all *began* to ⁴grumble, saying, "He has gone ⁵to be the guest of a man who is a sinner."

8 And Zaccheus ⁶stopped and said to the Lord, "Behold, Lord, half of my possessions I will give to the poor, and if I have defrauded anyone of anything, I will give back four times as much."

9 And Jesus said to him, "Today salvation has come to this house, because he, too, is ᵛa son of Abraham.

10 "For the Son of Man has come to seek and to save that which was lost."

¹I.e., Collector of Roman taxes for profit. ²I.e., fig-mulberry. ³Lit., *rejoicing*. ⁴Lit., *grumble among themselves*. ⁵Or, *to find lodging*. ⁶Lit., *stood*.

Sec. 184   Parable to teach responsibility while the Kingdom is delayed (cf. Sec. 207)
– *Jericho and the final ascent to Jerusalem* –

Luke 19:11-28

11 And while they were listening to these things, He went on to tell a parable, because He was near Jerusalem, and they supposed that the kingdom of God was going to appear ʷimmediately.

12 He said therefore, "'ˣA certain nobleman went to a distant country to receive a kingdom for himself, and *then* return.

13 "And he called ten of his slaves, and gave them ten ¹minas, and said to them, 'Do business *with this* ²until I come *back*.'

14 "But his citizens hated him, and sent ³a delegation after him, saying, 'We do not want this man to reign over us.'

15 "And it came about that when he returned, after receiving the kingdom, he ordered that these slaves, to whom he had given the money, be called to him in order that he might know what business they had done.

16 "And the first appeared, saying, '⁴Master, your ¹mina has made ten minas more.'

17 "And he said to him, "Well done, good slave, because you have been faithful in a very little thing, be in authority over ten cities.'

18 "And the second came, saying, 'Your ¹mina, ⁵master, has made five minas.'

19 "And he said to him also, 'And you are to be over five cities.'

20 "And another came, saying, 'Master, behold, your mina, which I kept put away in a handkerchief;

21 for I was afraid of you, because you are an exacting man; you take up what you did not lay down, and reap what you did not sow.'

22 "He *said to him, ⁶By your own words I will judge you, you worthless

---

ᵛ(Luke 19:9) The despised calling of tax-gatherer could not nullify the birthright of Zaccheus. It was a matter of divine compulsion (cf. "must," v. 5) that he be offered an opportunity to repent. Jesus' insistence on reaching out to the tax-gatherers (Luke 15:1-2, Sec. 166) had visible fruit in this instance.

ʷ(Luke 19:11) Spoken when the party was in Jericho, only fifteen miles from Jerusalem, these words were designed to prepare the listeners for what might be an extended delay before institution of the Kingdom on earth. By this time Jesus' followers fully expected Him to ascend the throne of David upon His arrival in Jerusalem.

ˣ(Luke 19:12) Archelaus, son of Herod the Great, who had built a palace at Jericho, had made a similar visit to Rome to receive for himself a vassal kingdom from the Roman government (cf. Matt. 2:22, Sec. 19). That historical incident may have suggested the structuring of this parable.

Luke 19:11-28 (cont'd)

slave. Did you know that I am an exacting man, taking up what I did not lay down, and reaping what I did not sow?

23   '⁷Then why did you not put the money in the bank, and having come, I would have collected it with interest?'

24   "And he said to the bystanders, 'Take the mina away from him, and give it to the one who has the ten minas.'

25   "And they said to him, 'Master, he has ten minas *already.*'

26   "I tell you, that ʸto everyone who has shall *more* be given, but from the one who does not have, even what he does have shall be taken away.

27   "But these enemies of mine, who did not want me to reign over them, bring them here and slay them in my presence."

28   And after He had said these things, He was going on ahead, ascending to Jerusalem.

¹A mina is equal to about 100 days' wages.   ²Lit., *while I am coming.*   ³Or, *an embassy.*   ⁴Lit., Lord.   ⁵Lit., *lord.*   ⁶Lit., *Out of your own mouth.*   ⁷Lit., *And.*

ʸ(Luke 19:26) The lesson of the parable is twofold:
1. While awaiting the Kingdom to be ushered in by the King's return, the disciples were to apply themselves diligently to the King's business.
2. The Jews who refused to acknowledge Him as King were given a stern warning regarding the heavy retribution brought on by their rejection (v. 27).

TRIUMPHAL ENTRY AND THE FIG TREE

Sec. 185   Arrival at Bethany
– Bethany near Jerusalem –

John 11:55—12:1

55   Now the Passover of the Jews was at hand, and many went up to Jerusalem out of the country ᶻbefore the Passover, to purify themselves.

56   Therefore they were seeking for Jesus, and were saying to one another, as they stood in the temple, "What do you think; that He will ᵃnot come to the feast at all?"

57   Now the chief priests and the Pharisees had given orders that if anyone knew where He was, he should report it, that they might seize Him.

1   Jesus, therefore, ᵇsix days before the Passover, came to Bethany where Lazarus was, whom Jesus had raised from the dead.

Sec. 186   Mary's anointing of Jesus for burial (cf. Sec. 77)
– Bethany –

Matt. 26:6-13	Mark 14:3-9	John 12:2-11
6 Now ᶜwhen Jesus was in Bethany, at the home of Simon the leper, **7** a woman came to Him with an alabaster vial of very costly perfume, and she poured it upon His head as He reclined *at the table.*	**3** And ᶜwhile He was in Bethany at the home of Simon the leper, and reclining *at the table,* came a woman with an alabaster vial of very costly perfume of pure nard; *and* she broke the vial and poured it over His head.	**2** ᶜSo they made Him a supper there, and Martha was serving; but Lazarus was one of those reclining *at the table* with Him. **3** Mary therefore took a pound of very costly perfume of pure nard, and anointed the feet of Jesus,

ᶻ(John 11:55) Because of the large number making this pilgrimage, ceremonial purification for the feast required more time than otherwise. Hence many came early, as much as a full week in some cases.

ᵃ(John 11:56) General opinion appears to have been that Jesus would not come to this feast. The command of the authorities (John 11:57) served to incriminate anyone who withheld information as to His whereabouts. Under such conditions Jesus' presence in Jerusalem was difficult for all who knew Him.

ᵇ(John 12:1) Jesus probably arrived on the Saturday before Passover, if we assume that the Passover fell on Friday that year. He must have already been in the vicinity. Otherwise, He would have exceeded the limit set for a Sabbath day's journey.

ᶜ(Matt. 26:6; Mark 14:3; John 12:2) Possibly this episode occurred later, two days before Passover as Matthew and Mark may imply (cf. Matt. 26:2; Mark 14:1, Sec. 209), instead of six days before as John places it. The placement of John is preferred in this *Harmony*, however, because it is easier to construe the synoptic accounts as flashbacks than to interpret John's account as an anticipation. The fourth gospel apparently gives the event in its chronological sequence. Matthew and Mark, on the other hand, introduce it out of sequence either to contrast the worship of Mary with the animosity of the high priest, chief priests, and scribes (Matt. 26:3-4; Mark 14:1; Luke 22:2, Sec. 209) or to show why Judas was so interested in obtaining additional funds (cf. Matt. 26:9; Mark 14:5; John 12:5-6; with Matt. 26:15; Mark 14:11; Luke 22:5, Sec. 210).

Matt. 26:6-13 (cont'd)	Mark 14:3-9 (cont'd)	John 12:2-11 (cont'd)
8 But the disciples were indignant when they saw *this*, and said, "Why this waste? **9** "For this *perfume* might have been sold for a high price and *the money* given to the poor." **10** But Jesus, aware of this, said to them, "Why do you bother the woman? For she has done a good deed to Me. **11** "For the poor you have with you always; but you do not always have Me. **12** "For when she poured this perfume upon My body, she did it to prepare Me for burial. **13** "Truly I say to you, wherever this gospel is preached in the whole world, what this woman has done shall also be spoken of in memory of her."	**4** But some were indignantly *remarking* to one another, "Why has this perfume been wasted? **5** "For this perfume might have been sold for over three hundred [1]denarii, and *the money* given to the poor." And they were scolding her. **6** But Jesus said, "Let her alone; why do you bother her? She has done a good deed to Me. **7** "For the poor you always have with you, and whenever you wish, you can do them good; but you do not always have Me. **8** "She has done what she could; she has anointed My body beforehand for the burial. **9** "And truly I say to you, wherever the gospel is preached in the whole world, that also which this woman has done shall be spoken of in memory of her."	and wiped His feet with her hair; and the house was filled with the fragrance of the perfume. **4** But Judas Iscariot, one of His disciples, who was intending to [2]betray Him, *said, **5** "Why was this perfume not sold for [3]three hundred denarii, and given to poor *people?*" **6** Now he said this, not because he was concerned about the poor, but because he was a thief, and as he had the money box, he used to pilfer what was put into it. **7** Jesus therefore said, "Let her alone, in order that she may keep [4]it for the day of My burial. **8** "For the poor you always have with you; but you do not always have Me." **9** The great multitude therefore of the Jews learned that He was there; and they came, not for Jesus' sake only, [d]but that they might also see Lazarus, whom He raised from the dead. **10** But the chief priests took counsel that they might put Lazarus to death also; **11** because on account of him many of the Jews were going away, and were believing in Jesus.

[1]The denarius was equivalent to one day's wage. [2]Or, *deliver Him up.* [3]Equivalent to 11 months' wages. [4]I.e., The custom of anointing for burial.

[d](John 12:9) The raising of Lazarus played a large part in attracting the throngs that witnessed the triumphal entry of Christ (cf. John 12:17-18, Sec. 187). The notoriety of Lazarus' resurrection resulted in an official decision to have him executed (John 12:10), a decision like the earlier one against Jesus (John 11:53, Sec. 172).

Sec. 187   Triumphal Entry into Jerusalem
– From Bethany to Jerusalem to Bethany –

Matt. 21:1-11, 14-17	Mark 11:1-11	Luke 19:29-44	John 12:12-19
1 And when they had approached Jerusalem and had come to Bethphage, to the Mount of Olives, then Jesus sent two disciples,	**1** And as they *approached Jerusalem at Bethphage and Bethany, near the Mount of Olives, He *sent two of His disciples,	**29** And it came about that when He approached Bethphage and Bethany, near the [3]mount that is called [4]Olivet, He sent two of the disciples,	
2 saying to them, "[e]Go into the village opposite you, and immediately you will find a [f]donkey tied *there* and a colt with her; untie *them*, and bring *them* to Me.	**2** and *said to them, "[e]Go into the village opposite you, and immediately as you enter it, you will find a [f]colt tied *there*, on which no one yet has ever sat; untie it and bring it here.	**30** saying, "[e]Go into the village opposite you, in which as you enter you will find a [f]colt tied, on which no one yet has ever sat; untie it, and bring it here.	
3 "And if anyone says something to you, you shall say, 'The Lord has need of them,' and immediately he will send them."	**3** "And if anyone says to you, 'Why are you doing this?' you say, 'The Lord has need of it'; and immediately he [2]will send it back here."	**31** "And if anyone asks you, 'Why are you untying it?' thus shall you speak, 'The Lord has need of it.'"	
6 And the disciples went and did just as Jesus had directed them,	**4** And they went away and found a colt tied at the door outside in the street; and they *untied it.	**32** And those who were sent went away and found it just as He had told them.	
	5 And some of the bystanders were saying to them, "What are	**33** And as they were untying the colt, its [5]owners said to them, "Why are you untying the colt?"	**12** On the next day [11]the great multitude who had come to the feast, when they heard that Jesus was coming to Jerusalem,
		34 And they said, "The Lord has need of it."	**13** took the

---

[e](Matt. 21:2; Mark 11:2; Luke 19:30) Jesus took great pains to demonstrate His office as King of Israel in fulfillment of Zechariah 9:9, a point that was not missed by the crowds (Matt. 21:9; Mark 11:9-10; Luke 19:38; John 12:13). According to John, the crowds who assembled came from three sources. In 12:12 a pilgrim throng approached Jerusalem from more distant areas. Probably most of them came from Galilee where they had witnessed a large part of Jesus' ministry. In 12:17 the crowd that had been in Bethany when Lazarus was raised bore witness (cf. John 11:42, Sec. 171). In 12:18 a large Jerusalem crowd flocked out of the city to see the one who had raised Lazarus.

The people's understanding of His mission was only partial, however. They grasped its political significance, namely, deliverance from foreign oppression, but failed to catch the spiritual requirements of His Kingdom. Therefore, the national aspirations of their generation were doomed to disappointment. This failure brought grief to Jesus, even in His hour of great public acclamation (Luke 19:41).

[f](Matt. 21:2; Mark 11:2; Luke 19:30; John 12:14) Matthew tells about two animals, a donkey and a colt, while the other writers mention only the colt. Here is another instance where Matthew recalls a second participant whereas the other accounts are more general and speak of one only (cf. note h, Sec. 94, and note t, Sec. 182). Matthew adds this detail to tie the event more closely with Zechariah 9:9 (Matt. 21:4-5; "even" in v. 5 may be translated "and") which mentions two animals. Jesus apparently rode on the colt only, as the other three gospels stipulate. "On which" (lit., "on them") in verse 7 means that He sat on the garments, not on both donkey and colt. The mother of the colt was probably led in front to make the colt more at ease in carrying its first rider.

Matt. 21:1-11, 14-17 (cont'd)	Mark 11:1-11 (cont'd)	Luke 19:29-44 (cont'd)	John 12:12-19 (cont'd)
	you doing, untying the colt?''	**35** And they brought it to Jesus, and they threw their garments on the colt, and put Jesus *on it*.	branches of the palm trees, and went out to meet Him, and *began* to cry out, "Hosanna! BLESSED IS HE WHO COMES IN THE NAME OF THE LORD [Psalm 118:26], even the King of Israel."
	6 And they spoke to them just as Jesus had told them, and they gave them permission.		
7 and brought the donkey and the colt, and laid on them their garments, ¹on which He sat.	**7** And they *brought the colt to Jesus and put their garments on it; and He sat upon it.		**14** And Jesus, finding a young ᶠdonkey, sat on it; as it is written,
4 Now this took place that what was spoken through the prophet might be fulfilled, saying,			**15** "FEAR NOT, DAUGHTER OF ZION; BEHOLD, YOUR KING IS COMING, SEATED ON A DONKEY'S COLT" [Zech. 9:9].
5 "SAY TO THE DAUGHTER OF ZION, ' BEHOLD YOUR KING IS COMING TO YOU, GENTLE, AND MOUNTED ON A DON-KEY, EVEN ON A COLT, THE FOAL OF A BEAST OF BURDEN'" [Isa. 62:11; Zech. 9:9].			**16** These things His disciples did not understand at the first; but when Jesus was glorified, then they remembered that these things were written of Him, and that they had done these things to Him. **17** And so the multitude who were with Him when He called Lazarus out of the tomb, and raised him from the dead, were bearing Him witness.
8 And most of the multitude spread their garments in the road, and others were cutting branches from the trees, and spreading them in the road.	**8** And many spread their garments in the road, and others *spread* leafy branches which they had cut from the fields.	**36** And as He was going, they were spreading their garments in the road. **37** And as He was now ap-proaching, near the descent of the Mount of Olives, the whole mul-titude of the disci-ples began to praise God ⁶joyfully with a loud voice for all	**18** For this cause also the mul-titude went and met Him, because they heard that He had performed this ¹²sign.
9 And the multitudes going before Him, and those who followed after were crying out, saying,	**9** And those who went before, and those who fol-lowed after, were crying out, "Hosanna! BLESSED IS HE WHO		**19** The Phari-sees therefore said to one another, "You see that you are not doing any good; look. the

Matt. 21:1-11, 14-17 (cont'd)	Mark 11:1-11 (cont'd)	Luke 19:29-44 (cont'd)	John 12:12-19 (cont'd)
"Hosanna to the Son of David; BLESSED IS HE WHO COMES IN THE NAME OF THE LORD [Psalm 118:26]; Hosanna in the highest!"	COMES IN THE NAME OF THE LORD [Psalm 118:26]; **10** Blessed is the coming king-dom of our father David; Hosanna in the high-est!"	the [7]miracles which they had seen, **38** saying, "BLESSED IS THE KING WHO COMES IN THE NAME OF THE LORD [Psalm 118:26]; Peace in heaven and glory in the highest!"	world has gone after Him."

39 And some of the Pharisees [8]in the multitude said to Him, "Teacher, rebuke Your disciples."

40 And He answered and said, "I tell you, if these become silent, the stones will cry out!"

41 And when He approached, He saw the city and wept over it,

42 saying, "If you had known in this day, even you, the things which make for peace! But now they have been hidden from your eyes.

43 "For the days shall come upon you [9]when your enemies will throw up a [10]bank before you, and surround you, and hem you in on every side,

44 and will level you to the ground and your children within you, and they will not leave in you one stone upon another, because you did not recognize the time of your visitation."

Matt. 21:1-11, 14-17 (cont'd)	Mark 11:1-11 (cont'd)
10 And when He had entered Jerusalem, all the city was stirred, saying, "Who is this?"	**11** And He entered Jerusalem
11 And the multitudes were saying, "This is the prophet Jesus, from Nazareth in Galilee."	
14 And the blind and the lame came to Him in the temple, and He healed them.	and came into the temple;
15 But when the chief priests and the scribes saw the wonderful things that He had done, and the children who were crying out in the temple and saying, "Hosanna to the Son of David," they became indignant,	
16 and said to Him, "Do You hear what these are saying?" And Jesus *said to them, "Yes; have you never read, 'OUT OF THE MOUTH OF INFANTS AND NURSING BABES THOU HAST PREPARED PRAISE FOR THYSELF'?" [Psalm 8:2].	

Matt. 21:1-11, 14-17 (cont'd)	Mark 11:1-11 (cont'd)
17 And He left them and went out of the city to Bethany, and lodged there.	and after looking all around, He departed for Bethany with the twelve, since it was already late.

¹Lit., *on them.* ²Lit., *sends.* ³Or, *hill.* ⁴Or, *Olive Grove.* ⁵Lit., *lords.* ⁶Lit., *as they were rejoicing.* ⁷Or, *works of power.* ⁸Lit., *from.* ⁹Lit., *and.* ¹⁰I.e., a dirt wall or mound for siege purposes. ¹¹Or, *the common people.* ¹²Or, *attesting miracle.*

Sec. 188   Cursing of the fig tree having leaves but no figs
– From Bethany to Jerusalem –

Matt. 21:18-19a	Mark 11:12-14
18 Now in the morning, when He returned to the city, He became hungry. **19** And seeing a lone fig tree by the road, He came to it, and found nothing on it except leaves only;	**12** And on the next day, when they had departed from Bethany, He became hungry. **13** And seeing at a distance a fig tree in leaf, He went *to see* if perhaps He would find anything on it; and when He came to it, He found nothing but leaves, for it was ᵍnot the season for figs.
and He *said to it, "No longer shall there ever be *any* fruit from you."	**14** And He answered and said to it, "May no one ever eat fruit from you again!" And His disciples were listening.

Sec. 189   Second cleansing of the Temple (cf. Sec. 34)
– Jerusalem, in the Temple –

Matt. 21:12-13	Mark 11:15-18	Luke 19:45-48
12 And Jesus entered the ʰtemple and cast out all those who were buying and selling in the temple, and overturned the tables of the moneychangers and the seats of those who were selling ¹doves.	**15** And they *came to Jerusalem. And He entered the ʰtemple and began to cast out those who were buying and selling in the temple, and overturned the tables of the moneychangers and the seats of those who were selling ¹doves; **16** and He would not permit anyone to carry ³goods through the temple.	**45** And He entered the ʰtemple and began to cast out those who were selling,

ᵍ(Mark 11:13) Jesus knew that Passover time was not the season for figs, but He used His own hunger and this leafy fig tree as an object lesson for the disciples. In the Old Testament the fig tree is often a symbol for Israel (Jer. 8:13; 29:17; Hos. 9:10, 16; Joel 1:7; Mic. 7:1-6). Such is the case here. The ritualism of national worship was hiding the absence of genuine piety among the people (cf. Sec. 189). Hence Jesus' curse of this fig tree (Matt. 21:19; Mark 11:14) was emblematic of God's judgment that was going to fall on Jerusalem (cf. Sec. 192).

ʰ(Matt. 21:12; Mark 11:15; Luke 19:45) The Court of the Gentiles was the scene of the cleansing. After His dramatic entrance into the city (Sec. 187), the King went right to the heart of the nation's problem: corruption in worship. This lack of true devotion to God was what kept His triumphal entry from being triumphal in a permanent sense.

Matt. 21:12-13 (cont'd)	Mark 11:15-18 (cont'd)	Luke 19:45-48 (cont'd)
13 And He *said to them, "It is written, 'MY HOUSE SHALL BE CALLED A HOUSE OF PRAYER'; but you are making it a ROBBERS' ²DEN" [Isa. 56:7; Jer. 7:11].	**17** And He *began* to teach and say to them, "Is it not written, 'MY HOUSE SHALL BE CALLED A HOUSE OF PRAYER FOR ALL THE NATIONS'? But you have made it a ROBBERS' ²DEN" [Isa. 56:7; Jer. 7:11]. **18** And the chief priests and the scribes heard *this*, and *began* seeking how to destroy Him; for they were afraid of Him, for all the multitude was astonished at His teaching.	**46** saying to them, "It is written, 'AND MY HOUSE SHALL BE A HOUSE OF PRAYER,' but you have made it a ROBBERS' ²DEN" [Isa. 56:7; Jer. 7:11]. **47** And He was teaching daily in the temple; but the chief priests and the scribes and the leading men among the people were trying to destroy Him, **48** and they could not find ⁴anything that they might do, for all the people were hanging upon ⁵His words.

¹Lit., *the doves.* ²Lit., *cave.* ³Lit., *a vessel;* i.e., a receptacle or implement of any kind. ⁴Lit., *what they might do.* ⁵Lit., *Him, listening.*

Sec. 190   Request of some Greeks and necessity of the Son of Man's being lifted up (cf. Sec. 119)

– Jerusalem –

John 12:20-36a

20 Now there were certain Greeks among those who were going up to worship at the feast;

21 these therefore came to Philip, who was from Bethsaida of Galilee, and *began to* ask him, saying, "Sir, we wish to see Jesus."

22 Philip *came and *told Andrew; Andrew and Philip *came, and they *told Jesus.

23 And Jesus *answered them, saying, "¹The hour has come for the Son of Man to be glorified.

24 "Truly, truly, I say to you, unless a grain of wheat falls into the earth and dies, it remains by itself alone; but if it dies, it bears much fruit.

25 "He who loves his ¹life loses it; and he who hates his ¹life in this world shall keep it to life eternal.

26 "If anyone serves Me, let him follow Me; and where I am, there shall My servant also be; if anyone serves Me, the Father will honor him.

27 "Now My soul has become troubled; and what shall I say, 'Father, save Me from this hour'? But for this purpose I came to this hour.

28 "Father, glorify Thy name." There came therefore a voice out of heaven: "I have both glorified it, and will glorify it again."

29 The multitude therefore, who stood by and heard it, were saying that it had thundered; others were saying, "An angel has spoken to Him."

30 Jesus answered and said, "This voice has not come for My sake, but for your sakes.

---

¹(John 12:23) Jesus' answer totally ignored the Greeks and their request. John's inclusion of the incident clearly indicates their importance, however. Indirectly, their coming to seek Jesus indicated to Him that the climax of His ministry had come. The time had now come for Him to conclude His ministry limited to the Jews and move out to include others such as these Greeks. This could happen only after His crucifixion, however (cf. John 12:24, 32).

John 12:20-36a (cont'd)

31   "Now judgment is upon this world; now the ruler of this world shall be cast out.

32   "And I, if I be lifted up from the earth, will draw all men to Myself."

33   But He was saying this to indicate the kind of death by which He was to die.

34   The multitude therefore answered Him, "We have heard out of the Law that ²the Christ is to remain forever; and how can You say, 'The Son of Man must be lifted up'? Who is this Son of Man?"

35   Jesus therefore said to them, "For a little while longer the light is among you. Walk while you have the light, that darkness may not overtake you; he who walks in the darkness does not know where he goes.

36   "While you have the light, believe in the light, in order that you may become sons of light."

¹Or, *soul.*   ²I.e., *the Messiah.*

Sec. 191   Departure from the unbelieving multitude and Jesus' response (cf. Sec. 83)

— Jerusalem —

John 12:36b-50

36   These things Jesus spoke, and He departed and ¹hid Himself from them.

37   But though He had performed so many ²signs before them, yet they were not believing in Him;

38   that the word of Isaiah the prophet might be fulfilled, which he spoke, "LORD, WHO HAS BELIEVED OUR REPORT? AND TO WHOM HAS THE ARM OF THE LORD BEEN REVEALED?" [Isa. 53:1].

39   For this cause they could not believe, for Isaiah said again,

40   "HE HAS BLINDED THEIR EYES, AND HE HARDENED THEIR HEART; LEST THEY SEE WITH THEIR EYES, AND PERCEIVE WITH THEIR HEART, AND ³BE CONVERTED, AND I HEAL THEM" [Isa. 6:10].

41   These things Isaiah said, because he saw His glory, and he spoke of Him.

42   Nevertheless ʲmany even of the rulers believed in Him, but because of the Pharisees they were not confessing *Him*, lest they should be ⁴put out of the synagogue;

43   for they loved the approval of men rather than the approval of God.

44   And Jesus cried out and said, "He who ᵏbelieves in Me does not believe in Me, but in Him who sent Me.

45   "And he who beholds Me beholds the One who sent Me.

46   "I have come *as* light into the world, that everyone who believes in Me may not remain in darkness.

47   "And if anyone hears My sayings, and does not keep them, I do not judge him; for I did not come to judge the world, but to save the world.

48   "He who rejects Me, and does not receive My sayings, has one who judges him; the word I spoke is what will judge him at the last day.

49   "For I did not speak ⁵on My own initiative, but the Father Himself who sent Me has given Me commandment, what to say, and what to speak.

50   "And I know that His commandment is eternal life; therefore the things I speak, I speak just as the Father has told Me."

¹Lit., *was hidden.*   ²Or, *attesting miracles.*   ³Lit., *should be turned;* i.e., turn about.   ⁴I.e., excommunicated.   ⁵Lit., *of Myself.*

ʲ(John 12:42) Nicodemus and Joseph of Arimathea must have been only two of a much larger number of leaders who had trusted Christ. What a pity that misplaced values (cf. John 12:43) may have kept them from speaking up in His defense.

ᵏ(John 12:44) Fittingly John closes his description of Jesus' public ministry with a final plea to believe. This along with other emphases of the earlier chapters are picked up in this summary para-

Sec. 192   Withered fig tree and the lesson on faith (cf. Sec. 69)
— Back to Bethany and return to Jerusalem —

Matt. 21:19b-22	Mark 11:19-25, [26]
	19 And whenever evening came, ¹they would go out of the city.
	20 And as they were passing by in the morning, they saw the fig tree withered from the roots up.
And at once the fig tree withered.	
20 And seeing this, the disciples marveled, saying, "How did the fig tree wither at once?"	21 And being reminded, Peter *said to Him, "Rabbi, behold, the fig tree which You cursed has withered."
21 And Jesus answered and said to them, "Truly I say to you, if you have faith, and do not doubt, you shall not only do what was done to the fig tree, but even if you say to this ¹mountain, 'Be taken up and cast into the sea,' it shall happen.	22 And Jesus *answered saying to them, "Have faith in God.
	23 "Truly I say to you, whoever says to this ¹mountain, 'Be taken up and cast into the sea,' and does not doubt in his heart, but believes that what he says is going to happen, it shall be granted him.
22 "And all things you ask in prayer, believing, you shall receive."	24 "Therefore I say to you, all things for which you pray and ask, believe that you have received them, and they shall be granted you.
	25 "And whenever you stand praying, forgive, if you have anything against anyone; so that your Father also who is in heaven may forgive you your transgressions.
	26 ["²But if you do not forgive, neither will your Father who is in heaven forgive your transgressions."]

¹I.e., Jesus and His disciples.   ²Many mss. do not contain this v.

OFFICIAL CHALLENGE OF CHRIST'S AUTHORITY

Sec. 193   A question by the chief priests, scribes, and elders
— Jerusalem, in the Temple —

Matt. 21:23-27	Mark 11:27-33	Luke 20:1-8
	27 And they *came again to Jerusalem. And as He was walking in the temple, the chief priests, and scribes, and elders *came to Him,	1 And it came about on one of the days while He was teaching the people in the temple and preaching the ᵐgospel, that the chief priests and
23 And when He had come into the temple, the		

graph (e.g., His being sent by the Father [vv. 44-45, 49], light and darkness [v. 46], present and future judgment [vv. 47-48], salvation for the world [v. 47], eternal life [v. 50]).

¹(Matt. 21:21; Mark 11:23) The mountain referred to was the Mount of Olives from which one could see the Dead Sea. For this mountain to have been cast into the Sea would have meant a fall of about four thousand feet. Whether Jesus intended a physical miracle or used the mountain only in a symbolic way cannot be discerned. The important lesson in either case was for the disciples to believe God.

ᵐ(Luke 20:1) It was probably the gospel of the Kingdom (Matt. 9:35; 24:14) to which these representatives of the Sanhedrin objected, but the cleansing of the Temple the day before was probably included also in "these things" (Matt. 21:23; Mark 11:28; Luke 20:2) about which they asked. This is the first in a series of verbal encounters with various groups of Jewish leaders. All of these came on Tuesday of Passion Week.

Matt. 21:23-27 (cont'd)	Mark 11:27-33 (cont'd)	Luke 20:1-8 (cont'd)
chief priests and the elders of the people came to Him as He was teaching, and said, "By what authority are You doing these things, and who gave You this authority?" **24** And Jesus answered and said to them, "I will ask you one ¹thing too, which if you tell Me, I will also tell you by what authority I do these things. **25** "The baptism of John was from what source, from heaven or from men?" And they began reasoning among themselves, saying, "If we say, 'From heaven,' He will say to us, 'Then why did you not believe him?' **26** "But if we say, 'From men,' we fear the multitude; for they all hold John to be a prophet." **27** And answering Jesus, they said, "We do not know." He also said to them, "Neither will I tell you by what authority I do these things.	**28** and *began* saying to Him, "By what authority are You doing these things, or who gave You this authority to do these things?" **29** And Jesus said to them, "I will ask you one question, and you answer Me, and *then* I will tell you by what authority I do these things. **30** "Was the baptism of John from heaven, or from men? Answer Me." **31** And they *began* reasoning among themselves, saying, "If we say, 'From heaven,' He will say, 'Then why did you not believe him?' **32** "But ²shall we say, 'From men'?" —they were afraid of the multitude, for all considered John to have been a prophet indeed. **33** And answering Jesus, they *said, "We do not know." And Jesus *said to them, "Neither ³will I tell you by what authority I do these things."	the scribes with the elders confronted *Him*, **2** and they spoke, saying to Him, "Tell us by what authority You are doing these things, or who is the one who gave You this authority?" **3** And He answered and said to them, "I shall also ask you a ¹question, and you tell Me: **4** "Was the baptism of John from heaven or from men?" **5** And they reasoned among themselves, saying, "If we say, 'From heaven,' He will say, 'Why did you not believe him?' **6** "But if we say, 'From men,' all the people will stone us to death, for they are convinced that John was a prophet." **7** And they answered that they did not know where *it came* from. **8** And Jesus said to them, "Neither ³will I tell you by what authority I do these things."

¹Lit., *word.*   ²Or, *if we say.*   ³Lit., *do I tell.*

Sec. 194   Faithful discharge of responsibility taught by three parables
– Jerusalem, in the Temple –

Matt. 21:28—22:14	Mark 12:1-12	Luke 20:9-19
28 "But what do you think? A man had two ¹sons, and he came to the first and said, '²Son, go work today in the vineyard.' **29** "And he answered and said, '³I will, sir'; and he did not go. **30** "And he came to the second and said ⁴the same thing. But he answered and said, '⁵I will		

Matt. 21:28—22:14 (cont'd)	Mark 12:1-12 (cont'd)	Luke 20:9-19 (cont'd)
not'; *yet* he afterward regretted *it* and went. **31** "Which of the two did the will of his father?" They *said, "The latter." Jesus *said of them, "Truly I say to you that the [6]tax-gatherers and harlots [7]will get into the kingdom of God before you. **32** "For John came to you in the way of righteousness and you did not believe him; but the tax-gatherers and harlots did believe him; and you, seeing this, did not even feel remorse afterward so as to believe him. **33** "Listen to another [n]parable. There was a [8]landowner who PLANTED A VINEYARD AND PUT A WALL AROUND IT AND DUG A WINE PRESS IN IT, AND BUILT A TOWER [Isa. 5:2], and rented it out to [9]vine-growers, and went on a journey. **34** "And when the [10]harvest time approached, he sent his slaves to the [9]vine-growers to receive his produce. **35** "And the [9]vine-growers took his slaves and beat one, and killed another, and stoned a third. **36** "Again he sent another group of slaves larger than the first; and they did [4]the same thing to them. **37** "But afterward he	**1** And He began to speak to them in [n]parables: "A man PLANTED A VINE-YARD, AND PUT A [18]WALL AROUND IT, AND DUG A VAT UNDER THE WINE PRESS, AND BUILT A TOWER [Isa. 5:2], and rented it out to [9]vine-growers and went on a journey. **2** "And at the *harvest* time he sent a slave to the vine-growers, in order to receive *some* of the produce of the vineyard from the vine-growers. **3** "And they took him, and beat him, and sent him away empty-handed. **4** "And again he sent them another slave, and they wounded him in the head, and treated him shamefully. **5** "And he sent another, and that one they killed; and *so with* many others, beating some, and killing others. **6** "He had one more	**9** And He began to tell the people this [n]parable: "A man planted a vineyard and rented it out to [9]vine-growers, and went on a journey for a long time. **10** "And at the *harvest* time he sent a slave to the vine-growers, in order that they might give him *some* of the produce of the vine-yard; but the [9]vine-growers beat him and sent him away empty-handed. **11** "And he proceeded to send another slave; and they beat him also and treated him shamefully, and sent him away empty-handed. **12** "And he proceeded to send a third; and this one also they wounded and cast out. **13** "And the [11]owner of the vineyard said, 'What shall I do? I will send my

[n](Matt. 21:33; Mark 12:1; Luke 20:9) This parable pictures the rejection of God's "beloved son" (Luke 20:13), while that of the two sons (Matt. 21:28-32) charges the listeners with the rejection of John the Baptist.

Matt. 21:28—22:14 (cont'd)	Mark 12:1-12 (cont'd)	Luke 20:9-19 (cont'd)

sent his son to them, saying, 'They will respect my son.'
 38 "But when the [9]vine-growers saw the son, they said among themselves, 'This is the heir; come, let us kill him, and seize his inheritance.'
 39 "And they took him, and threw him out of the vineyard, and killed him.
 40 "Therefore when the [11]owner of the [9]vineyard comes, what will he do to those vine-growers?"
 41 They *said to Him, "He will bring those wretches to a wretched end, and will rent out the vineyard to other vine-growers, who will pay him the proceeds at the *proper* seasons."
 42 Jesus *said to them, "Did you never read in the Scriptures,
  'THE STONE WHICH
  THE BUILDERS RE-
  JECTED,
  THIS BECAME THE
  CHIEF CORNER
  stone;
  THIS CAME ABOUT
  FROM THE LORD,
  AND IT IS MARVELOUS
  IN OUR EYES'?
  [Psalm 118:22-23].
 43 "Therefore I say to you, the kingdom of God will be [o]taken away from you, and be given to a nation producing the fruit of it.
 44 "And he who falls
	to send, a beloved son; he sent him last *of all* to them, saying, 'They will respect my son.'
	 7 "But those vine-growers said to one another, 'This is the heir; come, let us kill him, and the inheritance will be ours!'
	 8 "And they took him, and killed him, and threw him out of the vineyard.
	 9 "What will the [11]owner of the vineyard do?
	
	 He will come and destroy the vine-growers, and will give the vineyard to others.
	 10 "Have you not even read this Scripture:
	  'THE STONE WHICH
	  THE BUILDERS RE-
	  JECTED,
	  THIS BECAME THE
	  CHIEF CORNER
	  stone;
	 11 THIS CAME ABOUT
	  FROM THE LORD,
	  AND IT IS MARVELOUS
	  IN OUR EYES'?"
	  [Psalm 118:22-23].
		beloved son; perhaps they will respect him.'
		 14 "But when the [9]vine-growers saw him, they reasoned with one another, saying, 'This is the heir; let us kill him that the inheritance may be ours.'
		 15 "And they threw him out of the vineyard and killed him. What, therefore, will the [11]owner of the vineyard do to them?
		
		 16 "He will come and destroy these [9]vine-growers and will give the vineyard to others." And when they heard it, they said, "May it never be!"
		 17 But He looked at them and said, "What then is this that is written,
		  'THE STONE WHICH
		  THE BUILDERS RE-
		  JECTED,
		  THIS BECAME THE
		  CHIEF CORNER
		  stone '? [Psalm 118:22]
		
		 18 "Everyone who

[o](Matt. 21:43) God's rejection of this generation of Israelites because of their rejection of Jesus and His spiritual standards has received attention already (cf. Luke 19:41-44, Sec. 187; Matt. 21:19; Mark 11:13, Sec. 188). The new "nation" to whom the Kingdom will be given is either those who respond to the gospel during the present, whether they be Jews or Gentiles (cf. Matt. 22:8-10), or that future generation of Israel that will respond to His call to repentance (Matt. 23:39, Sec. 200). The Greek word for "nation" (v. 43) is without a definite article and hence stresses the quality of people to whom the Kingdom will be given rather than the identity of the nation.

Matt. 21:28—22:14 (cont'd)	Mark 12:1-12 (cont'd)	Luke 20:9-19 (cont'd)
on this stone will be broken to pieces; but on whomever it falls, it will scatter him like dust." **45** And when the chief priests and the Pharisees heard His parables, they understood that He was speaking about them.		falls on that stone will be broken to pieces; but on whomever it falls, it will scatter him like dust."
46 And when they sought to seize Him, they feared the multitudes, because they held Him to be a prophet. **1** And Jesus answered and spoke to them again in parables, saying, **2** "The kingdom of heaven may be compared to [12]a king, who [13]gave a wedding feast for his son.	**12** And they were seeking to seize Him; and yet they feared the multitude; for they understood that He spoke the parable against them. And so they left Him, and went away.	**19** And the scribes and the chief priests tried to lay hands on Him that very hour, and they feared the people; for they understood that He spoke this parable against them.

3 "And he sent out his slaves to call those who had been invited to the wedding feast, and they were unwilling to come.

4 "Again he sent out other slaves saying, 'Tell those who have been invited, "Behold, I have prepared my dinner; my oxen and my fattened livestock are *all* butchered and everything is ready; come to the wedding feast."'

5 "But they paid no attention and went their way, one to his own [14]farm, another to his business,

6 and the rest seized his slaves and mistreated them and killed them.

7 "But the king was enraged and sent his armies, and destroyed those murderers, and [p]set their city on fire.

8 "Then he *said to his slaves, 'The wedding is ready, but those who were invited were not worthy.

9 'Go therefore to the main highways, and as many as you find *there*, invite to the wedding feast.'

10 "And those slaves went out into the streets, and gathered together all they found, both evil and good; and the wedding hall was filled with [15]dinner guests.

11 "But when the king came in to look over the dinner guests, he saw there a man not dressed in wedding clothes,

12 and he *said to him, 'Friend, how did you come in here [16]without wedding clothes?' And he was speechless.

13 "Then the king said to the servants, 'Bind him hand and foot, and cast him into the outer darkness; in that place there shall be weeping and gnashing of teeth.'

14 "For many are [17]called, but few *are* chosen."

[1]Lit., *children* [2]Lit., *Child.* [3]Some mss. read '*I will not*'; *yet he afterward regretted and went.* [4]Lit., *likewise.* [5]Some mss. read '*I will*'; *and he did not go.* [6]I.e., Collectors of Roman taxes for profit. [7]Or, *are getting into.* [8]Lit., *a man, a householder.* [9]Or, *tenant farmers.* [10]Lit., *the season of the fruits.* [11]Lit., *lord.* [12]Lit., *a man, a king.* [13]Lit., *made.* [14]Or, *field.* [15]Lit., *those reclining at the table.* [16]Lit., *not having.* [17]Or, *invited.* [18]Or, *fence.*

[p](Matt. 22:7) This parabolic reference to the destruction of Jerusalem which came in A.D. 70 is one of several predictions about that event. Jesus had already referred to it (Luke 19:43-44, Sec. 187) and was to do so again (Matt. 23:37-38, Sec. 200; Matt. 24:1-2; Mark 13:1-2; Luke 21:5-6, Sec. 202).

Sec. 195   A question by the Pharisees and Herodians
— Jerusalem, probably in the Temple —

Matt. 22:15-22	Mark 12:13-17	Luke 20:20-26
15 Then the Pharisees went and counseled together how they might trap Him [1]in what He said. **16** And they *sent their disciples to Him, along with the [q]Herodians, saying, "Teacher, we know that You are truthful and teach the way of God in truth, and [2]defer to no one; for You are not partial to any. **17** "[3]Tell us therefore, what do You think? Is it [3]lawful to give a poll-tax to Caesar, or not?" **18** But Jesus perceived their [4]malice, and said, "Why are you testing Me, you hypocrites? **19** "Show Me the coin used for the poll-tax." And they brought Him a [5]denarius. **20** And He *said to them, "Whose likeness and inscription is this?" **21** They *said to Him, "Caesar's." Then He *said to them, "Then render to Caesar the things that are Caesar's; and to God the things that are God's." **22** And hearing this, they marveled, and leaving Him, they went away.	**13** And they *sent some of the [q]Pharisees and Herodians to Him, in order to trap Him in a statement. **14** And they *came and *said to Him, "Teacher, we know that You are truthful, and [6]defer to no one; for You are not partial to any, but teach the way of God in truth. Is it [3]lawful to pay a poll-tax to Caesar, or not? **15** "Shall we pay, or shall we not pay?" But He, knowing their hypocrisy, said to them, "Why are you testing Me? Bring Me a [5]denarius to look at." **16** And they brought one. And He *said to them, "Whose likeness and inscription is this?" And they said to Him, "Caesar's." **17** And Jesus said to them, "Render to Caesar the things that are Caesar's, and to God the things that are God's." And they [7]were amazed at Him.	**20** And they watched Him, and sent spies who [8]pretended to be righteous, in order that they might [9]catch Him in some statement, so as to deliver Him up to the rule and the authority of the governor. **21** And they questioned Him, saying, "Teacher, we know that You speak and teach correctly, and You [10]are not partial to any, but teach the way of God in truth. **22** "Is it [3]lawful for us to pay taxes to Caesar, or not?" **23** But He detected their trickery and said to them, **24** "Show Me a [5]denarius. Whose [11]likeness and inscription does it have?" And they said, "Caesar's." **25** And He said to them, "Then render to Caesar the things that are Caesar's, and to God the things that are God's." **26** And they were unable to [12]catch Him in a saying in the presence of the people; and marveling at His answer, they became silent.

[1]Lit., *in word.* [2]I.e., *you court no man's favor.* [3]Or, *permissible.* [4]Or, *wickedness.* [5]The denarius was equivalent to one day's wage. [6]Lit., *it is not a concern to You about anyone;* i.e., *You court no man's favor.* [7]Or, *were greatly marveling.* [8]Lit., *feigned themselves.* [9]Lit., *take hold of His word.* [10]Lit., *do not receive a face.* [11]Lit., *image.* [12]Lit., *take hold of His saying.*

[q](Matt. 22:16; Mark 12:13) For the Pharisees and Herodians to unite in a common cause was quite unusual. The Pharisees were strongly resentful of the Roman occupation of Palestine—particularly of Judea where the poll-tax was required (cf. Matt. 22:17; Mark 12:14). In contrast, the Herodians strongly supported the Roman presence in the land, because this was the source of power by which the Herod family ruled. In whatever way Jesus answered their question (Matt. 22:17; Mark 12:15; Luke 20:22), they assumed He must violate the tenets of one of the two groups. He would be proven guilty in the eyes of either the people (Luke 20:26) if He disagreed with the Pharisees, or the governor (Luke 20:20) if He disagreed with the Herodians. But Jesus avoided both pitfalls with His perceptive answer.

Sec. 196   A question by the Sadducees
— Jerusalem, probably in the Temple —

Matt. 22:23-33	Mark 12:18-27	Luke 20:27-40
23 On that day *some* Sadducees ([r]who say there is no resurrection) came to Him and questioned Him, **24** saying, "Teacher, Moses said, 'IF A MAN DIES, HAVING NO CHILDREN, HIS BROTHER AS NEXT OF KIN SHALL MARRY HIS WIFE, AND RAISE UP AN OFFSPRING TO HIS BROTHER' [Deut. 25:5].	**18** And some Sadducees [r]who say that there is no resurrection) *came to Him, and *began* questioning Him, saying, **19** "Teacher, Moses wrote for us that IF A MAN'S BROTHER DIES, and leaves behind a wife, AND LEAVES NO CHILD, HIS BROTHER SHOULD TAKE THE WIFE, AND RAISE UP OFFSPRING TO HIS BROTHER [Deut. 25:5].	**27** Now there came to Him some of the Sadducees ([r]who say that there is no resurrection), **28** and they questioned Him, saying, "Teacher, Moses wrote for us that IF A MAN'S BROTHER DIES, having a wife, AND HE IS CHILDLESS, HIS BROTHER SHOULD TAKE THE WIFE AND RAISE UP OFFSPRING TO HIS BROTHER [Deut. 25:5].
25 "Now there were seven brothers with us; and the first married and died, and having no offspring left his wife to his brother; **26** so also the second, and the third, down to the seventh. **27** "And last of all, the woman died. **28** "In the resurrection therefore whose wife of the seven shall she be? For they all had her." **29** But Jesus answered and said to them, "You are mistaken, not [1]understanding the Scriptures, or the power of God.	**20** "There were seven brothers; and the first took a wife, and died, leaving no offspring. **21** "And the second one took her, and died, leaving behind no offspring; and the third likewise; **22** and *so* [3]all seven left no offspring. Last of all the woman died also. **23** "In the resurrection, [4]when they rise again, which one's wife will she be? For [3]all seven had her as wife." **24** Jesus said to them, "Is this not the reason you are mistaken, that you do not [5]understand the Scriptures, or the power of God?	**29** "Now there were seven brothers; and the first took a wife, and died childless; **30** and the second **31** and the third took her; and in the same way [8]all seven [9]died, leaving no children. **32** "Finally the woman died also. **33** "In the resurrection therefore, which one's wife will she be? For [10]all seven had her as wife." **34** And Jesus said to them,
		"The sons of this age marry and are given in marriage, **35** but those who are considered worthy to attain to that age and the resurrection from the dead, neither marry, nor are given in marriage;
30 "For in the resurrection they neither marry, nor are given in marriage, but are like angels [2]in	**25** "For when they rise from the dead, they neither marry, nor are given in marriage, but are like	resurrection from the dead, neither marry, nor are given in marriage;

---

[r](Matt. 22:23; Mark 12:18; Luke 20:27) On a Tuesday filled with conflicts, the Sadducees thought they had a theological question that could not be answered by anyone who believed in resurrection as did Jesus (cf. John 11:23-26, Sec. 171). The law of levirate marriage (Deut. 25:7-10), they held, ruled out the possibility of resurrection. In response Jesus authoritatively expounded Exodus 3:6 (Matt. 22:32; Mark 12:26) and Exodus 3:15-16 (Luke 20:37) to show that Moses' words would have been entirely inappropriate if the Sadducean doctrine of extinction without hope of resurrection held true for Abraham, Isaac, and Jacob after their deaths.

Matt. 22:23-33 (cont'd)	Mark 12:18-27 (cont'd)	Luke 20:27-40 (cont'd)
heaven.	angels in heaven.	**36** for neither can they die anymore, for they are like angels, and are sons of God, being sons of the resurrection.
31 "But regarding the resurrection of the dead, have you not read that which was spoken to you by God, saying, **32** 'I AM THE GOD OF ABRAHAM, AND THE GOD OF ISAAC, AND THE GOD OF JACOB'? [Exod. 3:6]. He is not the God of the dead but of the living." **33** And when the multitudes heard *this*, they were astonished at His teaching.	**26** "But ⁶regarding the fact that the dead rise again, have you not read in the book of Moses, in the *passage about the burning* bush, how God spoke to him, saying, 'I AM THE GOD OF ABRAHAM, AND THE GOD OF ISAAC, AND THE GOD OF JACOB'? [Exod. 3:6]. **27** "He is not the God ⁷of the dead, but of the living; you are greatly mistaken."	**37** "But that the dead are raised, even Moses showed, in the *passage about the burning bush*, where he calls the Lord THE GOD OF ABRAHAM, AND THE GOD OF ISAAC, AND THE GOD OF JACOB [Exod. 3:6]. **38** "Now He is not the God of the dead, but of the living; for all live to Him." **39** And some of the scribes answered and said, "Teacher, You have spoken well." **40** For they did not have courage to question Him any longer about anything.

¹Or, knowing. ²Other mss. add *of God.* ³Lit., *the seven.* ⁴Most ancient mss. do not contain *when they rise again.* ⁵Or, *know.* ⁶Lit., *concerning the dead, that they rise.* ⁷Or, *of corpses.* ⁸Lit., *the seven also.* ⁹Lit., *left no children, and died.* ¹⁰Lit., *the.*

Sec. 197   A question by a Pharisaic scribe (cf. Sec. 141)
— Jerusalem, probably in the Temple —

Matt. 22:34-40	Mark 12:28-34
34 But when the Pharisees heard that He had put the Sadducees to silence, they gathered themselves together. **35** And one of them, ¹a lawyer, asked Him *a question*, testing Him, **36** "Teacher, which is the great commandment in the Law?"	**28** And one of the scribes came and heard them arguing, and recognizing that He had answered them well, asked Him, "What commandment is the ·²foremost of all?" **29** Jesus answered, "The foremost is, 'HEAR, O ISRAEL! THE LORD OUR GOD IS ONE LORD; **30** AND YOU SHALL LOVE THE LORD YOUR GOD WITH ALL YOUR HEART, AND WITH ALL YOUR SOUL, AND WITH ALL YOUR MIND, AND WITH ALL YOUR STRENGTH' [Deut. 6:4-5].
37 And He said to him, "'YOU SHALL LOVE THE LORD YOUR GOD WITH ALL YOUR HEART, AND WITH ALL YOUR SOUL, AND WITH ALL YOUR MIND' [Deut. 6:5]. **38** "This is the great and ²foremost commandment. **39** "The second is like it, 'YOU SHALL LOVE YOUR NEIGHBOR AS YOURSELF' [Lev. 19:18]. **40** "On these two commandments	**31** "The second is this, 'YOU SHALL LOVE YOUR NEIGHBOR AS YOURSELF' [Lev. 19:18]. There is no other commandment greater than these." **32** And the scribe said to Him, "Right, Teacher, You have truly stated

Matt. 22:34-40 (cont'd)	Mark 12:28-34 (cont'd)
depend the whole Law and the Prophets."	that HE IS ONE; AND THERE IS NO ONE ELSE BESIDES HIM;
	33 AND TO LOVE HIM WITH ALL THE HEART AND WITH ALL THE UNDERSTANDING AND WITH ALL THE STRENGTH, AND TO LOVE ONE'S NEIGHBOR AS HIMSELF [Deut. 4:35; 6:5], is much more than all burnt offerings and sacrifices."
	34 And when Jesus saw that [s]he had answered intelligently, He said to him, "You are not far from the kingdom of God." And after that, no one would venture to ask Him any more questions.

[1]I.e., an expert in the Mosaic Law.   [2]Or, *first.*

CHRIST'S RESPONSE TO HIS ENEMIES' CHALLENGES

Sec. 198   Christ's relationship to David as Son and Lord
— *Jerusalem, in the Temple* —

Matt. 22:41-46	Mark 12:35-37	Luke 20:41-44
41 Now while the Pharisees were gathered together, [1]Jesus asked them a question,		
42 saying, "What do you think about [1]the Christ, whose son is He?" They *said to Him, "*The son of David.*"	**35** And Jesus answering began to say, as He taught in the temple, "How is it that the scribes say that [1]the Christ is the son of David?	**41** And He said to them, "How is it that they say [1]the Christ is David's son?
43 He *said to them, "Then how does David [2]in the Spirit call Him 'Lord,' saying,	**36** "David himself said [2]in the Holy Spirit,	**42** "For David himself says in the book of Psalms,
44 'THE LORD SAID TO MY LORD, "SIT AT MY RIGHT HAND, UNTIL I PUT THINE ENEMIES BENEATH THY FEET"'? [Psalm 110:1].	'THE LORD SAID TO MY LORD, "SIT AT MY RIGHT HAND, UNTIL I PUT THINE ENEMIES BENEATH THY FEET"' [Psalm 110:1].	'THE LORD SAID TO MY LORD, "SIT AT MY RIGHT HAND, **43** UNTIL I MAKE THINE ENEMIES A FOOTSTOOL FOR THY FEET"' [Psalm 110:1].
45 "If David then calls Him 'Lord,' how is He his son?"	**37** "David himself calls Him 'Lord'; and so in what sense is He his son?" And the great crowd [3]enjoyed listening to Him.	**44** "David therefore calls Him 'Lord,' and how is He his son?"
46 And no one was		

[s](Mark 12:34) The favorable response of this lawyer to Jesus' answer must have caused alarm among his fellow Pharisees. It is a sign of Jesus' remarkable perception that He was able to recognize among such vicious opponents one whose heart was still open to the gospel, and who might still qualify for entrance into the Kingdom of God.

[t](Matt. 22:41) Having repulsed His opponents, Jesus now took the initiative. To the dismay of His enemies (Matt. 22:46) and the enjoyment of the crowd (Mark 12:37), by a single rhetorical question He proved from Old Testament Scripture that the Messiah must be both God and man ("Lord" and "son," Matt. 22:45; Mark 12:37; Luke 20:44).

Matt. 22:41-46
(cont'd)

able to answer Him a word,
nor did anyone dare from
that day on to ask Him
another question.

[1]I.e., the Messiah.   [2]Or, by.   [3]Lit., *was gladly hearing Him.*

Sec. 199   Seven woes against the scribes and Pharisees (cf. Secs. 68; 145)
– Jerusalem, in the Temple –

Matt. 23:1-36	Mark 12:38-40	Luke 20:45-47
1 Then Jesus spoke to the multitudes and to His disciples,	**38** And in His teaching He was saying: "Beware of the scribes	**45** And while all the people were listening, He said to the disciples,
2 saying, ''The scribes and the Pharisees have seated themselves in the chair of Moses;		**46** ''Beware of the scribes,
3 therefore [u]all that they tell you, do and observe, but do not do according to their deeds; for they say *things*, and do not do *them*.		
4 "And they tie up heavy loads, and lay them on men's shoulders; but they themselves are unwilling to move them with *so much as* a finger.		
5 "But they do all their deeds to be noticed by men; for they broaden their [1]phylacteries, and lengthen the tassels *of their garments.*	who like to walk around in long robes, and *like* respectful greetings in the market places,	who like to walk around in long robes, and love respectful greetings in the market places, and
6 "And they love the place of honor at banquets, and the chief seats in the synagogues,	**39** and chief seats in the synagogues, and places of honor at banquets,	chief seats in the synagogues, and places of honor at banquets,
7 and respectful greetings in the market places, and being called by men, Rabbi.		
8 "But do not be called Rabbi; for One is your Teacher, and you are all brothers.		

---

[u](Matt. 23:3) Even though He was about to denounce the scribes and Pharisees as hypocrites (Matt. 23:13, 15, 23, 25, 27, 29) and "blind guides" (Matt. 23:16), Jesus still recognized their official capacity as propagators of the Law of Moses. To the extent that they taught the Law faithfully, they were to be obeyed, but wherever their traditions missed the point of the Law (Matt. 5:21-48, Sec. 68) or nullified the teaching of the Law (Matt. 15:1-20; Mark 7:1-23, Sec. 111), they were not.

Matt. 23:1-36 (cont'd)	Mark 12:38-40 (cont'd)	Luke 20:45-47 (cont'd)
9 "And do not call *anyone* on earth your father; for One is your Father, He who is in heaven. **10** "And do not be called ²leaders; for One is your Leader, *that is,* Christ. **11** "But the greatest among you shall be your servant. **12** "And whoever exalts himself shall be humbled; and whoever humbles himself shall be exalted. **13** "But woe to ᵛyou, scribes and Pharisees, hypocrites, because you shut off the kingdom of heaven ³from men; for you do not enter in yourselves, nor do you allow those who are entering to go in.		
	40 who devour widows' houses, and for appearance's sake offer⸱ long prayers; these will receive greater condemnation."	**47** who devour widows' houses, and for appearance's sake offer long prayers; these will receive greater condemnation."
14 ⁴["Woe to you, scribes and Pharisees, hypocrites, because you devour widows' houses, even while for a pretense you make long prayers; therefore you shall receive greater condemnation.] **15** "Woe to you, scribes and Pharisees, hypocrites, because you travel about on sea and land to make one ⁵proselyte; and when he becomes one, you make him twice as much a son of ⁶hell as yourselves.		

ᵛ(Matt. 23:13) Whether the scribes and Pharisees were still present to hear these words has been debated. The natural impression is that they must have been, because the "woes" are addressed to the second person ("you"). Since Jesus was still in the Temple, it would be surprising if they had not been at least within earshot of His words. Aside from His two cleansings of the Temple (Secs. 34, 189), the wrath of Jesus shows itself more clearly here than at any other time. The failure of these religious leaders to qualify for entering the Kingdom of God was clearly delineated on this occasion.

Matt. 23:1-36 (cont'd)

16 "Woe to you, blind guides, who say, 'Whoever swears by the [7]temple, that is nothing; but whoever swears by the gold of the [7]temple, he is obligated.'

17 "You fools and blind men; which is [8]more important, the gold, or the [7]temple that sanctified the gold?

18 "And, 'Whoever swears by the altar, *that* is nothing, but whoever swears by the [9]offering upon it, he is obligated.'

19 "You blind men, which is [8]more important, the offering or the altar that sanctifies the [9]offering?

20 "Therefore he who swears, swears *both* by the altar and by everything on it.

21 "And he who swears by the [7]temple, swears *both* by [10]the temple and by Him who dwells within it.

22 "And he who swears by heaven, swears *both* by the throne of God and by Him who sits upon it.

23 "Woe to you, scribes and Pharisees, hypocrites! For you tithe mint and dill and [11]cummin, and have neglected the weightier provisions of the law: justice and mercy and faithfulness; but these are the things you should have done without neglecting the others.

24 "You blind guides, who strain out a gnat and swallow a camel!

25 "Woe to you, scribes and Pharisees, hypocrites! For you clean the outside of the cup and of the dish, but inside they are full [12]of robbery and self-indulgence.

26 "You blind Pharisee, first clean the inside of the cup and of the dish, so that the outside of it may become clean also.

27 "Woe to you, scribes and Pharisees, hypocrites! For you are like whitewashed tombs which on the outside appear beautiful, but inside they are full of dead men's bones and all uncleanness.

28 "Even so you too outwardly appear righteous to men, but inwardly you are full of hypocrisy and lawlessness.

29 "Woe to you, scribes and Pharisees, hypocrites! For you build the tombs of the prophets and adorn the monuments of the righteous,

30 and say, 'If we had been *living* in the days of our fathers, we would not have been partners with them in *shedding* the blood of the prophets.'

31 "Consequently you bear witness against yourselves, that you are [13]sons of those who murdered the prophets.

32 "[14]Fill up then the measure *of the guilt* of your fathers.

33 "You serpents, you brood of vipers, how shall you escape the [15]sentence of [6]hell?

34 "Therefore, behold, I am sending you prophets and wise men and scribes; some of them you will kill and crucify, and some of them you will scourge in your synagogues, and persecute from city to city,

35 that upon you may fall *the guilt of* all the righteous blood shed on earth, from the blood of righteous Abel to the blood of Zechariah, the son of Berechiah, whom you murdered between the [7]temple and the altar.

36 "Truly I say to you, all these things shall come upon this generation.

[1]I.e., small boxes containing Scripture texts worn for religious purposes. [2]Or, *teachers*. [3]Lit., in *front of*. [4]This v. not found in the earliest mss. [5]Or, *convert*. [6]Gr., *Gehenna*. [7]Or, *sanctuary*. [8]Lit., *greater*. [9]Or, *gift*. [10]Lit., *it*. [11]Similar to caraway seeds. [12]Or, *as a result of*. [13]Or, *descendants*. [14]Lit., *And fill up*. [15]Or, *judgment*.

Sec. 200   Lament over Jerusalem (cf. Sec. 163)
— *Jerusalem, in the Temple* —

Matt. 23:37-39

37 "'"O Jerusalem, Jerusalem, who kills the prophets and stones those who are sent to her! How often I wanted to gather your children together, the way a hen gathers her chicks under her wings, and you were unwilling.

38 "Behold, your house is being left to you [1]desolate!

39 "For I say to you, from now on you shall not see Me until [x]you say, 'BLESSED IS HE WHO COMES IN THE NAME OF THE LORD!' " [Psalm 118:26].

[1]Some mss. do not contain *desolate*.

Sec. 201   A poor widow's gift of all she had
— *Jerusalem, in the Temple* —

Mark 12:41-44	Luke 21:1-4
41 And He sat down opposite the treasury, and *began* observing how the multitude were putting [1]money into the treasury; and many rich people were putting in large sums.	**1** And He looked up and saw the rich putting their gifts into the treasury.
42 And a poor widow came and put in two [2]small copper coins, which amount to a [3]cent.	**2** And He saw a certain poor widow putting [7]in two [2]small copper coins.
43 And calling His disciples to Him, He said to them, "Truly I say to you, this poor widow put in more than all [4]the contributors to the treasury;	**3** And He said, "Truly I say to you, this poor widow put in more than all *of* them;
44 for they all put in out of their [5]surplus, but [y]she, out of her poverty, put in all she owned, [6]all she had to live on."	**4** for they all out of their [5]surplus put into the [8]offering; but [y]she out of her poverty put in all [9]that she had to live on."

[1]I.e., copper coins. [2]Gr., *lepta*. [3]Gr., *quadrans*; i.e., 1/64 of a denarius. [4]Lit., *those who were putting in*. [5]Or, *abundance*. [6]Lit., *her whole livelihood*. [7]Or, *therein*. [8]Lit., *gifts*. [9]Lit., *the living that she had*.

---

[w](Matt. 23:37) Jesus' deep concern for Jerusalem was voiced in similar language about three months earlier (Luke 13:34-35, Sec. 163) and also two days before in somewhat different language (Luke 19:41-44, Sec. 187). This city represented the whole nation of Israel for whom Jesus was deeply burdened, especially in light of her coming judgment.

[x](Matt. 23:39) At His second coming a far greater proportion of Israel will joyfully recognize Jesus as Messiah than did so at His first coming. This lament over Jerusalem was preparatory to what Jesus wanted to tell His disciples about His future coming and its relation to Jerusalem (cf. Sec. 202).

[y](Mark 12:44; Luke 21:4) Here was an example of true piety. In contrast to the corrupt leadership (cf. Matt. 23:23-24, Sec. 199), this woman gave from her heart, as evidenced by her self-sacrifice.

PART ELEVEN
PROPHECIES IN PREPARATION FOR THE DEATH OF CHRIST

THE OLIVET DISCOURSE: PROPHECIES ABOUT THE TEMPLE AND THE RETURN OF CHRIST

Sec. 202 Setting of the Discourse
— From the Temple to the Mount of Olives —

Matt. 24:1-3	Mark 13:1-4	Luke 21:5-7
1 And Jesus came out from the temple and was going away [1]when His disciples came up to point out the temple buildings to Him.	**1** And as He was going out of the temple, one of His disciples *said to Him, "Teacher, behold [3]what wonderful stones and [3]what wonderful buildings!"	**5** And while some were talking about the temple, that it was adorned with beautiful stones and votive gifts, He said,
2 And He answered and said to them, "Do you not see all these things? Truly I say to you, not one stone here shall be left upon another, which will not be torn down."	**2** And Jesus said to him, "Do you see these great buildings? Not one stone shall be left upon another which will not be torn down."	**6** *"As for* these things which you are looking at, the days will come in which there will not be left one stone upon another which will not be torn down."
3 And as He was sitting on the Mount of Olives, the disciples came to Him privately,	**3** And as He was sitting on the Mount of Olives opposite the temple, Peter and [4]James and John and Andrew were questioning Him privately,	
saying, "Tell us, [z]when will these things be, and what *will be* the sign of Your coming, and of the [2]end of the age?"	**4** "Tell us, [z]when will these things be, and what *will be* the [5]sign when all these things are going to be fulfilled?"	**7** And they questioned Him, saying, "Teacher, [z]when therefore will these things be? And what *will be* the [5]sign when these things are about to take place?"

[1]Lit., *and.*   [2]Or, *consummation.*   [3]Lit., *how great.*   [4]Or, *Jacob.*   [5]Or, *attesting miracle.*

---

[z](Matt. 24:3; Mark 13:4; Luke 21:7) The disciples apparently asked three questions. The first pertained to the destruction of the Temple (cf. Matt. 24:1-2; Mark 13:1-2; Luke 21:5-6), which subsequently happened in A.D. 70 at the hands of the Roman army. Another pertained to Jesus' future personal return and the consummation of the age associated with it. Though separated by many years, the two events are closely related in that both are part of God's ongoing program for the people of Israel. The other question related to the sign when "these things," probably the destruction of the Temple, were about to happen. The disciples assumed that the destruction of the Temple would be the prelude to Messiah's return to consummate that age and initiate His Kingdom on earth. Jesus did not deny a relationship between the two events, nor did He in the subsequent discourse reveal the long interval that would separate the two. Some predictions were fulfilled a few years after He spoke the words (e.g., Luke 21:20, Sec. 204), but others have as yet to be fulfilled (e.g., Matt. 24:30, Sec. 205).

Sec. 203 Beginning of birth pangs (cf. Secs. 99; 146)
— *Mount of Olives* —

Matt. 24:4-14	Mark 13:5-13	Luke 21:8-19
4 And Jesus answered and said to them, "See to it that no one misleads you. **5** "For many will come in My name, saying, 'I am the ¹Christ,' and will mislead many, **6** "And you will be hearing of wars and rumors of wars; see that you are not frightened, for *those things* must take place, but *that* is not yet the end. **7** "For nation will rise against nation, and kingdom against kingdom, and in various places there will be famines and earthquakes.	**5** And Jesus began to say to them, "See to it that no one misleads you. **6** "Many will come in My name, saying, 'I am He!' and will mislead many. **7** "And when you hear of wars and rumors of wars, do not be frightened; *those things* must take place; but *that* is not yet the end. **8** "For nation will arise against nation, and kingdom against kingdom; there will be earthquakes in various places; there will *also* be famines.	**8** And He said, "See to it that you be not misled; for many will come in My name, saying, 'I am He,' and, 'The time is at hand'; do not go after them. **9** "And when you hear of wars and disturbances, do not be terrified; for these things must take place first, but the end *does* not *follow* immediately." **10** Then He continued by saying to them, "Nation will rise against nation, and kingdom against kingdom, **11** and there will be great earthquakes, and in various places plagues and famines; and there will be terrors and great ⁹signs from heaven.
8 "But all these things are *merely* the beginning of ªbirth pangs. **9** "Then they will deliver you to tribulation, and will kill you, and you will be hated by all nations on account of My name.	These things are *merely* the beginning of ªbirth pangs. **9** "But ⁵be on your guard; for they will deliver you to the ⁶courts, and you will be flogged in the synagogues, and you will stand before governors and kings for My sake, as a testimony to them. **10** "And the gospel must first be preached to all the nations. **11** "And when they ⁷arrest you and deliver you up, do not be anxious beforehand about what you are to say, but say whatever is given you in that hour; for it is not you who speak, but it is the Holy Spirit.	**12** "But before all these things, they will lay their hands on you and will persecute you, delivering you to the synagogues and prisons, ¹⁰bringing you before kings and governors for My name's sake. **13** "It will lead to an ¹¹opportunity for your testimony. **14** "So make up your minds not to prepare beforehand to defend yourselves; **15** for I will give you ¹²utterance and wisdom

ª(Matt. 24:8; Mark 13:8) "Birth pangs" is a frequent figure of speech to depict the time of Israel's tribulation, which is the initial phase of "the day of the Lord" in Scripture (Isa. 13:8; 26:17-19; 66:7-9; Jer. 30:7-8; Mic. 4:9-10; 1 Thess. 5:3). This period of growing human agony will be climaxed by Messiah's second coming to earth.

Matt. 24:4-14 (cont'd)	Mark 13:5-13 (cont'd)	Luke 21:8-19 (cont'd)
10 "And at that time many will ²fall away and will deliver up one another and hate one another.	**12** "And brother will deliver brother to death, and a father *his* child; and children will rise up against parents and ⁸have them put to death. **13** "And you will be hated by all on account of My name,	which none of your opponents will be able to resist or refute.　. **16** "But you will be delivered up even by parents and brothers and relatives and friends, and they will put *some* of you to death, **17** and you will be hated by all on account of My name. **18** "Yet not a hair of your head will perish. **19** "By your endurance you gain your ¹³lives.
11 "And many false prophets will arise, and will mislead many. **12** "And because lawlessness is increased, ³most people's love will grow cold. **13** "But the one who endures to the end, he shall be saved. **14** "And this gospel of the kingdom shall be preached in the whole ⁴world for a witness to all the nations, and then the end shall come.	but the one who endures to the end, he shall be saved.	

¹I.e., Messiah.　²Lit., *be caused to stumble.*　³Lit., *the love of many.*　⁴Lit., *inhabited earth.*　⁵Lit., *look to yourselves.*　⁶Or, *Sanhedrin* or *council.*　⁷Lit., *lead.*　⁸Lit., *put them to death.*　⁹Or, *attesting miracles.*　¹⁰Lit., *being brought.*　¹¹Lit., *a testimony for you.*　¹²Lit., *a mouth.*　¹³Or, *soul.*

Sec. 204　Abomination of desolation and subsequent distress (cf. Sec. 174)
― Mount of Olives ―

Matt. 24:15-28	Mark 13:14-23	Luke 21:20-24
15 "Therefore when you see the ᵇABOMINATION OF DESOLATION [Dan. 9:27; 11:31; 12:11] which was spoken of through Daniel the prophet, standing in the holy place (let the reader understand),	**14** "But when you see the ᵇABOMINATION OF DESOLATION [Dan. 9:27; 11:31; 12:11] standing where it should not be (let the reader understand),	

ᵇ(Matt. 24:15; Mark 13:14) This feature of Daniel's seventy-week prophecy (Dan. 9:27) had not been fulfilled by this time. Neither has it been fulfilled since Jesus' time. As the midpoint of the future seventieth week of the prophecy, the "abomination of desolation" furnishes one of the most conspicuous signs of Jesus' coming (cf. Matt. 24:3, Sec. 202).

Matt. 24:15-28 (cont'd)	Mark 13:14-23 (cont'd)	Luke 21:20-24 (cont'd)
		20 "But when you see Jerusalem surrounded by armies, then [8]recognize that her desolation is at hand.
16 then let those who are in Judea flee to the mountains; **17** let him who is on the housetop not go down to get the things out that are in his house; **18** and let him who is in the field not turn back to get his cloak.	then let those who are in Judea flee to the mountains. **15** "And let him who is on the housetop not go down, or enter in, to get anything out of his house; **16** and let him who is in the field not turn back to get his cloak.	**21** "Then let those who are in Judea flee to the mountains, and let those who are in the midst of the [9]city depart, and let not those who are in the country enter [9]the city;
		22 because these are days of vengeance, in order that all things which are written may be fulfilled.
19 "But woe to those who are with child and to those who nurse babes in those days! **20** "But pray that your flight may not be in the winter, or on a Sabbath; **21** for then there will be a great tribulation, such as has not occurred since the beginning of the world until now, nor ever shall. **22** "And unless those days had been cut short, no [1]life would have been saved; but for the sake of the [2]elect those days shall be cut short.	**17** "But woe to those who are with child and to those who nurse babes in those days! **18** "But pray that it may not happen in the winter. **19** "For those days will be a *time of* tribulation such as has not occurred since the beginning of the creation which God created, until now, and never shall. **20** "And unless the Lord had shortened *those* days, no [1]life would have been saved; but for the sake of the [2]elect whom He chose, He shortened the days.	**23** "Woe to those who are with child and to those who nurse babes in those days;
		for there will be great distress upon the [10]land, and wrath to this people, **24** and they will fall by the edge of the sword, and will be led captive into all the nations; and Jerusalem will be trampled under foot by the Gentiles until the times of the Gentiles be fulfilled.
23 "Then if anyone says to you, 'Behold, here	**21** "And then if anyone says to you, 'Behold,	

Matt. 24:15-28 (cont'd)	Mark 13:14-23 (cont'd)
is the [3]Christ,' or '[4]There *He is,*' do not believe *him.*	here is the [3]Christ'; or 'Behold, *He is* there'; do not believe *him;*
24 "For false Christs and false prophets will arise and will show great [5]signs and wonders, so as to mislead, if possible, even the [2]elect.	**22** for false Christs and false prophets will arise, and will show [5]signs and wonders, in order, if possible, to lead the elect astray.
25 "Behold, I have told you in advance.	**23** "But take heed; behold, I have told you everything in advance.
26 "If therefore they say to you, 'Behold, He is in the wilderness,' do not go forth, or, 'Behold, He is in the inner rooms,' do not believe *them.*	
27 "For just as the lightning comes from the east, and flashes even to the west, so shall the [6]coming of the Son of Man be.	
28 "Wherever the corpse is, there the [7]vultures will gather.	

[1]Lit., *flesh.* [2]Or, *chosen ones.* [3]I.e., Messiah. [4]Lit., *Here.* [5]Or, *attesting miracles.* [6]Or, *presence.* [7]Or, *eagles.* [8]Lit., *know.* [9]Lit. *her.* [10]Or, *earth.*

Sec. 205   Coming of the Son of Man (cf. Sec. 174)
– *Mount of Olives* –

Matt. 24:29-31	Mark 13:24-27	Luke 21:25-27
29 "But immediately after the tribulation of those days THE SUN WILL BE DARKENED, AND THE MOON WILL NOT GIVE ITS LIGHT, AND THE STARS WILL FALL [Isa. 13:10; 34:4; Ezek. 32:7; Joel 2:10, 31; 3:15] from [1]the sky,	**24** "But in those days, after that tribulation, THE SUN WILL BE DARKENED, AND THE MOON WILL NOT GIVE ITS LIGHT, **25** AND THE STARS WILL BE FALLING [Isa. 13:10; 34:4; Ezek. 32:7; Joel 2:10, 31; 3:15] from heaven,	**25** "And there will be [3]signs in sun and moon and stars, and upon the earth dismay among nations, in perplexity at the roaring of the sea and the waves, **26** men fainting from fear and the expectation of the things which are coming upon the [4]world;
and the powers of the heavens will be shaken, **30** and then the sign of the [c]Son of Man will appear in the sky, and then all the tribes of the earth	and the powers that are in [1]the heavens will be shaken.	for the powers of [1]the heavens will be shaken.

[c](Matt. 24:30; Mark 13:26; Luke 21:27) The return of "the Son of Man" to earth will climax all the

Matt. 24:29-31 (cont'd)	Mark 13:24-27 (cont'd)	Luke 21:25-27 (cont'd)
will mourn, and they will see the ^cSON OF MAN COMING ON THE CLOUDS OF THE SKY [Dan. 7:13] with power and great glory. **31** "And He will send forth His angels with A GREAT TRUMPET and THEY WILL GATHER TOGETHER [Isa. 27:13] His ²elect from the four winds, from one end of the sky to the other.	**26** "And then they will see THE ^cSON OF MAN COMING IN CLOUDS [Dan. 7:13] with great power and glory. **27** "And then He will send forth the angels, and will gather together His ²elect from the four winds, from the farthest end of the earth, to the farthest end of heaven.	**27** "And then they will see THE ^cSON OF MAN COMING IN A CLOUD [Dan. 7:13] with power and great glory.

¹Or, heaven.   ²Or, chosen ones.   ³Or, attesting miracles.   ⁴Lit., inhabited earth.

Sec. 206   Signs of nearness, but unknown time (cf. Sec. 174)
— *Mount of Olives* —

Matt. 24:32-41	Mark 13:28-32	Luke 21:28-33
		28 "But when these things begin to take place, straighten up and lift up your heads, because your redemption is drawing near."
32 "Now learn the parable from the fig tree: when its branch has already become tender, and puts forth its leaves, you know that summer is near; **33** even so you too, when you see all ^dthese things, ¹recognize that ²He is near, *right* at the ³door. **34** "Truly I say to you, this ⁴generation will not pass away until all these things take place. **35** "Heaven and earth	**28** "Now learn the parable from the fig tree: when its branch has already become tender, and puts forth its leaves, you know that summer is near. **29** "Even so, you too, when you see ^dthese things happening, ¹recognize that ²He is near, *right* at the ³door. **30** "Truly I say to you, this ⁴generation will not pass away until all these things take place.	**29** And He told them a parable: "Behold the fig tree and all the trees; **30** as soon as they put forth *leaves*, you see it and ¹know for yourselves that summer is now near. **31** "Even so you, too, when you see ^dthese things happening, ¹recognize that the kingdom of God is near. **32** "Truly I say to you, this ⁴generation will not pass away until all things

hopes and aspirations of Israel. Coming, as it does, immediately after her time of tribulation (Matt. 24:29), the return will be the occasion for regathering the dispersed of Israel (Matt. 24:31; Mark 13:27). Throughout the Old Testament this national deliverance is a recurring theme of Jewish eschatological hope (Deut. 30:3-4; Isa. 11:12; 27:13; 56:8; Jer. 23:3; 31:8; Ezek. 11:17; 20:34, 41; 28:25; 34:13; cf. Rom. 11:26).

^d(Matt. 24:33; Mark 13:29; Luke 21:31) "These things" are events the Lord has described in earlier verses of this discourse, such as the "birth pangs" (Matt. 24:8; Mark 13:9, Sec. 203) and "the abomination of desolation" (Matt. 24:15; Mark 13:14, Sec. 204). When Israel sees these things beginning to happen, she can recognize that her "redemption is drawing near" (Luke 21:28) and that "the Kingdom of God is near" (Luke 21:31). She will experience this national deliverance through the coming of the Son of Man (cf. Sec. 205).

Matt. 24:32-41 (cont'd)	Mark 13:28-32 (cont'd)	Luke 21:28-33 (cont'd)
will pass away, but My words shall not pass away. **36** "But of that day and hour no one knows, not even the angels of heaven, nor the Son, but the Father alone. **37** "For ⁵the coming of the Son of Man will be just like the days of Noah.	**31** "Heaven and earth will pass away, but My words will not pass away. **32** "But of that day or hour no one knows, not even the angels in heaven, nor the Son, but the Father alone.	take place. **33** "Heaven and earth will pass away, but My words will not pass away.

38 "For as in those days which were before the flood they were eating and drinking, they were marrying and giving in marriage, until the day that Noah entered the ark [Gen. 7:7],
39 and they did not ¹understand until the flood came and took them all away; so shall the coming of the Son of Man be.
40 "Then there shall be two men in the field; one ⁶will be taken, and one ⁶will be left.
41 "Two women *will* be grinding at the ⁷mill; one ⁶will be taken, and one ⁶will be left.

¹Lit., *know.* ²Or, *it.* ³Lit., *doors.* ⁴Or, *race.* ⁵Lit., *just as . . . were the days.* ⁶Lit., *is.* ⁷I.e., *handmill.*

Sec. 207   ᵉFive parables to teach watchfulness and faithfulness (cf. Secs. 148; 184)
– Mount of Olives –

Matt. 24:42—25:30	Mark 13:33-37	Luke 21:34-36
	33 "Take heed, keep on the alert; for you do not know when the *appointed* time is. **34** "*It is* like a man, away on a journey, *who* upon leaving his house and ¹¹putting his slaves in charge, *assigning* to each one his task, also commanded the doorkeeper to stay on the alert.	**34** "Be on guard, that your hearts may not be weighted down with dissipation and drunkenness and the worries of life, and that day come on you suddenly like a trap; **35** for it will come upon all those who dwell on the face of all the earth.
42 "Therefore be on the alert, for you do not know which day your Lord is coming.	**35** "Therefore, be on the alert — for you do not know when the ³master of the house is coming, whether in the evening, at midnight, at cockcrowing, or in the morning —	**36** "But keep on the alert at all times, praying in order that you may have strength to escape all these things that are about to take place, and to stand before the Son of Man."

ᵉOf the five parables, one is in Mark alone (13:34-36), and four are in Matthew only (24:43, 45-51; 25:1-12, 14-30). In the first, second, and fourth parables the dominant lesson is watchfulness. The lesson of the third and fifth parables is that faithfulness in service must accompany alertness for the Lord's return.

Matt. 24:42—25:30 (cont'd)	Mark 13:33-37 (cont'd)
	36 lest he come suddenly and find you asleep. **37** "And what I say to you I say to all, 'Be on the\ alert!'"
43 "But [1]be sure of this, that if the head of the house had known at what time of the night the thief was coming, he would have been on the alert and would not have allowed his house to be [2]broken into.	

44 "For this reason you be ready too; for the Son of Man is coming at an hour when you do not think *He will.*

45 "Who then is the faithful and sensible slave whom his [3]master put in charge of his household to give them their food at the proper time?

46 "Blessed is that slave whom his [3]master finds so doing when he comes.

47 "Truly I say to you, that he will put him in charge of all his possessions.

48 "But if that evil slave says in his heart, 'My [3]master [4]is not coming for a long time,'

49 and shall begin to beat his fellow slaves and eat and drink with [5]drunkards;

50 the [3]master of that slave will come on a day when he does not expect *him* and at an hour which he does not know,

51 and shall [6]cut him in pieces and [7]assign him a place with the hypocrites; weeping shall be there and the gnashing of teeth.

1 "Then the kingdom of heaven will be comparable to ten virgins, who took their lamps, and went out to meet the bridegroom.

2 "And five of them were foolish, and five were prudent.

3 "For when the foolish took their lamps, they took no oil with them,

4 but the prudent took oil in flasks along with their lamps.

5 "Now while the bridegroom was delaying, they all got drowsy and *began* to sleep.

6 "But at midnight there was a shout, 'Behold, the bridegroom! Come out to meet *him.*'

7 "Then all those virgins rose, and trimmed their lamps.

8 "And the foolish said to the prudent, 'Give us some of your oil, for our lamps are going out.'

9 "But the prudent answered, saying, 'No, there will not be enough for us and you *too*; go instead to the dealers and buy *some* for yourselves.'

10 "And while they were going away to make the purchase, the bridegroom came, and those who were ready went in with him to the wedding feast; and the door was shut.

11 "And later the other virgins also came, saying, 'Lord, lord, open up for us.'

12 "But he answered and said, 'Truly I say to you, I do not know you.'

13 "Be on the alert then, for you do not know the day nor the hour.

14 "For *it is* just like a man *about* to go on a journey, who called his own slaves, and entrusted his possessions to them.

15 "And to one he gave five [8]talents, to another, two, and to another, one,

Matt. 24:42—25:30 (cont'd)

each according to his own ability; and he went on his journey.

16 "Immediately the one who had received the five talents went and traded with them, and gained five more talents.

17 "In the same manner the one who had *received* the two *talents* gained two more.

18 "But he who received the one *talent* went away and dug in the ground, and hid his ⁹master's money.

19 "Now after a long time the master of those slaves *came and *settled accounts with them.

20 "And the one who had received the five talents came up and brought five more talents, saying, 'Master, you entrusted five talents to me; see, I have gained five more talents.'

21 "His master said to him, 'Well done, good and faithful slave; you were faithful with a few things, I will put you in charge of many things, enter into the joy of your ³master.'

22 "The one also who had *received* the two talents came up and said, 'Master, you entrusted to me two talents; see, I have gained two more talents.'

23 "His master said to him, 'Well done, good and faithful slave; you were faithful with a few things, I will put you in charge of many things; enter into the joy of your master.'

24 "And the one also who had received the one talent came up and said, 'Master, I knew you to be a hard man, reaping where you did not sow, and gathering where you scattered no *seed.*

25 'And I was afraid, and went away and hid your talent in the ground; see, you have what is yours.'

26 "But his master answered and said to him, 'You wicked, lazy slave, you knew that I reap where I did not sow, and gather where I scattered no *seed.*

27 'Then you ought to have put my money ¹⁰in the bank, and on my arrival I would have received my *money* back with interest.

28 'Therefore take away the talent from him, and give it to the one who has the ten talents.'

29 "For to everyone who has shall *more* be given, and he shall have an abundance; but from the one who does not have, even what he does have shall be taken away.

30 "And cast out the worthless slave into the outer darkness; in that place there shall be weeping and gnashing of teeth.

¹Lit., *know this.* ²Lit., *dug through.* ³Or, *lord.* ⁴Lit., *lingers.* ⁵Lit., *those who get drunk.* ⁶Or, *severely scourge him.* ⁷Lit., *appoint his portion.* ⁸A talent was $1,000 in silver content, much more in buying power. ⁹Or, *lord's.* ¹⁰Lit., *to the bankers.* ¹¹Lit., *giving the authority to.*

Sec. 208   Judgment at the Son of Man's coming
– Mount of Olives –

Matt. 25:31-46

31 "But when the Son of Man comes in His glory, and all the angels with Him, then He will sit on His glorious ᶠthrone.

ᶠ(Matt. 25:31) The throne on which the Son of Man will sit when He comes (cf. Matt. 24:30; Mark 13:26; Luke 21:27, Sec. 205) will be located at His destination, that is, on earth. It is the throne of His father David to which He is heir (Luke 1:32-33, Sec. 5). From here He will judge the survivors of the period of the Great Tribulation (Matt. 24:21-22; Mark 13:19-20, Sec. 204; Matt. 24:29; Mark 13:24, Sec. 205).

Matt. 25:31-46 (cont'd)

32 "And all the nations will be gathered before Him; and He will separate them from one another, as the shepherd separates the sheep from the goats;
33 and He will put the sheep on His right, and the goats on the left.
34 "Then the King will say to those on His right, 'Come, you who are blessed of My Father, inherit the kingdom prepared for you from the foundation of the world.
35 'For I was hungry, and you gave Me *something* to eat; I was thirsty, and you gave Me drink; I was a stranger, and you invited Me in;
36 naked, and you clothed Me; I was sick, and you visited Me; I was in prison, and you came to Me.'
37 "Then the righteous will answer Him, saying, 'Lord, when did we see You hungry, and feed You, or thirsty, and give You drink?
38 'And when did we see You a stranger, and invite You in, or naked, and clothe You?
39 'And when did we see You sick, or in prison, and come to You?'
40 "And the King will answer and say to them, 'Truly I say to you, to the extent that you did it to one of these brothers of Mine, *even* the least *of them*, you did it to Me.'
41 "Then He will also say to those on His left, 'Depart from Me, accursed ones, into the eternal fire which has been prepared for the devil and his angels;
42 for I was hungry, and you gave Me *nothing* to eat; I was thirsty, and you gave Me nothing to drink;
43 I was a stranger, and you did not invite Me in; naked, and you did not clothe Me; sick, and in prison, and you did not visit Me.'
44 "Then they themselves also will answer, saying, 'Lord, when did we see You hungry, or thirsty, or a stranger, or naked, or sick, or in prison, and did not ¹take care of You?'
45 "Then He will answer them, saying, 'Truly I say to you, to the extent that you did not do it to one of the least of these, you did not do it to Me.'
46 "And these will go away into eternal punishment, but the righteous into eternal life."

¹Or, *serve.*

ARRANGEMENTS FOR BETRAYAL

Sec. 209   Plot by the Sanhedrin to arrest and kill Jesus
   – Mount of Olives and the court of the high priest –

Matt. 26:1-5	Mark 14:1-2	Luke 21:37—22:2
		37 Now ¹during the day He was teaching in the temple, but ²at evening He would go out and spend the night on ³the mount that is called ⁴Olivet.
		38 And all the people would get up early in the morning to come to Him in the temple to listen to Him.
1 And it came about that when Jesus had finished all these words, He said to His disciples,	**1** Now the Passover and Unleavened Bread was two days off;	**1** Now the Feast of Unleavened Bread, which is called the Passover, was approaching.

Matt. 26:1-5 (cont'd)	Mark 14:1-2 (cont'd)	Luke 21:37—22:2 (cont'd)
2 "You know that after two days the Passover is coming, and the Son of Man is *to be* delivered up for crucifixion."		
3 Then ᵍthe chief priests and the elders of the people were gathered together in the court of the high priest, named Caiaphas;	and the chief priests and the scribes were seeking how	
4 and they plotted together to seize Jesus by stealth, and kill *Him.*	to seize Him by stealth, and kill *Him;*	**2** And the chief priests and the scribes were seeking how they
5 But they were saying, "Not during the festival, lest a riot occur among the people."	**2** for they were saying, "Not during the festival, lest there be a riot of the people."	might put Him to death; for they were afraid of the people.

¹Lit., *days.* ²Lit., *nights.* ³Or, *the hill.* ⁴Or, *Olive Grove.*

Sec. 210   Judas' agreement to betray Jesus
— *Jerusalem* —

Matt. 26:14-16	Mark 14:10-11	Luke 22:3-6
14 Then one of the twelve, named Judas Iscariot,	**10** And Judas Iscariot, who was one of the twelve,	**3** And ʰSatan entered into Judas who was called Iscariot, ⁵belonging to the number of the twelve.
went to the chief priests,	went off to the chief priests, in order to ⁴betray Him to them.	**4** And he went away and discussed with the chief priests and officers how he might betray Him to them.
15 and said, "What are you willing to give me ¹to ²deliver Him up to you?" And they weighed out to		
	11 And they were glad	**5** And they were glad,

ᵍ(Matt. 26:3) The Sanhedrin, represented by two of its three groups and presided over by Caiaphas, met to lay plans as to how it could implement the decision already reached (cf. John 11:53, Sec. 172). Because of Jesus' great popularity (Luke 21:38; 22:2), particularly among the visitors from Galilee and Perea, they decided to wait until after the feast (Matt. 26:5; Mark 14:2) when these pilgrims would have gone home. Their schedule of action was accelerated, however, when they received an unexpected offer of cooperation from one of the twelve (Sec. 210). This enabled them to arrest Jesus privately (Luke 22:6, Sec. 210; Sec. 227). In this way God's predetermined schedule for the Lamb of God to be slain on the Passover, and not after, (Matt. 26:2) was kept.

ʰ(Luke 22:3) The Scripture does not tell what form of deception Satan used to persuade Judas to follow this calamitous course. Judas could have been moved by any one of a number of motives or a combination of several. Covetousness seems to have played some part (John 12:6, Sec. 186). He may have wanted to make it appear to the rest of the twelve that he, like them, was concerned for the poor (Matt. 26:8-9; Mark 14:4-5, Sec. 186). He possibly felt his obligation as a citizen to obey the recent ruling about reporting Jesus' whereabouts to the authorities (John 11:57, Sec. 185). He may have been more disappointed than the rest of the twelve over the outcome of the triumphal entry: that Jesus and the Jewish leaders did not enter into an agreement to make Him King (Matt. 21:15-17; Luke 19:39-40, Sec. 187). Perhaps he thought by this action he could force Jesus to assume the throne. After what he had witnessed over the last three years, in all likelihood he never dreamed that his action would result in Jesus' crucifixion (Sec. 232). Whatever the case, his motives must have been selfish. Otherwise, Satan could not have gained control over him.

Matt. 26:14-16 (cont'd)	Mark 14:10-11 (cont'd)	Luke 22:3-6 (cont'd)
him thirty [3]pieces of silver. **16** And from then on he *began* looking for a good opportunity to [4]betray Him.	when they heard *this,* and promised to give him money. And he *began* seeking how to betray Him at an opportune time.	and agreed to give him money. **6** And he consented, and *began* seeking a good opportunity to betray Him to them [6]apart from the multitude.

[1]Lit., *and I will.* [2]Or, *betray.* [3]Or, *silver shekels.* [4]Or, *deliver Him up.* [5]Lit., *being of.* [6]Or, *without a disturbance.*

THE LAST SUPPER

Sec. 211   Preparation for the Passover meal
– *Jerusalem* –

Matt. 26:17-19	Mark 14:12-16	Luke 22:7-13
17 Now on the first day of Unleavened Bread the disciples came to Jesus, saying, "Where do You want us to [1]prepare for You to eat the Passover?" **18** And He said,	**12** And on the first day of Unleavened Bread, when [1]the Passover *lamb* was being sacrificed, His disciples *said to Him, "Where do You want us to go and [1]prepare for You to eat the Passover?" **13** And He *sent two of His disciples, and *said to them,	**7** Then came the *first* day of Unleavened Bread on which the Passover *lamb* had to be sacrificed. **8** And He sent Peter and John, saying, "Go and [1]prepare the Passover for us, that we may eat it." **9** And they said to Him, "Where do You want us to prepare it?" **10** And He said to them, "Behold, when you have entered the city, a man will meet you carrying a pitcher of water; follow him into the house that he enters. **11** "And you shall say to the owner of the house, 'The Teacher says to you, "Where is the guest room in which I may eat the Passover with My disciples?"' **12** "And he will show you a large, furnished,
"Go into the city to a certain man, and say to him, 'The Teacher says, "My time is at hand; I am to keep the Passover at your house with My disciples."'"	"Go into the city, and a man will meet you carrying a pitcher of water; follow him; **14** and wherever he enters, say to the owner of the house, 'The Teacher says, "Where is My guest room in which I may eat the Passover with My disciples?"' **15** "And he himself will show you a large upper room furnished *and*	

[1](Matt. 26:17; Mark 14:12; Luke 22:8) These preparations came during the daylight hours on Thursday, the fourteenth of Nisan. Lambs were customarily sacrificed in the afternoon in preparation for the Passover supper, which was eaten in the evening.

Matt. 26:17-19 (cont'd)	Mark 14:12-16 (cont'd)	Luke 22:7-13 (cont'd)
	ready; and prepare for us there."	upper room; prepare it there."
19 And the disciples did as Jesus had directed them; and they prepared the Passover.	**16** And the disciples went out, and came to the city, and found *it* just as He had told them; and they prepared the Passover.	**13** And they departed and found *everything* just as He had told them; and t h e y p r e p a r e d t h e Passover.

¹Lit., *they were sacrificing.*

Sec. 212 Beginning of the Passover meal
— Jerusalem, in the upper room —

Matt. 26:20	Mark 14:17	Luke 22:14-16
20 Now when evening had come, He was reclining *at the table* with the twelve disciples.	**17** And when it was evening He *came with the twelve.	
		14 And when the hour had come He reclined *at the table,* and the apostles with Him.
		15 A n d H e s a i d t o them, "I have earnestly desired to eat this ʲPassover with you before I suffer;
		16 for I say to you, I shall never again eat it until it is fulfilled in the kingdom of God."

Sec. 213 Washing the disciples' feet (cf. Secs. 70, 99, 220; 127)
— Jerusalem, in the upper room —

John 13:1-20

1 Now ᵏbefore the Feast of the Passover, Jesus knowing that His hour had come that He should depart out of this world to the Father, having loved His own who were in the world, He loved them ¹to the end.

2 And during supper, the devil having already put into the heart of Judas Iscariot, *the son* of Simon, to betray Him,

3 Jesus, knowing that the Father had given all things into His hands, and that He had come forth from God, and was going back to God,

4 *rose from supper, and *laid aside His garments; and taking a towel, girded Himself about.

ʲ(Luke 22:15) Matthew, Mark, and Luke leave no doubt that this Last Supper was the Passover meal. This means that it took place on the fifteenth of Nisan (Lev. 23:5), that is, Thursday evening after sundown which was the evening that closed the fourteenth and began the fifteenth.

ᵏ(John 13:1) Apparently John intends this as a chronological note to locate the supper (John 13:2) described in the rest of the chapter. It is also apparent that this is the same supper described as the Passover in the synoptic gospels (cf. Secs. 211-212). Therefore, John seems to have in mind a different scheme for reckoning when the Passover began. For further discussion, see essay 10, "The Day and-Year of Christ's Crucifixion" (pp. 320-323).

John 13:1-20 (cont'd)

5 Then He *poured water into the basin, and began to wash the disciples' feet, and to wipe them with the towel with which He was girded.

6 And so He *came to Simon Peter. He *said to Him, "Lord, do You wash my feet?"

7 Jesus answered and said to him, "What I do you do not realize now; but you shall understand hereafter."

8 Peter *said to Him, "Never shall You wash my feet!" Jesus answered him, "If I do not wash you, you have no part with Me."

9 Simon Peter *said to Him, "Lord, not my feet only, but also my hands and my head."

10 Jesus *said to him, "He who has bathed needs only to wash his feet, but is completely clean; and you are clean, but not all *of you.*"

11 For He knew the one who was betraying Him; for this reason He said, "Not all of you are clean."

12 And so when He had washed their feet, and taken His garments, and re-clined *at the table* again, He said to them, "Do you know what I have done to you?

13 "You call Me Teacher and Lord; and ²you are right; for *so* I am.

14 "If I then, the Lord and the Teacher, washed your feet, you also ought to wash one another's feet.

15 "For I gave you an ¹example that you also should do as I did to you.

16 "Truly, truly, I say to you, a slave is not greater than his master; neither *is* one who is sent greater than the one who sent him.

17 "If you know these things, you are blessed if you do them.

18 "I do not speak of all of you. I know the ones I have chosen; but *it is* that the Scripture may be fulfilled, 'HE WHO EATS MY BREAD HAS LIFTED UP HIS HEEL AGAINST ME' [Psalm 41:9].

19 "From now on I am telling you before *it* comes to pass, so that when it does occur, you may believe that I am He.

20 "Truly, truly, I say to you, he who receives whomever I send receives Me; and he who receives Me receives Him who sent Me."

¹Lit., *to the uttermost; or, eternally.*   ²Lit., *you say well.*

Sec. 214   Identification of the betrayer
— *Jerusalem, in the upper room* —

Matt. 26:21-25	Mark 14:18-21	Luke 22:21-23	John 13:21-30
21 And as they were eating, He said, "Truly I say to you that one of you will betray Me."	**18** And as they were reclining *at the table* and eating, Jesus said, "Truly I say to you that one of you will ³betray Me — ⁴one	**21** "But behold, ᵐthe hand of the one betraying Me is	**21** When Jesus had said this, He became troubled in spirit, and testified, and said, "Truly, truly, I say to you, that one of you will

¹(John 13:15) What Jesus did while the supper was in progress was intended to be an example of self-sacrificing humility. The disciples would do well to imitate their Teacher in possessing this quality (John 13:14, 16-17; cf. Secs. 181, 215).

ᵐ(Matt. 26:23, 25; Mark 14:20; Luke 22:21; John 13:26) Mark and Luke do not identify the traitor by name, but Matthew and John do. The rest present apparently did not grasp that Judas was the betrayer (John 13:28). Judas was an honored member of the twelve. He was their treasurer (John 13:29; cf. John 12:6, Sec. 186), and normally was the one to administer benevolences to the poor on their behalf (John 13:29, cf. John 12:4-5, Sec. 186). In fact, he seemingly was seated in the place of honor at this supper, that is at Jesus' left hand, while John the apostle was on His right (John 13:23, 26). Surely, the rest of the disciples must have reasoned, one so respected as Judas could not be the betrayer.

Matt. 26:21-25 (cont'd)	Mark 14:18-21 (cont'd)	Luke 22:21-23 (cont'd)	John 13:21-30 (cont'd)
	who is eating with Me."	with Me on the table. **22** "For indeed, the Son of Man is going as it has been determined; but woe to that man by whom He is betrayed!"	[3]betray Me."
22 And being deeply grieved, they [1]each one began to say to Him, "Surely not I, Lord?" **23** And He answered and said, " [m]He who dipped his hand with Me in the bowl is the one who will betray Me. **24** "The Son of Man *is to* go, just as it is written of Him; but woe to that man by whom the Son of Man is betrayed! It would have been good [2]for that man if he had not been born."	**19** They began to be grieved and to say to Him one by one, "Surely not I?" **20** And He said to them, " [m]It *is* one of the twelve, [4]one who dips with Me in the bowl. **21** "For the Son of Man *is to* go, just as it is written of Him; but woe to that man [5]by whom the Son of Man is betrayed! It *would have been* good [2]for that man if he had not been born."	**23** And they began to discuss among themselves which one of them it might be who was going to do this thing.	**22** The disciples *began* looking at one another, at a loss *to know* of which one He was speaking.
			23 There was reclining on Jesus' breast one of His disciples, whom Jesus loved. **24** Simon Peter therefore *gestured to him, and *said to him, "Tell us who it is of whom He is speaking." **25** He, leaning back thus on Jesus' breast, *said to Him, "Lord, who is it?" **26** Jesus therefore *answered, " [m]That is the one for whom I shall dip the morsel and give it to him." So

Matt. 26:21-25
(cont'd)

John 13:21-30
(cont'd)

when He had dipped the morsel, He *took and *gave it to Judas, *the son* of Simon Iscariot.

25 And ᵐJudas, who was betraying Him, answered and said, "Surely it is not I, Rabbi?" He *said to him, "You have said *it* yourself."

27 And after the morsel, Satan then entered into him, Jesus therefore *said to him, "What you do, do quickly."
28 Now no one of those reclining *at the table* knew for what purpose He had said this to him.
29 For some were supposing, because Judas had the money box, that Jesus was saying to him, "Buy the things we have need of for the feast"; or else, that he should give something to the poor.
30 And so after receiving the morsel he went out immediately; and it was night.

¹Or, *one after another.* ²Lit., *for him if that man had not been born.* ³Or, *deliver Me up.* ⁴Or, *the one.* ⁵Or, *through.*

Sec. 215   Dissension among the disciples over greatness (cf. Sec. 181)
— Jerusalem, in the upper room —

Luke 22:24-30

24 And there arose also a [n]dispute among them *as to* which one of them was regarded to be greatest.

25 And He said to them, "The kings of the Gentiles lord it over them; and those who have authority over them are called 'Benefactors.'

26 "But not so with you, but let him who is the greatest among you become as the youngest, and the leader as the servant.

27 "For who is greater, the one who reclines *at the table,* or the one who serves? Is it not the one who reclines *at the table?* But I am among you as the one who serves.

28 "And you are those who have stood by Me in My trials;

29 and just as My Father has granted Me a kingdom, I grant you

30 that you may eat and drink at My table in My kingdom, and you will sit on thrones judging the twelve tribes of Israel.

Sec. 216   First prediction of Peter's denial (cf. Secs. 225, 228, 230)
— Jerusalem, in the upper room —

Luke 22:31-38	John 13:31-38
	31 When therefore he had gone out, Jesus *said, "Now [3]is the Son of Man glorified, and God [3]is glorified in Him;
	32 [4]if God is glorified in Him, God will also glorify Him in Himself, and will glorify Him immediately.
	33 "Little children, I am with you a little while longer. You shall seek Me; and as I said to the Jews, I now say to you also, 'Where I am going, you cannot come.'
	34 "A new commandment I give to you, that you love one another, even as I have loved you, that you also love one another.
	35 "By this all men will know that you are My disciples, if you have love for one another."
31 "Simon, Simon, behold, Satan has [1]demanded *permission* to sift you like wheat;	**36** Simon Peter *said to Him, "Lord, where are You going?" Jesus answered, "Where I go, you cannot follow Me now; but you shall follow later."
32 but I have prayed for you, that your faith may not fail; and you, when once you have turned again, strengthen your brothers."	

---

[n](Luke 22:24) Quite possibly this dispute immediately preceded and was the occasion for the example of footwashing (Sec. 213). Yet there seems to be no strong reason for departing from Luke's placement of the argument after the identification of the betrayer (Sec. 214). Jesus' words about the destruction of Jerusalem and His second coming (Secs. 202-208) again provoked the disciples to ambition in relation to their roles of leadership when the promised Kingdom on earth becomes a reality (cf. Sec. 181). On the night before His crucifixion, Jesus' patience must have been taxed, because they had still not learned His oft repeated lesson on humility. Jesus, nevertheless, corrected them in regard to this important character trait once again (Luke 22:26-27) but did not correct their anticipations about the Kingdom. He rather confirmed them (Luke 22:28-30).

Luke 22:31-38 (cont'd)	John 13:31-38 (cont'd)
33 And he said to Him, "Lord, with You I am ready to go both to prison and to death!"	**37** Peter *said to Him, "Lord, why can I not follow You right now? I will lay down my life for You."
34 And He said, "I say to you, Peter, the cock will not crow today until °you have denied three times that you know Me."	**38** Jesus *answered, "Will you lay down your life for Me? Truly, truly, I say to you, a cock shall not crow, until °you deny Me three times."
35 And He said to them, "When I sent you out without purse and bag and sandals, you did not lack anything, did you?" And they said, "No, nothing."	
36 And He said to them, "But now, let him who has a purse take it along, likewise also a bag, and let him who has no sword sell his ²robe and buy one.	
37 "For I tell you, that this which is written must be fulfilled in Me, 'AND HE WAS NUMBERED WITH TRANSGRESSORS' [Isa. 53:12]; for that which refers to Me has *its* fulfillment."	
38 And they said, "Lord, look, here are two swords." And He said to them, "It is enough."	

¹Or, *obtained by asking.*   ²Or, *outer garment.*   ³Or, *was.*   ⁴Some ancient mss. do not contain this phrase.

Sec. 217   Conclusion of the meal and the Lord's Supper instituted
— Jerusalem, in the upper room —

Matt. 26:26-29	Mark 14:22-25	Luke 22:17-20	1 Cor. 11:23-26
		17 And when He had taken a cup *and* given thanks, He said, "Take this and share it among yourselves;	
		18 for I say to you, I will not drink of the fruit of the vine from now on until the kingdom of God comes."	
26 And while they were eating, Jesus took *some* bread, and ¹after a blessing, He broke it and gave *it* to the disciples, and said,	**22** And while they were eating, He took *some* bread, and ¹after a blessing He broke it; and gave *it* to them, and said,	**19** And when He had taken *some* bread *and* given thanks, He broke *it*, and gave *it* to them, saying, "This is My body ²which is	**23** For I received from the Lord that which I also delivered to you, that the Lord Jesus in the night in which He was be-

°(Luke 22:34; John 13:38) Since Luke and John make Peter's denial an integral part of the events in the upper room (cf. Luke 22:39; John 18:1, Sec. 225), it appears wiser to allow for two predictions of Peter's denial. The second prediction, described by Matthew and Luke, came while the company was at the Mount of Olives (Matt. 26:34; Mark 14:30, Sec. 225). In connection with this second prediction, Peter and the other disciples claimed they would never deny Him (Matt. 26:35; Mark 14:31, Sec. 225).

Matt. 26:26-29 (cont'd)

"Take, eat; this is My body."
27 And when He had taken a [p]cup and given thanks, He gave *it* to them, saying, "Drink from it, all of you;
28 for this is My blood of the covenant, which is poured out for many for forgiveness of sins.
29 "But I say to you, I will not drink of this fruit of the vine from now on until that day when I drink it new with you in My Father's kingdom."

Mark 14:22-25 (cont'd)

"Take *it;* this is My body."
23 And when He had taken a [p]cup, *and* given thanks, He gave *it* to them; and they all drank from it.
24 And He said to them, "This is My blood of the covenant, which is poured out for many.
25 "Truly I say to you, I shall never again drink of the fruit of the vine until that day when I drink it new in the kingdom of God."

Luke 22:17-20 (cont'd)

given for you; do this in remembrance of Me."
20 And in the same way *He took* the [p]cup after they had eaten, saying, "This cup which is poured out for you is the new covenant in My blood.

I Cor. 11:23-26 (cont'd)

trayed took bread;
24 and when He had given thanks, He broke it, and said, "This is My body which [3]is for you; do this in remembrance of Me."
25 In the same way *He took* the [p]cup also, after supper, saying, "This cup is the new covenant in My blood; do this, as often as you drink *it,* in remembrance of Me."
26 For as often as you eat this bread and drink the cup, you proclaim the Lord's death until He comes.

[1]Lit., *having blessed.* [2]Some ancient mss. do not contain the remainder of v. 19 nor any of v. 20. [3]Some ancient mss. read *is broken.*

DISCOURSES AND PRAYERS FROM THE UPPER ROOM TO GETHSEMANE

Sec. 218 Questions about His destination, the Father, and the Holy Spirit answered

– Jerusalem, in the upper room –

John 14:1-31

1 "[q]Let not your heart be troubled; [1]believe in God, believe also in Me.
2 "In My Father's house are many dwelling places; if it were not so, I would
have told you; for I go to prepare a place for you.
3 "And if I go and prepare a place for you, I will come again, and receive
you to Myself; that where I am, *there* you may be also.

[p](Matt. 26:27; Mark 14:23; Luke 22:20; 1 Cor. 11:25) Like the bread (Matt. 26:26; Mark 14:22; Luke 22:19; 1 Cor. 11:23), this cup was part of the traditional Passover meal among the Jews. It was the third of four times that participants took the cup during the meal. Traditionally the third cup related to the third of four promises of God to Israel in Exodus 6:6-7: "I will also redeem you with an outstretched arm and with great judgment." It becomes symbolic of the shedding of Jesus' blood for redemption (Matt. 26:28; Mark 14:24; Luke 22:20; 1 Cor. 11:25). The final cup, relating to the fourth promise, that of the restoration of Israel, will not be taken by Jesus until the establishing of the Kingdom of God (Matt. 26:29; Mark 14:25).

[q](John 14:1) This discourse (Secs. 218-224), given on Thursday evening of Passion Week, was delivered to the same group as the Olivet discourse given on Tuesday (Secs. 202-208). Yet the two differ radically from one another. A good reason for this difference lies in the dual capacity in which they were addressed. On Tuesday the focus of interest was the future of the nation Israel of which they were members (cf. Sec. 202). On Thursday, the issue was the state of the disciples and other believers during the period of Jesus' absence (John 13:33, 36, Sec. 216; John 16:5-7, Sec. 221). Anticipations of the latter group, many of whom are not Israelites, differ markedly from the national aspirations of Israel.

John 14:1-31 (cont'd)

4 "²And you know the way where I am going."

5 Thomas *said to Him, "Lord, we do not know where You are going, how do we know the way?"

6 Jesus *said to him, "I am the way, and the truth, and the life; no one comes to the Father, but through Me.

7 "If you had known Me, you would have known My Father also; from now on you know Him, and have seen Him."

8 Philip *said to Him, "Lord, show us the Father, and it is enough for us."

9 Jesus *said to him, "Have I been so long with you, and yet you have not come to know Me, Philip? He who has seen Me has seen the Father; how do you say, 'Show us the Father'?

10 "Do you not believe that I am in the Father, and the Father is in Me? The words that I say to you I do not speak on My own initiative, but the Father abiding in Me does His works.

11 "Believe Me that I am in the Father, and the Father in Me; otherwise believe on account of the works themselves.

12 "Truly, truly, I say to you, he who believes in Me, the works that I do shall he do also; and greater *works* than these shall he do; because I go to the Father.

13 "And whatever you ask in My name, that will I do, that the Father may be glorified in the Son.

14 "If you ask Me anything in My name, I will do *it*.

15 "If you love Me, you will keep My commandments.

16 "And I will ask the Father, and He will give you another ³Helper, that He may be with you forever;

17 *that is* the Spirit of truth, whom the world cannot receive, because it does not behold Him or know Him, *but* you know Him because He abides with you, and will be in you.

18 "I will not leave you as orphans; I will come to you.

19 "⁴After a little while the world will behold Me no more; but you *will* behold Me; because I live, you shall live also.

20 "In that day you shall know that I am in My Father, and You in Me, and I in you.

21 "He who has My commandments and keeps them, he it is who loves Me; and he who loves Me shall be loved by My Father, and I will love him, and will disclose Myself to him."

22 Judas (not Iscariot) *said to Him, "Lord, what then has happened that You are going to disclose Yourself to us, and not to the world?"

23 Jesus answered and said to him, "If anyone loves Me, he will keep My word; and My Father will love him, and We will come to him, and make Our abode with him.

24 "He who does not love Me does not keep My words; and the word which you hear is not Mine, but the Father's who sent Me.

25 "These things I have spoken to you, while abiding with you.

26 "But the Helper, the Holy Spirit, whom the Father will send in My name, He will teach you all things, and bring to your remembrance all that I said to you.

27 "Peace I leave with you; My peace I give to you; not as the world gives, do I give to you. Let not your heart be troubled, nor let it be fearful.

28 "You heard that I said to you, 'I go away, and I will come to you.' If you loved Me, you would have rejoiced, because I go to the Father; for the Father is greater than I.

29 "And now I have told you before it comes to pass, that when it comes to pass, you may believe.

30 "I will not speak much more with you, for the ruler of the world is coming, and he has nothing in Me;

John 14:1-31 (cont'd)

31   but that the world may know that I love the Father, and as the Father gave Me commandment, even so I do. ʳArise, let us go from here.

¹Or, *you believe in God.*   ²Some mss. read *And where I go you know, and the way you know.*   ³Gr., *Paracletos,* one called alongside to help; or, *Intercessor.*   ⁴Lit., *Yet a little and the world.*

Sec. 219   The Vine and the branches
— Jerusalem, in the upper room —

John 15:1-17

1   "I am the ˢtrue vine, and My Father is the vinedresser.

2   "Every branch in Me that does not bear fruit, He takes away; and every branch that bears fruit, He ¹prunes it, that it may bear more fruit.

3   "You are already clean because of the word which I have spoken to you.

4   "Abide in Me, and I in you. As the branch cannot bear fruit of itself, unless it abides in the vine, so neither *can* you, unless you abide in Me.

5   "I am the vine, you are the branches; he who abides in Me, and I in him, he bears much fruit; for apart from Me you can do nothing.

6   "If anyone does not abide in Me, he is thrown away as a branch, and dries up; and they gather them, and cast them into the fire, and they are burned.

7   "If you abide in Me, and My words abide in you, ask whatever you wish, and it shall be done for you.

8   "By this is My Father glorified, ²that you bear much fruit, and *so* prove to be My disciples.

9   "Just as the Father has loved Me, I have also loved you; abide in My love.

10   "If you keep My commandments, you will abide in My love; just as I have kept My Father's commandments, and abide in His love.

11   "These things I have spoken to you, that My joy may be in you, and *that* your joy may be made full.

12   "This is My commandment, that you love one another, just as I have loved you.

13   "Greater love has no one than this, that one lay down his life for his friends.

14   "You are My friends, if you do what I command you.

15   "No longer do I call you slaves, for the slave does not know what his master is doing; but I have called you friends, for all things that I have heard from My Father I have made known to you.

16   "You did not choose Me, but I chose you, and appointed you, that you

---

ʳ(John 14:31) Apparently Jesus' words, "Arise, let us go from here," expressed the intent to leave the upper room shortly, not the actual departure. Thus, the discourse and prayer of John 15-17 was given while they were still in the upper room, and their actual departure was recorded in Matthew 26:30, Mark 14:26, Luke 22:39, and John 18:1 (Sec. 225). However, it is also possible to argue that their departure from the upper room is indicated by John 14:31, with Matthew 26:30, Mark 14:26, and Luke 22:39 as parallels. John 18:1 would then refer to departure from the city. This of course would mean that the discourse and prayer of John 15-17 were given as they walked in the city on the way to Gethsemane. While such a reconstruction of events is possible, it has certain problems. It introduces an unnatural change of subject (second prediction of Peter's denial, Matt. 26:30-35; Mark 14:26-31) between John 14 and 15. Also, is it likely that such a long discourse and prayer (John 15-17) would be delivered while walking through the streets?

ˢ(John 15:1) The vine as a symbol for Israel was well known from the Old Testament. (Psalm 80:8; Isa. 5:1-7; Jer. 2:21; Ezek. 15:1-8; 19:10; Hos. 10:1), but the generation of the nation at Jesus' first coming turned its back on Him. Hence they were not a part of the "true" vine. Only by abiding in Him who is the true vine does one belong to it (John 15:4). Through such a spiritual relationship, the disciples were enabled to bear fruit after His departure (John 15:16).

John 15:1-17 (cont'd)

should go and bear fruit, and *that* your fruit should remain, that whatever you ask of the Father in My name, He may give to you.

17   "This I command you, that you love one another.

¹Lit., *cleanses.*   ²Another reading is *that you bear much fruit, and become My disciples.*

Sec. 220   Opposition from the world (cf. Secs. 70, 99, 213)
— *Jerusalem, in the upper room* —

John 15:18—16:4

18   "If ¹the world hates you, ¹you know that it has hated Me before *it hated* you.

19   "If you were of the world, the world would love its own; but because you are not of the world, but I chose you out of the world, therefore the world hates you.

20   "Remember the word that I said to you. 'A slave is not greater than his master.' If they persecuted Me, they will also persecute you; if they kept My word, they will keep yours also.

21   "But all these things they will do to you for My name's sake, because they do not know the One who sent Me.

22   "If I had not come and spoken to them, they would not have ²sin, but now they have no excuse for their sin.

23   "He who hates Me hates My Father also.

24   "If I had not done among them the works which no one else did, they would not have ²sin; but now they have both seen and hated Me and My Father as well.

25   "But *they have done this* in order that the word may be fulfilled that is written in their Law, 'THEY HATED ME WITHOUT A CAUSE' [Psalm 35:19, 69:4].

26   "When the ³Helper comes, whom I will send to you from the Father, *that is* the Spirit of truth, who proceeds from the Father, He will bear witness of Me,

27   ⁴and you *will* bear witness also, because you have been with Me from the beginning.

1   "These things I have spoken to you, that you may be kept from stumbling.

2   "⁵They will make you outcasts from the synagogue, but an hour is coming for everyone who kills you to think that he is offering service to God.

3   "And these things they will do, because they have not known the Father, or Me.

4   "But these things I have spoken to you, that when their hour comes, you ⁶may remember that I told you of them. And these things I did not say to you at the beginning, because I was with you.

¹Or, (imperative) *know that.*   ²I.e., *guilt.*   ³Gr., *Paracletos,* one called alongside to help; or, *Intercessor.*   ⁴Or, (imperative) *and bear witness.*   ⁵Or, *They will make you excommunicated.*   ⁶Lit., *may remember them, that I told you.*

Sec. 221   Coming and ministry of the Spirit
— *Jerusalem, in the upper room* —

John 16:5-15

5   "But now I am going to Him who sent Me; and ᵘnone of you asks Me, 'Where are You going?'

ᵗ(John 15:18) Because of His departure Jesus had to add this word about opposition. As long as He was present there was no need (John 16:4b), for the persecution fell on Him, not them. After His departure they would have to rely on the Holy Spirit to help them (John 15:26-27).

ᵘ(John 16:5) This statement at first appears to ignore the questions already asked by Peter (John

John 16:5-15 (cont'd)

6 "But because I have said these things to you, sorrow has filled your heart.

7 "But I tell you the truth, it is to your advantage that I go away; for if I do not go away, the [1]Helper shall not come to you; but if I go, [v]I will send Him to you.

8 "And He, when He comes, will convict the world concerning sin, and righteousness, and judgment;

9 concerning sin, because they do not believe in Me;

10 and concerning righteousness, because I go to the Father, and you no longer behold Me;

11 and concerning judgment, because the ruler of this world has been judged.

12 "I have many more things to say to you, but you cannot bear them now.

13 "But when He, the Spirit of truth, comes, He will guide you into all the truth; for He will not speak on His own initiative, but whatever He hears, He will speak; and He will disclose to you what is to come.

14 "He shall glorify Me; for He shall take of Mine, and shall disclose it to you.

15 "All things that the Father has are Mine; therefore I said, that He takes of Mine, and will disclose it to you.

[1]Gr., *Paracletos,* one called alongside to help; or, *Intercessor.*

Sec. 222   Prediction of joy over His resurrection
– Jerusalem, in the upper room –

John 16:16-22

16 "A little while, and you will no longer behold Me; and again a little while, and [w]you will see Me."

17 *Some* of His disciples therefore said to one another, "What is this thing He is telling us, 'A little while, and you will not behold Me; and again a little while, and you will see Me'; and, 'because I go to the Father'?"

18 And so they were saying, "What is this that He says, 'A little while'? We do not know what He is talking about."

19 Jesus knew that they wished to question Him, and He said to them, "Are you deliberating together about this, that I said, 'A little while, and you will not behold Me, and again a little while, and you will see Me'?

20 "Truly, truly, I say to you, that you will weep and lament, but the world will rejoice; you will be sorrowful, but your sorrow will be turned to joy.

21 "Whenever a woman is in travail she has sorrow, because her hour has

---

13:36, Sec. 216) and Thomas (John 14:5; Sec. 218). What Jesus meant by this statement was that the earlier questions were prompted by their concern over being separated from Him, not by a genuine interest in where He was going. Now that He had explained about His return to the Father, they should have asked more intelligently about the meaning of such a destination.

[v](John 16:7) The coming of the Holy Spirit (i.e., the "Helper") to inaugurate the new age beginning at Pentecost would mark a new phase of His ministry. His new activity was to be a leading characteristic of that age. The ministry of the Spirit is described here in a twofold manner: His ministry to the world (John 16:7-11) and His ministry to the disciples and others who would become believers through their testimony (John 16:12-15; cf. John 17:20).

[w](John 16:16) It is difficult to be sure what Jesus meant by these words. Though elsewhere in the discourse He seemed to refer to the coming of the Spirit as His own coming (John 14:17-18, Sec. 218), the promise "you will see Me" is an unlikely way of referring to the Spirit's coming at Pentecost. He also referred to His second advent earlier in the address (John 14:3, Sec. 218), but "a little while" (John 16:17) seems inadequate to refer to the entire present age which separates His two comings. The impending sorrow over His death followed quickly by an impartation of joy (John 16:20-21) favors a reference to the historical experience of the disciples when they viewed the resurrected Christ (John 16:22).

John 16:16-22 (cont'd)

come; but when she gives birth to the child, she remembers the anguish no more, for joy that a [1]child has been born into the world.

22 "Therefore you too now have sorrow; but I will see you again, and your heart will rejoice, and no one takes your joy away from you.

[1]Lit., *human being.*

Sec. 223   Promise of answered prayer and peace
— *Jerusalem, in the upper room* —

John 16:23-33

23 "And in that day you will [1]ask Me no question. Truly, truly, I say to you, if you shall ask the Father for anything, He will give it to you in My name.

24 "Until now you have asked for nothing in My name; ask, and you will receive, that your joy may be made full.

25 "These things I have spoken to you in [2]figurative language; an hour is coming when I will speak no more to you in [2]figurative language, but will tell you plainly of the Father.

26 "In that day you will ask in My name, and I do not say to you that I will request the Father on your behalf;

27 for the Father Himself loves you, because you have loved Me, and have believed that I came forth from the Father.

28 "I came forth from the Father, and have come into the world; I am leaving the world again, and going to the Father."

29 His disciples *said, "Lo, now You are speaking plainly, and are not using a [3]figure of speech.

30 "Now we know that You know all things, and have no need for anyone to question You; by this we believe that You came from God."

31 Jesus answered them, "Do you now believe?

32 "Behold, an hour is coming, and has *already* come, for you to be scattered, each to his own *home*, and to leave Me alone; and *yet* I am not alone, because the Father is with Me.

33 "These things I have spoken to you, that in Me you may have peace. In the world you have tribulation, but take courage; I have overcome the world."

[1]Lit., *question Me nothing.*   [2]Lit., *proverbs; or, figures of speech.*   [3]Lit., *proverb.*

Sec. 224   Jesus' prayer for His disciples and all who will believe
— *Jerusalem, in the upper room* —

John 17:1-26

1 These things Jesus spoke; and lifting up His eyes to heaven, He said, "[x]Father, the hour has come; glorify Thy Son, that the Son may glorify Thee,

2 even as Thou gavest Him authority over all [1]mankind, that to [2]all whom Thou hast given Him, He may give eternal life.

3 "And this is eternal life, that they may know Thee, the only true God, and Jesus Christ whom Thou hast sent.

---

[x](John 17:1) The prayer of this chapter is high priestly in the sense of Romans 8:34 and Hebrews 7:25. In His own thoughts Jesus was at this point thrust forward beyond the time of being offered as a sacrifice for sin to the time when in heaven He will engage in a continuing ministry of intercession. In other words, we have here a preview of His work as our advocate (1 John 2:1). The three parts of the prayer are: His prayer for His own glorification (17:1-5), His prayer for the disciples (17:6-19), and His prayer for future believers (17:20-26).

John 17:1-26 (cont'd)

4 "I glorified Thee on the earth, having accomplished the work which Thou hast given Me to do.

5 "And now, glorify Thou Me together with Thyself, Father, with the glory which I had with Thee before the world was.

6 "I manifested Thy name to the men whom Thou gavest Me out of the world; Thine they were, and Thou gavest them to Me, and they have kept Thy word.

7 "Now they have come to know that everything Thou hast given Me is from Thee;

8 for the words which Thou gavest Me I have given to them; and they received *them*, and truly understood that I came forth from Thee, and they believed that Thou didst send Me.

9 "I ask on their behalf; I do not ask on behalf of the world, but of those whom Thou hast given Me; for they are Thine;

10 and all things that are Mine are Thine, and Thine are Mine; and I have been glorified in them.

11 "And I am no more in the world; and *yet* they themselves are in the world, and I come to Thee. Holy Father, keep them in Thy name, *the name* which Thou hast given Me, that they may be one, even as We *are*.

12 "While I was with them, I was keeping them in Thy name which Thou hast given Me; and I guarded them, and not one of them perished but the son of perdition, that the Scripture might be fulfilled.

13 "But now I come to Thee; and these things I speak in the world, that they may have My joy made full in themselves.

14 "I have given them Thy word; and the world has hated them, because they are not of the world, even as I am not of the world.

15 "I do not ask Thee to take them out of the world, but to keep them [3]from [4]the evil one.

16 "They are not of the world, even as I am not of the world.

17 "Sanctify them in the truth; Thy word is truth.

18 "As Thou didst send Me into the world, I also have sent them into the world.

19 "And for their sakes I sanctify Myself, that they themselves also may be sanctified in truth.

20 "I do not ask in behalf of these alone, but for those also who believe in Me through their word;

21 that they may all be one; even as Thou, Father, *art* in Me, and I in Thee, that they also may be in Us; that the world may [5]believe that Thou didst send Me.

22 "And the glory which Thou hast given Me I have given to them; that they may be one, just as We are one;

23 I in them, and Thou in Me, that they may be perfected [6]in unity, that the world may [7]know that Thou didst send Me, and didst love them, even as Thou didst love Me.

24 "Father, [8]I desire that they also, whom Thou hast given Me, be with Me where I am, in order that they may behold My glory, which Thou hast given Me; for Thou didst love Me before the foundation of the world.

25 "O righteous Father, [9]although the world has not known Thee, yet I have known Thee; and these have known that Thou didst send Me;

26 and I have made Thy name known to them, and will make it known; that the love wherewith Thou didst love Me may be in them, and I in them."

[1]Lit., *flesh*.   [2]Lit., *all that which Thou hast given Him, to them He*.   [3]Or, *out of the power of*.   [4]Or, *evil*.   [5]Gr. tense indicates *continually believe*.   [6]Lit., *into a unit*.   [7]Gr. tense indicates *continually know*.   [8]Some mss. read *that which Thou hast given Me, I desire that where I am, they also may be with Me, that*.   [9]Lit., *and*.

Sec. 225   Second prediction of Peter's denial (cf. Secs. 216, 228, 230)
– Garden of Gethsemane on Mount of Olives –

Matt. 26:30-35	Mark 14:26-31	Luke 22:39-40a	John 18:1
30 And after singing a hymn, they went out to the Mount of Olives. **31** Then Jesus *said to them, "You will all ¹fall away because of Me this night, for it is written, 'I WILL STRIKE DOWN THE SHEPHERD, AND THE SHEEP OF THE FLOCK SHALL BE SCATTERED'[Zech. 13:7]. **32** "But after I have been raised, I will go before you to Galilee." **33** But Peter answered and said to Him, "Even though all may ¹fall away because of You, I will never fall away." **34** Jesus said to him, "Truly I say to you that this very night, before a ʸcock crows, you shall deny Me three times." **35** Peter *said to Him, "Even if I have to die with You, I will not deny You." All the disciples said the same thing too.	**26** And after singing a hymn, they went out to the Mount of Olives. **27** And Jesus *said to them, "You will all ¹fall away, because it is written, 'I WILL STRIKE DOWN THE SHEPHERD, AND THE SHEEP SHALL BE SCATTERED' [Zech. 13:7]. **28** "But after I have been raised, I will go before you to Galilee." **29** But Peter said to Him, "Even though all may ¹fall away, yet I will not." **30** And Jesus *said to him, "Truly I say to you, that you yourself ²this very night, before a ʸcock crows twice, shall three times deny Me." **31** But Peter kept saying insistently, "Even if I have to die with You, I will not deny You!" And they all were saying the same thing, too.	**39** And He came out and proceeded as was His custom to the Mount of Olives; and the disciples also followed Him. **40** And when He arrived at the place, He said to them,	**1** When Jesus had spoken these words, He went forth with His disciples over the ³ravine of the Kidron, where there was a garden, into which He Himself entered, and His disciples.

¹Or, *stumble.*   ²Lit., *today, on this night.*   ³Lit., *winter-torrent.*

ʸ(Matt. 26:34; Mark 14:30) The third of the four "watches" of the night (12:00 A.M. to 3:00 A.M.) was called "cockcrowing" (cf. Mark 13:35, Sec. 207). The cock would crow early in this period and again toward the period's end. In Mark's account Jesus referred to the second crowing so as to be quite specific. Matthew records a reiteration of His prediction in more general terms, that is, he refers to only one crowing, the second, which was the more commonly known of the two. Before dawn the next morning Peter was to deny His Lord three times.

Sec. 226 Jesus' three agonizing prayers in Gethsemane

Matt. 26:36-46	Mark 14:32-42	Luke 22:40b-46
36 Then Jesus *came with them to a place called Gethsemane, and *said to His disciples, "Sit here while I go over there and pray." **37** And He took with Him Peter and the two sons of Zebedee, and began to be ²grieved and distressed. **38** Then He *said to them, "My soul is deeply grieved, to the point of death; remain here and keep watch with Me." **39** And He went a little beyond *them,* and fell on His face and prayed, saying, "My Father, if it is possible, let this cup pass from Me; yet not as I will, but as Thou wilt."	**32** And they *came to a place named Gethsemane; and He *said to His disciples, "Sit here until I have prayed." **33** And He *took with Him Peter and ²James and John, and began to be very ²distressed and troubled. **34** And He *said to them, "My soul is deeply grieved to the point of death; remain here and keep watch." **35** And He went a little beyond *them,* and ³fell to the ground, and *began* to pray that if it were possible, the hour might ⁴pass Him by. **36** And He was saying, "Abba! Father! All things are possible for Thee; remove this cup from Me; yet not what I will, but what Thou wilt."	"Pray that you may not enter into temptation." **41** And He withdrew from them about a stone's throw, and He knelt down and *began* to pray, **42** saying, "Father, if Thou art willing, remove this cup from Me; yet not My will, but Thine be done." **43** ⁷Now an angel from heaven appeared to Him, strengthening Him. **44** And being ²in agony He was praying very fervently; and His sweat became like drops of blood, falling down upon the ground. **45** And when He rose from prayer, He came to the disciples and found them sleeping from sorrow,
40 And He *came to the disciples and *found them sleeping, and *said to Peter, "So, you *men* could not keep watch with Me for one hour? **41** "Keep watching and praying, that you may not enter into temptation; the spirit is willing, but the flesh is weak." **42** He went away again a second time and prayed, saying, "My Father, if this cannot pass away unless I drink it, Thy will be done."	**37** And He *came and *found them sleeping, and *said to Peter, "Simon, are you asleep? Could you not keep watch for one hour? **38** "Keep watching and praying, that you may not come into temptation; the spirit is willing, but the flesh is weak." **39** And again He went away and prayed, saying the same ⁵words.	**46** and said to them, "Why are you sleeping? Rise and pray that you may not enter into temptation."

---

²(Matt. 26:37; Mark 14:33; Luke 22:44) Jesus' agony is not attributable primarily to His dread of physical pain or to the prospect of being deserted by His friends and associates. The "cup" from which He prayed three times to be delivered (Matt. 26:39, 42, 44; Mark 14:36, 39; Luke 22:42) was the ultimate horror of separation from the Father (Matt. 27:46; Mark 15:34, Sec. 239). He was willing to undergo even this, however, if it were the Father's will, and it was (cf. Acts 2:22-23).

Matt. 26:36-46 (cont'd)	Mark 14:32-42 (cont'd)
43 And again He came and found them sleeping, for their eyes were heavy.	**40** And again He came and found them sleeping, for their eyes were very heavy; and they did not know what to answer Him.
44 And He left them again, and went away and prayed a third time, saying the same thing once more.	
45 Then He *came to the disciples, and *said to them, "¹Are you still sleeping and taking your rest? Behold, the hour is at hand and the Son of Man is being betrayed into the hands of sinners.	**41** And He *came the third time, and *said to them, "¹Are you still sleeping and taking your rest? It is enough; the hour has come; behold, the Son of Man is being ⁶betrayed into the hands of sinners.
46 "Arise, let us be going; behold, the one who betrays Me is at hand!"	**42** "Arise, let us be going; behold, the one who betrays Me is at hand!"

¹Or, *Keep on sleeping therefore.* ²Or, *Jacob.* ³Lit., *was falling.* ⁴Lit., *pass from Him.* ⁵Lit., *word.* ⁶Or, *delivered up.* ⁷Some ancient mss. do not contain vv. 43 and 44.

BETRAYAL AND ARREST

Sec. 227   Jesus betrayed, arrested, and forsaken
– Gethsemane –

Matt. 26:47-56	Mark 14:43-52	Luke 22:47-53	John 18:2-12
			2 Now Judas also, who was [9]betraying Him, knew the place; for Jesus had often met there with His disciples.
47 And while He was still speaking, behold, Judas, one of the twelve, came up, [1]accompanied by a great multitude with swords and clubs, from the chief priests and elders of the people.	43 And immediately while He was still speaking, Judas, one of the twelve, *came up, [1]accompanied by a multitude with swords and clubs, from the chief priests and the scribes and the elders.	47 While He was still speaking, behold, a multitude *came,* and the one called Judas, one of the twelve, was preceding them;	3 Judas then, having received the [10]Roman [a]cohort, and officers from the chief priests and the Pharisees, *came there with lanterns and torches and weapons.
			4 Jesus therefore, knowing all the things that were coming upon Him, went forth, and *said to them, "Whom do you seek?"
			5 They answered Him, "Jesus the Nazarene." He *said to them, "I am *He."* And Judas also who was betraying Him, was standing with them.
			6 When therefore He said to them, "I am *He,"* they drew back,

[a](John 18:3) In connection with their intention of putting Jesus to death, the Sanhedrin, represented by the chief priests and Pharisees, had called upon the Romans to help in the arrest. A Roman cohort was normally made up of 600 soldiers. Although the Romans were known to use large numbers to handle one prisoner (cf. Acts 23:23), it is doubtful that the whole cohort was involved in this arrest. In light of Matthew's "great multitude" (Matt. 26:47) and the "multitude" of Mark and Luke (Mark 14:43; Luke 22:47), the number of soldiers probably was still quite substantial.

Matt. 26:47-56 (cont'd)	Mark 14:43-52 (cont'd)	Luke 22:47-53 (cont'd)	John 18:2-12 (cont'd)
			and fell to the ground. **7** Again therefore He asked them, "Whom do you seek?" And they said, "Jesus the Nazarene." **8** Jesus answered, "I told you that I am *He*; if therefore you seek Me, let these go their way," **9** that the word might be fulfilled which He spoke, "Of those whom Thou hast given Me I lost not one."
48 Now he who was betraying Him gave them a sign, saying, "Whomever I shall kiss, He is the one; seize Him."	**44** Now he who was betraying Him had given them a signal, saying, "Whomever I shall kiss, He is the one; seize Him, and lead Him away [5]under guard."		
49 And immediately he went to Jesus and said, "Hail, Rabbi!" and kissed Him.	**45** And after coming, he immediately went to Him, saying, "Rabbi!" and kissed Him.	and he approached Jesus to kiss Him. **48** But Jesus said to him, "Judas, are you betraying the Son of Man with a kiss?" **49** And when those who were around Him saw what was going to happen, they said, "Lord, shall we strike with the sword?"	
50 And Jesus said to him, "Friend, *do* what you have come for." Then they came and laid hands on Jesus and seized Him. **51** And behold, one of those who were with Jesus	**46** And they laid hands on Him, and seized Him. **47** But a certain one of those who stood by drew his sword, and struck	**50** And a certain one of them struck the slave of the high priest and cut off his right ear.	**10** Simon Peter

Matt. 26:47-56 (cont'd)	Mark 14:43-52 (cont'd)	Luke 22:47-53 (cont'd)	John 18:2-12 (cont'd)
[2]reached and drew out his sword, and struck the slave of the high priest, and [3]cut off his ear. **52** Then Jesus *said to him, "Put your sword back into its place; for all those who take up the sword shall perish by the sword. **53** "Or do you think that I cannot appeal to My Father, and He will at once put at My disposal more than twelve [4]legions of angels? **54** "How then shall the Scriptures be fulfilled, that it must happen this way?"	the slave of the high priest, and [3]cut off his ear.		therefore having a sword, drew it, and struck the high priest's slave, and cut off his right ear; and the slave's name was Malchus. **11** Jesus therefore said to Peter, "Put the sword into the sheath; the cup which the Father has given Me, shall I not drink it?" **12** So the Roman [11]cohort and the [12]commander, and the officers of the Jews, arrested Jesus and bound Him,
		51 But Jesus answered and said, "[7]Stop! No more of this." And He touched his ear and healed him.	
55 At the time Jesus said to the multitudes, "Have you come out with swords and clubs to arrest Me as against a robber? Every day I used to sit in the temple teaching and you did not seize Me. **56** "But all this has taken place that the Scriptures of the prophets may be fulfilled." Then all the disciples left Him and fled.	**48** And Jesus answered and said to them, "Have you come out with swords and clubs to arrest Me, as against a robber? **49** "Every day I was with you in the temple teaching, and you did not seize Me; but [6]this has happened that the Scripture might be fulfilled." **50** And they all left Him and fled. **51** And a certain young man was following Him, wearing *nothing but* a linen sheet over *his* naked *body*; and they *seized him. **52** But he left the linen sheet behind, and escaped naked.	**52** And Jesus said to the chief priests and officers of the temple and elders who had come against Him, "Have you come out with swords and clubs as against a robber? **53** "While I was with you daily in the temple, you did not lay hands on Me; but [8]this hour and the power of darkness are yours."	

[1]Lit., *and with him.* [2]Lit., *extended the hand.* [3]Lit., *took off.* [4]A legion equaled 6,000 troops. [5]Lit., *safely.* [6]Or possibly, *let the Scriptures be fulfilled.* [7]Or, *"Let Me at least do this,"* and *He touched.* [8]Lit., *this is your hour and power of darkness.* [9]Or, *delivering Him up.* [10]Normally 600 men; *a battalion.* [11]Or, *battalion.* [12]I.e., chiliarch, in command of a thousand troops.

TRIAL

Sec. 228   First Jewish phase, before Annas (cf. Secs. 216, 225, 230)
– Jerusalem, court of Annas –

John 18:13-24

13 and led Him to Annas first; for he was father-in-law of Caiaphas, who was high priest that year.

14 Now Caiaphas was the one who had advised the Jews that it was expedient for one man to die on behalf of the people.

15 And Simon Peter was following Jesus, and *so was* another disciple. Now that disciple was known to [b]the high priest, and entered with Jesus into the court of the high priest,

16 but Peter was standing at the door outside. So the other disciple, who was known to the high priest, went out and spoke to the doorkeeper, and brought in Peter.

17 The slave-girl therefore who kept the door *said to Peter, "You are not also *one* of this man's disciples, are you?" He *said, "[c]I am not."

18 Now the slaves and the officers were standing *there*, having made a charcoal fire, for it was cold and they were warming themselves; and Peter also was with them, standing and warming himself.

19 The high priest therefore questioned Jesus about His disciples, and about His teaching.

20 Jesus answered him, "I have spoken openly to the world; I always taught in [1]synagogues, and in the temple, where all the Jews come together; and I spoke nothing in secret.

21 "Why do you question Me? Question those who have heard what I spoke to them; behold, these know what I said."

22 And when He had said this, one of the officers standing by gave Jesus a blow, saying, "Is that the way You answer the high priest?"

23 Jesus answered him, "If I have spoken wrongly, bear witness of the wrong; but if rightly, why do you strike Me?"

24 Annas therefore sent Him bound to Caiaphas the high priest.

[1]Lit., *the synagogue.*

Sec. 229   Second Jewish phase, before Caiaphas and the Sanhedrin
– Jerusalem, house of Caiaphas –

Matt. 26:57-68	Mark 14:53-65	Luke 22:54
57 And those who had seized Jesus led Him away to Caiaphas, the high	**53** And they led Jesus away to the high priest; and all the [d]chief priests	**54** And having arrested Him, they led Him away, and brought Him to

[b](John 18:15) Here and in verses 16, 19, and 22 John calls Annas "the high priest," but he says in verse 13 that Caiaphas was high priest. Caiaphas was the official high priest, having taken the office in A.D. 18, three years after his father-in-law Annas had been deposed. Though no longer in office, Annas still wielded great influence and bore the title of courtesy granted to former high priests.

[c](John 18:17) John places this denial in the courtyard of Annas prior to the convening of the Sanhedrin, whereas the synoptic gospels and John locate the other denials in Caiaphas' courtyard after the Sanhedrin had met (cf. Sec. 230). Jesus' stability under stress is thus contrasted with Peter's fickleness.

[d](Mark 14:53) Mark lists the three groups who composed the Sanhedrin of Jerusalem, the supreme Jewish court of law:
1. "the chief priests," comprising those who were former high priests (including Annas probably), the commander of the Temple guard, the steward of the Temple, and the three Temple treasurers
2. "the elders," some of the wealthy and influential lay persons of Jerusalem
3. "the scribes," who were primarily drawn from the middle class of society.

Matt. 26:57-68 (cont'd)	Mark 14:53-65 (cont'd)	Luke 22:54 (cont'd)
priest, where the scribes and the elders were gathered together.	and the elders and the scribes *gathered together.	the house of the high priest;
58 But Peter also was following Him at a distance as far as the courtyard of the high priest, and entered in, and sat down with the [1]officers to see the outcome.	**54** And Peter had followed Him at a distance, right into the couryard of the high priest; and he was sitting with the [1]officers, and warming himself at the [10]fire.	but Peter was following at a distance.
59 Now the chief priests and the whole [2]Council kept trying to obtain false testimony against Jesus, in order that they might put Him to death;	**55** Now the chief priests and the whole [2]Council kept trying to obtain testimony against Jesus to put Him to death; and they were not finding any.	
60 and they did not find *any*, even though many false witnesses came forward. But later on two came forward,	**56** For many were giving false testimony against Him, and *yet* their testimony was not consistent.	
61 and said, "This man stated, 'I am able to destroy the [3]temple of God and to rebuild it [4]in three days.'"	**57** And some stood up and *began* to give false testimony against Him, saying,	
	58 "We heard Him say, 'I will destroy this [3]temple made with hands, and in three days I will build another made without hands.'"	
	59 And not even in this respect was their testimony consistent.	
62 And the high priest stood up and said to Him, "Do You make no answer? What is it that these men are testifying against You?"	**60** And the high priest stood up *and came* forward and questioned Jesus, saying, "Do You make no answer? [11]What is it that these men are testifying against You?"	
63 But Jesus kept silent. And the high priest said to Him, "I [5]adjure You by the living God, that You tell us whether You are [6]the Christ, the Son of God."	**61** But He kept silent, and made no answer. Again the high priest was questioning Him, and [12]saying to Him, "Are You [6]the Christ, the Son of the Blessed One?"	
64 Jesus *said to him,		

The first two groups were predominantly Sadducean and the last Pharisaic. In meeting at the house of Caiaphas rather than in its usual meeting place, the Sanhedrin evidenced its haste to carry out its predetermined plan to convict Jesus (Mark 14:55; cf. Matt. 26:4; Mark 14:1, Sec. 209). For further discussion of Jesus' arrest and trial, see essay 12 (pp. 329-337).

Matt. 26:57-68 (cont'd)	Mark 14:53-65 (cont'd)
"You have said it *yourself;* nevertheless I tell you, [7]hereafter you shall see THE SON OF MAN SITTING AT THE RIGHT HAND OF POWER, and COMING ON THE CLOUDS OF HEAVEN" [Psalm 110:1; Dan. 7:13].	**62** And Jesus said, "I am; and you shall see THE SON OF MAN SITTING AT THE RIGHT HAND OF POWER, and COMING WITH THE CLOUDS OF HEAVEN" [Psalm 110:1; Dan. 7:13].
65 Then the high priest tore his [8]robes, saying, "He has blasphemed! What further need do we have of witnesses? Behold, you have now heard the blasphemy;	**63** And tearing his clothes, the high priest *said, "What further need do we have of witnesses?
66 what do you think?" They answered and said, "He is deserving of death!"	**64** "You have heard the blasphemy; how does it seem to you?" And they all condemned Him to be deserving of death.
67 Then they spat in His face and beat Him with their fists; and others [9]slapped Him,	**65** And some began to spit at Him, and to [13]blindfold Him, and to beat Him with their fists, and to say to Him, "Prophesy!" And the officers [14]received Him with [15]slaps in *the face.*
68 and said, "Prophesy to us, You [6]Christ; who is the one who hit You?"	

[1]Or, servants. [2]Or, Sanhedrin. [3]Or, sanctuary. [4]Or, after. [5]Or, charge You under oath. [6]I.e., the Messiah. [7]Or, from now on. [8]Or, outer garments. [9]Or possibly, beat Him with rods. [10]Lit., light. [11]Or, what do these testify. [12]Lit., says. [13]Or, cover over His face. [14]Or, treated. [15]Or possibly, blows with rods.

Sec. 230   Peter's denials (cf. Secs. 216, 225, 228)
– *Jerusalem, courtyard of Caiaphas* –

Matt. 26:69-75	Mark 14:66-72	Luke 22:55-65	John 18:25-27
		55 And after they had kindled a fire in the middle of the courtyard and had sat down together, Peter was sitting among them.	
69 Now Peter was sitting outside in the courtyard, and a certain servant-girl came to him and said,	**66** And as Peter was below in the courtyard, one of the servant-girls of the high priest *came,	**56** And a certain servant-girl, seeing him as he sat in the firelight, and looking intently at him, said, "This man was with Him too."	**25** Now Simon Peter was standing and warming himself. They said therefore to him, "You are not also one of His disciples, are you?" He
"You too were with Jesus	**67** and seeing Peter warming himself, she looked at him, and *said, "You, too, were with Jesus the		

Matt. 26:69-75 (cont'd)	Mark 14:66-72 (cont'd)	Luke 22:55-65 (cont'd)	John 18:25-27 (cont'd)
the Galilean."	Nazarene."	**57** But he denied *it*, saying, "Woman, I do not know Him."	denied *it*, and said, "I am not."
70 But he denied *it* before them all, saying, "I do not know what you are talking about."	**68** But he denied *it*, saying, "I neither know nor understand what you are talking about." And he went out onto the ²porch³.		
71 And when he had gone out to the gateway, another *servant-girl* saw him and *said to those who were there, "This man was with Jesus of Nazareth."	**69** And the maid saw him, and began once more to say to the bystanders, "This is one of them!"	**58** And a little later, another saw him and said, "You are one of them too!" But Peter said, "Man, I am not!"	
72 And again he denied *it* with an oath, "I do not know the man."	**70** But again he was denying it. And after a little while the bystanders were again saying to Peter, "Surely you are one of them, for you are a Galilean too."	**59** And after about an hour had passed, another man *began* to insist, saying, "Certainly this man also was with Him, for he is a Galilean too."	
73 And a little later the bystanders came up and said to Peter, "Surely you too are one of them; for the way you talk ¹gives you away."			**26** One of the slaves of the high priest, being a relative of the one whose ear Peter cut off, *said, "Did I not see you in the garden with Him?"
74 Then he began to curse and swear, "I do not know the man!" And immediately a cock crowed.	**71** But he began to ⁴curse and swear, "I do not know this man you are talking about!"	**60** But Peter said, "Man, I do not know what you are talking about." And immediately, while he was still speaking, a cock crowed.	**27** Peter therefore denied *it* again; and immediately a cock crowed.
	72 And immediately a cock crowed a second time.	**61** And the Lord turned and looked at Peter. And Peter remembered the word of the Lord, how He had told him, "Before a cock crows today, you will deny Me ᵉthree times."	
75 And Peter remembered the word which Jesus had said, "Before a cock crows, you will deny Me ᵉthree times." And he went out and wept bitterly.	And Peter remembered how Jesus had made the remark to him, "Before a cock crows twice, you will deny Me ᵉthree times." ⁵And he began to weep.	**62** And he went out and wept bitterly. **63** And the men who were holding	

ᵉ(Matt. 26:75; Mark 14:72; Luke 22:61) Jesus' prediction of a threefold denial by Peter need not exclude a fourth denial. Each writer, including John, records three denials to show the prediction's fulfillment, but John records only two denials at the house of Caiaphas as compared to three described by the others. According to the combined accounts (cf. Sec. 228), Peter apparently denied Jesus at least four times.

Luke 22:55-65
(cont'd)

⁶Jesus in custody were mocking Him, and beating Him,

64 and they blindfolded Him and were asking Him, saying, "Prophesy, who is the one who hit You?"

65 And they were saying many other things against Him, blaspheming.

¹Lit., *makes you evident.* ²Or, *forecourt, gateway.* ³Later mss. add *and a cock crowed.* ⁴Or, *put himself under a curse.* ⁵Or, *Thinking of this, he began weeping* or *Rushing out, he began weeping.* ⁶Lit., *Him.*

Sec. 231   Third Jewish phase, before the Sanhedrin
— *Jerusalem, meeting place of Sanhedrin* —

Matt. 27:1	Mark 15:1a	Luke 22:66-71
1 Now when morning had come, all the chief priests and the elders of the people took counsel against Jesus to put Him to death;	**1** And early in the morning the chief priests with the elders and scribes, and the whole ¹Council, immediately held a consultation;	**66** And when it was ʰday, the ¹Council of elders of the people assembled, both chief priests and scribes, and they led Him away to their council chamber, saying, **67** "If You are the ²Christ, tell us." But He said to them, "If I tell you, you will not believe; **68** and if I ask a question, you will not answer. **69** "But from now on THE SON OF MAN WILL BE SEATED AT THE RIGHT HAND [Psalm 110:1] of the power OF GOD." **70** And they all said, "Are You the Son of God, then?" And He said to them, "³Yes, I am." **71** And they said, "What further need do we have of testimony? For we have heard it ourselves from His own mouth."

¹Or, *Sanhedrin.*   ²I.e., *Messiah.*   ³Lit., *You say that I am.*

ᶠ(Luke 22:66) The traditional Christian explanation has been that no trial of the Jewish Sanhedrin was legal if held during the hours of darkness. Hence the council had to get together again and formalize the illegal verdict it had already settled upon a few hours earlier (Matt. 26:66; Mark 14:64, Sec. 229). However, the question of legality is a moot point, and is discussed in essay 12 (pp. 329-337).

Sec. 232   Remorse and suicide of Judas Iscariot
— In the Temple and the Potter's Field —

Matt. 27:3-10	Acts 1:18-19
3 Then when Judas, who had betrayed Him, saw that He had been condemned, he felt remorse and returned the thirty [1]pieces of silver to the chief priests and elders,	
4 saying, "I have sinned by betraying innocent blood." But they said, "What is that to us? See to that yourself!"	
5 And he threw the pieces of silver into the sanctuary and departed; and he went away and [g]hanged himself.	**18** (Now this man acquired a field with the price of his wickedness; and falling headlong, he [g]burst open in the middle and all his bowels gushed out.
6 And the chief priests took the pieces of silver and said, "It is not lawful to put them into the temple treasury, since it is the price of blood."	
7 And they counseled together and with [2]the money bought the Potter's Field as a burial place for strangers.	**19** And it became known to all who were living in Jerusalem; so that in their own language that field was called [5]Hakeldama, that is, Field of Blood).
8 For this reason that field has been called the Field of Blood to this day.	
9 Then that which was spoken through Jeremiah the prophet was fulfilled, saying, "AND [3]THEY TOOK THE THIRTY PIECES OF SILVER, THE PRICE OF THE ONE WHOSE PRICE HAD BEEN SET by the sons of Israel;	
10 AND [4]THEY GAVE THEM FOR THE POTTER'S FIELD, AS THE LORD DIRECTED ME" [Zech. 11:12-13; cf. Jer. 18:2; 19:2, 11; 32:6-9].	

[1]Or, *silver shekels.* [2]Lit., *them.* [3]Some mss. read *I took.* [4]Some mss. read *I gave.* [5]Some early mss. read *Hakeldamach.*

Sec. 233   First Roman phase, before Pilate
— Jerusalem, at the Praetorium —

Matt. 27:2, 11-14	Mark 15:1b-5	Luke 23:1-5	John 18:28-38
2 and they bound Him, and led Him away, and delivered Him up to Pilate the governor.	and binding Jesus, they led Him away, and delivered Him up to Pilate.	**1** Then the whole body of them arose and brought Him before Pilate.	**28** They *led Jesus therefore from Caiaphas into the [4]Praetorium, and it was early; and they themselves did not enter into the [4]Praetorium in order that they might not be

[g](Matt. 27:5; Acts 1:18) There is no reason to question the usual harmonization of these two accounts of Judas' death, that is, that he hanged himself from a tree on a cliff overlooking a valley, and that the tree limb or rope broke, causing him to plunge to the valley below.

Matt. 27:2, 11-14 (cont'd)	Mark 15:1b-5 (cont'd)	Luke 23:1-5 (cont'd)	John 18:28-38 (cont'd)
			defiled, but might eat the Passover. **29** Pilate therefore went out to them, and *said, "What accusation do you bring against this Man?"
		2 And they began to accuse Him, saying, "We found this man misleading our nation and forbidding to pay taxes to Caesar, and saying that He Himself is ³Christ, a King."	**30** They answered and said to him, "If this Man were not an evildoer, we would not have delivered Him up to you." **31** Pilate therefore said to them, "Take Him yourselves, and judge Him according to your law." The Jews said to him, "We are not permitted to put anyone to death," **32** that the word of Jesus might be fulfilled, which He spoke, signifying by what kind of death He was about to die. **33** Pilate therefore entered again into the ⁴Praetorium, and summoned Jesus,
11 Now Jesus stood before the governor, and the governor questioned Him, saying,	**2** And Pilate questioned Him,	**3** And Pilate asked Him, saying,	and said to Him,
"Are You the King of the Jews?" And Jesus said to him, "It is as you say."	"Are You the King of the Jews?" And answering He *said to him, "It is as you say."	"Are You the King of the Jews?" And He answered him and said, "It is as you say."	"Are You the King of the Jews?" **34** Jesus answered, "Are you saying this ⁵on your own initiative, or did others tell you about Me?" **35** Pilate answered, "I am not a Jew, am I? Your

Matt. 27:2, 11-14 (cont'd)	Mark 15:1b-5 (cont'd)	Luke 23:1-5 (cont'd)	John 18:28-38 (cont'd)
			own nation and the chief priests delivered You up to me; what have You done?"
			36 Jesus answered, "My kingdom ⁶is not ʰof this world. If My kingdom were of this world, then My servants would be fighting, that I might not be delivered to the Jews; but as it is, My kingdom is not ⁷of this realm."
			37 Pilate therefore said to Him, "So You are a king?" Jesus answered, "You say *correctly* that I am a king. For this I have been born, and for this I have come into the world, to bear witness to the truth. Everyone who is of the truth hears My voice."
			38 Pilate *said to Him, "What is truth?" And when he had said this, he went out again to the Jews, and *said to them, "I find no guilt in Him.
		4 And Pilate said to the chief priests and the multitudes, "I find no guilt in this man."	
12 And while He was being accused by the chief priests and elders, He made no answer.	**3** And the chief priests *began* to accuse Him ²harshly.		
13 Then Pilate *said to Him, "Do You not hear now	**4** And Pilate was questioning Him again, saying,		

ʰ(John 18:36) Jesus denied that His Kingdom had an earthly origin. If it had, He would have proceeded to round up and equip a conventional army to set it into operation. He did not deny, however, that the Kingdom will consist of an earthly realm such as the scripturally oriented Jew expected Messiah to establish (Dan. 7:13-14, 22-23, 27). Since this Kingdom on earth did not represent a rebellion against his Roman authority, Pilate was willing to release Jesus (Luke 23:4; John 18:38).

Matt. 27:2, 11-14 (cont'd)	Mark 15:1b-5 (cont'd)	Luke 23:1-5 (cont'd)
many things they testify against You?" 　　**14** And He did not answer him with regard to even a *single* [1]charge, so that the governor was quite amazed.	"Do You make no answer? See how many charges they bring against You!" 　　**5** But Jesus made no further answer; so that Pilate was amazed.	**5** But they kept on insisting, saying, "He stirs up the people, teaching all over Judea, starting from Galilee, even as far as this place."

[1]Lit., *word.* [2]Or, *of many things.* [3]I.e., *Messiah.* [4]I.e., governor's official residence. [5]Lit., *from yourself.* [6]Or, *is not derived from.* [7]Lit., *from here.*

Sec. 234　Second Roman phase, before Herod Antipas
– Jerusalem, before Herod Antipas –

Luke 23:6-12

6　But when Pilate heard it, he asked whether the man was a Galilean.

7　And when he learned that He belonged to Herod's jurisdiction, he sent Him to [1]Herod, who himself also was in Jerusalem [1]at that time.

8　Now Herod was very glad when he saw Jesus; for he had wanted to see Him for a long time, because he had been hearing about Him and was hoping to see some [2]sign performed by Him.

9　And he questioned Him [3]at some length; but He answered him nothing.

10　And the chief priests and the scribes were standing there, accusing Him vehemently.

11　And Herod with his soldiers, after treating Him with contempt and mocking Him, dressed Him in a gorgeous robe and sent Him back to Pilate.

12　Now Herod and Pilate became friends with one another that very day; for before they had been at enmity with each other.

[1]Lit., *in these days.* [2]Or, *attesting miracle.* [3]Lit., *in many words.*

Sec. 235　Third Roman phase, before Pilate
– Jerusalem, at the Praetorium –

Matt. 27:15-26	Mark 15:6-15	Luke 23:13-25	John 18:39—19:16
15 Now at *the* feast the governor was accustomed to release for the multitude *any one*	**6** Now at *the* feast he used to release for them *any* one prisoner whom they requested.		

[1](Luke 23:7) This is Herod Antipas, tetrarch of Galilee and Perea, who rather than repenting because of the preaching of John had the Baptist beheaded (cf. Sec. 102). Since much of Jesus' public ministry had been in Galilee, Pilate thought he had found a way to avoid condemning an innocent person, but Herod did not pronounce Jesus guilty or innocent. Luke had contacts within Herod's household (cf. Luke 8:3, Sec. 78) that enabled him to describe a phase of the trial not found in the other gospels, just as John had access to information about what happened at Annas' house (cf. Sec. 228).

Matt. 27:15-26 (cont'd)	Mark 15:6-15 (cont'd)	Luke 23:13-25 (cont'd)	John 18:39—19:16 (cont'd)
prisoner whom they wanted. **16** And they were holding at that time a notorious prisoner, called ʲBarabbas.	**7** And the man named ʲBarabbas had been imprisoned with the insurrectionists who had committed murder in the insurrection. **8** And the multitude went up and began asking him *to do* as he had been accustomed to do for them.		
		13 And Pilate summoned the chief priests and the rulers and the people, **14** and said to them, ''You brought this man to me as one who incites the people to rebellion, and behold, having examined Him before you, I have found no guilt in this man regarding the charges which you make against Him. **15** ''No, nor has Herod, for he sent Him back to us; and behold, nothing deserving death has been done by Him.	
			39 ''But you have a custom, that I should release someone ⁶for you at the Passover; do you wish then that I release for you the King of the Jews?''
17 When therefore they were gathered together, Pilate said to them, ''Whom do you want me to release for you? Barabbas,	**9** And Pilate answered them, saying, ''Do you want me to release for you the King of the Jews?'' **10** For he was	**16** ''I will therefore punish Him and release Him.''	

ʲ(Matt. 27:16; Mark 15:7; Luke 23:19; John 18:40) Barabbas was a well-known member of a local resistance movement dedicated to overthrowing Roman rule in Judea. Even though he was a thief and a murderer, he was a hero to many Jews who disliked Roman control. Hence the chief priests and elders had little difficulty persuading the crowd to prefer the release of Barabbas (Matt. 27:20; Mark 15:11). It is ironic that these leaders sought the release of one who was clearly guilty of the crime they had accused Jesus of committing (cf. Luke 23:2, Sec. 233; John 19:12).

Matt. 27:15-26 (cont'd)	Mark 15:6-15 (cont'd)	Luke 23:13-25 (cont'd)	John 18:39—19:16 (cont'd)

or Jesus who is called Christ?"

18 For he knew that because of envy they had delivered Him up.

19 And while he was sitting on the judgment seat, his wife sent to him, saying, "Have nothing to do with that righteous Man; for [1]last night I suffered greatly in a dream because of Him."

20 But the chief priests and the elders persuaded the multitudes to ask for Barabbas, and to put Jesus to death.

21 But the governor answered and said to them, "Which of the two do you want me to release for you?" And they said, "Barabbas."

---

aware that the chief priests had delivered Him up because of envy.

11 But the chief priests stirred up the multitude *to ask* him to release Barabbas for them instead.

---

17 [5][Now he was obliged to release to them at the feast one prisoner.]

18 But they cried out all together, saying, "Away with this man, and release for us Barabbas!"

19 (He was one who had been [j]thrown into prison for a certain insurrection made in the city, and for murder.)

---

40 Therefore they cried out again, saying, "Not this Man, but Barabbas." Now [j]Barabbas was a robber.

1 Then Pilate therefore took Jesus, and [7]scourged Him.

2 And the soldiers wove a crown of thorns and put it on His head, and arrayed Him in a purple robe;

3 and they *began* to come up to Him, and say,

Matt. 27:15-26 (cont'd)	Mark 15:6-15 (cont'd)	Luke 23:13-25 (cont'd)	John 18:39—19:16 (cont'd)
			"Hail, King of the Jews!" and to give Him blows in the face. **4** And Pilate came out again, and *said to them, "Behold, I am bringing Him out to you, that you may know that I find no guilt in Him." **5** Jesus therefore came out, wearing the crown of thorns and the purple robe. And
22 Pilate *said to them, "Then what shall I do with Jesus who is called Christ?" They all *said, "Let Him be crucified!" **23** And he said, "Why, what evil has He done?"	**12** And answering again, Pilate was saying to them, "Then what shall I do with Him whom you call the King of the Jews?" **13** And they shouted ⁴back, "Crucify Him!" **14** But Pilate was saying to them, "Why, what evil has He done?"	**20** And Pilate, wanting to release Jesus, addressed them again, **21** but they kept on calling out, saying, "Crucify, crucify Him!" **22** And he said to them the third time, "Why, what evil has this man done? I have found in Him no guilt *demanding* death; I will therefore punish Him and release Him."	Pilate *said to them, "Behold, the Man!" **6** When therefore the chief priests and the officers saw Him, they cried out, saying, "Crucify, crucify!" Pilate *said to them, "Take Him yourselves, and crucify Him, for I find no guilt in Him." **7** The Jews answered him, "We have a law, and by that law He ought to die because He made Himself out *to be* the Son of God." **8** When Pilate therefore heard this statement, he was the more afraid; **9** and he entered into the ⁸Praetorium again, and *said to Jesus, "Where are You from?" But Jesus gave him no answer.
But they kept shouting all the more, saying, "Let Him be crucified!"	But they shouted all the more, "Crucify Him!"		

Matt. 27:15-26 (cont'd)	Mark 15:6-15 (cont'd)	Luke 23:13-25 (cont'd)	John 18:39—19:16 (cont'd)
			10 Pilate therefore *said to Him, "You do not speak to me? Do You not know that I have authority to release You, and I have authority to crucify You?"
			11 Jesus answered, ''You would have no authority [9]over Me, unless it had been given you from above; for this reason he who delivered Me up to you has *the* greater sin."
			12 As a result of this Pilate [10]made efforts to release Him, but the Jews cried out, saying, "If you release this Man, you are no friend of Caesar; everyone who makes himself out *to be* a king [11]opposes Caesar."
			13 When Pilate therefore heard these words, he brought Jesus out, and sat down on the judgment seat at a place called [12]The Pavement, but in [13]Hebrew, Gabbatha.
			14 Now it was the day of preparation for the Passover; it was about the [14]sixth hour. And he *said to the Jews, "Behold, your King!"
		23 But they were insistent, with loud voices asking that He be crucified.	**15** They therefore cried out, "Away with *Him*, away with *Him*, crucify Him!" Pi-

Matt. 27:15-26 (cont'd)	Mark 15:6-15 (cont'd)	Luke 23:13-25 (cont'd)	John 18:39—19:16 (cont'd)
			late *said to them, "Shall I crucify your King?" The chief priests answered, "We have no king but Caesar."
24 And when Pilate saw that he was accomplishing nothing, but rather that a riot was starting, he took water and washed his hands in front of the multitude, saying, "I am innocent of ²this Man's blood; see *to that* yourselves." **25** And all the people answered and said, "His blood *be* on us and on our children!"		And their voices *began to* prevail.	
	15 And wishing to satisfy the multitude,	**24** And Pilate pronounced sentence that their demand should be granted. **25** And he released the man they were asking for who had been thrown into prison for insurrection and murder, but he delivered Jesus to ᵏtheir will.	
26 Then he released Barabbas ³for them; but after having Jesus scourged, he delivered Him to be crucified.	Pilate released Barabbas for them, and after having Jesus scourged, he delivered *Him* to be crucified.		**16** So he then delivered Him to ᵏthem to be crucified.

¹Lit., *today.* ²Many mss. read *the blood of this righteous Man.* ³Or, *to them.* ⁴Or, *again.* ⁵Many mss. do not contain this v. ⁶Or, *to you.* ⁷Or, *had Him scourged.* ⁸I.e., governor's official residence. ⁹Lit., *against.* ¹⁰Lit., *was seeking to.* ¹¹Or, *speaks against.* ¹²Gr., *The Lithostrotos.* ¹³I.e., Jewish Aramaic. ¹⁴Perhaps 6 a.m. (Roman time).

ᵏ(Luke 23:25; John 19:16) "Their" and "them" naturally refers to the chief priests, the rulers, and the people mentioned in Luke 23:13 and John 19:15. Yet the Jews had no authority to carry out capital punishment (John 18:31, Sec. 233). Even if they had such authority, their method of execution was by stoning (cf. Acts 7:58-60). Luke and John obviously mean that Pilate acceded to the wishes of the Jews in delivering Jesus to the Roman soldiers who would execute Him by crucifixion (Luke 23:36; John 19:23, Sec. 238).

CRUCIFIXION

Sec. 236   Mockery by the Roman soldiers
– Jerusalem, in the Praetorium –

Matt. 27:27-30	Mark 15:16-19
27 Then the soldiers of the governor took Jesus into the Praetorium and gathered the whole *Roman* [1]cohort around Him.	**16** And the soldiers took Him away into the [3]palace (that is, the Praetorium), and they *called together the whole *Roman* [1]cohort.
28 And they stripped Him, and put a scarlet robe on Him.	**17** And they *dressed Him up in [4]purple, and after weaving a crown of thorns, they put it on Him;
29 And after weaving a crown of thorns, they put it on His head, and a [2]reed in His right hand; and they kneeled down before Him and mocked Him, saying, "[1]Hail, King of the Jews!"	**18** and they began to acclaim Him, "[1]Hail, King of the Jews!"
30 And they spat on Him, and took the reed and *began* to beat Him on the head.	**19** And they kept beating His head with a [2]reed, and spitting at Him, and kneeling and bowing before Him.

[1]Or, *battalion.*   [2]Or, *staff* (made of a reed).   [3]Or, *court.*   [4]A term for shades varying from rose to purple.

Sec. 237   Journey to Golgotha

Matt. 27:31-34	Mark 15:20-23	Luke 23:26-33a	John 19:17
31 And after they had mocked Him, they took His robe off and put His garments on Him, and led Him away to crucify *Him.*	**20** And after they had mocked Him, they took the purple off Him, and put His garments on Him. And they *led Him out to crucify Him.		**17** They took Jesus therefore, and He went out, [4m]bearing His own cross,
32 And as they were coming out, they found a man of Cyrene named Simon, [1]whom they [m]pressed into service to bear His cross.	**21** And they *[m]pressed into service a passer-by coming from the country, Simon of Cyrene (the father of Alexander and Rufus), to bear His cross.	**26** And when they led Him away, they laid hold of one Simon of Cyrene, coming in from the country, and [m]placed on him the cross to carry behind Jesus.	
		27 And there were following Him a great mul-	

[1](Matt. 27:29; Mark 15:18) The mockery and crude treatment of Jesus came in two stages of which this is the second. Before His condemnation, Pilate seems to have allowed ill-treatment in hopes of provoking the crowd's sympathy toward Jesus and thereby persuading them to ask for His release (John 19:1-5, Sec. 235). In this section, however, following His condemnation the soldiers took the initiative and carried the brutal mockery to a much greater extreme.

[m](Matt. 27:32; Mark 15:21; Luke 23:26; John 19:17) At the outset of the journey to Golgotha, Jesus appears to have carried the cross (or the transverse beam of the cross) Himself, in accordance with John's description. Being so weakened from lack of sleep and the cruel scourging, however, He was unable to complete the journey. The soldiers therefore forced Simon of Cyrene to carry it for Him. It is possible that Simon's son Rufus, who appears to have been known to Mark's Roman readers (Mark 15:21), is the person whom Paul greets in Romans 16:13.

Matt. 27:31-34 (cont'd)	Mark 15:20-23 (cont'd)	Luke 23:26-33a (cont'd)	John 19:17 (cont'd)
		titude of the people, and of women who were ²mourning and lamenting Him. **28** But Jesus turning to them said, "Daughters of Jerusalem, stop weeping for Me, but weep for yourselves and for your children. **29** "For behold, the days are coming when they will say, 'Blessed are the barren, and the wombs that never bore, and the breasts that never nursed.' **30** "Then they will begin TO SAY TO THE MOUNTAINS, 'FALL ON US,' AND TO THE HILLS, 'COVER US' [Hos. 10:8]. **31** "For if they do these things in the green tree, what will happen in the dry?" **32** And two others also, who were criminals, were being led away to be put to death with Him.	
33 And when they had come to a place called Golgotha, which means Place of a Skull, **34** they gave Him wine to drink mingled with gall; and after tasting *it,* He was unwilling to drink.	**22** And they *brought Him to the place Golgotha, which is translated, Place of a Skull. **23** And they tried to give Him wine mixed with myrrh; but He did not take it.	**33** And when they came to the place called ³The Skull,	to the place called the Place of a Skull, which is called in ⁵Hebrew, Golgotha.

¹Lit., *this one.* ²Lit., *beating the breast.* ³In Lat., *Calvarius;* or, *Calvary.* ⁴Lit., *bearing the cross for Himself.* ⁵I.e., Jewish Aramaic.

Sec. 238   First three hours of crucifixion
– Golgotha –

Matt. 27:35-44	Mark 15:24-32	Luke 23:33b-43	John 19:18-27
35 And when they had crucified Him, they divided up His garments among themselves, casting [1]lots; **36** and sitting down, they *began* to keep watch over Him there.	**24** And they *crucified Him, and *divided up His garments among themselves, casting [5]lots for them, *to decide* [6]what each should take.	there they crucified Him and the criminals, one on the right and the other on the left. **34** [11]But Jesus was saying, "[n]Father, forgive them; for they do not know what they are doing." And they cast lots, dividing up His garments among themselves.	**18** There they crucified Him, and with Him two other men, one on either side, and Jesus in between. **23** The soldiers therefore, when they had crucified Jesus, took His outer garments and made four parts, a part to every soldier and *also* the [15]tunic; now the tunic was seamless, woven [16]in one piece. **24** They said therefore to one another, "Let us not tear it, but cast [1]lots for it, *to decide* whose it shall be"; that the Scripture might be fulfilled, "THEY DIVIDED MY OUTER GARMENTS AMONG THEM, AND FOR MY CLOTHING THEY CAST [1]LOTS" [Psalm 22:18]. **25** Therefore the soldiers did these things.
37 And they put up above His head the charge against Him [2]which	**25** And it was the [7][o]third hour [8]when they crucified Him.	**38** Now there was also an inscription above Him, "[p]THIS IS	**19** And Pilate wrote an inscription also, and put it on the cross. And it

[n](Luke 23:34) This prayer for forgiveness is the first of Jesus' sayings from the cross. The others are the promise to the repentant criminal (Luke 23:43), the provision for His mother (John 19:26-27), the cry of separation from the Father (Matt. 27:46; Mark 15:34, Sec. 239), the acknowledgement of thirst (John 19:28, Sec. 239), the cry of accomplishment (John 19:30, Sec. 239), and the cry of resignation (Luke 23:46, Sec. 239).

[o](Mark 15:25) Jesus' hours on the cross extended from 9:00 A.M. to 3:00 P.M. The last three hours were distinct because of a darkness into which the area was plunged beginning at noon (Matt. 27:45; Mark 15:33; Luke 23:44-45a, Sec. 239).

Matt. 27:35-44 (cont'd)	Mark 15:24-32 (cont'd)	Luke 23:33b-43 (cont'd)	John 19:18-27 (cont'd)
read, "ᴾTHIS IS JESUS THE KING OF THE JEWS."	**26** And the inscription of the charge against Him ⁹read, "ᴾTHE KING OF THE JEWS."	THE KING OF THE JEWS."	was written, "ᴾJESUS THE NAZARENE, THE KING OF THE JEWS."
38 At that time two robbers *were crucified with Him, one on the right and one on the left.	**27** And they *crucified two robbers with Him, one on His right and one on His left.		**20** Therefore this inscription many of the Jews read, for the place where Jesus was crucified was near the city; and it was written in ¹⁴Hebrew, Latin, *and* in Greek.
	28 [¹⁰And the Scripture was fulfilled which says, "And He was numbered with transgressors."]		**21** And so the chief priests of the Jews were saying to Pilate, "Do not write, 'The King of the Jews'; but that He said, 'I am King of the Jews.'"
			22 Pilate answered, "What I have written I have written."
39 And those passing by were ³hurling abuse at Him, wagging their heads,	**29** And those passing by were ³hurling abuse at Him, wagging their heads, and saying, "Ha! You who are going to destroy the temple and rebuild it in three days,	**35** And the people stood by, looking on.	
40 and saying, "You who are going to destroy the temple and rebuild it in three days, save Yourself! If You are the Son of God, come down from the cross."	**30** save Yourself, and come down from the cross!"		
41 In the same way the chief priests also, along with the scribes and elders, were mocking *Him*, and saying,	**31** In the same way the chief priests also, along with the scribes, were mocking *Him* among themselves and saying, "He saved others; ⁴He cannot save Himself.	And even the rulers were sneering at Him, saying, "He saved others; let Him save Himself if this is the ¹²Christ of God, His Chosen	
42 "He saved others; ⁴He cannot			

ᴾ(Matt. 27:37; Mark 15:26; Luke 23:38; John 19:19) Each writer records only a portion of the inscription. The full inscription is reconstructed by combining the four accounts: "This is Jesus the Nazarene, the King of the Jews."

Matt. 27:35-44 (cont'd)	Mark 15:24-32 (cont'd)	Luke 23:33b-43 (cont'd)	John 19:18-27 (cont'd)
save Himself. He is the King of Israel; let Him now come down from the cross, and we shall believe in Him. **43** "HE TRUSTS IN GOD; LET HIM DELIVER *Him* now, IF HE TAKES PLEASURE IN HIM [Psalm 22:8]; for He said, 'I am the Son of God.'" **44** And the robbers also who had been crucified with Him were casting the same insult at Him.	**32** "Let *this* Christ, the King of Israel, now come down from the cross, so that we may see and believe!" And those who were crucified with Him were casting the same insult at Him.	One." **36** And the soldiers also mocked Him, coming up to Him, offering Him sour wine, **37** and saying, "If You are the King of the Jews, save Yourself!"	

39 And one of the criminals who were hanged *there* was ³hurling abuse at Him, saying, "Are You not the ¹²Christ? Save Yourself and us!"
40 But the other answered, and rebuking him said, "Do you not even fear God, since you are under the same sentence of condemnation?
41 "And we indeed justly, for we are receiving ¹³what we deserve for our deeds; but this man has done nothing wrong."
42 And he was saying, "Jesus, remember me when You come in Your kingdom!"
43 And He said to him, "Truly I say to you, today you shall be with Me in Paradise."

But there were

			John 19:18-27 (cont'd)

standing by the cross of Jesus His mother, and His mother's sister, Mary the *wife* of Clopas, and Mary Magdalene.

26 When Jesus therefore saw His mother, and the disciple whom He loved standing nearby, He *said to His mother, "Woman, behold, your son!"

27 Then He *said to the disciple, "Behold, your mother!" And from that hour the disciple took her into his own *household*.

¹Lit., *a lot.* ²Lit., *written.* ³Or, *blaspheming.* ⁴Or, *can He not save Himself?* ⁵Lit., *a lot upon.* ⁶Lit., *who should take what.* ⁷I.e., 9 a.m. ⁸Lit., *and.* ⁹Lit., *had been inscribed.* ¹⁰Many mss. do not contain this v. ¹¹Some mss. do not contain *But Jesus was saying . . . doing.* ¹²I.e., Messiah. ¹³Lit., *things worthy of what we have done.* ¹⁴I.e., Jewish Aramaic. ¹⁵Gr., *khiton,* the garment worn next to the skin. ¹⁶Lit., *woven from the upper part through the whole.*

Sec. 239   Last three hours of crucifixion
– *Golgotha* –

Matt. 27:45-50	Mark 15:33-37	Luke 23:44-45a, 46	John 19:28-30
45 Now from the ¹sixth hour darkness ²fell upon all the land until the ³ninth hour. **46** And about the ninth hour Jesus cried out with a loud voice, saying, "ᵍELI, ELI, LAMA SABACHTHANI?" that is, "MY GOD, MY GOD, WHY HAST	**33** And when the ¹sixth hour had come, darkness ²fell over the whole land until the ³ninth hour. **34** And at the ninth hour Jesus cried out with a loud voice, "ᵍELOI, ELOI, LAMA SABACHTHANI?" which is translated,	**44** And it was now about ⁷the sixth hour, and darkness ²fell over the whole land until ³the ninth hour, **45** the sun⁸being obscured;	

ᵍ(Matt. 27:46; Mark 15:34) This cry of dereliction reflects the heart of Jesus' purpose in His first advent and death: to bear the penalty for human sin (Heb. 9:28). Since sin separates from a holy God, He had to endure that separation in the moment of His death. Otherwise, the penalty could not have been paid.

Matt. 27:45-50 (cont'd)	Mark 15:33-37 (cont'd)	Luke 23:44-45a, 46 (cont'd)	John 19:28-30 (cont'd)
THOU FORSAKEN ME?" [Psalm 22:1]. **47** And some of those who were standing there, when they heard it, *began saying*, "This man is calling for Elijah." **48** And immediately one of them ran, and taking a sponge, he filled it with sour wine, and put it on a reed, and gave Him a drink. **49** But the rest *of them* said, "4Let us see whether Elijah will come to save Him.5"	"MY GOD, MY GOD, WHY HAST THOU FORSAKEN ME?" [Psalm 22:1]. **35** And when some of the bystanders heard it, they *began* saying, "Behold, He is calling for Elijah." **36** And someone ran and filled a sponge with sour wine, put it on a reed, and gave Him a drink, saying, "6Let us see whether Elijah will come to take Him down."		**28** After this, Jesus, knowing that all things had already been accomplished, in order that the Scripture might be fulfilled, *said, "I am thirsty." **29** A jar full of sour wine was standing there; so they put a sponge full of the sour wine upon *a branch of* hyssop, and brought it up to His mouth.
		46 And Jesus, crying out with a loud voice, said, "Father, INTO THY HANDS I COMMIT MY SPIRIT" [Psalm 31:5]. And having	**30** When Jesus therefore had received the sour wine,
50 And Jesus cried out again with a loud voice,	**37** And Jesus uttered a loud cry,		He said, "rIt is finished!"
and yielded up *His* spirit.	and breathed His last.	said this, He breathed His last.	And He bowed His head, and gave up His spirit.

1I.e., noon.   2Or, *occurred*.   3I.e., 3 p.m.   4Lit., *Permit that we see*.   5Some early mss. add *And another took a spear and pierced His side, and there came out water and blood*.   6Lit., *Permit that we see; or, Hold off, let us see*.   7I.e., 12 noon.   8Lit., *failing*.

---

r(John 19:30) These words look back to "all things" in John 19:28. They refer to "all things" that the Father had given Jesus to do (John 17:4, Sec. 224; cf. John 3:35, Sec. 37; John 13:3, Sec. 213). Included in His commission was the complete fulfillment of Scripture (John 19:28) which the words "it is finished" also reflect.

Sec. 240   Witnesses of Jesus' death
– Temple and Golgotha –

Matt. 27:51-56	Mark 15:38-41	Luke 23:45b, 47-49
51 And behold, the veil of the temple was torn in two from top to bottom, and the earth shook; and the rocks were split,	**38** And the veil of the temple was torn in two from top to bottom.	and the veil of the temple was torn [9]in two.
52 and the tombs were opened; and many bodies of the [1]saints who had fallen asleep were raised;		
53 and coming out of the tombs after His resurrection they entered the holy city and appeared to many.		
54 Now the centurion, and those who were with him keeping guard over Jesus, when they saw the earthquake and the things that were happening, became very frightened and said, "Truly this was [2]the Son of God!"	**39** And when the centurion, who was standing [4]right in front of Him, saw [5][s]the way He breathed His last, he said, "Truly this man was [2]the Son of God!"	**47** Now when the centurion saw what had happened, he *began* praising God, saying, "Certainly this man was [10]innocent."
55 And many women were there looking on from a distance, who had followed Jesus from Galilee, [3]ministering to Him,	**40** And there were also *some* women looking on from a distance,	**48** And all the multitudes who came together for this spectacle, when they observed what had happened, *began* to return, beating their breasts.
56 among whom was [t]Mary Magdalene, *along with* Mary the mother of James and Joseph, and the mother of the sons of Zebedee.	among whom *were* [t]Mary Magdalene, and Mary the mother of [6]James the [7]Less and Joses, and Salome.	**49** And all His acquaintances and the [t]women who accompanied Him from Galilee, were standing at a distance, seeing these things.
	41 And when He was in Galilee, they used to follow Him and [8]minister to Him; and *there were* many other women who had come up with Him to Jerusalem.	

[1]Or, *holy ones.* [2]Or possibly, *a son of God* or *a son of a god.* [3]Or, *waiting on.* [4]Or, *opposite Him.* [5]Lit., *that He thus.* [6]Or, *Jacob.* [7]Lit., *little* (either in stature or age). [8]Or, *wait on.* [9]Lit., *in the middle.* [10]Lit., *righteous.*

---

[s](Mark 15:39) The centurion was impressed not only by the earthquake and other signs (Matt. 27:54) but also by the manner of Jesus' death. That Jesus possessed enough strength to cry loudly at the moment of death (Matt. 27:50; Mark 15:37; Luke 23:46, Sec. 239) was remarkable to one who was accustomed to seeing crucified criminals die from sheer exhaustion.

[t](Matt. 27:56; Mark 15:40; Luke 23:49) These women were eyewitnesses to the events that compose the heart of the gospel message: Jesus' death (in this section), His burial (Matt. 27:61; Mark 15:47; Luke 23:55, Sec. 243), and His resurrection (Matt. 28:1; Mark 16:1, Sec. 244). Compare 1 Corinthians 15:3-4.

BURIAL

Sec. 241   Certification of death and procurement of the body
   – Golgotha and the Praetorium –

Matt. 27:57-58	Mark 15:42-45	Luke 23:50-52	John 19:31-38
			31 The Jews therefore, because it was the day of preparation, so that the bodies should not remain on the cross on the Sabbath (¹for that Sabbath was a high *day*), asked Pilate that their legs might be broken, and *that* they might be taken away. **32** The soldiers therefore came, and broke the legs of the first man, and of the other man who was crucified with Him; **33** but coming to Jesus, when they saw that He was already dead, they did not break His legs; **34** but one of the soldiers pierced His side with a spear, and immediately there came out ᵘblood and water. **35** And he who has seen has borne witness, and his witness is true; and he knows that he is telling the truth, so that you also may believe. **36** For these things came to pass, that the Scripture might be

ᵘ(John 19:34) The issuance of blood and water from Jesus' side, though difficult to explain medically, actually happened as John describes it (John 19:35). This signified that Jesus was already dead and was the basis for a report to this effect brought back to Pilate (Mark 15:44-45). In the midst of uncertainty regarding the cause of this phenomenon, the possibility that Jesus died of a ruptured heart must remain one of the possible explanations (cf. Psalm 69:20).

Matt. 27:57-58 (cont'd)	Mark 15:42-45 (cont'd)	Luke 23:50-52 (cont'd)	John 19:31-38 (cont'd)
			fulfilled, "NOT A BONE OF HIM SHALL BE ²BROKEN" [Psalm 34:20]. **37** And again another Scripture says, "THEY SHALL LOOK ON HIM WHOM THEY PIERCED" [Zech. 12:10].
57 And when it was evening,	**42** And when evening had already come, because it was the preparation day, that is, the day before the Sabbath,		
there came a rich man from Arimathea, named Joseph,	**43** Joseph of Arimathea came, a prominent member of the Council,	**50** And behold, a man named Joseph, who was a member of the Council, a good and righteous man **51** (he had not consented to their plan and action), *a* man from Arimathea, a city of the Jews, who was	**38** And after these things Joseph of Arimathea,
who himself had also become a disciple of Jesus. **58** This man went to Pilate and asked for the body of Jesus.	who himself was waiting for the kingdom of God; and he gathered up courage and went in before Pilate, and asked for the body of Jesus. **44** And Pilate wondered if He was dead by this time, and summoning the centurion, he questioned him as to whether He was already dead.	waiting for the kingdom of God; **52** this man went to Pilate and asked for the body of Jesus.	being a disciple of Jesus, but a secret *one*, for fear of the Jews, asked Pilate that he might take away the body of Jesus;
Then Pilate ordered *it* to be given over *to him*.	**45** And ascertaining this from the centurion, he granted the body to Joseph.		and Pilate granted permission. He came therefore, and took away His body.

¹Lit., *for the day of that Sabbath was great.* ²Or, *crushed or shattered.*

Sec. 242   Jesus' body placed in a tomb
– the garden tomb at Golgotha –

Matt. 27:59-60	Mark 15:46	Luke 23:53-54	John 19:39-42
			39 And [v]Nicodemus came also, who had first come to Him by night; bringing a [2]mixture of myrrh and aloes, about a hundred [3]pounds *weight.*
59 And [v]Joseph took the body and wrapped it in a clean linen cloth,	**46** And Joseph bought a linen cloth, took Him down, wrapped Him in the linen cloth,	**53** And he took it down and wrapped it in a linen cloth,	**40** And so they took the body of Jesus, and bound it in linen wrappings with the spices, as is the burial custom of the Jews.
60 and laid it in his own new tomb, which he had hewn out in the rock; and he rolled a large stone against the entrance of the tomb and went away.	and laid Him in a tomb which had been hewn out in the rock; and he rolled a stone against the entrance of the tomb.	and laid Him in a tomb cut into the rock, where no one had ever lain. **54** And it was the preparation day, and the Sabbath was about to [1]begin.	**41** Now in the place where He was crucified there was a garden; and in the garden a new tomb, in which no one had yet been laid. **42** Therefore on account of the Jewish day of preparation, because the tomb was nearby, they laid Jesus there.

[1]Lit., *dawn.*   [2]Another reading is *package of.*   [3]I.e., 100 litras (12 oz. each).

Sec. 243   Tomb watched by the women and guarded by the soldiers
– Bethany, Golgotha, and the Praetorium –

Matt. 27:61-66	Mark 15:47	Luke 23:55-56
61 And Mary Magdalene was there, and the other Mary, sitting opposite the grave.	**47** And Mary Magdalene and Mary the mother of Joses were looking on *to see* where He was laid.	**55** Now the women who had come with Him out of Galilee followed after, and saw the tomb and how His body was laid. **56** And they returned and prepared spices and perfumes. And on the Sabbath they rested according to the commandment.

[v](Matt. 27:59; John 19:39) The disciples who had openly followed Jesus during His lifetime ran away at the end, but the two who had kept their faith secret while He was alive (cf. John 19:38, Sec. 241) came forward publicly to give Him an appropriate burial.

Matt. 27:61-66 (cont'd)

62 Now on the next day, which is *the one* after the preparation, the chief priests and the Pharisees gathered together with Pilate,

63 and said, "Sir, ^wwe remember that when He was still alive that deceiver said, 'After three days I *am to* rise again.'

64 "Therefore, give orders for the grave to be made secure until the third day, lest the disciples come and steal Him away and say to the people, 'He has risen from the dead,' and the last deception will be worse than the first."

65 Pilate said to them, "You have a guard; go, make it *as* secure as you know how."

66 And they went and made the grave secure, and along with the guard they set a seal on the stone.

---

^w(Matt. 27:63) How strange it is that Jesus' disciples failed to grasp His plainly spoken prophecies to them about His resurrection (cf. Secs. 119, 125, 180), whereas these Sadducees and Pharisees understood and remembered the ones He had spoken to them in figurative language (Matt. 12:40, Sec. 80; Matt. 16:4, Sec. 115; John 2:19-20, Sec. 34).

PART THIRTEEN
THE RESURRECTION AND ASCENSION OF CHRIST

THE EMPTY TOMB

Sec. 244 The tomb visited by the women
– Bethany and Golgotha –

Matt. 28:1

1 Now after the Sabbath, as it began to dawn toward the first *day* of the week, [x]Mary Magdalene and the other Mary came to look at the grave.

Mark 16:1

1 And when the Sabbath was over, [x]Mary Magdalene , and Mary the *mother* of [1]James, and Salome, bought spices, that they might come and anoint Him.

[1]Or, *Jacob.*

Sec. 245 The stone rolled away
– Golgotha –

Matt. 28:2-4

2 And behold, a [y]severe earthquake had occurred, for an angel of the Lord descended from heaven and came and rolled away the stone and sat upon it.
3 And his appearance was like lightning, and his garment as white as snow;
4 and the guards shook for fear of him, and became like dead men.

Sec. 246 The tomb found to be empty by the women
– Golgotha –

Matt. 28:5-8	Mark 16:2-8	Luke 24:1-8	John 20:1
	2 And very early on the first day of the week, they *came to the tomb [z]when the sun had risen.	**1** But on the first day of the week, at early dawn, they came to the tomb, bringing the spices which	**1** Now on the first *day* of the week Mary Magdalene *came early to the tomb, [z]while it *was still dark,

[x](Matt. 28:1; Mark 16:1) The number of women involved in various visits to the tomb is indefinite. The following are named: Mary Magdalene (Matt. 28:1; Mark 16:1; Luke 24:10, Sec. 247; John 20:1, Sec. 246), Mary the mother of James or "the other Mary" (Matt. 28:1; Mark 16:1; Luke 24:10, Sec. 247), Salome (Mark 16:1), and Joanna (Luke 24:10, Sec. 247). How many "other women" (Luke 24:10, Sec. 247) were with them we are not told.

[y](Matt. 28:2) Perhaps the moment of Christ's resurrection coincided with this "severe earthquake," because so often in Scripture the earthquake signifies a divine visitation (cf. Matt. 27:51, 54, Sec. 240). Yet the exact time cannot be fixed with certainty, since no one saw Jesus rise. The early witnesses of His resurrection (cf. Acts 1:22) were those who saw Him after He rose (cf. Secs. 248-249, 251, 253-259), not when He rose. The angel's coming to roll away the stone was not designed to allow the risen Jesus to leave. He did not need this (cf. John 20:19, Sec. 253). Removal of the stone was designed to let witnesses see the empty tomb (cf. Mark 16:5; Luke 24:3, Sec. 246; John 20:5-8, Sec. 247).

[z](Mark 16:2; John 20:1) "When the sun had risen" in Mark 16:2 does not contradict "while it was

252

Matt. 28:5-8 (cont'd)	Mark 16:2-8 (cont'd)	Luke 24:1-8 (cont'd)	John 20:1 (cont'd)
		they had prepared.	
	3 And they were saying to one another, "Who will roll away the stone for us from the entrance of the tomb?"	**2** And they found the stone rolled away from the tomb,	and *saw the stone *already* taken away from the tomb.
	4 And looking up, they *saw that the stone had been rolled away, [2]although it was extremely large.	**3** but when they entered, they did not find the body of the Lord Jesus.	
5 And the angel answered and said to the women, "[1]Do not be afraid; for I know that you are looking for Jesus who has been crucified.	**5** And entering the tomb, they saw a young man sitting at the right, wearing a white robe; and they were amazed.	**4** And it happened that while they were perplexed about this, behold, two men suddenly stood near them in dazzling apparel;	
6 "He is not here, for He has risen, just as He said. Come, see the place where He was lying.	**6** And he *said to them, "Do not be amazed; you are looking for Jesus the Nazarene, who has been crucified. He has risen; He is not here; behold, *here is* the place where they laid Him.	**5** and as *the women* were terrified and bowed their faces to the ground, *the men* said to them, "Why do you seek the living One among the dead?	
7 "And go quickly and tell His disciples that He has risen from the dead; and behold, He is going before you into Galilee, there you will see Him; behold, I have told you."	**7** "But go, tell His disciples and Peter, 'He is going before you into Galilee; there you will see Him, just as He said to you.'"	**6** "[3]He is not here, but He has [4]risen. Remember how He spoke to you while He was still in Galilee,	
8 And they departed quickly from the tomb with fear and great joy and ran to report it to His disciples.	**8** And they went out and fled from the tomb, for trembling and astonishment had gripped them; and they said nothing to anyone, for they were afraid.	**7** saying that the Son of Man must be delivered into the hands of sinful men, and be crucified, and the third day rise again."	
		8 And they remembered His words,	

[1]Or, *Stop being afraid.*   [2]Lit., *for.*   [3]Some ancient mss. do not contain *He is not here, but He has risen.*   [4]Or, *been raised.*

---

still dark" in John 20:1. Quite possibly Mary Magdalene ran ahead of the other women and arrived before the sun rose, as John describes, whereas the rest reached the tomb after sunrise, as Mark records. Another possible explanation is that it was dark when the party of women departed, and after sunrise when they arrived at the tomb.

Sec. 247   The tomb found to be empty by Peter and John
   − Golgotha −

Luke 24:9-11, [12]

9 and returned from the tomb and reported all these things to the eleven and to all the rest.

10 Now they were Mary Magdalene and Joanna and Mary the *mother of* James; also the other women with them were telling these things to the apostles.

11 And these words appeared [1]to them as nonsense, and they would not believe them.

12 [2][But Peter arose and ran to the tomb; stooping and looking in, he *saw the linen wrappings [3]only; and he went away to his home, marveling at that which had happened.]

John 20:2-10

2 And so she *ran and *came to Simon Peter, and to the other disciple whom Jesus [4]loved, and *said to them, "They have taken away the Lord out of the tomb, and we do not know where they have laid Him."

3 Peter therefore went forth, and the other disciple, and they were going to the tomb.

4 And the two were running together; and the other disciple ran ahead faster than Peter, and came to the tomb first;

5 and stooping and looking in, he *saw the linen wrappings lying *there;* but he did not go in.

6 Simon Peter therefore also *came, following him, and entered the tomb; and he *beheld the [a]linen wrappings lying *there,*

7 and the face-cloth, which had been on His head, not lying with the linen wrappings, but rolled up in a place by itself.

8 So the other disciple who had first come to the tomb entered then also, and he saw and believed.

9 For as yet they did not understand the Scripture, that He must rise again from the dead.

10 So the disciples went away again to their own homes.

[1]Lit., *in their sight.* [2]Some ancient mss. do not contain v. 12. [3]Or, *by themselves.* [4]Lit., *was loving.*

THE POSTRESURRECTION APPEARANCES

Sec. 248   Appearance to Mary Magdalene
   − Golgotha and Jerusalem −

[Mark 16:9-11]

John 20:11-18

11 But Mary was standing outside the tomb weeping; and so, as she wept, she stooped and looked into the tomb;

12 and she *beheld two angels in white sitting, one at the head, and one at

[a](John 20:6) John's description of the linen wrappings and face-cloth (John 20:7) does not necessarily mean that Jesus rose from the dead without disturbing the grave clothes in which He was wrapped. The record rather presents a picture of the orderly arrangement of these grave clothes, such as would not have been the case if grave robbers, the disciples, or anyone else had taken the body away. This neatness was sufficient to convince John that Jesus had risen (John 20:8).

[Mark 16:9-11] (cont'd)

9 [¹Now after He had risen early on the first day of the week, He first appeared to Mary Magdalene, from whom He had cast out seven demons.

10 She went and reported to those who had been with Him, while they were mourning and weeping.

11 And when they heard that He was alive, and had been seen by her, they refused to believe it.]

John 20:11-18 (cont'd)

the feet, where the body of Jesus had been lying.

13 And they *said to her, "Woman, why are you weeping?" She *said to them, "Because they have taken away my Lord, and I do not know where they have laid Him."

14 When she had said this, she turned around, and *beheld Jesus standing *there*, and did not know that it was Jesus.

15 Jesus *said to her, "Woman, why are you weeping? Whom are you seeking?" Supposing Him to be the gardener, she *said to Him, "Sir, if you have carried Him away, tell me where you have laid Him, and I will take Him away."

16 Jesus *said to her, "Mary!" She *turned and *said to Him in ²Hebrew, "Rabboni!" (which means, Teacher).

17 Jesus *said to her, " ᵇStop clinging to Me, for I have not yet ascended to the Father; but go to My brethren, and say to them, 'I ascend to My Father and your Father, and My God and your God.'"

18 Mary Magdalene *came, announcing to the disciples, "I have seen the Lord," and *that* He had said these things to her.

¹Some of the oldest mss. do not contain vv. 9-20.   ²I.e., Jewish Aramaic.

Sec. 249   Appearance to the other women
— *Jerusalem* —

Matt. 28:9-10

9 And behold, Jesus met ᶜthem ¹and greeted them. And they came up and took hold of His feet and worshiped Him.

10 Then Jesus *said to them, "²Do not be afraid; go and take word to My brethren to leave for Galilee, and there they shall see Me."

¹Lit., *saying hello.*   ²Or, *Stop being afraid.*

ᵇ(John 20:17) The force of Jesus' words apparently was to inform Mary that He was not returning to the old life as Lazarus had (cf. John 12:2, 9, Sec. 186). By clinging to Him, Mary responded to His presence as though He were. His postresurrection appearances were to occupy only a brief time because He must soon return to the Father's house (cf. Sec. 259; John 14:2, Sec. 218). He therefore instructed Mary to go and tell the disciples this.

ᶜ(Matt. 28:9) Mary Magdalene had returned to the tomb after contacting Peter and John (John 20:11, Sec. 248) and was therefore no longer with this company of women when they left the tomb (Matt. 28:8; Mark 16:8, Sec. 246). This group now could report to the disciples not only the empty tomb and the words of the angelic messenger (Matt. 28:7-8; Mark 16:7, Sec. 246), but also that they themselves had seen their risen Lord (Matt. 28:10).

Sec. 250   Report of the soldiers to the Jewish authorities
– Jerusalem –
Matt. 28:11-15

11   Now while they were on their way, behold, some of the guard came into the city and reported to the chief priests all that had happened.

12   And when they had assembled with the elders and counseled together, they gave a large sum of money to the soldiers,

13   and said, "You are to say, '^dHis disciples came by night and stole Him away while we were asleep.'

14   "And if this should come to the governor's ears, we will win him over and ¹keep you out of trouble."

15   And they took the money and did as they had been instructed; and this story was widely spread among the Jews, *and is* to this day.

¹Lit., *make you free from care.*

Sec. 251   Appearance to two disciples traveling to Emmaus
– On the road to Emmaus –

[Mark 16:12-13]	Luke 24:13-32
12 [And after that, He appeared in a different form to two of them, while they were walking along on their way to the country.	**13** And behold, two of them were going that very day to a village named Emmaus, which was ¹about seven miles from Jerusalem.
13 And they went away and reported it to the others, but they did not believe them either.]	**14** And they were conversing with each other about all these things which had taken place.
	15 And it came about that while they were conversing and discussing, Jesus Himself approached, and *began* traveling with them.

16   But their eyes ²were prevented from recognizing Him.

17   And He said to them, "What are these words that you are exchanging with one another as you are walking?" And they stood still, ^elooking sad.

18   And one of them, named Cleopas, answered and said to Him, "³Are You the only one visiting Jerusalem and unaware of the things which have happened here in these days?"

19   And He said to them, "What things?" And they said to Him, "The things about Jesus the Nazarene, who was a prophet mighty in deed and word in the sight of God and all the people,

20   and how the chief priests and our rulers delivered Him up to the sentence of death, and crucified Him.

21   "But we were hoping that it was He who was going to redeem Israel. Indeed, besides all this, it is the third day since these things happened.

22   "But also some women among us amazed us. When they were at the tomb early in the morning,

23   and did not find His body, they came, saying that they had also seen a vision of angels, who said that He was alive.

---

^d(Matt. 28:13) The absurdity of this story invented by the Sanhedrin in official session (Matt. 28:11-12) reveals the desperation to which they had been driven by recent developments. Surely the disciples in removing the heavy stone from the tomb would have made enough noise to have awakened at least one of the soldiers. Furthermore, if the soldiers were asleep, how could they have known the grave robbers to be the disciples? Yet for twenty centuries attempts to explain the empty tomb have continued to come forth and have proven just as futile as this original one. The only plausible explanation is that God raised Jesus from the dead, thus allowing Him to leave the tomb under His own power.

^e(Luke 24:17) The sorrow and despondency of Jesus' followers, even after they had received word about the empty tomb, show how ridiculous is the explanation that they invented the story of Jesus' resurrection. Their state of mind was completely opposed to the possibility of doing such a thing.

Luke 24:13-32 (cont'd)

24 "And some of those who were with us went to the tomb and found it just exactly as the women also had said; but Him they did not see."

25 And He said to them, "O foolish men and slow of heart to believe in all that the prophets have spoken!

26 "Was it not necessary for the [4]Christ to suffer these things and to enter into His glory?"

27 And beginning [5]with Moses and with all the prophets, He explained to them the things concerning Himself in all the Scriptures.

28 And they approached the village where they were going, and He acted as though He would go farther.

29 And they urged Him, saying, "Stay with us, for it is *getting* toward evening, and the day [6]is now nearly over." And He went in to stay with them.

30 And it came about that when He had reclined *at the table* with them, He took the bread and blessed *it*, and breaking *it*, He *began* giving *it* to them.

31 And their eyes were opened and they recognized Him; and He vanished from [7]their sight.

32 And they said to one another, "[8]Were not our hearts burning within us while He was speaking to us on the road, while He was [9]explaining the Scriptures to us?"

[1]I.e., 60 stadia, one stadion was about 600 ft. [2]Lit., *were being prevented*. [3]Or, *visiting Jerusalem alone*. [4]I.e., *Messiah*. [5]Lit., *from*. [6]Lit., *has now declined*. [7]Lit., *them*. [8]Lit., *Was not our heart*. [9]Lit., *opening*.

Sec. 252 Report of the two disciples to the rest
– Jerusalem –

Luke 24:33-35	1 Cor. 15:5a
33 And they arose that very hour and returned to Jerusalem, and found gathered together the eleven and those who were with them,	
34 saying, "The Lord has really risen, and has appeared to [f]Simon."	**5** and that He appeared to [f]Cephas,
35 And they *began* to relate [1]their experiences on the road and how He was recognized by them in the breaking of the bread.	

[1]Lit., *the things*.

Sec. 253 Appearance to the ten assembled disciples (cf. Secs. 256, 258)
– Jerusalem –

[Mark 16:14]	Luke 24:36-43	John 20:19-25
		19 When therefore it was evening, on that day, the first *day* of the week, and when the doors were

[f](Luke 24:34; 1 Cor. 15:5a) This private appearance to Peter is not described in the four gospels, though Paul alludes to it in his first Corinthian epistle. It apparently happened after the two disciples started for Emmaus (Luke 24:13, Sec. 251), but before the eleven disciples assembled in Jerusalem (Luke 24:33).

[Mark 16:14] (cont'd)	Luke 24:36-43 (cont'd)	John 20:19-25 (cont'd)
14 [And afterward He appeared to the eleven themselves as they were reclining *at the table;* and He reproached them for their unbelief and hardness of heart, because they had not believed those who had seen Him after He had risen.]	**36** And while they were telling these things, He Himself stood in their midst.[1] **37** But they were startled and frightened and thought that they were seeing a spirit. **38** And He said to them, "Why are you troubled, and why do doubts arise in your [2]hearts? **39** "See My hands and My feet, that it is I Myself; touch Me and see, for a spirit does not have flesh and bones as you see that I have." **40** [3][And when He had said this, He showed them His hands and His feet.] **41** And while they still [4]could not believe *it* for joy and were marveling, He said to them, "Have you anything here to eat?" **42** And they gave Him a piece of a broiled fish; **43** and He took it and ate *it* before them.	shut where the disciples were, for fear of the Jews, Jesus came and [g]stood in their midst, and *said to them, "[5]Peace *be* with you." **20** And when He had said this, He showed them both His hands and His side. The disciples therefore rejoiced when they saw the Lord. **21** Jesus therefore said to them again, "[5]Peace *be* with you; as the Father has sent Me, I also send you." **22** And when He had said this, He breathed on them, and *said to them, "Receive the Holy Spirit. **23** "If you forgive the sins of any, *their sins* [6]have been forgiven them; if you retain the *sins* of any, they have been retained." **24** But Thomas, one of the twelve, called [7]Did-

[g](John 20:19) This section reveals several things about Jesus' resurrection body. In this verse He was able to pass through a shut (and locked) door. The wounds of His crucifixion were still visible (Luke 24:39; John 20:20). The body was composed of material substance that could be felt (Luke 24:39, Sec. 253; John 20:25, 27, Secs. 253-254). It consisted of flesh and bone as contrasted to flesh and blood (Luke 24:39). It was capable of consuming food as a mortal body does (Luke 24:43).

John 20:19-25
(cont'd)

ymus, was not with them when Jesus came.

25 The other disciples therefore were saying to him, "We have seen the Lord!" But he said to them, "Unless I shall see in His hands the imprint of the nails, and put my finger into the place of the nails, and put my hand into His side, I will not believe."

¹Some ancient mss. insert *And He says to them, "Peace be to you."* ²Lit., *heart.* ³Many mss. do not contain this v. ⁴Lit., *were disbelieving.* ⁵Lit., *Peace to you.* ⁶I.e., have previously been forgiven. ⁷I.e., the Twin.

Sec. 254   Appearance to the eleven assembled disciples
— *Jerusalem* —

John 20:26-31

26 And ¹after eight days again His disciples were inside, and Thomas with them. Jesus *came, the doors having been ²shut, and stood in their midst, and said, "Peace be with you."

27 Then He *said to Thomas, "Reach here your finger, and see My hands; and reach here your hand, and put it into My side; and be not unbelieving, but believing."

28 Thomas answered and said to Him, "My Lord and ʰmy God!"

29 Jesus *said to him, "Because you have seen Me, have you believed? Blessed are they who did not see, and yet believed."

30 Many other ³signs therefore Jesus also performed in the presence of the disciples, which are not written in this book;

31 but these have been written that you may believe that Jesus is ⁴the Christ, the Son of God; and that believing you may have life in His name.

1 Cor. 15:5b

then to the twelve.

¹Or, *a week later.* ²Or, *locked.* ³Or, *attesting miracles.* ⁴I.e., the Messiah.

Sec. 255   Appearance to seven disciples while fishing
— *Sea of Galilee* —

John 21:1-25

1 ¹After these things Jesus ¹manifested Himself again to the disciples at the Sea of Tiberias; and He manifested *Himself* in this way.

ʰ(John 20:28) Once he overcame his skepticism, Thomas made the strongest confession of all. Prior to this no one had addressed Jesus in this way. To call Jesus "God" was tantamount to putting Him on an equal plane with the Father (cf. John 5:23, Sec. 59).

ⁱ(John 21:1) The viewpoint that makes John 21 a later addition to the fourth gospel cannot be substantiated. The absence of manuscript support for this theory and the fact that the writing style used in chapters 1-20 continues in chapter 21 strongly support the traditional position that this chapter was an integral part of the gospel from the time John the apostle penned it.

John 21:1-25 (cont'd)

2 There were together Simon Peter, and Thomas called [2]Didymus, and Nathanael of Cana in Galilee, and the sons of Zebedee, and two others of His disciples.

3 Simon Peter *said to them, "I am going fishing." They *said to him, "We will also come with you." They went out, and got into the boat; and that night they caught nothing.

4 But when the day was now breaking, Jesus stood on the beach; yet the disciples did not know that it was Jesus.

5 Jesus therefore *said to them, "Children, you do not have any [3]fish, do you?" They answered Him, "No."

6 And He said to them, "Cast the net on the right-hand side of the boat, and you will find a catch." They cast therefore, and then they were not able to haul it in because of the great number of fish.

7 That disciple therefore whom Jesus [4]loved *said to Peter, "It is the Lord." And so when Simon Peter heard that it was the Lord, he put his outer garment on (for he was stripped for work), and threw himself into the sea.

8 But the other disciples came in the little boat, for they were not far from the land, but about [5]one hundred yards away, dragging the net full of fish.

9 And so when they got out upon the land, they *saw a charcoal fire already laid, and fish placed on it, and bread.

10 Jesus *said to them, "Bring some of the fish which you have now caught."

11 Simon Peter went up, and drew the net to land, full of large fish, a hundred and fifty-three; and although there were so many, the net was not torn.

12 Jesus *said to them, "Come and have breakfast." None of the disciples ventured to question Him, "Who are You?" knowing that it was the Lord.

13 Jesus *came and *took the bread, and *gave them, and the fish likewise.

14 This is now the third time that Jesus [1]was manifested to the disciples, after He was raised from the dead.

15 So when they had finished breakfast, Jesus *said to Simon Peter, "Simon, [6]son of John, do you [7]love Me more than these?" He *said to Him, "Yes, Lord; You know that I [8]love You." He *said to him, "Tend My lambs."

16 He *said to him again a second time, "Simon, son of John, do you [7]love Me?" He *said to Him, "Yes, Lord; You know that I [8]love You." He *said to him, "Shepherd My sheep."

17 He *said to him the third time, "Simon, son of John, do you [8]love Me?" Peter was grieved because He said to him the third time, "Do you [8]love Me?" And he said to Him, "Lord, You know all things; You know that I [8]love You." Jesus *said to him, "Tend My sheep.

18 "Truly, truly, I say to you, when you were younger, you used to gird yourself, and walk wherever you wished; but when you grow old, you will stretch out your hands, and someone else will gird you, and bring you where you do not wish to go."

19 Now this He said, signifying by what kind of death he would glorify God. And when He had spoken this, He *said to him, "Follow Me!"

20 Peter, turning around, *saw the disciple whom Jesus loved following them; the one who also had leaned back on His breast at the supper, and said, "Lord, who is the one who betrays You?"

21 Peter therefore seeing him *said to Jesus, "Lord, and what about this man?"

22 Jesus *said to him, "If I want him to remain until I come, what is that to you? You follow Me!"

23 This saying therefore went out among the brethren that that disciple would not die; yet Jesus did not say to him that he would not die, but only, "If I want him to remain until I come, what is that to you?"

John 21:1-25 (cont'd)

24 This is the disciple who bears witness of these things, and wrote these things; and we know that his witness is true.

25 And there are also many other things which Jesus did, which if they *were written in detail, I suppose that even the world itself *would not contain the books which *were written.

[1]Or, *made Himself visible.* [2]I.e., *the Twin.* [3]Lit., *something eaten with bread.* [4]Lit., *was loving.* [5]Lit., *200 cubits.* [6]Here and in vv. 16 and 17 some mss. read *son of Jonas.* [7]Gr., *agapao.* [8]Gr., *phileo.*

Sec. 256   Appearance to the eleven in Galilee (cf. Secs. 253, 258)
– A mountain in Galilee –

Matt. 28:16-20	[Mark 16:15-18]	1 Cor. 15:6
16 But the eleven disciples proceeded to [1]Galilee, to the mountain which Jesus had designated.		
17 And when they saw Him, they worshiped Him; but some were doubtful.		**6** After that He appeared to more than five hundred brethren at one time, most of whom remain until now, but some have fallen asleep;
18 And Jesus came up and spoke to them, saying, "All authority has been given to Me in heaven and on earth.		
19 "Go therefore and make disciples of all the nations, baptizing them in the name of the Father and the Son and the Holy Spirit,	**15** [And He said to them, "Go into all the world and preach the gospel to all creation.	
20 teaching them to observe all that I commanded you;		
	16 "He who has believed and has been baptized shall be saved; but he who has disbelieved shall be condemned.	
	17 "And these [2]signs will accompany those who have believed: in My name they will cast out demons, they will speak with new tongues;	
	18 they will pick up serpents, and if they drink any deadly *poison,* it shall	

[1](Matt. 28:16) For some reason great prominence is given to this rendezvous in Galilee (Matt. 26:32; Mark 14:28, Sec. 225; Matt. 28:7; Mark 16:7, Sec. 246; Matt. 28:10, Sec. 249; cf. John 21:1, Sec. 255). Perhaps this site was chosen because it was convenient to many of Jesus' loyal followers who lived in Galilee. In addition, the mountain probably furnished a location that would be free from distractions and outside disturbances.

Matt. 28:16-20 (cont'd)	[Mark 16:15-18] (cont'd)
	not hurt them; they will lay hands on the sick, and they will recover."]
and lo, I am with you [1]always, even to the end of the age."	

[1]Lit., all the days. [2]Or, attesting miracles.

Sec. 257 Appearance to James, His brother

1 Cor. 15:7

7 then He appeared to [1][k]James, then to all the apostles;

[1]Lit., Jacob.

Sec. 258 Appearance to the disciples in Jerusalem (cf. Secs. 253, 256)

Luke 24:44-49	Acts 1:3-8
44 [1]Now He said to them, "These are My words which I spoke to you while I was still with you, that all things which are written about Me in the Law of Moses and the Prophets and the Psalms must be fulfilled."	
45 Then He opened their [1]minds to understand the Scriptures,	**3** To [5]these He also presented Himself alive, after His suffering, by many convincing proofs, appearing to them over a period of forty days, and speaking of the things concerning the kingdom of God.
46 and He said to them, "Thus it is written, that the [2]Christ should suffer and rise again from the dead the third day;	
47 and that repentance [3]for forgiveness of sins should be proclaimed [4]in His name to all the nations, beginning from Jerusalem.	**4** And [6]gathering them together, He commanded them not to leave Jerusalem, but to wait for [7]what the Father had promised, "Which," He said, "you heard of from Me;
	5 for John baptized with water, but you shall be baptized [8]with the Holy Spirit [9]not many days from now."
	6 And so when they had come together, they were asking Him, saying, "Lord, is it at this time You are restoring the kingdom to Israel?"

[k](1 Cor. 15:7) This is probably James, the half-brother of Jesus. The time of this appearance is not given, but that it happened was well-known. James, an unbeliever before Jesus' crucifixion, became a believer and leader of the Jerusalem church after this experience. Seeing the risen Jesus not only resulted in his conversion but was also a basis for his appointment to the apostolic office (cf. Gal. 1:19).

[l](Luke 24:44) It must not be surmised that this meeting was the same as that in Section 253 and therefore took place on the same day as the resurrection. Luke clarifies this point in his second book when he points out that forty days had transpired since the resurrection (Acts 1:3). Hence there was ample time for a journey to Galilee (Secs. 255-256) and back.

Luke 24:44-49 (cont'd)	Acts 1:3-8 (cont'd)
48 "You are witnesses of these things.	**7** He said to them, "It is not for you to know times or epochs which the Father has fixed by His own authority;
49 "And behold, I am sending forth the promise of My Father upon you; but you are to stay in the city until you are clothed with power from on high."	**8** but you shall receive power when the Holy Spirit has come upon you; and you shall be My witnesses both in Jerusalem, and in all Judea and Samaria, and even to the remotest part of the earth."

[1]Lit., *mind.* [2]I.e., *Messiah.* [3]Some mss. read *and forgiveness.* [4]Or, *on the basis of.* [5]Lit., *whom.* [6]*eating with;* or possibly, *lodging with.* [7]Lit., *the promise of the Father.* [8]Or, *in.* [9]Lit., *after these many days.*

THE ASCENSION

Sec. 259 Christ's parting blessing and departure
– From Jerusalem to the Mount of Olives (toward Bethany) –

[Mark 16:19-20]	Luke 24:50-53	Acts 1:9-12
	50 And He led them out as far as Bethany, and He lifted up His hands and blessed them.	
19 [So then, when the Lord Jesus had spoken to them, He was received up into heaven,	**51** And it came about that while He was blessing them, He parted from them.[4]	**9** And after He had said these things, He was lifted up while they were looking on, and a cloud received Him out of their sight.
and sat down at the right hand of God.		
		10 And as they were gazing intently into [7]the sky while He was departing, [8]behold, two men in white clothing stood beside them;
		11 and they also said, "Men of Galilee, why do you stand looking into [7]the sky? This Jesus, who has been taken up from you into heaven, will come in just the same way as you have watched Him go into heaven."
	52 And they[5] returned to Jerusalem with great joy, **53** and were continually in the [m]temple, [6]praising God.	**12** Then they returned to Jerusalem from the [9]mount called [10]Olivet, which is near Jerusalem, a Sabbath day's journey away.
20 And they went out and preached everywhere,		

[m](Luke 24:53) Only gradually did the earliest Christians learn that they had been freed from the old forms of Temple worship (cf. Heb. 8:13). Hence right after Jesus' ascension they went back to the only form of worship they knew. Over a period of years, however, their understanding grew to the point that the Temple's destruction in A.D. 70 proved no hindrance to their worship.

[Mark 16:19-20] (cont'd)

while the Lord worked with them, and confirmed the word by the [1]signs that followed.[2]]

[[3]And they promptly reported all these instructions to Peter and his companions. And after that, Jesus Himself sent out through them from east to west the sacred and imperishable proclamation of eternal salvation.]

[1]Or *attesting miracle.*   [2]Many mss. add *Amen.*   [3]A few later mss. and versions contain this paragraph, usually after v. 8; a few have it at the end of chap.   [4]Some mss. add *and was carried up into heaven.*   [5]Some mss. insert *worshiped Him, and.*   [6]Lit., *blessing.*   [7]Or, *heaven.*   [8]Lit., *and behold.*   [9]Or, *hill.*   [10]Or, *Olive Grove.*

ESSAYS RELATED TO HARMONISTIC STUDIES

ESSAY 1

Is a Harmony of the Gospels Legitimate?

Until the nineteenth or twentieth century it was rather a foregone conclusion that constructing a harmony of the gospels was a legitimate undertaking. Since the rise of modern criticism, however, harmonization is no longer universally admitted to be a valid procedure. An increasing number of people are concerned as to whether or not research into the life of Jesus—in other words, compiling a harmony of the biblical records of that life—can or should be undertaken.

Opposition to this type of project has followed several approaches:

1. One thrust has been to emphasize that the four gospels were not designed to be histories but gospels. With such admitted bias on the part of the writers, it is held, one could hardly expect to derive much value in drawing up a biography of Jesus. This objection to harmonization is logically weak, however. An evangelistic interest and purpose does not necessarily preclude historical accuracy. In fact, the wise evangelist will make his account accurate so that the cause he seeks to promote will not be undermined by being shown to be fallacious (Luke 1:3-4). Furthermore, a principal ethic of Christianity and the gospels is honesty. It appears unlikely that those who wrote of this ethic would have practiced distortions of historical truth in the very books where it is taught.

2. Another attempt to discredit the harmonizing approach to the gospels has come from some who doubt that such a historical person as Jesus ever existed. To these extremists, who incidentally are few in number, Jesus is no more than a mythological figure such as those encountered in the nature myths and mystery religions of the Graeco-Roman world. However, that Jesus Christ was a historical person is subscribed to by an impressive collection of ancient documents, including those from Jewish and Roman writers as well as Christian. In addition, the existence of that institution known as the Christian church is explicable only on the ground of His being a historical person.

3. Others attempt to demonstrate the fruitlessness of harmonies by placing strong emphasis on alleged loose handling of traditions by

the earliest Christian churches. Supposedly, the church took fragmentary reports about the person Jesus and elaborated upon them so as to attribute to Jesus sayings and actions that would meet their own needs. The process held to be necessary in separating the facts from the elaborations is called Form Criticism (see essay 4, pp. 280-286). Several difficulties confront such criticism of the gospels' historical worth. Among them is the critics' assumption that those who had the utmost reason for being interested in the historical facts of Jesus' life had little or no interest in ascertaining and transmitting those facts. Form Criticism also maintains that eyewitnesses of Jesus' life stood by in silence while falsehood about Jesus was actively promoted as the truth. This is inconceivable.

4. A more recent theory, Redaction Criticism, has also proposed obstacles to accepting the gospels at face value (see essay 5, pp. 287-294). This discipline takes special note of the gospel writers and their distinctive theological purposes. The writers purportedly took the traditions handed down to them and molded them so as to reflect the church's and their own understanding of the kerygma (i.e., proclamation; the preached Word; gospel). In so doing, Redaction Criticism claims, they beclouded the historical Jesus and His teachings even more than the generation before them had done. It may be agreed that each gospel writer had a distinctive purpose in mind, but it is unwarranted to conclude that he altered the facts at hand in order to attain this purpose. Matthew, Mark, Luke, and John were truthful men writing about a system of truth built around Him who is the Truth. To arbitrarily attribute to them an almost endless stream of lies, even "white lies," as does the redaction critic, is to impugn the truth itself. No tangible grounds have as yet been forthcoming to support this objection to harmonizing the gospels.

5. Another problem, insuperable to some, is the extreme difficulty encountered in attempting to harmonize parallel accounts (see essay 7, "Problems and Principles of Harmonization," pp. 302-308). So difficult are some areas that the only solution is the presumption that there is no solution. This viewpoint is often associated with a lower estimate of biblical inspiration than orthodox Christianity has traditionally held. It unfortunately reflects a willingness to concede a point here and there to those who actively support biblical errancy. Yet this is not necessary. For those who are willing to approach the Bible from the perspective of what it says about itself, namely, that it is free from error, satisfactory explanations for most problems of harmonization can be found. The remaining problems can be explained reasonably, although it is granted that completely satisfactory solutions to them must await further discoveries.

6. Others, who represent a more conservative approach to the gospels, object to attempts to harmonize them simply on the basis of not wishing to "tamper" with the text of Scripture. If God had wanted us to have a harmony of the life of Christ, they say, He would have given us one gospel instead of four. In response, it should be noted that a harmony of the gospels, especially one such as this where the text of each gospel is retained in its entirety in a separate column, is not an attempt to destroy the distinctive contribution of each gospel. The grammatical and historical interpretation of each gospel as an entity must remain the basic element in understanding God's revelation of Jesus Christ. At the same time, however, much can be added to that grammatical-historical understanding through a systematic comparison of the light the gospels shed on each other. Harmonization is not contradictory, but supplementary, to exegesis of the individual books.

7. One last objection may be cited. Some contend that the gospel writers, principally Luke, disagree with secular sources on points of history. If so, then it is foolish to try to combine the four gospels as though they were historical documents. However, although discrepancies of this type have been proposed, none has as yet been verified. In fact, the findings of archaeological and historical research have consistently verified the accuracy of the scriptural record. No convincing reason, therefore, has emerged for believing that the gospels err by violating secular findings. In fact, it is possible that secular sources, or our interpretation of them, may at times be in error.

On the other hand, very good reasons exist for arranging the gospels so as to point out their parallels as well as their distinctive contributions.

1. In the first place, harmonization grants deserved recognition to these writings as historical documents. Places in the gospels have geographical significance. Dates and chronological notations are also components worthy of historical note (see essay 10, "The Day and Year of Christ's Crucifixion," pp. 320-323, and essay 11, "Chronology of the Life of Christ," pp. 324-328). The people mentioned in the gospels were actual people. A harmony clarifies relationships among these places, times, and people as would the arrangement of any other set of historical data in order to obtain greater clarity.

2. Second, a harmony highlights the historical basis of Christianity. Without such a factual basis, Christianity becomes but another world religion that has been concocted by the imaginations of men. Unfortunately, a delusion being widely and increasingly propagated today reasons that it does not really matter what Jesus said and did; the important thing is that Christianity meet the needs of

men right now. What Jesus said and did does matter, however. It is essential that Christianity have the historical Jesus as He is described in the four gospels. It is essential that Christianity be built on the solid foundation of His resurrection from the dead. Without historical foundation, any system becomes a self-deceptive sham. A harmony of the gospels helps demonstrate how very solid is the historical foundation of Christianity.

3. Third, a harmony of the gospels greatly enhances our knowledge of the historical Jesus. Large amounts of additional insight are gained by allowing the gospels to fill in gaps in one another's accounts. The result is a fuller record of the Lord's life. Some instances of this type of mutual help are included in the explanatory footnotes of this work.

4. Finally, the twentieth century church should note that the Body of Christ has found harmonies to be conducive to her growth since very early in her existence (see essay 2, "A History of Harmonies," pp. 269-273). Though the nature of these harmonies has varied, the principle of the need for them remains. The replacement of harmonies by synopses in more recent years is doubtless attributable to the rise of the aforementioned objections. But the church can hardly afford to deprive herself of this means of growth because some have for flimsy reasons doubted the validity of harmonization. Furthermore, she can rejoice in this added opportunity to know Jesus Christ better, especially in a day when historical research is enhancing our knowledge of the times in which He lived.

In summary, let it be recalled that the objections to the practice of harmonizing the gospels are not formidable. Each argument seems to be based on ill-founded presuppositions about Jesus, the gospels, or the objectives of harmonization. On the other side, very good reasons exist for study of the gospels in relation to one another. In fact, it may be affirmed that harmonies of the gospels are not only legitimate but also absolutely necessary for comprehending to a maximum degree the person and work of Jesus Christ.

Selected Reading List

Guthrie, Donald. *A Shorter Life of Christ*. Grand Rapids: Zondervan, 1970.
Harrison, Everett F. *A Short Life of Christ*. Grand Rapids: Eerdmans, 1968.

ESSAY 2

A History of Harmonies

Harmonies of the gospels are by no means recent innovations. In spite of the difficulties and limitations involved in putting together the four accounts of the life, death, and resurrection of Jesus, obvious practical advantages were recognized very early in the history of the church. The earliest known attempt at combination was Tatian's *Diatessaron*, compiled about A.D. 170. Present knowledge of the *Diatessaron* is sketchy and indirect. Nevertheless, Tatian appears to have woven the four gospel accounts into one continuous narrative of the life and words of Jesus Christ. He retained so far as possible the words of all the evangelists. On what principles or with what success he did his work is simply not known.

In the early third century, Ammonius of Alexandria devised a system which made it possible to compare passages in Mark, Luke, and John with parallel passages in Matthew. He gave the full text of Matthew and then copied alongside what he regarded to be the parallel portions of the other gospels. Consequently, only those portions of Mark, Luke, and John that parallel Matthew were reproduced, and they were presented in the sequence of Matthew. In the next century, Eusebius of Caesarea developed a system of cross-references which preserved the sequential arrangement of each gospel and yet allowed the reader to find and study similar passages in the other gospels.

Although there were a few occasional attempts in subsequent centuries to establish sequence and parallels among the gospels, an outpouring of harmonies of various types has appeared since the Protestant Reformation. In the sixteenth century itself such works came from Andreas Osiander, R. Stephanus, John Calvin, Cornelis Jansen, Molinaeus, Codomanus, Paul Crell, and Martin Chemnitz. Between Chemnitz and the nineteenth century, the trickle of harmonies became a flood. Well-known men producing harmonies during this period were John Lightfoot, Jean LeClerc, J. A. Bengel, Joseph Priestly, and J. J. Greisbach. Greisbach's work is especially noteworthy; in 1776 he established a new format for published harmonies with his *Synopsis Evangeliorum Matthaei Marci et Lucae una cum iis Johannis pericopis*. He hit upon the device of printing the gospels in parallel columns when they recorded the same or similar material.

269

Since Greisbach's time, most harmonies have either been of the diatessaron type (one continuous narrative with the material from the four accounts interwoven and changed as little as possible) or of the parallel-column type. The parallel column format has two variations. One type attempts no rearrangement of the text to achieve a probable chronological order. Instead, the text of each gospel is given in its original sequence. However, most who have taken this approach also print the same or similar material which occurs in a different sequence in the other gospels alongside the material with which it seems to be at least a secondary parallel. Usually some printer's device (brackets, or smaller or lighter type) is used to indicate that such material has been removed from its original context. Works taking this approach often have the word synopsis in their title. This saves the editor from the necessity of making difficult, and sometimes arbitrary, decisions of probable chronological sequence and yet allows the reader to have on one page an overview of all primary and secondary parallels for comparative purposes. However, sometimes this approach also reflects the editor's skepticism that harmonization is possible or that basically accurate chronological sequence can be established.

New Testament scholars have a primary concern for the Greek text of the gospels, and there has been no lack of harmonies placing the Greek text in parallel columns. The better known of these were prepared by Robinson (1846), Tischendorf (1851), Stroud (1853), Strong (1859), Gardiner (1876), Huck (1892), Wright (1896), Campbell (1899), Burton and Goodspeed (1920), Huck, Lietzmann, and Cross˙ (1935), Mgr. de Solages (edition with notes in English, 1959), and Aland (1963). Some of these are more accurately described as synopses than harmonies, and some deal only with the text of the first three gospels. Several were issued in more than one edition. The work of Edward Robinson had an especially long and useful history. In the twentieth century, *A Harmony of the Synoptic Gospels in Greek* by Ernest De Witt Burton and Edgar Johnson Goodspeed long held the field, and Huck's *Synopsis of the First Three Gospels* has been periodically revised and is still widely used. However, Kurt Aland's *Synopsis Quattuor Evangeliorum* is now unmatched in utility and completeness. It has also been published with the English Revised Standard Version text on facing pages. For the serious student who uses Greek, Aland's work is indispensable for a comparative study of the gospels.

The average reader, though, must use a harmony of the English text. Since the mid-nineteenth century, English harmonies have been even more numerous. Unfortunately, the care with which many of these have been executed leaves much to be desired, and results are mixed. This is especially true of the diatessaron type. Their primary purpose is to create a continuous narrative of the life, works, and words of Jesus Christ. If done carefully, this method can communicate a sense of the course of development of Christ's life and ministry. But the approach, even in its best forms, also has severe limitations. Passages are taken from their original contexts. The distinctive purposes of each evangelist are almost hopelessly obscured. The method does not allow for comparative study of parallel passages. And when their wording differs, the texts of parallel passages are combined in an arbitrary manner. But apparently the desire to produce such "lives of Christ" has been compelling. The following is a partial listing of such works appearing since the mid-nineteenth century:

C. F. Holley and J. E. Holley, *Jesus the Christ: A Complete Gospel Harmony* (n.d.), KJV.
R. Mimpriss, *A Harmony of the Four Gospels, Arranged as a Continuous History* (1845), KJV.
J. Glentworth Butler, *Bible Reader's Commentary, New Testament*, vol. 1, *The Fourfold Gospel* (1878), KJV.
Arthur T. Pierson, *The One Gospel* (1889), KJV.
William Pittenger, *The Interwoven Gospels* (1890), ERV.
Fred'k L. Chapman, *The True Life of Christ* (1899), KJV.
Horace J. Cossar, *The Four Gospels Unified* (1911), KJV.
Eva Livingston, *His Life: The Story of Christ's Life* (1912), ASV.
Helen Barrett Montgomery, *The Story of Jesus As Told by His Four Friends* (1927), Centenary translation.
Robert Edgar Beall, *The Short Story Combined Gospels, and Reference Harmony Supplement* (1928), ASV.
Andrew J. Reynolds, *Jesus of Nazareth, "The Prince of Life"* (1933), KJV.
Loraine Boettner, *A Summary of the Gospels* (1933), ASV.
Vaughan Stock, *The Life of Christ* (1934), KJV.
J. W. Lea, *The Unified Gospels: The Complete Life of Christ in the Words of the Evangelist* (1935), KJV.
Russell Hubbard White, *The Combined Gospels of Matthew, Mark, Luke and John* (1947), KJV.
Freeman Wills Crofts, *The Four Gospels in One Story* (1949), an original paraphrase.
Edward F. Cary, *The Life of Jesus in the Words of the Four Gospels* (1951), an original translation.
Thomas U. Fann, *Behold the Son of Man! Or the Complete Gospel Interwoven from the Four Gospels* (1955), ASV.
William F. Beck, *The Christ of the Gospels* (1959), an original translation.
Who is This Man Jesus? The Complete Life of Jesus from the Living Bible (1967).
Johnston M. Cheney, *The Life of Christ in Stereo: The Four Gospels Combined as One*, ed. Stanley A. Ellison (1969). "We have sought to preserve the beauty of the 'King James' version, testing each rendering by the original."
Chester Wilkins, *The Four Gospels Arranged as a Single Narrative* (1976), KJV.

Harmonies using the parallel column format are obviously much more useful for careful comparative study of the text of the gospels. When skillfully arranged and outlined, they can also portray the course of development in Christ's life and ministry. Although rearrangement of

271

some of the materials is necessary if there is to be chronological sequence in the text of the harmony, at least the wording of each
evangelist is allowed to stand in its own integrity rather than being
amalgamated with the others. Still, the individual success or failure of a
harmony primarily depends on the care with which the editor has done
his work. The following harmonies appearing since the mid-nineteenth
century are of varying value:

Benjamin Davies, *Harmony of the Four Gospels* (n.d.), KJV.
Adam Fahling, *A Harmony of the Gospels* (n.d.), KJV.
J. M. Fuller, *The Four Gospels Arranged in the Form of a Harmony* (n.d.), KJV.
Edward Robinson, *A Harmony of the Four Gospels in English* (1846), KJV.
Simon Greenleaf, *The Testimony of the Evangelists Examined by the Rules of
    Evidence Administered in Courts of Justice* (1874), KJV.
John A. Broadus, *A Harmony of the Gospels* (1893), ERV.
William Arnold Stevens and Ernest DeWitt Burton, *A Harmony of the Gospels
    for Historical Study* (1893), ERV.
I. N. Johns and J. F. Kempfer, *The Parallel Gospels* (1896), KJV.
E. S. Young, *The Life of Christ: A Harmony of the Four Gospels* (1898), KJV.
John H. Kerr, *A Harmony of the Gospels* (1903), ASV.
Ernest DeWitt Burton and Edgar Johnson Goodspeed, *A Harmony of the Synoptic
    Gospels for Historical and Critical Study* (1917), ASV.
A. T. Robertson, *A Harmony of the Gospels for Students of the Life of Christ*
    (1922), ERV.
G. C. Savage, *Time and Place Harmony of the Gospels* (1927), original transla-
    tion.
Walter E. Bundy, *A Syllabus and Synopsis of the First Three Gospels* (1932),
    ASV.
Ralph Daniel Heim, *A Harmony of the Gospels for Students* (1947), RSV.
Albert Cassel Wieand, *A New Harmony of the Gospels: The Gospel Records of
    the Message and Mission of Jesus Christ* (1947), RSV.
Henry J. Cadbury, Frederick C. Grant, and Clarence T. Craig, *Gospel Parallels: A
    Synopsis of the First Three Gospels* (1949), RSV.
John Franklin Carter, *A Layman's Harmony of the Gospels* (1961), ASV.
H. F. D. Sparks, *A Synopsis of the Gospels* (1964), ERV.
Frederick R. Coulter, *A Harmony of the Gospels in Modern English* (1974), origi-
    nal translation.

Edward Robinson's work went through many editions, was eventually revised by M. B. Riddle and also served as the basis for the work of
other harmonists. The year 1893 marked the advent of two harmonies
that were long to be standards, those by Broadus, and Stevens and Burton. Both used the English Revised Version of 1881, and both used divisions that showed the historical unfolding of Christ's life; previous
practice had been to divide according to the feasts. Broadus' harmony
contained end notes by his younger colleague, A. T. Robertson. In 1922
Robertson's revision of Broadus' work and the Burton and Goodspeed
harmony of 1917 became the new standards in the field. Robertson's revision has had an especially long and useful life, even in the face of

272

more recent entries into the field, such as Sparks's widely used *Synopsis*

In 1975 Reuben J. Swanson presented to students of the gospels a completely new concept in *The Horizontal Line Synopsis of the Gospels* (Dillsboro, North Carolina: Western North Carolina). Swanson's innovation grew out of the frustration students experience in identifying the details of similarity and difference among the gospel accounts. Even when put in parallel columns, one's eye must still jump from column to column to pick out the points of comparison and contrast. To eliminate this tedious work, Swanson hit upon the idea of placing the parallel material in parallel horizontal lines rather than in parallel vertical columns. Thus the similarities and differences would be immediately apparent. Using the text of the Revised Standard Version, he gives the text of Matthew, line by line. Parallel with each line he gives whatever corresponding material there might be from any of the other three gospels, again line by line. The same procedure is then followed with the text of Mark, Luke, and John. This method has obvious advantage for the kind of detailed comparison Swanson has in mind. Also, each gospel in its original sequence can be examined and compared with line by line parallels from the other gospels placed there for handy reference.

However, if such detailed comparison is not one's primary purpose, the horizontal line format has severe limitations. It is difficult to read with any feeling for continuity of thought even in the lead line of the lead gospel. Furthermore, since this method presents each gospel line by line with parallels to each line, it does not integrate all the materials and give an overall picture of the historical unfolding of Christ's life and ministry.

Thus, while Swanson's innovation should receive appropriate recognition, its value is quite limited for the general student or reader. Unless one is primarily concerned to discover possible literary interrelationships among the gospels, the parallel column format, in spite of its own limitations, is still superior for general study of the life of Christ, because the material from all four gospels is integrated.

Selected Reading List
Ebrard, J. H. A. *The Gospel History: A Compendium of Critical Investigations In Support of the Historical Character of the Four Gospels.* Edinburgh: T. and T. Clark, 1873. Pp. 47-55.

ESSAY 3

Source Criticism

Matthew, Mark, and Luke have in modern times been referred to as the "synoptic gospels" since the three take a more or less common view of the Lord Jesus' life. Supposing that extensive agreement among the three indicates some sort of direct literary collaboration, much New Testament scholarship of the past century or so has attempted to explain the nature of that literary relationship. A complicating factor in these studies, however, has been a substantial number of instances where one gospel describes matters differently from one or both of the others. The difficulty encountered in devising a scheme of literary dependence to account for the combinations of similarities and dissimilarities has been labeled the *Synoptic Problem* and the field of studies devoted to solving the problem as *Source Criticism*.

Ancient Christianity was not too bothered by this difficulty. It was generally assumed that the gospel writers drew upon personal memory and firsthand reports rather than upon one another's writings or some common written source. The church historian Eusebius indicated that Matthew, one of the twelve apostles, was first to write. About to leave the Palestinian area, he supplied a written substitute for his oral ministry which apparently in turn was drawn largely from his apostolic experience. Luke, according to his own word (Luke 1:1-4), drew from numbers of sources, both oral and written, none of which had the authority of Matthew or Mark. Mark is said by Clement of Alexandria to have based his gospel on the apostolic tradition through Peter. John alone, writing at a much later time a gospel quite different from the synoptics, was in possession of the other gospels before he wrote. He could have copied from them, yet he did not. Instead, he verified their truthfulness and supplemented their contents with material not found in the other three.

In spite of this early consensus, scholars, particularly in the nineteenth century, explored various hypotheses as to how one writer might have depended on the others or on a single source also available to the others. Theories of one source used by all three and of various orders of writing, with the second writer depending on the first and the third on the other two, were typical forerunners of the *Two-Source theory*, an approach which eventually gained wide acceptance among New Testament authorities. This theory advocates that Mark was written

274

first, and that Matthew and Luke were based on this and another source called Q, now nonextant.

Streeter has ably supported the prior writing of Mark on five grounds:

1. Most of the material in Mark (93 percent according to Westcott) is found in Matthew and Luke. Since it seemed inconceivable to him that Mark would have abbreviated the other two, Streeter concluded that Matthew and Luke must have expanded Mark.

   Answers to this argument note that Mark may have had special reason for condensing one or both of the other gospels. Then too, material common to two or three gospels may have come to be there by some means other than copying. For example, it may be traceable to a common oral tradition. In other words, Mark may not have seen the gospels of Matthew and Luke before writing his own, and vice versa.

2. Though agreeing often with Mark in actual words used, Matthew and Luke do not agree with each other when they diverge from Mark. Allowing for exceptions to this generalization, Streeter explained these exceptions as either irrelevant, or deceptive, or that they were agreements because of an overlap of Mark and Q (Matthew's and Luke's other major source), or agreements because of textual corruption. This Matthean-Lucan diversity is taken to prove their dependence on Mark.

   Like Streeter's first proposition, however, this one too can be turned to prove the priority of Matthew or Luke. Depending on the parallel passages chosen and on which two gospels are pitted against the other, one could prove the priority of either Matthew or Luke as well. Though not numerous, agreements between Matthew and Luke where Mark has something different are substantial enough to indicate their independence of Mark in almost all sections where the Two-Source theory says they were dependent. No convincing explanation that would allow this premise to stand has accounted for these "exceptions."

3. The order of events in Mark is original, for wherever Matthew departs from Mark, Luke supports Mark's order, and wherever Luke departs from Mark, Matthew agrees with Mark's order. This, it is said, demonstrates Marcan priority and that the other two gospels are secondary since they never follow each other when departing from Mark's order.

   Again, however, the conclusion does not necessarily follow. For example, Mark may have worked from Matthew and Luke; he may have followed their order when they agreed and followed one or the other of them when they disagreed. Other explanations also offer plausible alternatives for the observed phenomena. One option which must remain open is that all three were working from an order dictated by a tradition agreed upon by eyewitnesses and transmitted in varieties of ways among early Christians. All three writers, then, as occasion arose, deviated from this traditional sequence in their gospels.

4. The primitive nature of Mark as compared with Matthew and Luke demonstrates Mark's priority. To illustrate, Matthew uses *kurie* ("Lord") nineteen times and Luke sixteen times, compared to the word's appearing only once in Mark. This is taken to indicate a more developed reverential attitude and hence a later date for the two longer gospels.

Yet the same type of evidence may be used otherwise. Question may be raised as to a reverential connotation in *kurie* since Matthew uses such an address seven times when referring to mere man (Matt. 13:27; 21:29; 25:11, 20, 22, 24; 27:63). Certainly this was not a form of address Matthew reserved for deity. Consequently, nothing chronological can be built on its use or nonuse in any of the gospels.

The same disposition may be made of other alleged marks of primitivity, such as Mark's Aramaisms. According to most standards of judgment, Matthew is much more Semitic than Mark. Couple this with Mark's Latinisms and his translation of Aramaic expressions for the sake of those who knew no Aramaic, and one has good reason for postulating the priority of Matthew.

5. The distribution of Marcan and non-Marcan material in Matthew and Luke shows their dependence on Mark. Matthew uses Mark as a framework and arranges his material into that structure, while Luke gives Marcan and non-Marcan material in alternate blocks.

It is just as plausible, however, to suppose the opposite procedure. Rather than Matthew's picking words or phrases here and there and weaving them into a smooth polished narrative, Mark, in coming up with his account, just as feasibly may have taken the book of Matthew and added details for vividness. If the assumption of Mark's priority be dropped, it can be shown how Luke could have extracted sections from Matthew and, in turn, Mark could have done the same from Luke. Another possible explanation is that all three could have drawn from a common core of tradition among early Christians.

Thus Streeter's support of the Two-Source theory, though widely accepted, in some cases presupposes the point to be proven and in others rests on overgeneralizations that fail to account for substantial exceptions. The case has therefore met with considerable opposition in some quarters.

Furthermore the Two-Source theory clashes directly with the strong testimony of ancient Christendom to the effect that Matthew wrote first. That he composed an Aramaic work before his Greek gospel does not seem to concern the early Fathers. They apparently took the Greek writing to be a natural sequel of the Aramaic when Matthew left Palestine to undertake a ministry among non-Aramaic-speaking people. Coupled with this, inherent weaknesses in support of Mark and Q as sources for Matthew and Luke have given rise to a growing movement to reexamine the Two-Source theory's validity. A few of the theory's more prominent shortcomings may be mentioned:

1. The Two-Source theory cannot account for what has been labeled "The Great Omission." If Luke used Mark as a source, no feasible explanation has as yet come as to why he omitted any reference to Mark 6:45—8:26. This important section includes Jesus' walking on the water, the healing at Gennesaret, a major conflict over the tradition of the elders, the Syrophoenician woman's faith, the healing of a deaf and dumb man, the feeding of the four thousand, the Pharisees' demand for a sign, the instruction regarding the leaven of the Pharisees and that of Herod, and the healing of a blind man at Bethsaida. Though Luke may have had reasons for omitting such a long, consecutive body of material, it is simpler to suppose he had no access to Mark's gospel when he wrote.

2. Recent archaeological findings and increased knowledge about first century Palestinian conditions have made it increasingly difficult to sustain the argument for Q as a single written body of tradition. Furthermore, if Q is insisted on as a single source, the changes made by Matthew and Luke are anomalous. It is more satisfying to explain Q, if the symbol is to be retained, as gospel material belonging to many different strands of tradition, both written and oral. Since the Two-Source theory rests on the foundation of a homogeneous Q, the theory is essentially disproved with such a redefining of Q.

3. In sections of triple tradition (i.e., those covered by Matthew, Mark, and Luke) a considerable number (about 230) of agreements between Matthew and Luke are different from a parallel portion of Mark. ("Different from" does not mean that Mark contradicts the other two, but that his wording varies.) Such agreements are admittedly not as numerous as agreements of Matthew and Mark where Luke differs, and Mark and Luke where Matthew differs, but they are sufficient, and their arrangement is such as to prove a common source other than Mark for Matthew and Luke. For example, Matthew 9:1-8 and Luke 5:17-26 agree with one another verbatim in nine separate expressions, whereas Mark 2:1-12 records different wording. In Matthew 8:1-4 and Luke 5:12-16 seven identical words or expressions are found, whereas Mark 1:40-45 deviates.

Perhaps each of these agreements individually could be explained as accidental or as a textual corruption, but when their proximity to one another is considered, possibility of coincidence is rendered quite remote. The fact of the matter is that the Two-Source theory cannot account for such agreements between Matthew and Luke when Mark reads differently.

4. The priority of Mark poses a serious challenge to the heretofore un-challenged testimony of early Christianity that Matthew the apostle wrote the first gospel. It necessitates understanding that Matthew, an eyewitness of Jesus' ministry, depended on Mark, a non-eyewitness, for his information. This dependence extends even to Matthew's reliance on Mark for a description of his own conversion. Eventually a choice must be made between accepting what the early Fathers said about Matthean authorship or accepting the "findings" of nineteenth century rationalism. The latter, uncon-cerned about retaining Matthean authorship of Matthew, placed the first gospel's composition much later. Probability of accuracy is on the side of the ancient church in such a choice, since the church was much nearer the time the gospels were written. No good reason for doubting the accuracy of these ancient sources has appeared, so the Two-Source theory comes short in another respect.

5. The Two-Source theory takes insufficient notice of personal contacts between the synoptic writers. Unless one does not accept the tradi-tional authorship of the three synoptics, he must be impressed by the opportunities available to the three writers to exchange infor-mation about the life of Christ orally, without having to resort to a form of documentary dependence. Matthew and Mark must have been close associates immediately following Pentecost, while Jerusalem Christians used Mark's home as a meeting place (cf. Acts 12:12). Mark and Luke were associated during Paul's Roman im-prisonment (Col. 4:10, 14). Quite likely Luke encountered Matthew during his two-year stay with Paul in Palestine in the late fifties (cf. Acts 24:27). If not, in the process of his gospel research he must have talked to some very close to Matthew. Personal contacts like these render unnecessary the literary dependence advocated by the Two-Source theory.

Since the Two-Source theory appears inadequate, and in the absence of any other satisfactory scheme as to how the synoptic writers de-pended directly on each other's writings or on a single common source, it is preferable to endorse the tradition of ancient Christianity: each of the three synoptic gospels arose in relatively independent circum-stances. The three writers probably exchanged information on a personal basis before writing, but each had sources of information separate from the others. Matthew's contacts with the Lord were primarily personal.

Mark's were predominately through Peter. Luke utilized what he could derive through interviews and whatever accurate written records he could find. All three drew heavily on various oral traditions that accumulated rapidly around Jerusalem through the concentrated post-Pentecostal preaching of the first Christians. Constant repetition directed toward Spirit-quickened minds (John 14:26; 16:13) was more than adequate to account for the large number of agreements in the synoptic gospels. It was unnecessary that any of the writers see another's work, or that all three draw upon one or two common sources. The times and places of composition were sufficiently scattered to constitute these as three independent witnesses of Jesus' life.

Selected Reading List

Albright, C. F., and Mann, C.S. *Matthew*. The Anchor Bible. Garden City, New York: Doubleday, 1971. Pp. xix-cxcviii.

Cole, R. A. *The Gospel According to Mark*. The Tyndale New Testament Commentaries. Grand Rapids: Eerdmans, 1961. Pp. 23-48.

Farmer, William. R. *The Synoptic Problem*. New York: Macmillan, 1964. Pp. 1-198.

Hiebert, D. Edmond. *An Introduction to the New Testament. The Gospels and Acts*. Vol. 1. Chicago: Moody, 1975. Pp. 160-190.

Pamphilus, Eusebius. *The Ecclesiastical History of Eusebius Pamphilus*. Translated by Christian Frederick Cruse. Grand Rapids, Michigan: Baker, 1955. Pp. 12-478.

Sanders, E. P. *The Tendencies of the Synoptic Tradition*. Cambridge: Cambridge U., 1969. Pp. 1-285.

Streeter, B. H. *The Four Gospels, A Study of Origins*. London: Macmillan, 1936. Pp. 150-360.

Thomas, Robert L., "An Investigation of the Agreements Between Matthew and Luke Against Mark," *Journal of the Evangelical Theological Society*, 19 (1976): 103-112.

Form Criticism

THE NATURE OF FORM CRITICISM

In the early twentieth century a new variety of gospel criticism came on the scene. In Germany, its place of origin, it has been known as *Formgeschichte*, meaning "form history." Its English name has been "form criticism." Source Criticism attempted to solve the Synoptic Problem by analysis of the gospels in terms of positing source documents upon which the gospel writers were supposedly dependent. Thus Source Criticism generally held that Mark was the earliest gospel and that Matthew and Luke drew upon Mark and another conjectural written source known as Q, which mainly contained sayings. By this means the similarities and divergencies among the synoptics were to be explained. Form critics for the most part accept some form of the Source Criticism theory. but they have not been content to let the matter rest there.

The reasons for this discontent are significant. In the effort to account for all the phenomena of the synoptics, source critics found it necessary to multiply the hypothetical written sources; this in itself tended to discredit the theory as an adequate solution. Furthermore, as a literary method, Source Criticism could not push behind the written sources. Yet the written sources did not appear for at least twenty years following Jesus' death. What had been the status of the gospel tradition during this period? Then W. Wrede and others challenged the historicity of the Marcan account by arguing that the framework of Mark was the author's own creation. Thus Mark could not be considered reliable chronologically or geographically; Mark and those dependent upon him were not biographically accurate. With the elimination of the integrity of the chronological-geographical framework of the synoptics, the units of gospel material which had been tied together by that framework were left in isolation, subject to critical analysis in their own right.

The intent of Form Criticism has been to investigate these units of gospel tradition in the twenty-year oral period before they were edited into the first written sources proposed by source critics. Form critics attempt to classify this material into "forms" of oral tradition and to discover the historical situation *(Sitz im Leben)* within the early church which gave rise to each of these forms. In other words, Form Criticism generally accepts Source Criticism as far as it goes, but Form Criticism aims to push the inquiry of gospel origins behind the written sources into the oral period. The New Testament scholars most readily identified as form critics have been Martin Dibelius, Rudolf Bultmann, Burton S. Easton, Frederick C. Grant, Edwin B. Redlick, R. H. Lightfoot, Vincent Taylor, and D. E. Nineham.

However, even these leading advocates represent widely different perspectives. For some form critics the study of the forms of gospel material is simply and only a matter of literary analysis. At the other extreme are those whose theories are highly speculative and whose evaluation of the historical worth of the material is very skeptical. To such scholars the units of tradition are products of the earliest Christian community. The units usually reflect more of the life and teaching of the early church than of the life and teaching of Jesus. The "forms" in which the units are cast are clues to their relative historical value. Among form critics there are also differences of judgment as to what forms the units of tradition are cast in, what they should be named, and what the significance of each form is. Dibelius spoke of paradigms, tales, legends, sayings, and myths. Bultmann divided the traditional material into three general categories: miracle stories, apophthegmata (i.e., utterances of Jesus resulting from the controversies that followed Jesus' miracles), and sayings of Jesus.

Analysis and comparison of the form critical theories of classification and interpretation would require very detailed discussion and is outside the scope of this essay. This type of discussion, however, is not necessary to the evaluation of Form Criticism. To get to the heart of the matter, one must evaluate the fundamental assumption of Form Criticism in its more thoroughgoing forms as typified by Dibelius and Bultmann. If the foundation of radical Form Criticism is without footing, there is little point in giving serious consideration to the details of its superstructure. And if Form Criticism is viewed only as a method of literary analysis devoid of value judgments, there is no cause for it to create much stir.

But what is the fundamental assumption of Form Criticism? Form tradition first existed as brief, rounded units, circulating orally in the Christian community, and that their contextual connections in the gospels are the creations of the evangelists. This assumption in itself could be quite innocuous. Indeed, when stated in this manner, it nearly corresponds to the oral tradition theory regarding the origin of the gospels. But by this assumption, the thoroughgoing form critic means something entirely different. He means that the primitive Christian church not only transmitted the accounts of the words and deeds of Jesus, but it also molded and changed the tradition to fit its own changing perspectives and needs. It even created new words and deeds of Jesus if the occasion demanded. The evangelists, in turn, took over the units of this tradition with little change or discrimination. They arranged the material in an artificial context so as to serve the purposes of their compositions.

This assumption contains two key elements. First, it holds that the early Christian community was so lacking in genuine biographical interest or honesty that it thought nothing of creating and transforming the tradition which it passed on. Supposedly this was done in order to meet certain types of needs within the community. These needs allegedly are discernible now from the various forms which the units of the tradition assumed. Thus, the gospels become primary sources of knowledge concerning the life of the primitive church and only secondary sources concerning the words and deeds of Jesus. The second element of the basic assumption is that the evangelists were merely editors of these individual, isolated units of tradition. Without regard for historical reality, they likewise arranged and rearranged material to suit their own purposes. Virtually all descriptions of place and time which connect the individual units are regarded as editorial creations and therefore historically unreliable. This view of the early church and of the gospel writers is open to serious challenge.

THE EVIDENCE OF EYEWITNESSES

The first and most obvious factor to be considered is the evidence of eyewitnesses. The failure of Form Criticism to account adequately for the role of eyewitnesses in the early church is sufficient to discredit its basic assumption and implications. If there were eyewitnesses, there could have been no "creative" community that formed and transformed tradition to suit its own needs without regard to the readily accessible facts. Yet the form critic ignores the possibility of eyewitnesses.

In effect form critics see Christianity as cut off from its founder and His disciples by an inexplicable ignorance. The new sect had to invent situations for the words of Jesus and put into His mouth words that memory could not check and that He may not have said. But still living in those early days were leaders and disciples who had heard and seen what they recounted (Acts 2:1-4). The form critic either forgets or ignores the fact that Jesus had a surviving mother and followers who had many vivid memories of His life and ministry. There is no reason to suppose that the individuals mentioned in Mark 3:31-35; 4:10; 15:40, and 16:1-8 would not have remembered these things.

Form critics call into question the integrity of the disciples. The disciples had seen and heard Jesus. They had even been a part of his ministry. Yet, if the form critics are correct, they did not control the accuracy of the tradition. Such however could hardly have been the case. Is it conceivable that in its own discussions and disputes the early church would not have examined doubtful statements concerning Jesus' ministry? If the church, in fact, did not scrutinize such statements, why is there such close agreement as to the nature and details of that ministry? A community that was purely imaginative and lacking in discrimination would have found it impossible to form a consistent tradition. The tradition must have been under the control of eyewitnesses within the church.

Equally important is the fact that outside the church the opponents of Christianity also had been eyewitnesses of Jesus' ministry. Again, is it possible that opponents would have allowed false statements to pass as facts concerning His life as they knew it? Christianity would have become hopelessly vulnerable if it had created such stories in order to perpetuate itself. Peter not only said, "We are all witnesses" (Acts 2:32), but he also said to the men of Israel, "You yourselves know" (Acts 2:22).

THE BIOGRAPHICAL INTEREST OF THE COMMUNITY

The assumption that the primitive Christian community was imaginative not only disregards the eyewitnesses who could have checked the accuracy of the developing tradition, but also disregards the fact that the early church would surely have wanted to guard the accuracy of the tradition. In other words, the early church did have a biographical interest in the life of Jesus. Form Criticism, asserting the opposite, claims that early Christians were so absorbed by the possibility of the Lord's return that they were not interested in the factual life of Jesus. However, it is inconceivable that memories of Jesus would not have been carefully and accurately retained. No solid evidence proves that the early church was preoccupied with other interests. In fact, all indicators point to the opposite conclusion.

If no biographical interest in Jesus existed in the early church, why did Paul distinguish between his words and the Lord's (1 Cor. 7:10, 12, 25)? Why had many taken in hand to draw up narratives of the events of Jesus' life, and why had they used the material of eyewitnesses (Luke 1:1-2)? Why did Luke, after careful research, add to this collection his own accurate account of the Lord's ministry (Luke 1:3-4)? Why did early Christians appeal constantly to the fact they were eyewitnesses of the events about which they spoke? The form critics must thoroughly discredit Luke's prologue and his Acts account if they are to eliminate a case for the early church's biographical interest.

Besides the evidence of eyewitnesses appealed to in Acts, the book also directly proves that the early church had a biographical interest extending beyond the bounds of the passion story. This is seen in the choice of Matthias to replace Judas (Acts 1:21-22), in Peter's sermon at Pentecost (Acts 2:12-24), in Peter's words to Cornelius' household (Acts 10:36-43), and in Paul's message in Antioch of Pisidia (Acts 13:23-31).

Contrary to what form critics say, it can be confidently asserted that early Christians had an intense desire to know Jesus. The form critic forgets that the person of Jesus is central to the Christian faith. That faith would have no meaning if an accurate picture of Him were withdrawn. Faith in Christ is central; but this is impossible without a knowledge of who and what He was. Thus the historical Jesus, being identical with the Christ of Christianity, was the heart of the Christian message no matter who was preaching (cf. Acts 2:32; 3:12-26; 4:10-20; 5:30-32; 8:35).

THE IMPOSSIBILITY OF A CREATIVE COMMUNITY

The fundamental assumption of Form Criticism also involves the concept of an imaginative, creative community; that is, the primitive Christian church supposedly exercised the power of creating and changing tradition about Jesus to suit its own needs.

To the form critic, Jesus is a faint and remote figure. The community was supposedly alert and ready for every enterprise of corruption or creation. But could this have been the case? Sayings as striking and pointed as those preserved in the gospels are not created by communities but by individuals. In this case the individual could only have been Jesus. Nor would the sayings have necessarily been taken from Hellenistic or rabbinic sources and put into Jesus' mouth. Even great teachers may say familiar things.

Nevertheless, for the sake of argument, let it be supposed that the community did have the inclination to create a tradition about Jesus, including sayings and stories about Him. If such were the case, where did that community get the wisdom to select the best? That such selection would have had to be made is evident from the consistency of synoptic tradition. No contradiction is found between Jesus' doctrine and actions. A logical and chronological sequence marks the gospel story from beginning to end. Accuracy in the descriptions of contemporary Palestine is acknowledged. But if the early church had been "creative," it would have had no standard by which to govern its selections and thus form such a harmonious tradition.

The impossibility of such a creative church is demonstrated by noting that gospel history created the community, not vice versa. To put it another way, if early Christian faith created the gospel record, what created Christian faith? The idea of a creative community responsible for originating synoptic tradition supposes the almost spontaneous appearance of an organized religious life built upon an intense faith in the deity of a crucified Jew—all without the dominant influence of Jesus or any other man. Such speculation contradicts the facts.

THE EVIDENCE FOR RELIABLE HISTORICAL CONTEXTS

Form critics also question the reliability of historical contexts into which the units of tradition are woven. In fact, their first task is to free the units from alleged artificial contexts. But such artificiality is without proof. The character of the gospels themselves leads to the opposite conclusion.

To support the idea of artificial contexts, the form critics hold that most historical, geographical, chronological, and biographical references in the gospels are a fictional means by which the evangelists combined isolated units of tradition. However, an examination of the references to place, time, sequence, and persons shows these to be so interwoven with the other material of the units, and to present such a natural ordered sequence when considered separately, that to view them as editorial creations of the evangelists is highly speculative. The contexts, as well as the sayings and events, are rooted in history.

The gospel of Mark is a good example. Close examination of his sequence and his chronological and geographical notations reveals an integration and development that is natural, not artificial, and that is confirmed by close parallels with the outlines, or partial outlines, of the gospel story in Acts. These accounts cover the period from the preaching of John the Baptist to the resurrection of Christ, and especially emphasize the passion story (cf. Acts 10:37-40; 13:23-31). Here is the heart of the message of the early church. This is also exactly the scope of the gospel of Mark.

THE REAL SIGNIFICANCE OF STEREOTYPED FORMS

It would be difficult to deny that some parts included in the gospels originally circulated in the early church as isolated units. However, even form critics recognize that the passion story existed as a long, continuous narrative. Why not also recognize other continuous sections such as Mark 1:21-39 and 2:1—3:6? It is evident from synoptic material that probably some stereotyped forms existed, although the extent of these has been greatly exaggerated by the form critics. The real question is, Do the stereotyped forms indicate particular historical situations (Sitz im Leben) in which each kind of form supposedly originated to fill certain needs in the primitive church? That is, do forms give relative historical value to what is related?

The answer to this question can only be an emphatic no. Forms do not give the related material a relative historical value. Form is in no way related to truth or falsity. Nothing can be inferred from stereotyped forms other than that the church customarily related episodes in a certain way or that Jesus taught in certain patterns.

Accounts of miracles would naturally be related in similar ways, for the general outline of conditions and events is likely to be the same. The same may be said of controversies with the scribes and the Pharisees. As for the poetic form of many of Jesus' sayings, what would have been more natural for Him, speaking to Jews, than to cast His declarations in poetic form? Such, in fact, was normal Semitic style. This practice would have made it easier for His followers, whether Jews or not, to remember His words. It makes just as much sense, perhaps more, to say that the real originator of the forms of those sayings attributed to Jesus is Jesus Himself.

Selected Reading List

Bultmann, Rudolf. *History of the Synoptic Tradition.* New York: Harper & Row, 1963.

Dibelius, Martin. *From Tradition to Gospel.* New York: Scribner's, 1935.

———. *Gospel Criticism and Christology.* London: Nicholson and Watson, 1935.

Easton, Burton Scott. *The Gospel Before the Gospels.* New York: Scribner's, 1928.

Gundry, Stanley N. "A Critique of the Fundamental Assumption of Form Criticism." *Bibliotheca Sacra* 123 (1966): 32-39 and 123 (1966): 140-49.

Guthrie, Donald. *New Testament Introduction.* Downers Grove, Illinois: InterVarsity, 1970. Pp. 188-219.

ESSAY 5

Redaction Criticism

Just as Form Criticism originated as a further refinement of source criticism, so Form Criticism has itself given birth to a further subdiscipline called *Redaction Criticism (Redaktionsgeschichte)*. With the amount of attention being devoted to synoptic gospel forms and church theology *(Gemeindetheologie)*, the question was not whether but when the scrutiny of New Testament scholarship would be redirected to the gospel writers who put together Matthew, Mark, and Luke. Though not recognized in all quarters as separate from Form Criticism, Redaction Criticism has with most gained the status of a separate discipline.

The theology of the evangelists as distinguished from that of the Christian community is the primary focus of Redaction Criticism. A clear-cut line of demarcation between the two is not easily drawn. In fact, in some cases overlap must be acknowledged. Since the gospel writers were part of the community, inevitably they would reflect the community's theological outlook at least in part. Otherwise, these composers must be unnaturally separated from the people whom they served.

Redaction critics, for the most part, do not embrace traditional viewpoints of authorship. They look upon the originators of the synoptics as later theological editors to whose works the names of Matthew, Mark, and Luke were attached for the sake of prestige. These anonymous compilers are, then, the ones whose theological views are in question in this type of research. Such views are assumed to be quite distinct from any specific, systematic teaching delivered by Jesus.

The emergence of Redaction Criticism as a separate discipline dates from the mid-twentieth century. Most prominent among its early advocates are Günther Bornkamm, Hans Conzelmann, and Willi Marxsen. Each of these has concentrated his efforts on one gospel—Bornkamm on Matthew, Conzelmann on Luke, and Marxsen on Mark. In the discussion to follow, these three along with Werner Kümmel and Norman Perrin will be representatives of Redaction Criticism.

THEOLOGY OF MARK

Since the Two-Source theory and Form Criticism endorse the priority of Mark, so does Redaction Criticism. This gospel is then a suitable starting point for theological analysis. Redactional analysis of Mark is more difficult because of the unavailability of sources used by him.

According to Marxsen, Mark joins, edits, and expands isolated units of tradition in accordance with four guidelines:

1. The passion story is linked to the rest by the addition of predictions of its coming.
2. The Messianic-secret theory is invented to explain the late (post-Easter) emergence of Messianic teaching.
3. The new literary concept of a "gospel" (euangelion) is introduced. It is the "proclamation of a message of salvation" and is derived from Paul.
4. A geographical orientation toward Galilee is woven into the narrative. The resultant force of the gospel is, therefore, not an historical account of Jesus' life but a proclamation of the salvation to be expected by Christians subsequent to the Easter (i.e., resurrection) "experience." The evangelist anticipates an imminent return of Christ and directs his readers to make their way to Galilee where he expects the parousia ("coming") to happen.

THEOLOGY OF MATTHEW

For the redaction critic the theologies of Matthew and Luke are more easily discernible since these gospels were based on a known source (Mark) and a reconstructed source (Q). Bornkamm contends that Matthew was written in the eighties or nineties somewhere between Palestine and Syria. The book reflects a deep cleavage between Judaism and Christianity and, more specifically, a turmoil within the church between Jewish Christianity and Gentile Christianity. In siding with the Gentile position, this evangelist arranges his sources (Mark and Q plus some special Matthean material) and adds material so as to create a Teacher who has captured the true essence of the Law that had been missed by Pharisaic Judaism. Unlike His predecessors this "Rabbi" teaches with authority supported by miracles, and His disciples never cease to be pupils. While having much in common with Judaism, this new system is distinct from it and earns its own title of "church" (ekklesia), a term put into the mouth of the earthly Jesus by the Christian community. The "church" has become universal and is not local like a Jewish synagogue. The presence of the Lord with His church replaces the Law and the Temple as a unifying factor. Yet ultimate perfection has not been attained in the church. Need still exists to obey Jesus' teachings in light of future judgment that will issue in promised salvation.

In Matthew's scheme, then, Mark's exclusive attention to Christ's imminent return has been replaced by a joint emphasis on ecclesiology and eschatology. Late first century Christian thought came to grips with the fact that Messiah's return was not to be immediate and therefore originated the concept of a new institution, the church, to fill the interval before the return.

THEOLOGY OF LUKE

In Conzelmann's view, Luke, coming at about the time of Matthew or later (perhaps around A.D. 90 or after), delineates three distinct periods: the period of Israel, the period of Jesus' ministry, and the period since the ascension. The second and third periods are kept quite distinct by this writer. The former, when Jesus was alive ministering on earth, was the time of salvation when Satan was far removed and temptation was nonexistent. Since His passion, however, Satan has returned and temptations are very real. The work of the Spirit in the church is presented as essentially fulfilling prophecies of the "last days." Hence Luke reflects a more general, weakened, eschatological expectation in the church of his time. The delay of Christ's return is, then, Luke's motif.

This means that Luke shifts from his predecessors' focus on a short time of waiting to deal with a Christian life of longer duration. This shift entails a development of ethical standards among which perseverance is prominent. It also leads to development of a complete redemptive plan and the replacement of an imminent end by one that is "endlessly" remote.

CHARACTERISTICS OF THE METHOD

Several additional observations will provide a better understanding of Redaction Criticism:
1. The following are a few examples of how the gospel writers allegedly incorporated their theological emphases:
   a. In the narrative connected with Caesarea Philippi (Mark 8:27—9:1), the writer reports questions and answers as from the lips of Jesus and Peter. In reality, Redaction Criticism alleges, the titles are from the Christological vocabulary of the early Christian community. Furthermore, though persons bear the names of individuals and groups connected with Jesus' ministry, the principal reference is to circumstances in the church of the late sixties. "Jesus" and His sayings represent the Lord from heaven and His message to this church. "Peter" pictures misled believers who confess correctly but interpret their own confession erroneously. "The multitude" stands for the total church membership for whom the teaching is intended. In other words, Redaction Criticism sees this story as bearing the form of a history about Jesus, but its actual purpose was the conveying of the risen Lord's message to His church, as conceived by Mark. The historical impression is

only a vehicle and is not to be equated with actual happenings.

b. Matthew took over the same incident at Caesarea Philippi and reworked it. Dominated by an ecclesiological interest, Matthew reshaped the Marcan narrative by inserting a formal blessing of Peter on the basis of which Peter assumed full authority as founder and leader of the early church (Matt. 16: 17-19). For Matthew the church was the sole medium of salvation. In fact, to the person within this church salvation is assured. In effect, Matthew moved the "Son of man" reference from 16:21 (cf. Mark 8:31) to 16:13, because, unlike Mark, he was not interested in generating a Christological discussion. Matthew's interest was in a formal proclamation by Jesus regarding the Christian church.

c. In the Lucan parallel (Luke 9:18-27) Luke removed the Marcan urgency based on an imminent return in favor of highlighting a consistent life of testimony over a considerable period of time. Such touches as the addition of "daily" to Luke 9:23 and the omission of "in this adulterous and sinful generation" and "come with power" from 9:26-27 changed the account's complexion drastically. This resulted when Luke rethought Mark's outlook regarding eschatology and introduced his own emphasis on delay. By attention to details such as these, the redaction critic supposes he has captured this or that theological point being made by the gospel writers.

2. The above examples demonstrate in a small way how the redaction critic conceives the gospel writers' method. Mark, supposedly, was wholly dependent on the isolated units that have been identified by Form Criticism. Matthew and Luke each had access to some special sources of their own which they utilized along with Mark and Q. The task of these three consisted of adapting and connecting these units in ways that seemed best to them, so as to attribute to Jesus the viewpoints and emphases which they deemed most crucial for nurturing the faith of the church of their time. The writers, then, were theologians or theological editors, not historians. It was quite inconsequential to them that they falsely attributed to Jesus and His associates many things they never said or did. Their prime concern was to construct a theology that would meet the needs of the church, even if doing so successfully meant fabricating a life of Jesus in order to give the system more credibility.

3. The philosophical basis by which the redactionist attempts to grant respectability to this system of falsification is similar to that behind the neoorthodoxy of Karl Barth and the demythologizing of Rudolf Bultmann. Besides the obvious realm of reality where space, time,

and the physical senses prevail, another realm is visualized: the realm of faith. Anything which one is inwardly persuaded to be true is taken to be quite real whether or not it could ever be regarded as historic fact. For example, the postresurrection faith of early Christians was so strong that it became confused with space-time happenings to the point that many were fully convinced that the physical body of Jesus rose from death and departed, leaving an empty tomb. To the redaction critic, as to the form critic, this mental persuasion is not wrong, even though Jesus' resurrection cannot be advocated as a fact of history. To him the resurrection is a fact of faith which proved to be health-giving for the early church, and this is enough. It need not coincide with history. Similarly, as a whole, the synoptic gospels need not portray the historical Jesus in toto. It is sufficient that they proved beneficial in the development of the early Christian community.

4. The above philosophical basis of Redaction Criticism raises the question whether or not it is valid to think of reconstructing a life of Jesus from the gospels. This discipline says it is not. Redaction Criticism also finds improper any attempt to reconstruct a life of Jesus theology. These endeavors are impossible because early Christians allegedly were not guided by the modern concept of "historical" (i.e., "factual"). Motivated by a strong religious experience, they had no qualms about imputing to the historical Jesus words that He never spoke. The gospels and the traditions behind them, therefore, are to the redaction critic primarily reflections of the early church's experience and theology. Only by stringent application of very carefully contrived criteria for authenticity can one hope to derive accurate data about Jesus' life and teachings. Whatever is derived will be at best minimal, says the redactionist.

EVALUATION

An evaluation of Redaction Criticism must incorporate a notice of certain constructive features:

1. Redaction Criticism corrects the tendency of Form Criticism, which looks upon the gospel writers as mere compilers of tradition. It gives due recognition to them as men who wrote with a purpose.

2. Redaction Criticism notes that each writer has a distinct contribution. It sees him with specific emphases all his own that must not be omitted in quest of an adequate understanding of the New Testament.

3. Redaction Criticism focuses on the differences between the gospels, whereas criticism previously tended to emphasize the similarities. These differences are oftentimes basic to an understanding of the writer's meaning.

4. Redaction Criticism has revived interest in a comparative study of the gospels. Such interest had for some time lagged because of earlier efforts to merge the three into a single strand of tradition.
5. Redaction Criticism looks at each gospel as a whole instead of as an assortment of miscellaneous units of tradition. This is only proper for a self-contained piece of literature.
6. In its efforts to discover theological motivation, Redaction Criticism induces very close attention to the situation of first century Christianity. Research into this historical situation is bound to result in much help in understanding the New Testament.

These elements of value, associated as they are with Redaction Criticism, are nevertheless no more than by-products of a system beset with deep-seated weaknesses:
1. Since Redaction Criticism is founded on the Two-Source solution to the Synoptic Problem and on Form Criticism, it automatically inherits all their difficulties. Presupposing the validity of the other two disciplines renders the redactionist methodology vulnerable at the very same points as they.
2. For no valid reason the redaction critic supposes that events and sayings were invented or reshaped for a purely theological purpose. He assumes the nonhistorical character of the bulk of gospel literature as though some immense barrier separated the gospel writers from any interest in real happenings of the earlier portion of their century. This is quite uncharacteristic of other teachers in the ancient world, both Jewish and Greek. The unanswered evidence to the contrary says that early Christians did have considerable historical interest in Jesus of Nazareth. The writers' theological purposes, therefore, were not separate from but rather anchored in history.
3. The philosophical basis of Redaction Criticism is quite questionable. To grant recognition to a set of "faith realities" that stand in conspicuous opposition to physically observable historical data can, after serious analysis, only be rejected. Only the mind thoroughly preconditioned by theories of modern rationalism can envisage two realms of reality in conflict with each other and yet regard both as equally valid. In endorsing such a state of affairs one's intuitive concepts of reality are called into serious question. Such a dualistic concept is artificial, to say the least.
4. An unregulated subjectivism also characterizes Redaction Criticism. This is an outgrowth of the system's underlying philosophy. The redactor becomes his own norm with the result that interpretations are quite often stretched. For example, Marxsen's explanation of "Peter" as Mark's representation of misled believers must be traced

to Marxsen, not to Mark (cf. Mark 8:27—9:1). "Peter" in his confession could just as easily be taken by someone else to represent discerning believers. Only the factual data about who Peter was can rescue from the dilemma of endless conflicting opinions about him. An objective control on these must be found. In other words, "faith realities" must be reduced to one "faith reality" by reaffirming the only reality to be that which is historical. "Peter" was either a historical person or the figment of someone's imagination. He cannot be both.

5. Differences of opinion among redaction critics reflect the shallowness of their assumptions. That they have taken unjustified liberties in arguing for various emphases in each author could not be more clearly reflected than it is by their disagreements with one another. For example, theories of Mark's purpose variously hold his guideline to be typological fulfillment of Old Testament texts, the liturgical calendar, stages in the revelation of Messianic dignity, a geographical-theological outline, Pauline theology, and others. If redaction proponents cannot agree what theological theme Mark sought to inaugurate, it is quite plausible he was not trying to inaugurate any such theme. In fact, the theological theme originates in the mind of the modern redactionist, not the gospel writer. Differing foundational assumptions by different modern scholars create different opinions which are then read back into the gospel. This is a great injustice to the ancient record.

6. Redaction Criticism's method for recognizing "authentic Jesus material" is also quite subjective. Their three criteria, "distinctiveness," "multiple attestation," and "consistency," stem from the presupposition that tradition about Jesus contains much that is unhistorical. If this be the foregone conclusion, it is impossible to examine historical sources without bias. With the verdict already passed before the trial's beginning, the accused can never receive a fair trial. It is not a question of whether he will be found guilty, but how and when he will be condemned. Thus Redaction Criticism has determined in advance what it will discover. The results of the process can therefore be nothing less than devastating to the synoptic gospels as historical records.

To the person convinced of the gospels' historicity, Redaction Criticism has but limited value. Benefit may be derived only with greatest caution. It must be remembered that the theological themes in the synoptic gospels are traceable to Jesus, not to the gospel writers, and they do not conflict with but rather supplement one another. The part of the writer was only to emphasize this or that theme in accord with his particular purpose.

Selected Reading List

Bornkamm, Günther; Barth, Gerhard; and Held, Heinz Joachim. *Tradition and Interpretation in Matthew.* Translated by Percy Scott. Philadelphia: Fortress, 1963.

Bornkamm, Günther. *The New Testament: A Guide to Its Writings.* Translated by Reginald H. Fuller and Ilse Fuller. Philadelphia: Fortress, 1973. Pp. 50-66.

Conzelmann, Hans. *The Theology of St. Luke.* Translated by Geoffrey Buswell. New York: Harper, 1960.

Feine, Paul; and Behm, Johannes. *Introduction to the New Testament.* Re-edited by Werner Georg Kümmel. Translated by A. J. Mattill, Jr. Nashville: Abingdon, 1966. Pp. 62-68, 75-84, 91-102.

Guthrie, Donald. *New Testament Introduction.* Downers Grove, Ill.: InterVarsity, 1970. Pp. 214-19.

Harrison, Everett F. "Gemeindetheolgie: The Bane of Gospel Criticism." In *Jesus of Nazareth: Saviour and Lord,* edited by Carl F. H. Henry. Grand Rapids: Eerdmans, 1966. Pp. 157-73.

Hiebert, D. Edmond. *An Introduction to the New Testament. The Gospels and Acts.* Vol. 1. Chicago: Moody, 1975. Pp. 184-88.

Marshall, I. Howard. *Luke: Historian and Theologian.* Grand Rapids: Zondervan, 1970.

Marxsen, Willi. *Introduction to the New Testament.* Translated by G. Buswell. Philadelphia: Fortress, 1964. Pp. 136-42, 147-52, 155-61.

———. *Mark The Evangelist.* Translated by James Boyce, Donald Juel, and William Poehlmann with Roy A. Harrisville. Nashville: Abingdon, 1969.

Perrin, Norman. *What Is Redaction Criticism?* Philadelphia: Fortress, 1969.

ESSAY 6

Criticism of the Gospel of John

The gospel of John and its historical integrity have long been objects of severe attack. With some it is a foregone conclusion that the gospel could not have been written by John the apostle because no contemporary of Jesus could have held such a high view of His person. Past attitudes have at times bordered on extreme skepticism toward the value of a work that would picture the deity of Jesus Christ so clearly. Because of further research and discoveries this near skepticism has largely disappeared. Nevertheless, many are still reticent to endorse the gospel as completely reliable.

One frequently mentioned difficulty has related to the problems encountered by any theory of unified authorship. The differences in the gospel's Greek style, problems of sequence, and repetitions in discourse material have been cited as proving that more than one author was involved. So various attempts to explain the manner of composition have been made. One group of theories explains the alleged confusion in the gospel by suggesting that some sections were displaced accidentally; it seeks to correct the problem by rearranging the order. Another approach accounts for apparent stylistic differences and other problems by proposing that the gospel's compiler used a number of independent written sources in putting the work together. A third proposed solution has been to suggest that the gospel went through a number of editions before arriving at its present form. Still another theory, called "gradual composition," combines elements of the other theories and identifies five stages in the gospel's development. This approach sees two dominant figures, a master preacher (or evangelist) and a redactor, as presiding over this process. All the above explanations have in common that they question the gospel's historical integrity.

Yet all are so speculative and lacking in substantial foundation that their significance to those interested in what tangible evidence dictates is small. Other issues are far more relevant because they pertain to objective data at hand. To this type of criticism the following discussion is devoted. Evaluation of these grounds for questioning the fourth gospel's integrity is much more beneficial.

The critical questions surrounding the fourth gospel are nearly all interrelated. Thus, discussion of any one area of critical questions necessarily presupposes matters relating to another area. This is true whether one discusses authorship, date, or the relationship existing between John's gospel and the synoptics. Choice of a starting point for discussion is somewhat arbitrary, but the last of these issues may be the best way into the other two.

The first three gospels in the traditonal order are commonly spoken of as the *synoptic gospels* because they treat the life and ministry of Jesus from a similar perspective (*synoptic* means "seeing together"). Striking and extensive similarities of content, arrangement, and wording occur. One may readily see their similarity by examining the parallel columns of material in this *Harmony*.

But also evident is the fact that the gospel of John is in a class by itself. One notes more differences than similarities between John and the synoptics. Differences in material content are the most obvious. John does not record the virgin birth, the baptism, the temptation, the transfiguration, the institution of the Lord's Supper, the agony in the garden of Gethsemane, or the ascension. Synoptic type parables and cures of demoniacs and lepers are notably absent. Many omissions of less significant material occur also.

Just as critical is the fact that John includes much material that is unique to him. John's prologue is without parallel (1:1-18). It is John who records the early Judean ministry (chaps. 2-3), including such notable events as the first miracle and the discussion with Nicodemus. It is John who details the journey through Samaria to Galilee, including the encounter with the Samaritan woman at Sychar. High points of the remaining material unique to John are the Sabbath healing of the lame man in Jerusalem, Jesus' failure in Capernaum to conform to popular Messianiac ideas, the healing of the blind man in Jerusalem, the Good Shepherd discourse, the raising of Lazarus, the washing of the disciples' feet, the discourse in the upper room, Christ's intercessory prayer, and the miraculous catch of fish. In sum, there is an obvious difference in material content between the synoptics and John.

These, however, by no means exhaust the differences that set John apart. John's manner of presentation is different. The material content cited has already hinted at this. John has less narrative and more discourse, in contrast to the short aphorisms and parables characteristic of the synoptics. He portrays Jesus more in the role of the Jewish rabbi. Jesus' manner of teaching in the synoptics would be more appropriate to the common people of Galilee, that in John to the more educated populace in and around Jerusalem.

Differences of chronology between John and the synoptics are also found. There is the question of whether there were one or two cleansings of the Temple. The dating of the Last Supper is also a problem. Even more far-reaching in its implication is the duration of Christ's ministry. The synoptic accounts apparently require a ministry of only one year, although their chronological details are vague. But John's requires nearly four years.

Our discussion of John's relationship to the synoptics must also embrace their similarities, although these are not so obvious. Indeed, since the differences do not necessarily involve contradiction or incompatibility, the similarities become especially significant. At least two of the synoptists and John include material on John the Baptist, the feeding of the five thousand, the storm at sea, the triumphal entry into Jerusalem, Mary's anointing of Jesus, and parts of the Last Supper and passion narratives. In addition, similar material often occurs in the same order in John as in the synoptics. However, very little verbal similarity exists between John and the synoptics, except in some cases of the words spoken by Jesus or others.

To identify these similarities and differences is not enough. What relationship between the synoptics and John do they evidence?

1. One solution offered is that John wrote with the intention of replacing the synoptic gospels. But taken by itself, John is an incomplete account of the life and ministry of Jesus. That any author would suppose that this account could replace any one or all of the synoptics is stretching imagination too far.

2. A second proposal is that the book of John is an interpretation of Jesus and His teaching designed for Gentile readers. Those who hold this view, though, usually assume that John's intentions are not historical; if the assumption is wrong, the theory collapses. And if John is interpreting the other gospels, why is so little material held in common with them?

3. Closely akin are the views holding that John, having been written later, was dependent on one or more of the synoptics. John supposedly is a reworking of synoptic material. Attempts to identify sections of John that are dependent on written sources result in failure, however, because John is stylistically uniform. Again it must be said that the similarities are not significant enough to justify the assumption of John's actual dependence on the synoptics. Variation is much more characteristic. John cites incidents not even in the synoptics, and his accounts of the same incidents differ in detail.

4. These considerations suggest a fourth view—that John is independent of the synoptics, that he writes neither to interpret nor to replace

them, that he is in no sense dependent on them. This independence theory is certainly preferable to the first three and has much more to commend it. It challenges the assumption of much gospel criticism that the gospels form a documentary series in literary dependence on one another.

Advocates of the independence view point out that in supposed instances of John's using synoptic or Marcan material, he so drastically alters it that either John's credibility is called into question or the theory of literary dependence is itself called into question. Yet nothing in John's account itself casts doubt on his credibility. As for the points of similarity and contact that do exist between John and the synoptics, these are precisely what would be expected from authors drawing upon an interlocking oral tradition about Christ. The tradition was stable and held great respect for the historical verities; John, as well as the synoptists, would have drawn on this and on his own recollections (assuming he was John the apostle).

Such a view of John's relationship to the synoptics has much to commend it and is a helpful corrective to those views already discussed. However, some advocates of the independence theory maintain that John either was unaware of the synoptics or that he wrote without any reference to their content and purpose. Since it is difficult to imagine a situation later in the first century in which the synoptics would be unknown, some have postulated an early date for John, perhaps earlier than any of the synoptics. But such an extreme view of John's independence is neither necessary nor the best accounting of the evidence.

It would seem preferable to combine the theory accepting John's essential literary independence with the supplemental view of John's relationship to the synoptics. According to this view John did not use the synoptics as sources, but he did apparently write with a knowledge of their contents. He assumed his readers also knew their contents. Among his purposes seems to have been conscious supplementation of synoptic material; John filled in the gaps and avoided unnecessary duplication. Thus, John concentrated on the Judean, rather than on the Galilean, ministry of Jesus. By his mention of three, perhaps four, Passovers, he made clear that Jesus' ministry lasted between three and four years. This is not clear from the synoptics. On the other hand, John's omission of so much important synoptic material, such as Kingdom teaching and the institution of the ordinances, is extremely difficult to explain unless we assume that he knew the synoptics and saw no need to repeat their content. Thus, a view that accepts John's literary independence but that also sees his purpose as that of supplementing the synoptics best accounts for both the similarities on the one hand and the many significant differences on the other. This seems to be the relationship of the fourth gospel to the first three.

Traditionally, John the apostle has been thought to be the author of the fourth gospel. A recent variation of this view of apostolic authorship holds the apostle John to be the source of the gospel's historical data but suggests that a disciple or disciples of John actually wrote it. Under John's influence, it is said, they preached and developed John's reminiscences even further so as to meet the needs of the community to which they ministered. This viewpoint aligns itself with modern theories of composition connected with the synoptic gospels (see essays 4 and 5, "Form Criticism" and "Redaction Criticism," pp. 280-294). The proposal does injustice to the gospel of John itself, however, when it fails to recognize the gospel's own claim that the beloved disciple of Jesus wrote the book (John 21:20, 24).

Others have proposed that the John to whom early tradition ascribed authorship is John the Elder, referred to by Papias as quoted by Eusebius. Eusebius's interpretation of Papias's statement distinguishes between two persons in Ephesus by the name of John. Motivation for such a distinction is probably traceable to influential Christian leaders in Alexandria who questioned the millennial views of Revelation and therefore were seeking to dispense with the apostolic authorship of this last book of the Bible. By postulating another John in Ephesus at the time it was written, they thought they had grounds for doing this. However, it is not at all clear that Papias intended to distinguish John the Elder from John the apostle in his quoted statement. A good argument can be advanced that the two were one and the same person, so that no confusion in the traditional ascription of authorship to John results.

Some theories of non-Johannine authorship discredit the external evidence for a John as author and argue that internal evidence makes apostolic authorship impossible. Actually, though, both external and internal evidence firmly support authorship by John the apostle.

Irenaeus (c. A.D. 180) is the first to clearly say that John the apostle wrote this gospel and that it was published by John at Ephesus where he resided. Other late second century evidence testifies to John the apostle's residence in Ephesus late in the first century. But Irenaeus' testimony is especially important; he was a disciple of Polycarp, and Polycarp had known the apostle John personally. Here then is a direct line between Irenaeus and John with only one connecting link—Polycarp. Writers after Irenaeus assume apostolic authorship of the fourth gospel without question.

At one time, New Testament critics of the school following F. C. Baur argued that the fourth gospel was not written until about A.D. 160, so that John could not have been its author. However, the discovery of a papyrus fragment of this gospel in the collection of the John Rylands Library demolished this view. Dated at least at A.D. 150 and perhaps as early as A.D. 130, the fragment (P⁵²) came from a community along the Nile River in the hinterland of Egypt. When one allows for the time necessary for the processes of copying and circulation in order for this fragment to reach a remote Egyptian community, the origins of this gospel are easily pushed back into at least the late first century when John was probably still alive.

Nowhere in the fourth gospel does the author identify himself by name, and the interpretation of internal evidence is subject to the preconceptions of the individual critic. Nevertheless, this evidence fits well (many would say best) with apostolic and Johannine authorship. The writer claims to be an eyewitness (1:14; 19:35; 21:24-25). He has an accurate knowledge of Jewish customs and Palestinian topography before Jerusalem's destruction in A.D. 70. He employs the kind of vivid, incidental detail one would expect of an eyewitness (2:6; 6:19; 21:8). His writing style is Semitic. Even more specifically, the author seems to identify himself as the "disciple whom Jesus loved" (21:20, 24). James, John, and Peter formed the inner circle of disciples closest to Jesus (Mark 5:37; 9:2; Luke 22:8). James was martyred early in the history of the church (Acts 12:1-5), too early to have written the gospel. "The disciple whom Jesus loved" is distinguished from Peter in 13:23 and 21:7. By process of elimination, it must be John the son of Zebedee, one of the group from whom Jesus singled out "the disciple whom Jesus loved" (John 20:2; 21:20). Although the beloved disciple is not identified by name, this very anonymity is best explained by John the apostle's authorship.

DATE OF THE FOURTH GOSPEL

Although it is impossible to date this gospel with certainty, most writers today place it in the last ten or fifteen years of the first century or very early in the second. This view finds support in the early church Fathers. As already noted, the early dating of the P⁵² fragment hardly allows for a much later date. Critics who view this gospel either as corrective of or supplemental to the synoptics obviously must place its writing after one or more of the synoptics. Thus, they usually prefer a later date, although it is difficult to place apostolic authorship after A.D. 100.

Scholars who maintain that the author either did not know or use the synoptics find it possible to place the writing very early, perhaps as the earliest of the gospels. In fact, those who maintain that John neither knew nor consciously supplemented the synoptics find a pre-A.D. 70 date to be the easiest to maintain. However, there are no compelling reasons to insist on such an early date; those who see John as a conscious supplement to the synoptics usually date it between A.D. 85 and A.D. 100.

Since the gospel of John presents no insuperable problems in its relationship to the synoptic gospels and encounters no insurmountable difficulties as to its apostolic authorship and date, no valid reason exists for questioning its right to respect as another accurate report of the life of Christ. Jesus was recognized as God by His contemporaries even as John represents Him to be.

Selected Reading List

Guthrie, Donald. *New Testament Introduction.* Downers Grove, Ill.: InterVarsity, 1970. Pp. 241-271, 282-287.

Harrison, Everett F. *Introduction to the New Testament.* Grand Rapids: Eerdmans, 1964. Pp. 204-214.

Hiebert, D. Edmond. *An Introduction to the New Testament. The Gospels and Acts.* Vol. 1. Chicago: Moody, 1975. Pp. 192-213, 222-226.

Morris, Leon, *Studies in the Fourth Gospel.* Grand Rapids: Eerdmans, 1969.

————. *The Gospel According to John.* Grand Rapids: Eerdmans, 1971. Pp. 8-35.

ESSAY 7

Problems and Principles of Harmonization

Distinct advantages accrue from studying the gospels in a harmony. All available information on the same or similar events, conversations, and discourses is put side by side on the same page. Narratives describing different occasions from all four gospels are integrated into probable chronological sequence so that one has an overview of the course of Jesus' life from His conception to His postresurrection ministry. For many readers this will be a new experience with great benefit.

But the first careful reading of a harmony can also be a disturbing experience, especially for the reader who accepts the inspiration and historical integrity of the gospels. While most readers recognize the obvious fact that there are *four* gospels and that they are not identical, many have never explored the implications of that fact. But when reading a harmony, one can hardly avoid noting the differences. The reader begins to notice that the accounts of Christ's words sometimes differ. One evangelist's report of the same conversation, saying, or discourse may be more or less complete than another's. Differences may occur in grammatical construction. Synonyms may be substituted, verb voice or tense changed, or nouns replaced by pronouns. There may be differences in the order of discussion. Sometimes the differences in details reported even involve what appear to be contradictions. Occasionally, the same or similar statements will be found in contexts which appear to reflect different situations. The Beatitudes as recorded by Matthew and Luke contain a number of typical variations. Which report is correct? Or are both correct? How are the variations to be accounted for?

Similarly, when reading of the activities of Jesus, one may notice that somewhat similar events occur in different situations. Are they different events, or are they the same events erroneously reported? To complicate matters, sometimes what really appears to be the same event will be reported in a different order in another gospel. Sometimes diverse descriptive details are given for what appears to be the same event; and sometimes these details may have the appearance of discrepancy. A few readers may be surprised to find that the gospel writers do not always report the same events.

The questions arising from these phenomena are as significant as they are obvious. Do these phenomena undermine the historical integrity of the gospels? Or are they fully consistent with historical integrity? Do they call in question the inspiration and inerrancy of the gospels? Or are they consistent with the orthodox concept of inspiration? One thing seems certain: if the evangelists really are guilty of inaccuracies, misrepresentations, and contradictions, their reliability and the claim to inspiration are suspect.

It is neither possible nor necessary within these notes to give answers to all the harmonistic problems that might be raised in a comparative reading of the gospels. But the editors of this *Harmony* without equivocation hold to both the historical integrity and verbal plenary inspiration of the gospels. They also believe that most harmonistic problems can be resolved adequately when certain obvious and common sense principles of reporting and writing are applied in the interpretation of the evidence. The remainder of the problems have reasonable explanations, though further information about them would help in reaching more clear-cut solutions.

Some general considerations especially apply to the manner in which Jesus' words are reported. Jesus spoke three languages, as did many of His contemporaries. It must not be forgotten that in many cases the Greek text reporting what someone said is actually a translation of what was originally said in Aramaic or Hebrew. In translation a certain amount of variation is possible; seldom, if ever, is there only one legitimate way to translate from one language into another. At times, the evangelists may even have deemed it more suited to their purposes to depart from a strictly literal translation than to translate literally what Jesus said. So long as what Jesus intended is faithfully represented in language that accurately and effectively communicates to the intended readership, they cannot properly be faulted for this. Sometimes a more free translation may have been employed in reporting what Jesus said, for occasionally free translation can communicate the impact of what was originally said with gestures, intonation, and expression better than a verbatim account.

Aside from the inevitable variations arising from literal and free translations of Jesus' words, there are other equally significant considerations. Modern writing style employs various devices to indicate direct and verbatim quotations. Words included within quotation marks are assumed to be the exact words of the speaker. Ellipses are used to indicate words left out of the original statement, and brackets indicate words added by the reporter to clarify the sense of the quotation even though they were not originally part of the quotation. Footnotes may be employed to distinguish quotations coming from different sources or made at different times. None of these devices was available to first century writers, and it is wrong to impose upon them standards of writing which presuppose their availability.

Furthermore, the exacting rules for quotation in modern writing may presuppose the mechanical means by which oral speech can be exactly recorded. Obviously early writers had no tape recorders, but shorthand techniques were widely used in the first century. Matthew, a tax collector accustomed to keeping records, may have acquired this skill. It has even been suggested he may have kept records of Christ's words and deeds, thus creating a core of written tradition upon which early Christians, including the gospel writers, could draw. This would partially explain the remarkable similarities among the gospels. But it would not eliminate differences, because he was only one of a number who contributed to this core of tradition.

With these general considerations in mind, then, one should examine the theory that accounts of what Jesus or other individuals said are instances of unavoidable inaccuracy. Is this a necessary conclusion? By no means. The gospels should not be called inaccurate when there are at least two viable options for defending their accuracy.

1. One approach is to note that the writers were not necessarily bound to conform to standards of verbal exactitude that later times developed. This explanation does not see verbatim reproduction of Jesus' words as the real question always. Rather, the issue is, do the words of the evangelists which report what Jesus said faithfully represent what Jesus in fact said; and, apart from verbal differences, are the reports of what Jesus said as given by the different evangelists consistent with one another in meaning? If the answer is yes, then their accuracy cannot be impugned.

   Actually, in ordinary oral discourse this manner of reporting what others have said is still followed, and so long as it is done carefully, no one questions the integrity of what has been said. To repeat word for word the speech of another is not in every case the natural thing. It would sometimes be impossible and unnatural to repeat every little word and phrase. What one does expect to be reproduced in ordinary discussion are the striking or important statements, the leading thoughts, the major divisions or topics, and the general drift of discussion including transitions from one topic to another. While different reports are expected to agree on these matters, it is also expected that there will be differences on details reflecting the interests and purposes of the reporters. Modifications such as changes of person, substitution of pronouns for nouns or vice versa, changes in tense, voice, or mood of the verbs, and substitution of synonyms are too trivial to be taken as serious objections to a reporter's accuracy in ordinary discussion. While wording is important, meaning can be conveyed in a variety of ways. Verbal inspiration does not imply that truth can be accurately communicated in only one way. Rather, it means that the manner in which the Holy Spirit did speak through the human agents is inspired and hence accurate, word for word.

2. A second option for defending the gospels' accuracy despite differing parallel accounts of the same speech is based on the possibility that these accounts do in fact retain verbatim utterances of Jesus and others. These of course would be the occasions when the Greek language was used. It is certainly not inconceivable that those recording Jesus' teachings in shorthand did so in a manner so as to retain the very words spoken. In addition, sufficient allowance should be made for the highly trained memories among the Jewish people of this time. It is generally acknowledged that they were much more adept in remembering details than the average Western mind of the twentieth century.

Beyond the use of shorthand and memory, allowance must also be made for the activity of the Holy Spirit in calling to mind the words which Jesus had spoken. Jesus had promised such a Helper when He said, "The Holy Spirit, whom the Father will send in My name, He will teach you all things, and bring to your remembrance all that I said to you" (John 14:26). If the Spirit could provide for verbally inspired utterances in the composition of other parts of Scripture, He could surely do the same in the gospels.

If one follows this approach, differences between parallel accounts of the same discourse or conversation are explained by noting that no single gospel records everything spoken on a single occasion. In fact, it is doubtful that any combination of parallel accounts records the entirety of a speech or dialogue. Christ undoubtedly repeated some of His teachings in slightly differing forms on different occasions. He very possibly did so on the same occasion too. Thus, instances where parallel accounts report the same substance in slightly different forms may easily be due to different but similar statements on the same occasion, each writer selecting only a part of what was said for his account. A sample of this may be seen in the first Beatitude. Matthew relates, "Blessed are the poor in spirit, for theirs is the kingdom of heaven" (Matt. 5:3), while Luke writes, "Blessed are you who are poor, for yours is the kingdom of God" (Luke 6:20). Jesus probably repeated this Beatitude in at least two different forms on the occasion of His Sermon on the Mount. If so, He used third person once, second person another time, and referred to the Kingdom by two different titles. Since we know that neither gospel records the whole sermon, this explanation is quite plausible.

The parable of the mustard tree (Matt. 13:32; Mark 4:32) may also illustrate Jesus on the same occasion repeating something in slightly different form. According to Matthew He said that the birds of the air rest "in its branches," but according to Mark they rest "under its shade." Which did Jesus say? The chances are good that He said both. According to Matthew, Jesus in His Olivet discourse gives the claim of future impostors as "I am the Christ" (Matt. 24:5), but Mark and Luke quote Him as saying, "I am (He)" (Mark 13:6; Luke 21:8). Minor variations of this type are quite numerous.

In other places the variations are not minor. The difference between "because" (Matt. 13:13) and "in order that" (Mark 4:12) has far reaching implications as to meaning. Did Jesus use parables because His rejectors were already spiritually blind or so as to produce their blindness? He probably said both. The alleged displacement of Matthew 13:12 in Mark (4:25) and Luke (8:18b) most likely has the same explanation: in Matthew's account the words speak of Jesus' enemies and in the other two, of His disciples. Again the difference in meaning is substantial. Differences of this magnitude are not infrequent and can well be resolved by postulating that Jesus often repeated the same essential meaning in more than one form on one occasion.

Either of the options, then, or a combination of the two is sufficient to show that inaccuracy is not an inevitable or even a likely means of accounting for differences between parallel accounts. Whether we have an accurate summary of what Jesus said or the very words He spoke is difficult for us to determine at this point. It may very well be that we have some cases of both. The important thing is to recognize the Holy Spirit's part in inspiring what was written so as to guarantee an accurate report. It is not difficult to see this in light of the many instances where the gospels confirm rather than differ from one another.

What is to be said of events that are put in different order by the evangelists? First, it is quite possible for two different occurrences, happening within the same sphere and under similar circumstances, to resemble each other in several respects. However, if the leading features of the accounts differ, they should not be understood to be reports of the same event. Thus apparent divergency of order may in fact indicate different events with differing detail at certain crucial points. The fact that the gospels do not always give their material, whether of word or event, in the same order is a problem only if it is assumed that they must follow a strict and uniform chronological sequence, or if they categorically state that they will use only a chronological sequence and then proceed to violate it. The latter cannot be shown to be the case, and the former assumption is clearly inappropriate. While some sort of chronological arrangement might usually be expected to prevail, such is not a necessary condition of good writing. At his own discretion, an author is free to arrange his materials according to subject rather than chronological sequence if that better serves his purposes. Many variations of order in the gospels are due to this freedom which authors may legitimately exercise. This of course creates problems for the harmonist who is seeking to establish a chronological sequence. Which evangelist preserves that order? Sometimes indications of time or place will give the necessary clue, but not always. However this is the problem of the harmonist, not the fault of the author.

Finally, the careful reader of a harmony will eventually notice cases of what appear to be discrepancies in the recounting of events by two or more gospel writers. He may discover that a few such instances may in fact be different events, so that no discrepancy, real or apparent, exists at all. In most cases this is not the solution, but the solution is not hard to find. It is both possible and probable that when several writers narrate the same occurrence, they will differ at several points in their descriptions of what was said, what happened, and the attendant circumstances.

This fact is confirmed in daily experience. Referees are stationed at different positions on the court or playing field precisely because they can see different things. Equally calm and intelligent observers stationed on different corners of an intersection will report an automobile accident somewhat differently. Equally competent reporters of a convention will differ in their accounts of what happened. Why? Each reports from the angle of his own vantage point or that of his sources. Each chooses and narrates his material in a manner which is consistent with his purposes. What one reports, another might pass over altogether without falsity occurring in either account. In fact, reports that are too closely identical provide grounds for suspecting collusion.

Although gospel accounts might superficially *appear* to conflict with one another, the variety of perspective and selectivity of reporting they exhibit are themselves marks of accuracy and reliability. In such instances the contradictions are *apparent,* not *real.* Careful analysis will generally resolve the apparent conflicts and harmonize the accounts. Even in those cases where clear or persuasive resolution of conflicting descriptions is lacking, one is not forced to the conclusion that the contradictions are real. Just as possibly, not enough information is available to bring to the surface the *real underlying harmony* between *apparently conflicting* accounts.

These considerations do not solve all the problems which comparative study of the gospels in a harmony may raise. However they are valid principles, assumed to be true and operative in other areas, and they are equally apropos in study of the gospels. They successfully resolve most of the problems of harmonization. For those matters where no satisfactory solution is evident, it is better to leave the matter unresolved than to resort to strained and artificial exegesis of the text. Textual corruption in copying manuscripts is a possibility, but this is a plea easily abused. The student believing in the inspiration of Scripture is not obligated to find a solution to every difficulty therein. In view of the repeatedly established integrity of the gospels, is it not presumptuous for anyone to claim sufficient knowledge to conclude that the gospels are in fact contradictory? Historical accounts of whatever kind are selective in the material they include and exclude. Such is an inescapable necessity. The gospel writers did not write with the idea in mind that one day someone would try to put together a harmony. Their purposes were much different, although we have no credible reason to doubt their reliability in reporting history. Had they wanted to produce accounts more easily harmonized, they could have done so and made the present task much easier. But that would have diverted them from the direction in which the Spirit led them and radically changed the literary character of the gospels. In the process their character as gospels, four independent accounts of the good news, would have been rendered ineffective.

The Languages Jesus Spoke

The language milieu of first century Palestine has more than a passing interest for the reader of the gospels. It involves the question of what language(s) Jesus spoke and indirectly may have implications for one's view of the origin and integrity of the gospels as historical documents. For instance, on the assumption that the language exclusively, or at least primarily, spoken by Jesus was Aramaic, it has been commonplace to argue that the closer the language and style of the gospels to the language and style of Aramaic, the greater the presumption for authenticity. Conversely, it has often been argued that the absence of Semitisms creates a presumption against authenticity.

What has been the state of the debate? Almost certainly Latin was not in common use in Palestine, for conquest by the Roman armies had not involved conquest by the Latin language. Stemming from Alexander the Great's conquests in the fourth century B.C. and the subsequent Hellenistic movement, Greek had already been established as the *lingua franca*, and the conquests of Rome made no significant change. What of the use of Greek in Palestine in the time of Christ? Was it a language of culture and commerce for an elite few, or was it also used by the common people? And if it were used by more than the elite, how extensive was that use? Or was Aramaic the language of almost universal usage by the masses? Commonly held since the Middle Ages is the view that, beginning with the Babylonian exile, Hebrew gradually ceased to exist as a living language and that among Jewish people Aramaic became the language of everyday discourse. But did Hebrew really cease to be a living language; did it come to be only the religious vernacular of Jewish scholars? Advocates for the dominance of any of these three languages in Palestine have not been lacking, and cogent arguments have been made for the common usage of *all three* languages among Jews in first century Palestine.

Perhaps this in itself should have alerted the advocates of the different viewpoints to the possibility that all three languages were in fact in common use. Robert H. Gundry has persuasively argued that this was the situation, and his work has been supplemented by that of Philip Edgcumbe Hughes.

Recently discovered archaeological data have done much to resolve the problem. Ossuaries, receptacles in which the bones of the dead were placed, often have writing on them. It is to be expected that in the presence of death the language(s) used would be those in which people customarily thought and spoke. Gundry briefly surveys ossuary finds in Palestine from the period in question and concludes that all three languages appear on them in roughly equal proportions.

This evidence for the currency of all three languages is further strengthened by discoveries coming from excavations in caves around the Dead Sea. In his two expeditions to the "Cave of Letters," Yigael Yadin and his associates unearthed some fifteen letters and over forty other papyrus documents such as contracts and receipts. These come from the last years of the first century to the time of Bar Kokhba's revolt, A.D. 132-135. The cave appears to have been the actual hiding place of Bar Kokhba and his guerrilla band, and the documents are apparently representative of their routine correspondence on everyday and military matters. All three languages—Greek, Hebrew, and Aramaic—are represented in both the correspondence and miscellaneous documents. These men were not academicians. That they understood and used these languages strongly suggests their use among the people of Palestine generally. It appears that Hebrew was not confined to the scholars of Judea, and that Greek was not merely the language of commerce and culture. Apparently both were in common usage alongside Aramaic, and therefore Jesus might easily have used any one of the three.

Impartial examination of the gospels seems to confirm that this was indeed the language environment of Jesus' day. Based on extensive research in Old Testament quotation material shared by Matthew and the other synoptic writers, Robert Gundry concludes that the text types of these quotations reflects the trilingual situation evidenced in the archaeological data. The presence of Semitisms in the Greek of the gospels does not necessarily indicate an exclusively Semitic (Aramaic or Hebrew) linguistic situation in the first century. In polylingual areas, languages tend to interpenetrate one another in their vocabulary and manner of expression. The Septuagint is full of Semitic forms of expression. This would have influenced powerfully the type of Greek spoken in Palestine. The fact that Greek had been imported into an originally Semitic language milieu also gives one reason to expect that the Greek spoken there will reflect Semitic idiom and thought patterns.

But the gospels (and Acts) offer more positive evidence for the common currency of Greek in Christ's day and among those whom He taught. Two of the twelve disciples, Andrew and Philip, had Greek names. John 12:20-23 strongly suggest that Philip, Andrew, and Jesus understood and spoke Greek. Peter, the foremost among the twelve, bears not only Hebrew and Aramaic names (Simon and Cephas) but also is referred to by his Greek name (Peter). It is also likely that this same Peter spoke Greek to Cornelius' household in Acts 10 and wrote in Greek

310

the two letters bearing his name. That a Galilean fisherman would have a Greek name and speak and write Greek testifies to the fact that those without formal education were competent in that language as well. In the Greek text of John 21 Jesus uses two different Greek words for love and for tending the flock, and Peter uses two different words for know. However, none of these pairs can be reproduced in Hebrew or Aramaic; this was apparently a conversation originally carried on in Greek. Also, the play on the Greek words *petra* and *petros* in Matthew 16:18 cannot be reproduced in Hebrew or Aramaic and is best explained as occurring in a discussion originally carried on in Greek. In all likelihood, Jesus' conversations with the Syrophoenician woman, the Roman centurion, and Pilate were in Greek. Stephen (Acts 7) and James (Acts 15) quote from the Septuagint, thus giving evidence of their facility in the Greek language.

That Aramaic was a language in popular usage in first century Palestine is so clear from both biblical and extrabiblical sources that it is unnecessary to argue the point. Indeed, some have found the evidence so compelling they have argued that the language of the Jewish people in all districts of Palestine had become Aramaic long before the time of Christ. Semitic forms of expression and thought patterns in the gospels were cited as general evidence; more specific evidence was found in what were thought to be a large number of Aramaic terms and names in the gospels. Aramaic as the only language for common discourse was commonly held to be so firmly established that Josephus', the biblical (John 19:20; Acts 21:40; 22:2; 26:14), and the patristic references to the Hebrew language were taken as really referring to Aramaic.

The obvious evidences of an Aramaic background for the gospels do not establish the exclusive use of Aramaic among the people of the land. But in addition, much recent research has challenged the opinion that the transliterated Aramaic terms in the Greek text of the gospels are really Aramaic (see, for example, Matt. 27:46; Mark 5:41; 7:34; 14:36; 15:34). It is now argued that at least some of these transliterations are really Hebrew, and that when Josephus, the biblical writers, or the church Fathers refer to the Hebrew language, they mean *Hebrew*. This is further confirmed by linguistic evidence that the Hebrew used by Jewish scholars was not a dead language. Instead it bears the earmarks of a typical vernacular language: coining new words, having a vocabulary that covers all of daily experience, and being simple and direct. In rabbinic literature, Hebrew is used in conversations, and the subject matter is not confined to scholarly questions but includes matters of everyday life. Also, a number of Qumran documents are written in Hebrew. Again, subject matter is not confined to scholarly pursuits and evidence suggests that the common person at Qumran understood it. Some have argued that one should not expect Aramaic to have so quickly and completely replaced Hebrew as the language of the common people. Aramaic initially was spoken in the commercial or governmental levels of Jewish society. Only gradually did it filter down to become the spoken and written language of the lower, uneducated community. Hebrew long remained the language of the common people; the final blow to it as a spoken language came from the wars of A.D. 132-135 when the Jewish revolutionaries were crushingly defeated.

Apparently, then, Greek, Hebrew, and Aramaic were all commonly spoken and/or understood among the Palestinian Jews of Jesus' day. To determine precise proportions of use is not possible, and perhaps one language tended to predominate in one area more than the others. But it was a mixed language milieu. Almost certainly Jesus spoke in all three languages, and evidences for this exist in the gospels themselves.

Selected Reading List

Gundry, Robert H. "The Language Milieu of First-Century Palestine." *Journal of Biblical Literature* 83 (1964): 404-408.

Hughes, Philip Edgcumbe. "The Languages Spoken by Jesus." In *New Dimensions in New Testament Study*. Edited by Richard N. Longenecker and Merrill C. Tenney. Grand Rapids: Zondervan, 1974. Pp. 125-143.

ESSAY 9

The Genealogies in Matthew and Luke

(Matt. 1:1-17; Luke 3:23b-38)

Both Matthew and Luke give a genealogical list for the descent of Jesus. When these are compared, differences and difficulties appear immediately. The most obvious difference is that Matthew's list begins with Abraham and descends to Jesus, whereas Luke's list begins with Jesus and ascends to Adam, the son of God. This in itself presents no difficulty; but when one of the lists is put in inverse order for convenience in comparing, it is quite another matter. Of course only Luke gives the generations from Adam to Abraham, and the lists of progenitors between Abraham and David as given by Matthew and Luke are nearly identical. No real problem comes until we compare the two versions of the succession from David to Jesus:

Matthew's list	Luke's list (in inverse order)
David	David
Solomon	Nathan
Rehoboam	Mattatha
Abijah	Menna
Asa	Melea
Jehoshaphat	Eliakim
Joram	Jonan
Uzziah	Joseph
Jotham	Judah
Ahaz	Simeon
Hezekiah	Levi
Manasseh	Matthat
Amon	Jorim
Josiah	Eliezer
Jeconiah	Joshua
Shealtiel	Er
Zerubbabel	Elmadam
Abiud	Cosam
Eliakim	Addi
Azor	Melchi
Zadok	Neri
Achim	Shealtiel
Eliud	Zerubbabel
Eleazer	Rhesa
Matthan	Joanan
Jacob	Joda
Joseph (husband of Mary	Josech
Jesus)	Semein

313

Mattathias
Maath
Naggai
Hesli
Nahum
Amos
Mattathias
Joseph
Jannai
Melchi
Levi
Matthat
Eli
Joseph
Jesus (supposedly)

For students of a harmony of the gospels the above comparison presents two problems: the difference in the number of generations and the dissimilarity of names. How can the two genealogies be harmonized without sacrificing the historical integrity of either?

Recent critical studies have generally regarded past attempts at harmonization as just so much frustrated effort and dissipated energy. Both H. C. Waetjen and M. D. Johnson summarily dismiss past efforts to preserve full historical authenticity as unconvincing, strained, and beside the point. In any event, it is said historicity will not affect significantly the reader's existential response or understanding of New Testament theology. Instead, each genealogy must be understood individually and theologically in relation to the gospel in which it appears and the thought of the evangelist that it is intended to express. The content and structure of each supposedly is arbitrary to suit the evangelist's purpose. What those specific purposes were need not occupy our attention here, for the analyses of scholars such as Johnson and Waetjen follow the assumptions and methodology of much recent New Testament critical scholarship. Their analyses will be no better than their assumptions and methodology. And the fundamental question of the historical reliability of the genealogies cannot be bypassed in so cavalier a fashion. Consequently, we turn our attention to the problems of harmonizing the two lists of Jesus' ancestoral descent.

The first problem, the difference in the number of generations, is the easier to resolve. While it is true that Matthew lists twenty-six progenitors between David and Jesus, compared to Luke's forty, two factors must be kept in mind. First, it is not uncommon for the generations in one line of descent to increase much more rapidly than in another. Second, and more important, in Jewish thinking "son" might mean "grandson," or even more generally "descendant" (as "Jesus Christ, the son of David, the son of Abraham," Matt. 1:1). Similarly, "begat" ("to 'X' was born," NASB) does not necessarily mean "was the actual father of" but instead simply may indicate real descent. Just the fact that Matthew casts his list in the form of three groups of fourteen generations suggests this was a convenient though arbitrary arrangement from which some generations may have been omitted. In fact, it can be shown that Matthew's list has omissions (cf. 2 Kings 8:24; 1 Chron. 3:11; 2 Chron. 22:1, 11; 24:27; 2 Kings 23:34; 24:6). Omission of generations in biblical genealogies is not unique to this case, and Jews are known to have done this freely. The purpose of a genealogy was not to account for every generation but to establish the fact of an undoubted succession, including especially the more important ancestors.

The second problem is much more difficult to resolve. In the two lists of succession between David and Joseph all the names are different except Shealtiel and Zerubbabel (connected above by dotted lines). How is this to be accounted for? Some exegetes unnecessarily despair of finding an adequate solution or even suggest the lists are in error. But four other proposals deserve consideration.

1. Julius Africanus (d. A.D. 240) suggested that Matthew gives the genealogy of Joseph through his actual father, Jacob, while Luke gives Joseph's genealogy through his legal father, Eli. In this view, Eli died childless. His half brother Jacob, who had the same mother but a different father, married Eli's widow and by her had Joseph. Known as levirate marriage, this action meant that *physically* Joseph was the son of Jacob and *legally* the son of Eli. Jacob was the descendant of David through David's son Solomon, and Eli was the descendant of David through David's son Nathan. Thus, by both *legal* and *physical* lineage Joseph had a rightful claim to the Davidic throne, and so would his *legal* (but not physical) son Jesus. Matthew gives Joseph's *physical* lineage, Luke his *legal* lineage.

2. In his classic work *The Virgin Birth of Christ*, J. Gresham Machen argued for the view that Matthew gives the *legal* descent of Joseph whereas for the most part (he does allow for levirate marriage and/or transfer of lineage to a collateral line in Joseph's physical line) Luke gives the physical descent. Although the physical and legal lines are reversed, the purpose is still to establish Joseph's rightful claim to the Davidic throne. This view holds that Solomon's line failed in Jeconiah (Jer. 22:30). But when the kingly line through Solomon became extinct, the living member of the collateral line (Shealtiel, Matt. 1:12, cf. Luke 3:27) of Nathan inherited the title to the throne. Thus, Machen asserts, Matthew is tracing the legal heirship to the throne from David, through Solomon, through Jeconiah, with transfer to a collateral line at that point. Luke traces the physical descent (with a possibility of jumps to a collateral line or levirate marriages) to David through Nathan. Matthew starts with

the question, "Who is the heir to David's throne?" Luke starts with the question, "Who is Joseph's father?"

A large number of scholars have preferred some form of this view, including A. Hervey, Theodor Zahn, Vincent Taylor, and Brooke F. Westcott.

3. A third view suggests that the apparent conflict between the two genealogies of Joseph results from *mistakenly* assuming Luke is intending to give Joseph's genealogy. Instead, it should be understood as Mary's genealogy. Joseph's name stands in for Mary's by virtue of the fact that he had become son or heir of Eli (Mary's father) by his marriage to her. This view holds that Eli died with no sons, and that Mary became his heiress (Num. 27:1-11; 36:1-12). The first of these passages seems to provide for the preservation of the name of the man who dies with daughters but no sons. In the case of Eli and his daughter Mary, this could have been accomplished by Joseph's becoming identified with Mary's family. Joseph would be included in the family genealogy, although the genealogy is really Mary's. Thus, the genealogies of Matthew and Luke diverge from David on because Matthew traces the Davidic descent of Joseph, and Luke the Davidic descent of Mary (with Joseph's name standing in).

Each of the three proposals discussed thus far would resolve the apparent conflict between the genealogies in Matthew and Luke. Each also appears to be within the realm of reasonable possibility. However, it must be pointed out that all three rely upon conjecture which is possible but far from certain. In the first two views one must appeal to levirate marriages or collateral lines to resolve difficulties. The third view rests on the conjecture that Joseph takes Mary's place in the genealogy. In addition, the first must explain why Luke rather than Matthew is interested in the legal lineage of Joseph. Both the first and second views must explain why Luke, in light of his apparent interest in and close association with Mary, would be concerned with Joseph's genealogy at all. Interested as he was in Jesus' humanity, birth, and childhood, why would Luke give the genealogy of the man who was Jesus' legal but not physical father? These questions are not unanswerable, but they do leave the field open for a view less dependent on conjecture, and that itself does not raise these questions.

4. There is such a view. Like the third proposed solution, this fourth view understands the genealogy in Luke really to be Mary's, but for different reasons. Here Eli is understood to be the progenitor of Mary, not of Joseph. Joseph is not properly part of the genealogy, and is mentioned only parenthetically. Luke 3:23 should then read,

"Jesus . . . being the son (as was supposed of Joseph) of Eli. . . ."
The support for this view is impressive.

a. Placing the phrase "as was supposed of Joseph" in parentheses, and thus in effect removing it from the genealogy, is grammatically justified. In the Greek text Joseph's name occurs without the article prefixed; every other name in the series has the article. By this device Joseph's name is shown to be not properly a part of the genealogy. Jesus was only thought to be his son. This would make Jesus the son (i.e., grandson or descendant) of Eli, Mary's progenitor, and is consistent with Luke's account of Jesus' conception, which makes clear that Joseph was not His physical father (Luke 1:26-38).

b. This view allows the most natural meaning of "begat" to stand. In other words, "begat" refers to actual physical descent rather than to jumps to collateral lines.

c. Matthew's interest in Jesus' relation to the Old Testament and the Messianic kingdom makes it appropriate that he give Joseph's real descent from David through Solomon—a descent that is also Jesus' *legal* descent—and thus gives Him legal claim to the Davidic throne.

d. Since Luke emphasizes the humanity of Jesus, His solidarity with the race, and the universality of salvation, it is fitting that Luke show His humanity by recording His human descent through His human parent Mary. His pedigree is then traced back to Adam.

e. The objection that Mary's name is not in Luke's version needs only the reply that women were rarely included in Jewish genealogies; though giving her descent, Luke conforms to custom by not mentioning her by name. The objection that Jews never gave the genealogy of women is met by the answer that this is a unique case; Luke is talking about a virgin birth. How else could the physical descent of one who had no human father be traced? Furthermore, Luke has already shown a creative departure from customary genealogical lists by starting with Jesus and ascending up the list of ancestors rather than starting at some point in the past and descending to Jesus.

f. This view allows easy resolution of the difficulties surrounding Jeconiah (Matt. 1:11), Joseph's ancestor and David's descendant through Solomon. In 2 Sam. 7:12-17 the perpetuity of the Davidic kingdom through Solomon (vv. 12-13) is unconditionally promised. Jeconiah later was the royal representative of that line of descent for which eternal perpetuity had been promised. Yet, for his gross sin, Jeconiah was to be written down as childless, and no descendant of his would prosper on the Davidic throne (Jer. 22:30). This poses a dilemma. It is Jeconiah through whom the Solomonic descent and legal right to the throne properly should be traced. Solomon's throne had already been unconditionally promised eternal perpetuity. Yet Jeconiah will have no physical descendants who will prosper on that throne. How may both the divine promise and the curse be fulfilled?

First, notice that Jeremiah's account neither indicates Jeconiah would have no seed, nor does it say Jeconiah's line has had its legal claim to the throne removed by his sin. The legal claim to the throne remains with Jeconiah's line, and Matthew records that descent down to Joseph. In 1:16, Matthew preserves the virgin birth of Jesus and at the same time makes clear that Jesus does not come under the curse upon Jeconiah. He breaks the pattern and carefully avoids saying Joseph begat Jesus. Instead he refers to "Joseph the husband of Mary, by whom was born Jesus." In the English translation the antecedent of "whom" is ambiguous. But in the Greek text, "whom" is feminine singular in form and can only refer back to Mary. As to human parentage, Jesus was born of Mary alone, though Joseph was His legal father. As Jesus' *legal* father, Joseph's legal claim passed to Jesus. But because Jesus was not actually of Jeconiah's seed, although of actual Davidic descent through Mary, descendant of Nathan, Jesus escaped the curse on Jeconiah's seed pronounced in Jeremiah 22:30.

Thus the problem is resolved.

What we have then are two different genealogies of two people. Probably even the Shealtiel and Zerubbabel of Matthew and Luke are different persons. This view does not depend on conjecture, rests on evidence within the texts themselves, fits the purposes of the evangelists, and easily resolves the problem surrounding Jeconiah. Of this view L. M. Sweet appropriately wrote, "Its simplicity and felicitous adjustment to the whole complex situation is precisely its recommendation."

Although it is not, strictly speaking, a harmonistic problem, one other difficulty of lesser significance found in Matthew's record of Joseph's genealogy needs discussion here. In 1:17, Matthew divides the generations from Abraham to Christ into three groups of fourteen generations: from Abraham to David, from David to the deportation to Babylon, and from the deportation to Christ. In part, this was likely a device used by Matthew to aid memory; it does not imply that he mentioned every progenitor. At least five names are omitted: Ahaziah, Joash,

Amaziah, Jehoiakim, and Eliakim. As previously stated, this procedure was not unusual and presents no real problem.

However, with three groups of fourteen generations one does expect to find forty-two names. But there are only forty-one. Although one set has thirteen names, the problem is only apparent. Matthew does not speak of forty-two different names but of three groups of fourteen generations which he divides for himself. David's name concludes the first set and stands first in the second set (cf. 1:17). In other words, David is counted twice and is thus given special prominence in the genealogy that shows Jesus' Davidic throne rights through His legal father, Joseph. Possibly the Davidic emphasis is further enhanced by the number fourteen. The sum of the numerical value of the Hebrew letters in the name David is fourteen. To the modern English reader this might seem overly subtle, but it was not necessarily so to the ancient Semitic mind. However, the numerical value of David's name is not necessary to the resolution of this problem.

Again, alleged discrepancies between and in the genealogical lists of Matthew and Luke are shown to be more apparent than real. Reasonable solutions to the problems exist and even throw further light on the text.

Selected Reading List

Johnson, Marshall D. *The Purpose of the Biblical Genealogies: With Special Reference to the Setting of the Genealogies of Jesus.* Cambridge: Cambridge U., 1969. Pp. 139-256.

Machen, J. Gresham. *The Virgin Birth of Christ.* New York: Harper, 1930.

The International Standard Bible Encyclopedia, s.v. "The Genealogy of Jesus Christ," by L. M. Sweet.

Waetjen, Herman C. "The Genealogy as the Key to the Gospel according to Matthew." *Journal of Biblical Literature* 95 (1976): 205-230.

The Day and Year of Christ's Crucifixion

Determining the day of the week, the date of the month, and the year of Christ's crucifixion is of greatest importance in settling upon a broad chronology of the life of Christ. For clarity's sake these three issues will be discussed in this article before we proceed to a study of other chronological aspects of the gospels. The three will be considered in the above order and kept separate from each other insofar as is possible.

THE DAY OF THE WEEK

The Christian church has traditionally looked upon Friday as the day on which Jesus died. No strong reason has been advanced for abandoning this understanding. The best biblical evidence favors a Friday crucifixion. Specifically, according to all four gospels, Jesus was crucified on the day called "preparation" (paraskeuē) (Matt. 27:62; Mark 15:42; Luke 23:54; John 19:14, 31, 42), a term well known among the Jews as referring to Friday.

Objections to the Friday view have been based largely on Matthew 12:40 which states that Jesus would be in the grave three days and three nights before rising. Yet it was common practice among the Jews to refer to a fractional part of a day or night as one day and one night (cf. Gen. 42:17-18; 1 Sam. 30:12-13; 1 Kings 20:29; 2 Chron. 10:5, 12; Esther 4:16; 5:1). Hence "three days and three nights" does not necessitate three twenty-four hour days between Christ's crucifixion and resurrection but is just another way of saying He was raised on "the third day" (Matt. 16:21; 17:23; 20:19; 27:64; Luke 9:22; 18:33; 24:7, 21, 46; Acts 10:40; 1 Cor. 15:4) or after "three days" (Matt. 26:61; 27:40, 63; Mark 8:31; 9:31; 10:34; 14:58; 15:29; John 2:19-20).

In light of the gospel accounts, then, it can be safely concluded that Jesus died at 3:00 P.M. on a Friday and was placed in the tomb later that same day. He remained there part of Friday (until sundown), all of the next day (from sundown Friday until sundown Saturday), and part of the third day (from sundown Saturday until early Sunday morning). This system of reckoning each day from sunset to sunset was followed by the Sadducees in Jerusalem. Another system of reckoning from sunrise to sunrise was also in vogue, but the sunset to sunset scheme was the more officially recognized of the two (cf. pp. 321-322 of this essay).

It is also of great moment to ascertain on which date of the Jewish calendar Christ was crucified. Was it on the fourteenth or the fifteenth of Nisan? The gospel of John gives an initial impression that it was the fourteenth, but the synoptic gospels appear to say the fifteenth. Stated another way, John seems to indicate that the Last Supper was not a Passover meal, while the synoptists say it was.

John 13:1 says the supper the night preceding Jesus' crucifixion was "before the Feast of the Passover." He also writes about Jesus' trial as being on "the day of preparation for (literally, 'of') the Passover" (John 19:14). He adds in John 18:28 that Jesus' Jewish accusers had not yet eaten the Passover. Also in John 13:29 the misimpression of the other disciples about the nature of Judas' mission also seems to be based on their anticipation of the Passover feast's coming on the next day. Since the Passover was normally eaten on the evening marking the end of the fourteenth and the beginning of the fifteenth (Lev. 23:5), it appears that John understands Jesus' death to have come on the fourteenth of Nisan.

On the other side of the question, Matthew, Mark, and Luke are specific in placing the Last Supper after sundown ending the fourteenth and beginning the fifteenth of the month (Matt. 26:17-20; Mark 14:12-17; Luke 22:7-16). They refer to the sacrifice of the lambs which occurred on the fourteenth and the meal following it that same evening.

Different attempts have been made to resolve this apparent contradiction. Some have proposed that the synoptic gospels are right, and John is wrong, while others have suggested the opposite. Another proposal has been to say both versions are correct and to strain the interpretation of one or the other account to make it match up with its opposite.

The best approach to the issue is to accept the accuracy of both methods of dating the crucifixion. This can be done because the Jews of Jesus' day apparently recognized a dual method of reckoning dates. In addition to the better known system which regarded each new day as starting at sundown, the policy of some was to reckon from sunrise to sunrise. Each of these customs finds support from the Old Testament, the former in such places as Genesis 1:5 and Exodus 12:18 and the latter in Genesis 8:22 and 1 Samuel 19:11.

The system of reckoning used by Jesus and His disciples and described by Matthew, Mark, and Luke was from sunrise to sunrise. John describes the events from the perspective of a sunset-to-sunset reckoning. Indications are that the difference in systems was also a point of disagreement between the Pharisees (sunrise to sunrise) and the Sadducees (sunset to sunset).

The synoptic accounts therefore see Jesus as eating a Passover meal the evening before His crucifixion. For those who followed the sunrise-to-sunrise reckoning, the Passover lambs had been slain a few hours earlier, in the afternoon. For them the slaughter took place on the fourteenth of Nisan, as did the Passover meal. The fifteenth did not begin until the next morning, Friday, at about 6:00.

The Johannine description, however, views the events from the standpoint of the Sadducees who controlled the Temple. Jesus was crucified at the normal time of killing the Passover lambs, that is, the afternoon of Nisan 14. Nisan 14 had begun at sunset Thursday and would not end until sunset Friday. This was the normal time for the lambs to be slain, but the Temple authorities had apparently compromised with those who followed the other calendar and allowed them to slay the lambs on Thursday afternoon. This difference explains why Jesus' accusers had not yet eaten the Passover (John 18:28). They were about to do it Friday evening, Nisan 15, which began at sunset.

If the above solution is correct (and it is impossible at this point to say dogmatically that it is, but it does seem to handle all the data more effectively than other proposals), then Jesus was crucified on Nisan 15 according to the sunrise-to-sunrise reckoning and on Nisan 14 according to the sunset-to-sunset method.

THE YEAR

The field of astronomy offers the most help in fixing the year of Christ's crucifixion. The Jewish calendar was based on lunar months. Hence by noting the dates of the new moons' appearances in the general period of Jesus' death, it is possible to determine in which years Nisan 14 (according to the sunset-to-sunset reckoning) fell between Thursday at sundown and Friday at sundown.

Jesus was crucified sometime between A.D. 26 and 36 because this was the period of Pontius Pilate's governorship (cf. John 19:15-16). Complex astronomical calculations reveal that during this period Nisan 14 fell on Friday twice, in A.D. 30 and in A.D. 33.

Deciding between 30 and 33 is no easy matter. To a large degree, the issue hinges upon chronological features regarding the life of Christ as a whole. Such matters as the time of Christ's birth, what Luke means by "the fifteenth year of the reign of Tiberius Caesar" (Luke 3:1-2) and "about thirty years of age" (Luke 3:23), what John means by "forty-six years to build this temple" (John 2:20), and other related matters must be analyzed before reaching a final decision as to the year of the crucifixion. The next essay will undertake this investigation.

Selected Reading List

Hoehner, Harold W. *Chronological Aspects of the Life of Christ.* Grand Rapids: Zondervan, 1977. Pp. 65-114.

Morris, Leon. *The Gospel According to John.* The New International Commentary on the New Testament. Grand Rapids: Eerdmans, 1971. Pp. 774-786.

Ogg, George. "Chronology of the New Testament." *Peake's Commentary on the Bible*. Nelson, 1962. Pp. 729-730.

⸻. *The Chronology of the Public Ministry of Jesus*. Cambridge: Cambridge U., 1940. Pp. 203-285.

ESSAY 11

Chronology of the Life of Christ

Much uncertainty pervades a study of the chronology of Christ's life. It is generally assumed that He was born in about A.D. 1 and died in about A.D. 30. Yet these are only generalizations. Our calendar which sought to use His birth as its reference point erred at that very point when it was initially established in A.D. 525. *Anno Domini* (A.D.) means "in the year of the Lord," but subsequent study has shown that Jesus was born prior to A.D. 1.

Though complete certainty regarding dates is impossible, a great deal of light can be shed on the subject of when Jesus lived. Certain selected happenings and statements will be discussed to give more detailed data.

THE DEATH OF HEROD THE GREAT

According to Matthew 2:1 and Luke 1:5, Herod the Great was still reigning as king over the Jews at the time of Jesus' birth. It is now known from other sources that Herod's death came in 4 B.C., soon after Nisan 1 of that year. Jesus must have been born within the two years prior to that, because Herod after ascertaining the time of the star's appearance (Matt. 2:7) gave orders to execute all the male children who were two years old and under (Matt. 2:16). Hence Jesus must have been born between 6 and 4 B.C.

THE CENSUS UNDER AUGUSTUS CAESAR

Luke 2:1-2 places the birth of Christ within the reign of the Roman emperor Augustus Caesar and also probably synchronizes it with Quirinius' governorship in Syria, though some understand Luke to say that the census came before this governorship. Augustus during his reign (30 B.C.-A.D. 14) established a system of census taking, and Luke refers to it in Luke 2:1. The particular census that brought Joseph and Mary to Bethlehem when Jesus was born was the first of these while Quirinius was governor (cf. Acts 5:37 for a reference to what was probably the second which came in A.D. 6).

Evidence has surfaced to the effect that a census was taken every fourteen years. By counting back from those taken in neighboring Egypt, one discovers that a census must have been scheduled in 8 B.C. It is quite

324

possible that turbulent conditions in Palestine and Syria at the time may have somewhat delayed the census.

Quirinius is known to have been governor of Syria in A.D. 6 at the time of a census, but this is about ten years too late for the birth of Jesus. Evidence from inscriptions, however, has shown the probability that Quirinius was involved in the Syrian government as joint ruler at an earlier time, about 8 B.C. His rule may well have extended until 6 B.C. when the governorship of Sentius Saturnius, alongside whom he ruled, ended.

THE FIFTEENTH YEAR OF TIBERIUS CAESAR

In Luke 3:1 the fifteenth year of the reign of Tiberius Caesar is given as the date when John the Baptist began his public ministry. Since John's ministry began a short time before Jesus', this chronological note is of great help in setting time limits for Jesus' ministry.

Exact placement of this fifteenth year is attended with a great deal of difficulty, however, because Tiberius' rule had two beginnings. He became coruler with Augustus his father at some time before his father's death, but at Augustus' death in A.D. 14 he became sole ruler of the empire. If Luke is using an earlier date, John's prophetic ministry was probably initiated some time in A.D. 26 or 27. If the later date is meant, the fifteenth year was probably A.D. 28 or 29.

The latter of these two possibilities looks more probable when compared with customary modes of dating practiced in ancient times, but the former finds more favor in light of biblical data yet to be discussed as this study proceeds. Specifically, A.D. 26-27 agrees better with the statement of Luke regarding Jesus' age at the outset of His ministry.

"ABOUT THIRTY YEARS OF AGE"

Luke says that Jesus at the beginning of His ministry was "about thirty years of age" (Luke 3:23). While this important expression may mean anything from twenty-eight through thirty-two, customs of the times and other details of Jesus' life seem to indicate that Jesus was within one year of His thirtieth birthday one way or the other when He began His ministry. A more limited age span also accords better with Luke's interest in furnishing chronological details (cf. Luke 1:5; 2:1-2; 3:1-2).

If His birth is placed in 6 B.C., He reached thirty sometime in A.D. 25. If in 5 B.C., He was thirty sometime in the year A.D. 26. The latter date is more probable, since Jesus' crucifixion cannot be placed earlier than A.D. 30, as shown in the previous essay, "The Day and Year of Christ's Crucifixion" (pp. 320-323).

It is extremely difficult to place the beginning of Jesus' ministry any later than A.D. 27, because this would put an intolerable strain on Luke's statement about His age. Furthermore, unless Jesus' ministry were only one or two years, He could not have completed it by A.D. 30. Also, unless His ministry were more extensive than commonly thought—about four or five years—it could not have lasted until A.D. 33, the other possible date discussed in the previous essay.

FORTY-SIX YEARS OF TEMPLE REMODELING

In John 2:20 Jesus' antagonists referred to a building or, more correctly, remodeling project that had been undertaken by Herod the Great forty-six years earlier. This consisted of the renovation of Zerubbabel's Temple. According to secular history Herod initiated the work some time in 20 or 19 B.C. This statement was addressed to Jesus at the first Passover after He began His public ministry. The "forty-six years" therefore furnishes another means for identifying the year when His ministry began.

This extensive project had not been completed when Herod died in 4 B.C. In fact, it was still in progress when the Jews uttered the words of John 2:20. Completion of it did not come until A.D. 64.

Though some disagreement has arisen regarding the word translated "temple" and the tense of the verb for "build," the more obvious meaning and the one that satisfies the context quite well is that the Jews were pointing to how long the project had taken up to that point in contrast to the three days in which Jesus said He could build the Temple (John 2:19).

By counting forty-six years from 20-19 B.C. one arrives at A.D. 26-27. Hence the first Passover of Jesus' ministry must have been in the spring of A.D. 27.

THE LENGTH OF JESUS' MINISTRY

A firm date having been established for the beginning of Christ's ministry, it remains to determine the length of that ministry before a firm date for His crucifixion can be set.

Some have argued for a one-year ministry because the first three gospels mention only one Passover during His ministry, the one when He was crucified (Matt. 26:17-20; Mark 14:12-17; Luke 22:7-16). The gospel of John is strongly opposed to this theory, however. John specifically names three Passovers in which Jesus was involved after He began public ministry (John 2:13; 6:4; 11:55).

Others favor a ministry of a little over two years. They take the three Passovers in John's gospel as opening and closing each of the two years. This theory, however, is most often defended on the basis of transposing John 5 and 6. Since no manuscript evidence exists for this rearrangement, the two-years theory is basically weak.

Attempts to prove a ministry of a little over four years have usually

326

rested on the assumption of two Passovers not mentioned by John. One of these additional Passovers comes between John 4:35, which indicates the time is the winter after the Passover of John 2:13, and John 5:1, which probably refers to the Feast of Tabernacles the following fall. To postulate this unmentioned Passover seems to be quite reasonable. The other additional Passover does not rest on good grounds, however. Some place it before the Passover of John 2:13, and others after the one mentioned in John 6:4. In neither case, however, has convincing proof been adduced for concluding that there was a fifth Passover.

The most widely held viewpoint is that Jesus' ministry extended a little more than three years. From Jesus' baptism by John (Matt. 3:13-17; Mark 1:9-11; Luke 3:21-23a) until His first Passover (John 2:13) was a period of several months which found Him in both Galilee and Judea. The first full year of ministry (between Passovers), also spent in Judea and Galilee, was terminated by a Passover, not mentioned in the biblical record, that came a few months after Jesus' statement of John 4:35 and six months before the Feast of Tabernacles mentioned in John 5:1. His second year, most of it spent in Galilee, ended with the Passover of John 6:4. The final year was spent in areas around Galilee, in Judea, and in Perea, and came to its conclusion with the Passover referred to in John 11:55.

The conclusion that Jesus had a ministry of a little over three years is, then, the one supported by the strongest evidence and the one most free from difficulty.

THE CRUCIFIXION

As is shown in the essay "The Day and Year of Christ's Crucifixion" (pp. 320-323), Nisan 14, the day of Passover, fell on Friday only twice between A.D. 26 and 36. This left two possible years for Christ's crucifixion, A.D. 30 or 33. If conclusions reached earlier in this essay are valid, the former possiblity must be chosen as the year in which Jesus was crucified.

Conclusions

It is helpful in summarizing the conclusions of this essay to do so in the form of a table into which more probable options from the above discussion are incorporated:

6 B.C. or	(late in the year) or	birth of Christ
5 B.C.	(early in the year)	
4 B.C.	(after Nisan 1)	death of Herod the Great
A.D. 26	(earlier part of year)	beginning of John's ministry
A.D. 26	(middle or latter part of year)	beginning of Christ's ministry

A.D. 27	(Nisan 14)	first Passover of Christ's ministry
A.D. 28	(Nisan 14)	second Passover of Christ's ministry
A.D. 29	(Nisan 14)	third Passover of Christ's ministry
A.D. 30	(Nisan 14)	crucifixion of Christ

While not free from difficulty, the above table of dates appears to provide a solution with stronger cumulative evidence than any other that has been proposed. It enables the student of the gospels to know more precisely when Jesus lived, ministered, and died.

Selected Reading List

Hoehner, Harold W. *Chronological Aspects of the Life of Christ.* Grand Rapids: Zondervan, 1977. Pp. 11-63.

Ogg, George. "Chronology of the New Testament." *Peake's Commentary on the Bible.* Nelson, 1962. Pp. 728-729.

———. *The Chronology of the Public Ministry of Jesus.* Cambridge: Cambridge U., 1940. Pp. 3-201.

Thompson, W. A. "Chronology of the New Testament." *The Zondervan Pictorial Encyclopedia of the Bible.* Grand Rapids: Zondervan, 1975. Pp. 816-821.

ESSAY 12

The Arrest and Trial of Jesus

When the evangelists came to the events that brought Jesus' earthly life to a close, they gave much more information than for the other periods of His life. In fact, when taken together, the gospels give a rather detailed description of Passion week. Their accounts of Jesus' arrest and trial in particular have long fascinated both Jewish and Christian scholars.

If we assume the evangelists have given us reliable information, events leading up to Jesus' crucifixion apparently took the following course:

1. On Thursday evening of Passion week, after the journey from the upper room to the Garden of Gethsemane, Judas, Jesus' betrayer, approached Jesus in the darkness of the garden. But Judas was not alone. What is described as a great multitude included representatives of the Sanhedrin, the Temple police, and a cohort (probably about 200 in this case) of Roman soldiers. Although Jesus readily identified Himself as the one whom they were seeking, Judas betrayed Him to His captors with a kiss. With that they took Jesus and arrested Him.

    Peter momentarily tried to thwart the arrest by drawing his sword and cutting off the right ear of the high priest's servant. But Jesus rebuked Peter and restored Malchus' ear. After being chastened for his bravado and misguided zeal, Peter, with all the disciples, left Jesus and fled. Peter did return to follow from a distance.

2. Jesus was then taken to Annas, the ex-high priest. In what constitutes the first phase of His Jewish trial, He was briefly questioned by Annas and then sent to Annas' son-in-law, the current high priest, Caiaphas.

3. In Caiaphas' house at least a quorum of the Sanhedrin had been brought together for a night session. This was to be the second Jewish phase of Jesus' trial. Witnesses were called to try to establish charges against Jesus, but no two witnesses could agree, and Jesus by His silence refused to confirm the charges. Finally, after badgering from Caiaphas, Jesus confessed He was the Messiah, the Son of God, the Son of Man. Caiaphas took this to be blasphemy and worthy of death. The assembled council concurred in this judg-

329

ment, passed sentence upon Him, and began to physically abuse Him.

4. The third Jewish phase of the trial took place early the next morning. While the earlier night session may have had only a quorum of the Sanhedrin, the entire council was clearly in attendance this time. The charge and sentence of the previous session were confirmed.

5. Now the trial of Jesus was to enter a new phase. Since the Jews did not have the general authority to administer a sentence of death, Jesus was taken before the Roman governor Pilate for the first Roman phase of the trial. The Sanhedrin presented a threefold charge against Jesus: "misleading our nation and forbidding to pay taxes to Caesar, and saying that He Himself is Christ, a King" (Luke 23:2).

   Rather than repeating the charge for which they had condemned Him (blasphemy), the Sanhedrin charged Jesus with insurrection. This was a charge that a Roman governor might be expected to give a more sympathetic hearing. However, Pilate's interrogation of Jesus failed to convince him that Jesus was guilty as charged, and his confession that he could find no fault only intensified the charge from the Jews that Jesus had been guilty of revolutionary activity in Judea and Galilee.

6. Mention of Galilee led to the second Roman phase of the trial, for much of Jesus' activity had been in Galilee, the jurisdiction of Herod Antipas. Herod was then in Jerusalem. Perhaps partly as a means of getting rid of a difficult case and perhaps partly as a means of gaining favor with Herod, Pilate sent Jesus to him. Herod was glad for the opportunity to question Jesus and make sport of Him; but he did not adjudicate the matter, and he sent Jesus back to Pilate.

7. With the case back in Pilate's hands, the trial entered its third Roman phase. Pilate restated the charges that had been brought against Jesus and reaffirmed his own judgment of Jesus' innocence. He observed that Herod also had not found Jesus worthy of death. But Pilate was caught between his own conviction of Jesus' innocence and the rising clamor of the Jewish leadership for His death.

   Then Pilate hit upon a scheme by which he thought he could solve the dilemma. He customarily released a prisoner to the Jews at Passover, and a crowd was gathering to demand the annual favor. Pilate decided to let them choose the release of either Jesus or an insurrectionist named Barabbas. Pilate knew that envy was behind the Jewish leadership's hatred for Jesus. Surely the multitudes would choose Jesus over Barabbas, and thus Pilate would be free of the case.

   But Pilate had not taken into account the persuasiveness of the chief priests and elders who incited the crowd, or the popularity of Barabbas. Confronted with the choice, the crowd demanded the release of Barabbas and the crucifixion of Jesus. All Pilate's efforts to dissuade them only increased the uproar. When Pilate made a move to release Jesus anyway, the Jews charged that Pilate could not then be Caesar's friend. Such an accusation could ruin Pilate. Putting career above conviction, he decided to accede to their demands. Hoping to absolve himself of responsibility for the death of an innocent man, Pilate washed his hands before the multitude and proclaimed his innocence of Jesus' blood. Barabbas was released. Jesus was scourged and delivered to the will of the Jews, a Roman crucifixion by Roman soldiers.

Such is the probable reconstruction of events surrounding the arrest and trial of Jesus. But there is a large body of contemporary literature that challenges this reconstruction by assuming the unreliability of the evangelists' accounts. The claim is often made that the tradition the evangelists drew upon was merely the creation of a Christian community having no biographical interest. This tradition, it is said, was adapted by the evangelists for their own purposes of propaganda. Thus, from beginning to end the gospels are biased literature. Many of the recent attempts to rescue the "few bits of objective information" embedded in the passion story, and then to reconstruct what may have actually happened, follow the methodology laid down by source critical, form critical, and redaction critical assumptions. Once the credibility of the gospel record is surrendered, that record becomes subject to the most arbitrary reinterpretive imagination. To illustrate, we cite several recent theories of the arrest and trial.

Haim Cohn, a justice of the Supreme Court of Israel, argued that Jesus appeared before the Jewish authorities in a hearing, not a trial. Rather than having as their purpose to find fault with and convict Jesus, the high priest and court were attempting to find a way to save Him.

Arguing that the gospel accounts of the arrest and trial contain incongruities and inconsistencies which prevent us from accepting them at face value, Cohn asserted that in fact the intention of the Jewish leaders was to prevent Jesus' execution by the Romans. Jesus enjoyed the love and affection of many of the people. The court tried to bring about His acquittal, or at least a suspension of sentence on condition of good behavior. But to achieve this, Jesus had to be persuaded not to plead guilty, and reliable witnesses to Jesus' innocence of the insurrection charge had to be found. Furthermore, they needed a commitment from Jesus not to participate in treasonable activities against Rome in the future. But reliable witnesses to His innocence were not to be found, and Jesus insisted on continuing to proclaim the teaching which Rome found seditious, and for which He was convicted and crucified. Thus, accord-

331

ing to Cohn, Jesus was executed in spite of the efforts of the high priest and Sanhedrin to save Him. Jesus had refused to cooperate and to bow to their authority, and nothing could be done to prevent a Roman trial from taking its course.

S. G. F. Brandon took quite a different approach to the accounts of the arrest and trial. He claimed Jesus was a nationalist patriot and either a member of or a sympathizer with the Zealots. His message clearly reflected these concerns and, according to Brandon, Jesus' nationalistic concerns were well understood by both the Jews and Romans. As one espousing the cause of Israel's freedom from the yoke of heathen Rome, Jesus had many sympathizers and followers among the Jewish populace. But Jesus was obviously a threat to Rome and to those Jewish leaders who had compromised themselves with Rome. Jesus' appearances before the Sanhedrin were enquiries resulting in charges of sedition against Rome. The cooperation of Jewish leaders with Pilate led to Jesus' crucifixion as a rebel against the Roman government.

Obviously, this is not how events are portrayed in the gospels. But that was no problem to Brandon. Following the assumptions and methodology of Source, Form, and Redaction Criticism, he argued that the purpose of the gospels, of which the accounts of the arrest and trial are an integral part, was not to provide an objective, historical account of the career of Jesus. Instead, he claimed, the evangelists consciously altered the facts to suit their apologetic purpose. The earliest Jewish followers of Jesus had not been troubled by the circumstances of Jesus' death. Indeed, in the tradition they developed they emphasized the Roman cross, for it enhanced the reputation of Jesus as the martyred Messiah of Israel.

According to Brandon the situation was quite different for later Gentile followers of Jesus. The Jewish revolt against Rome in A.D. 66, the initial atrocities against Gentiles, and the four years of bitter warfare that followed had inflamed an already existing anti-Semitism and had caused Jewish Messianism to be seen as a subversive force. The fact that Jesus had been executed by Pontius Pilate for sedition had become both embarrassing and a potential source of danger for Gentile followers of Jesus. The gospel accounts supposedly reflect this Gentile concern to shift the blame for Jesus' execution from Pilate to the Jews. Thus Mark, writing for Christians in Rome shortly after Flavian's triumph over rebel Judea in A.D. 71, initiated a different version of the trial of Jesus. While not denying that Jesus had been put to death as a rebel against Rome, he tried to modify the tradition. Mark, Brandon asserted, presented Jesus as endorsing Jewish obligation to pay tribute to Rome, and he showed the Jewish leaders as condemning Jesus for blasphemy and then forcing Pilate to crucify him. This set the pattern, drawn upon and elaborated by the later evangelists, of representing the Roman trial as a contest between Pilate, who was now represented as recognizing the innocence of

Jesus and seeking to save Him, and the Jews, who were intent upon His destruction.

Thus, Mark's account of the arrest and trial is essentially an apologetic, not sober history. Mark's record explained the scandal of a Roman cross; it showed the Jews to be criminally responsible; and it assured the Roman government that Christianity was not subversive. The later gospel writers accepted this apologetic and further developed in their own ways the picture of the pacific Christ. Their common purpose was to make Pilate a witness to Jesus' innocence and the Jews solely responsible for His death. The fact that their purpose was apologetic rather than historical explains why the four accounts are (according to Brandon) full of contradictions, elusiveness, and absurdities.

Brandon's assessment of the biased and apologetic nature of the gospels and the implications of this for the arrest and trial of Jesus is somewhat similar to the view of Paul Winter. He shares the opinion that Jesus was arrested, convicted, and executed as an insurrectionist against Rome, and that beginning with Mark the gospel writers were embarrassed by this fact. Indeed, writing in the post-A.D. 70 period, the evangelists portray Pilate as convinced of Jesus' innocence and unwilling to pass the death sentence. They do this to ingratiate Christians to the Romans and to avert persecution for Christians as subversives. But Winter is not convinced it can be shown that Jesus was closely aligned with the Zealots, or that the charge of insurrection was justified. The charge may have been concocted by His enemies, Jewish or Roman, but that would not necessarily indicate His own intentions. Winter feels it is impossible to make trustworthy, historical deductions from the gospels about Jesus' conflicts with other Jews before His last visit to Jerusalem.

However, Winter does argue that Jesus stood close to Phariseeism, indeed, that He was a Pharisee, and that His teaching was Pharisaic in ethics and eschatology. He does recognize that Jesus probably had altercations with (other) Pharisees, but whatever quarrels He may have had with any Jewish individual or group prior to His last visit to Jerusalem had no determining influence on His fate. It was not the content of His teaching that led to His arrest and conviction; it was the effect His teaching had on certain sections of the populace that induced the authorities to take action against Him. This would have been sufficient reason for Pilate to order His execution.

In widely read books and articles, Hugh Schonfield popularized still another view that assumes the gospel accounts to be historically unreliable. He contended that from before His baptism by John, Jesus had carefully mapped out a program of events that would have to be fulfilled if He were to successfully carry out what He regarded as His Messianic task. This meant not only that He would have to do and say certain things necessary to the plan, but He would have to contrive situations in such a way as to produce certain reactions on the part of others. It was a conspiracy, a plot, that would produce a contrived "fulfillment" of the Scriptures. Moves and situations would have to be engineered so that others involved would perform their function without their realizing they were being used. The road that Jesus mapped out was to culminate in the events of Passion Week. The arrest, trial, conviction, and crucifixion were the torturous conclusion of the contrived scenario.

If nothing else, one thing clearly emerges from this survey of contemporary reinterpretations of the arrest and trial of Jesus. When one gives up on the historical reliability of the accounts, he cannot be assured that he is any nearer the truth. Although he has no confidence in the trustworthiness of the gospels, Professor Samuel Sandmel is at least more consistent and realistic when he confesses that he does not know what happened historically, and that he sees no possibility of reconstructing a factual account of what really happened at the arrest and trial. Such would seem to be the inevitable conclusion if one surrenders the only accounts we have of the events to the whims of the reinterpreters.

But a significant segment of recent New Testament and historical scholarship has argued for at least the essential trustworthiness of the gospel accounts of the arrest and trial. Among these may be counted C. H. Dodd, A. N. Sherwin-White, and E. F. Harrison. However, the man whose work in this area, from a basically conservative critical viewpoint, towers over all others is the distinguished scholar, Josef Blinzler. For the most part, he accepted the essential historicity of the gospel accounts and the consequent traditional Christian understanding of the events as summarized in the opening part of this essay.

Many issues are raised by the radical reinterpretations of the arrest and trial. The most fundamental is that of the reliability of the gospel record. It is beyond the scope of this essay to argue the case for historical trustworthiness. But it should be noted that radical reinterpretations of the type mentioned above proceed on the *assumption* of untrustworthiness. Evidence to give credibility to this assumption is either absent or of the most flimsy and subjective nature. The supposition argues from silence, assumes that the gospels are contradictory rather than allowing that they might be complementary, or is based on a prior assumption that the gospels cannot be accepted as credible by their own testimony and evidence because they are fundamentally apologetic pieces. The assumptions that are behind the allegedly objective methodology of the radical critics are themselves tendentious. For this reason it is difficult to find a common ground with them. The reliability of the evangelists' statements is dismissed when it does not happen to fit the critics' theories. Nevertheless, some of the more important issues should be mentioned.

Was Jesus really a Pharisee, as Winter has argued? It must be granted that Jesus was often the guest of Pharisees, and that in some respects they held things in common. However, the gospels show the relationship, at least with the more legalistic branch of the Pharisees to be fundamentally negative. There were many conflicts between Jesus and Pharisees. Jesus spoke against their understanding of Sabbath laws, external defilement, fastings, and divorce. Their hypocritical self-righteousness was the object of His most scorching denunciations.

Was Jesus closely aligned with the Zealots, as Brandon has contended? A Zealot would never have advocated paying the taxes due the Roman emperor or loving one's enemies. A Zealot's message and concern were political; Jesus' was religious. To Him membership in the Kingdom depended on meeting moral and spiritual prerequisites.

One can make Jesus a Zealot or a Pharisee only by totally dismissing the portrayal of Him in the gospels.

John's statement (18:3) that a cohort of Roman soldiers participated in the arrest is frequently said to be a fabrication. That Roman soldiers would participate in an arrest that involved Jewish concerns is considered inconceivable. But that they would be present to keep the peace at the request of Jewish authorities does not stretch the imagination. Again, a cohort at full strength consisted of 600 men. Since it does seem strange that 600 soldiers should be required for this mission in the middle of the night, some have taken this as another evidence of historical untrustworthiness. However, the term can also be used of a detachment of 200 men, which may well have been the situation here.

One of the most serious claims is that there was no Sanhedrin trial at all. Grounds for this claim are various. It is pointed out that in the Jewish trial Jesus was convicted of blasphemy, which has no direct relation to the reason for conviction in the Roman trial, sedition. But there is no inconsistency in supposing that the Jews realized the difficulty of persuading Pilate to execute Jesus on religious grounds, so they assigned different charges when bringing Him before Pilate. It is also pointed out that death by stoning was the usual Jewish method of execution. However, crucifixion does not becloud the credibility of a Jewish trial for it is natural that an execution carried out by Roman soldiers would follow the Roman method, even if the original instigator were the Sanhedrin.

The most serious charge is that the Sanhedrin trial could not have taken place because it was so manifestly illegal. Instead, the Sanhedrin trial is argued to be the creation of early Christians, primarily Mark, in order to try to shift the blame for a Roman crucifixion from Pilate to the Jews. Thus, Christianity hoped to avoid the onus that its founder was an insurrectionist.

The Mishnah, in the Sanhedrin tractate, gives the procedures for the conduct of a trial in capital cases. It is true that the Sanhedrin trial, as recorded in the gospels, is in violation of these provisions at a number of crucial points. But that this indicates no such trial ever occurred does not follow. Possibly the Jewish leaders were so obsessed with quickly disposing of Jesus before the Sabbath and Passover Week that they knowingly violated their own procedures. This has been the traditional Christian explanation. More likely, however, the provisions of the Sanhedrin tractate were not operative in Jesus' time. The Mishnah was a collection of orally transmitted laws drawn up toward the close of the second century. By this time the ruling Sanhedrin, as it had existed historically, had ceased to exist and was only an academic institution having no authority. The regulations of the Sanhedrin tractate conflict with other Jewish sources closer to the first century, and its provisions are probably not a reflection of actual Sanhedrin procedures in the first third of the first century. Consequently, it is probably wrong to accuse the Sanhedrin of illegal procedures, and wrong to say such a trial could not have occurred.

Another focus for debate has been the statement attributed to the Jews in John 18:31, "We are not permitted to put any one to death." Critics assert that the Jews did have this authority and that this alleged statement was another device created to try to shift the blame for Jesus' execution from Pilate to the Jews. Harrison, though, shows that, of the arguments given to establish that the Jews had general authority to execute, none are convincing. Alleged evidences were either exceptional cases or illegal acts.

A. N. Sherwin-White, renowned historian of Roman law, convincingly argues for the credibility of John 18:31. It was not Roman practice to grant the authority of capital punishment to local officials. Otherwise, anti-Roman groups might be able to eliminate pro-Roman groups by judicial action. Sherwin-White confidently asserts that turbulent Judea is the last place where one would expect such an extraordinary concession. Indeed, on the basis of his knowledge of Roman law and practice, he is willing to grant credibility not only to John 18:31 but to the basic gospel portrayal of events moving from the Sanhedrin trial, to the conviction for blasphemy, to the alternative charge of sedition before Pilate.

Selected Reading List

Bammel, Ernst, ed. *The Trial of Jesus: Cambridge Studies in Honour of C. F. D. Moule*. Naperville, Ill.: Allenson, 1970.

Blinzler, Josef. *The Trial of Jesus*. Westminster, Md.: Newman, 1959.

Brandon, S. G. F. *The Trial of Jesus of Nazareth*. New York: Stein and Day, 1968.

Catchpole, David R. *The Trial of Jesus: A Study in the Gospels and Jewish Historiography from 1770 to the Present Day*. Leiden: Brill, 1971.

Chandler, Walter M. *The Trial of Jesus From a Lawyer's Standpoint*. 2 vols. New York: Empire, 1908.

Danby, H. "The Bearing of the Rabbinical Criminal Code on the Jewish Trial Narratives in the Gospels." *The Journal of Theological Studies* 21 (1919): 51-76.

Dodd, C. H. *More New Testament Studies.* Manchester, England: Manchester U., 1968. Pp. 84-101.

Harrison, Everett F. *A Short Life of Christ.* Grand Rapids: Eerdmans, 1968. Pp. 198-216.

Maier, Paul L. *Pontius Pilate.* Wheaton, Ill.: Tyndale, 1970.

Schonfield, Hugh J. *The Passover Plot: New Light on the History of Jesus.* New York: Random House, 1965. Pp. 45-46, 127-157.

Sherwin-White, A. N. *Roman Society and Roman Law in the New Testament.* Oxford: Oxford U., 1963. Pp. 24-47.

"The Trial of Jesus in the Light of History." *Judaism* 20 (1971): 6-74. This is a very helpful symposium of articles authored by Haim Cohn, Morton S. Enslin, David Flusser, Robert M. Grant, S. G. F. Brandon, Josef Blinzler, Gerard S. Sloyan, and Samuel Sandmel.

Winter, Paul. "The Trial of Jesus." *Commentary,* September 1964.

———. *On the Trial of Jesus.* Berlin: De Gruyter, 1961.

TABLE OF SECTION CROSS-REFERENCES
(with point of similarity)

Sec. No.	Cross-Referenced Sections	Point of Similarity
4	5, 11	foretelling a miraculous birth
5	4, 11	foretelling a miraculous birth
6	7, 9, 15	song because of a miraculous birth
7	6, 9, 15	song because of a miraculous birth
9	6, 7, 15	song because of a miraculous birth
11	4, 5	foretelling a miraculous birth
15	6, 7, 9	song because of a miraculous birth
24	29	a voice in the wilderness
26	29	preparatory nature of John's ministry
27	30	Spirit's descent on Jesus
	121	identification of the Son by the Father
29	24	a voice in the wilderness
	26	preparatory nature of John's ministry
30	27	Spirit's descent on Jesus
31	47, 51, 54	calling disciples
34	189	cleansing the Temple
38	102	John's imprisonment
42	43, 45, 97	no honor at home
43	42, 45, 97	no honor at home
44	73	healing at a distance
45	42, 43, 97	no honor at home
47	31, 51, 54	calling disciples
51	31, 47, 54	calling disciples
54	31, 47, 51	calling disciples
57-61	152, 155, 164	Sabbath controversies
63	99, Acts 1:13	twelve apostles listed
66	83, 144	lighting a lamp
	128, 165	salt of the earth
67	168	permanence of the Law
68	128	loss of hand or eye
	150	reconciliation
	168, 176	divorce and remarriage
	199	taking an oath
69	143	the disciple's prayer
	175	unhypocritical prayer
	192	forgiveness of men and forgiveness by God
70	83	measuring out
	83, 147	anxieties of life
	99, 213, 220	follower not above his leader
	144	lamp of the body
	146	value of sparrows
	147	danger of riches
	167	impossibility of being a slave to two masters

Sec. No.	Cross-Referenced Sections	Point of Similarity
71	79	recognition by fruit
	143	ask, seek, knock
	162	narrow entrance
73	44	healing at a distance
76	139	woes to the cities
77	186	anointing with perfume
79	71	recognition by fruit
	96, 144	casting out demons, and blasphemous statements
	128, 144	casting out demons, being for and against
	146	blasphemous statements
80	115, 144	request for a sign
83	66, 144	lighting a lamp
	70	measuring out
	70, 147	anxieties of life
	191	hardened hearts and blinded eyes
86	152	mustard tree
87	152	leaven
96	79, 144	casting out demons, and blasphemous statements
	182	healing the blind
97	42, 43, 45	no honor at home
98	99, 139	workers dispatched
99	63, Acts 1:13	twelve apostles listed
	70, 146	value of sparrows
	70, 213, 220	follower not above his leader
	98, 139	workers dispatched
	119, 165	cost of discipleship
	128	a cup of water
	146	confession before men
	149, 203	divided households
102	38	John's imprisonment
105	114, 116	feeding the multitudes
110	118	confessions of Jesus' identity
114	105, 116	feeding the multitudes
115	80, 144	request for a sign
116	105, 114	feeding the multitudes
	146	the leaven of hypocrisy
118	110	confessions of Jesus' identity
119	99, 165	cost of discipleship
	121, 122, 125, 180	prophecies of death and resurrection
	190	loving and hating life
121	27	identification of the Son by the Father
	119, 122, 125, 180	prophecies of death and resurrection
122	119, 121, 125, 180	prophecies of death and resurrection
125	119, 121, 122, 180	prophecies of death and resurrection
127	177	example of little children
	213	to receive the Son is to receive the Father
128	66, 165	salt of the earth
	68	loss of hand or eye
	79, 144	casting out demons, being for and against
	99	a cup of water

Sec. No.	Cross-Referenced Sections	Point of Similarity
	166	the ninety-nine
	169	warning against stumbling blocks
139	76	woes to the cities
	98, 99	workers dispatched
141	197	greatest commandment in the Law
143	69	the disciple's prayer
	71	ask, seek, knock
	175	importunate prayer
144	66, 83	lighting a lamp
	70	lamp of the body
	79, 128	being for and against
	79, 96, 128	casting out demons, and blasphemous statements
	80, 115	request for a sign
	146	blasphemous statements
145	199	woes against scribes and Pharisees
146	70, 99	value of sparrows
	70, 79, 144	blasphemous statements
	99	confession before men
	116	the leaven of hypocrisy
	203	trials before courts and rulers
147	70	danger of riches, anxieties of life
148	207	readiness for Christ's return
149	99	divided households
150	68	reconciliation
152	57-61, 155, 164	Sabbath controversies
	86	mustard tree
	87	leaven
155	57-61, 152, 164	Sabbath controversies
162	71	narrow entrance
	178, 179	last first and first last
163	200	lament over Jerusalem
164	57-61, 152, 155	Sabbath controversies
165	66, 128	salt of the earth
	99, 119	cost of discipleship
166	128	the ninety-nine
167	70	impossibility of being a slave to two masters
168	67	permanence of the Law
	68, 176	divorce and remarriage
169	128	warning against stumbling blocks
174	204-206	signs of Christ's return
175	69	unhypocritical prayer
	143	importunate prayer
176	68, 168	divorce and remarriage
177	127	example of little children
178	162, 179	last first and first last
179	162, 178	last first and first last
180	119, 121, 122, 125	prophecies of death and resurrection
181	215	rivalry over greatness
182	96	healing the blind

Sec. No.	Cross-Referenced Sections	Point of Similarity
184	207	faithful handling of the Lord's possessions
186	77	anointing with perfume
189	34	cleansing the Temple
190	119	loving and hating life
191	83	hardened hearts and blinded eyes
192	69	forgiveness of men and forgiveness by God
197	141	greatest commandment in the Law
199	68	taking an oath
	145	woes against scribes and Pharisees
200	163	lament over Jerusalem
203	99	divided households
	146	trials before courts and rulers
204	174	signs of Christ's return
205	174	signs of Christ's return
206	174	signs of Christ's return
207	148	readiness for Christ's return
	184	faithful handling of the Lord's possessions
213	70, 99, 220	follower not above his leader
	127	to receive the Son is to receive the Father
215	181	rivalry over greatness
216	225, 228, 230	Peter's denials
220	70, 99, 213	follower not above his leader
225	216, 228, 230	Peter's denials
228	216, 225, 230	Peter's denials
230	216, 225, 228	Peter's denials
253	256, 258	postresurrection appearances to the disciples
256	253, 258	postresurrection appearances to the disciples
258	253, 256	postresurrection appearances to the disciples

TABLES FOR FINDING PASSAGES IN THE HARMONY

MATTHEW

344

THE LIFE OF CHRIST

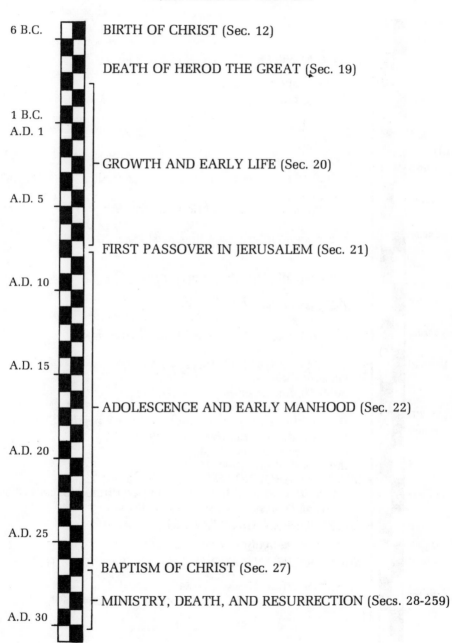

6 B.C. — BIRTH OF CHRIST (Sec. 12)

DEATH OF HEROD THE GREAT (Sec. 19)

1 B.C.
A.D. 1

GROWTH AND EARLY LIFE (Sec. 20)

A.D. 5

FIRST PASSOVER IN JERUSALEM (Sec. 21)

A.D. 10

A.D. 15

ADOLESCENCE AND EARLY MANHOOD (Sec. 22)

A.D. 20

A.D. 25

BAPTISM OF CHRIST (Sec. 27)

MINISTRY, DEATH, AND RESURRECTION (Secs. 28-259)

A.D. 30

347

THE MINISTRY OF CHRIST

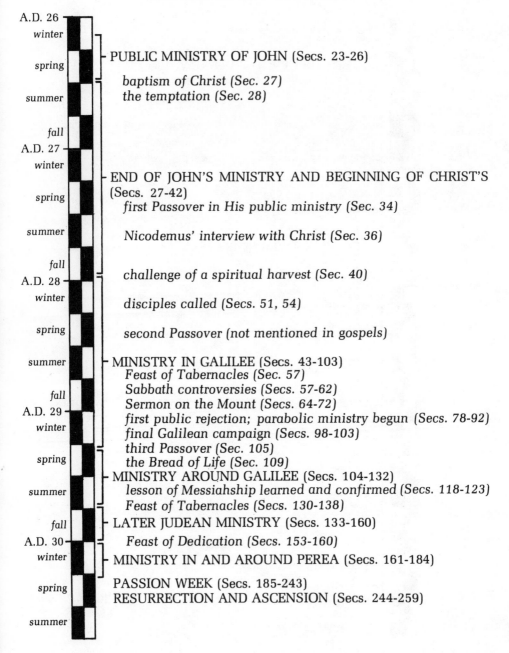

A.D. 26
winter

PUBLIC MINISTRY OF JOHN (Secs. 23-26)

spring

baptism of Christ (Sec. 27)
the temptation (Sec. 28)

summer

fall
A.D. 27
winter

END OF JOHN'S MINISTRY AND BEGINNING OF CHRIST'S
(Secs. 27-42)

spring

first Passover in His public ministry (Sec. 34)

summer

Nicodemus' interview with Christ (Sec. 36)

fall
A.D. 28

challenge of a spiritual harvest (Sec. 40)

winter

disciples called (Secs. 51, 54)

spring

second Passover (not mentioned in gospels)

summer

MINISTRY IN GALILEE (Secs. 43-103)
Feast of Tabernacles (Sec. 57)
Sabbath controversies (Secs. 57-62)

fall
A.D. 29

Sermon on the Mount (Secs. 64-72)
first public rejection; parabolic ministry begun (Secs. 78-92)

winter

final Galilean campaign (Secs. 98-103)
third Passover (Sec. 105)

spring

the Bread of Life (Sec. 109)
MINISTRY AROUND GALILEE (Secs. 104-132)

summer

lesson of Messiahship learned and confirmed (Secs. 118-123)
Feast of Tabernacles (Secs. 130-138)

fall

LATER JUDEAN MINISTRY (Secs. 133-160)

A.D. 30

Feast of Dedication (Secs. 153-160)

winter

MINISTRY IN AND AROUND PEREA (Secs. 161-184)

spring

PASSION WEEK (Secs. 185-243)
RESURRECTION AND ASCENSION (Secs. 244-259)

summer

PASSION WEEK

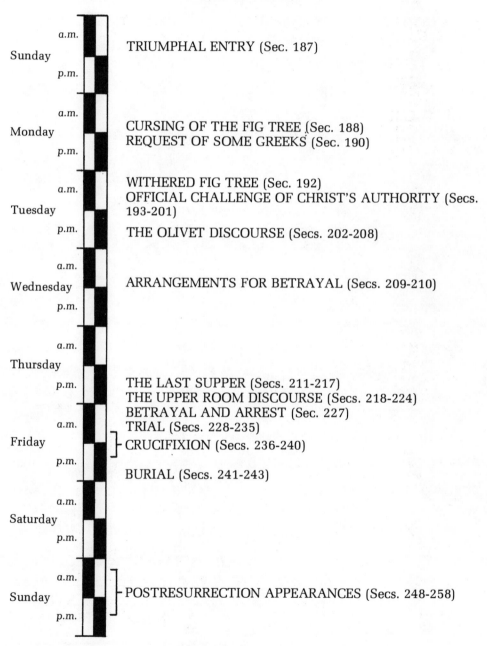

Sunday — a.m. / p.m.

TRIUMPHAL ENTRY (Sec. 187)

Monday — a.m. / p.m.

CURSING OF THE FIG TREE (Sec. 188)
REQUEST OF SOME GREEKS (Sec. 190)

Tuesday — a.m. / p.m.

WITHERED FIG TREE (Sec. 192)
OFFICIAL CHALLENGE OF CHRIST'S AUTHORITY (Secs. 193-201)

THE OLIVET DISCOURSE (Secs. 202-208)

Wednesday — a.m. / p.m.

ARRANGEMENTS FOR BETRAYAL (Secs. 209-210)

Thursday — a.m. / p.m.

THE LAST SUPPER (Secs. 211-217)
THE UPPER ROOM DISCOURSE (Secs. 218-224)
BETRAYAL AND ARREST (Sec. 227)
TRIAL (Secs. 228-235)

Friday — a.m. / p.m.

CRUCIFIXION (Secs. 236-240)

BURIAL (Secs. 241-243)

Saturday — a.m. / p.m.

Sunday — a.m. / p.m.

POSTRESURRECTION APPEARANCES (Secs. 248-258)

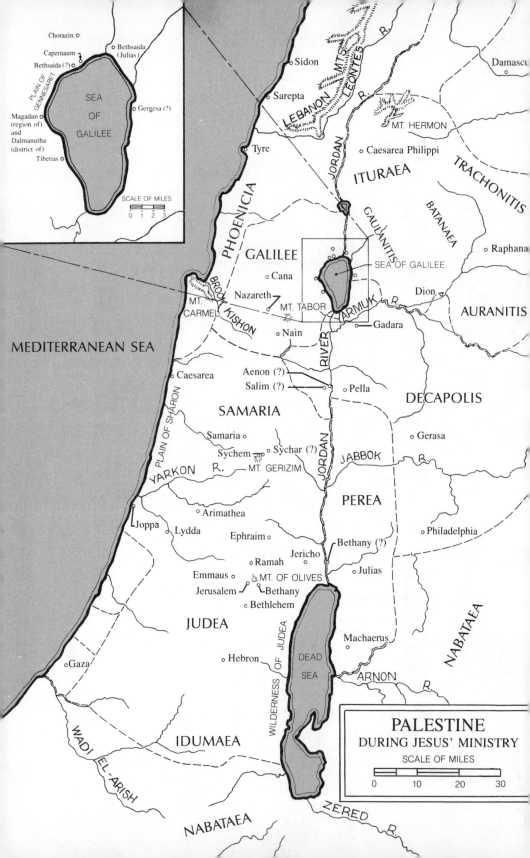

Chorazin ○

Capernaum ○
Bethsaida (?) ○   ○ Bethsaida
                      (Julias)

PLAIN OF GENNESARET

SEA
OF
GALILEE

Magadan
(region of)
and
Dalmanutha
(district of)

○ Gergesa (?)

Tiberias ○

SCALE OF MILES
0 1 2 3

○ Chorazin

Capernaum ○
Bethsaida (?) ○○   ○ Bethsaida (Julias)

○ Sidon

Damascu

MTS.
LEONTES R.

LEBANON

○ Sarepta

MT. HERMON

PHOENICIA

BROOK KISHON

○ Tyre

○ Caesarea Philippi

ITURAEA

GAULANITIS

TRACHONITIS

BATANAEA

GALILEE

○ Cana

SEA OF GALILEE

○ Raphana

Nazareth
MT. CARMEL
MT. TABOR

JORDAN

RIVER YARMUK R.

Dion ○

AURANITIS

○ Nain

○ Gadara

MEDITERRANEAN SEA

○ Caesarea

Aenon (?)
Salim (?)

○ Pella

DECAPOLIS

PLAIN OF SHARON

SAMARIA

Samaria ○

Sychem ○ ○ Sychar (?)
MT. GERIZIM

○ Gerasa

YARKON R.

JABBOK

JORDAN

PEREA

○ Arimathea

○ Philadelphia

Joppa ○ Lydda ○

Ephraim ○

Bethany (?) ○

Ramah ○   Jericho ○

○ Julias

Emmaus ○   MT. OF OLIVES
Jerusalem ○ ○ Bethany
○ Bethlehem

JUDEA

WILDERNESS OF JUDEA

DEAD SEA

○ Machaerus

NABATAEA

Gaza ○   ○ Hebron

ARNON R.

WADI EL-ARISH

IDUMAEA

ZERED R.

NABATAEA

PALESTINE
DURING JESUS' MINISTRY

SCALE OF MILES
0   10   20   30

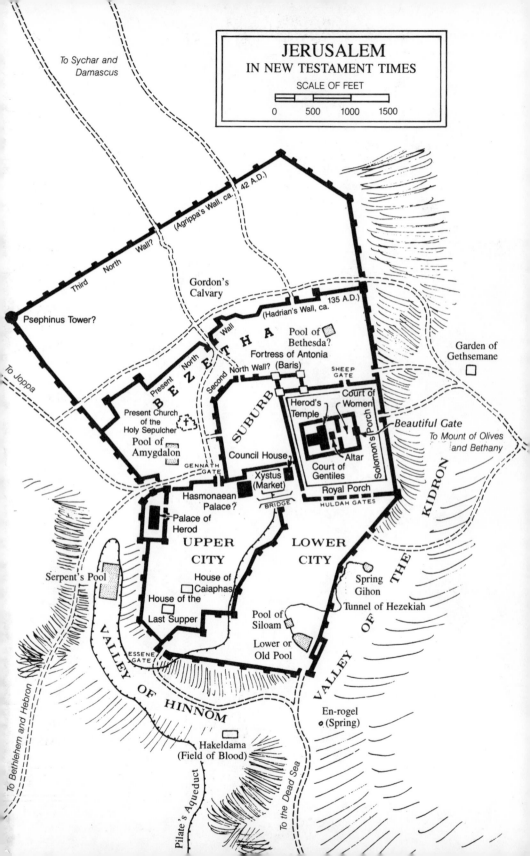

JERUSALEM
IN NEW TESTAMENT TIMES

SCALE OF FEET

0   500   1000   1500

To Sychar and Damascus

(Agrippa's Wall, ca., 42 A.D.)

Third   North   Wall?

Gordon's Calvary

Psephinus Tower?

(Hadrian's Wall, ca. 135 A.D.)

Wall

B E Z E T H A

Pool of Bethesda?

Fortress of Antonia (Baris)

Garden of Gethsemane

To Joppa

North   Second North Wall?

SHEEP GATE

SUBURB

Present Wall

Present Church of the Holy Sepulcher

Herod's Temple

Court of Women

Beautiful Gate

To Mount of Olives and Bethany

Pool of Amygdalon

Council House

Court of Gentiles

Altar

Solomon's Porch

GENNATH GATE

Xystus (Market)

Royal Porch

HULDAH GATES

Hasmonaean Palace?

BRIDGE

KIDRON

Palace of Herod

UPPER CITY

LOWER CITY

Serpent's Pool

House of Caiaphas

Spring Gihon

THE

House of the Last Supper

Pool of Siloam

Tunnel of Hezekiah

VALLEY OF

ESSENE GATE

Lower or Old Pool

VALLEY OF HINNOM

En-rogel (Spring)

To Bethlehem and Hebron

Hakeldama (Field of Blood)

Pilate's Aqueduct

To the Dead Sea